The Collected Essays, Journalism
and Letters of George Orwell

AS I PLEASE
1943-1945

III

Edited by
Sonia Orwell
and
Ian Angus

A Harvest Book

Harcourt Brace Jovanovich, Inc.
New York

ISBN 0-15-618622-5

Library of Congress Catalog Card Number: 68–12591

A B C D E F G H I J

Printed in the United States of America

Contents

Acknowledgements

The editors wish to express their grateful thanks to the following institutions and libraries, their trustees, curators and staffs for their co-operation and valuable help and for making copies of Orwell material available: Sir Frank Francis, Director and Principal Librarian of the British Museum (for: II: 37; III: 105; IV: 8); Dr John D. Gordan, Curator of the Henry W. and Albert A. Berg Collection of the New York Public Library, Astor, Lenox and Tilden Foundations (for: I: 18, 22, 23, 31, 33, 36, 38, 48, 50–2, 54, 58, 60, 61, 73, 75, 76, 86, 92, 98, 108, 112, 116, 121, 124, 128, 133, 139, 140, 141, 146, 154; III: 53, 97, 106; IV: 29, 59, 92, 95, 100, 106, 107, 110, 115, 121, 126, 136, 137, 142, 144, 159, 164, 165); Dr Warren Roberts, Director of the Humanities Research Center, University of Texas (for: I: 65, 66, 79, 102, 122, 123, 161; II: 4, 6, 10, 50; III: 52); S. C. Sutton, Librarian and Keeper of India Office Records (for: I: 115); Robert L. Collison, Librarian of the BBC Library (for: II: 38, 39, 52); Dr G. Chandler, Librarian of Liverpool City Library (for: I: 94); Wilbur Smith, Head of the Department of Special Collections, Library of the University of California, Los Angeles (for: I: 84); Anne Abley, Librarian of St Antony's College, Oxford (for: IV: 31, 32); and J. W. Scott, Librarian of University College London, for the material in the George Orwell Archive.

We are deeply indebted to all those recipients of letters from Orwell, or their executors, who have been kind enough to make available the correspondence published in these volumes.

We would like to thank the following publications for permission to reproduce material first published in their pages: *Commentary;* *Encounter;* the *Evening Standard; Forward; Life;* the *Listener;* the *London Magazine;* the *Manchester Evening News;* the *New Leader* (NY); the *New Statesman and Nation;* the *New Yorker;* the *New York Times Book Review;* the *Observer; Partisan Review; Peace News;* the *Socialist Leader; Time and Tide; The Times; Tribune;* and *Wiadomósci.*

We would like to thank the following for allowing us to use material whose copyright they own: the executors of the late Frank Richards for his "Reply to George Orwell" in *Horizon*; H. W. Wilson & Co. for Orwell's entry in *Twentieth Century Authors*; George Allen & Unwin Ltd for "The Rediscovery of Europe" in *Talking to India*; Professor George Woodcock and D. S. Savage for their contributions to the controversy "Pacifism and the War" in *Partisan Review*; Dr Alex Comfort for his contribution to the same controversy and for his "Letter to an American Visitor" in *Tribune*; William Collins Sons & Co. Ltd for *The English People*; the executors of the late James Agate for his contribution to the controversy in the *Manchester Evening News*; the executors of Gerard Manley Hopkins and the Oxford University Press for "Felix Randal"; Elek Books, Ltd for the Introduction to Jack London's *Love of Life*; Eyre & Spottiswoode, Ltd for the Introduction to Leonard Merrick's *The Position of Peggy Harper*; and the executors of the late Konni Zilliacus for his letter to *Tribune*.

We would like to thank the following for their co-operation and invaluable help: Mrs Evelyn Anderson, the Hon. David Astor, Frank D. Barber, Dennis Collings, Dr Alex Comfort, Jack Common, Lettice Cooper, Stafford Cottman, Humphrey Dakin, Mrs John Deiner, Mrs William Dunn, Mrs T. S. Eliot, Dr McDonald Emslie, Faber and Faber Ltd, Mr and Mrs Francis Fierz, Roy Fuller, T. R. Fyvel, Livia Gollancz, Victor Gollancz Ltd, Mrs Arthur Goodman, A. S. F. Gow, James Hanley, Rayner Heppenstall, Inez Holden, Mrs Humphry House, Mrs Lydia Jackson, Frank Jellinek, Dr Shirley E. Jones, Jon Kimche, Denys King-Farlow, Arthur Koestler, Mrs Georges Kopp, James Laughlin, F. A. Lea, John Lehmann, John McNair, Michael Meyer, Henry Miller, Raymond Mortimer, Mrs Middleton Murry, Mrs Rosalind Obermeyer, Laurence O'Shaughnessy, *Partisan Review*, Professor R. S. Peters, Ruth Pitter, Joyce Pritchard, Philip Rahv, Sir Herbert Read, Vernon Richards, the Rev. Herbert Rogers, the Hon. Sir Steven Runciman, Brenda Salkeld, John Sceats, Roger Senhouse, Oliver Stallybrass, Stephen Spender, Professor Gleb Struve, Julian Symons, F. J. Warburg and Professor George Woodcock. We would also like to thank: Angus Calder (for allowing us to consult his unpublished thesis on the Common Wealth Party); Howard Fink (for allowing us to consult his unpublished *Chronology of Orwell's Loci and Activities*); and I. R. Willison (whose *George Orwell: Some Materials for a*

Bibliography, School of Librarianship, London University, 1953, was indispensable).

Finally, this edition would not have been possible but for the patient and understanding editorial help of Aubrey Davis and the support and help of the Library staff of University College London, particularly that of J. W. Scott, the Librarian, Margaret Skerl, Karen Bishop, Mrs Michael Kraushaar, and Mrs Gordon Leitch.

A Note on the Editing

The contents are arranged in order of publication except where the time lag between writing and appearance in print is unusually large, when we have chosen the date of writing. There are one or two rare exceptions to this rule generally made for the sake of illustrating the development in Orwell's thought, but a note at the end of each article or review states when, and in which publication, it appeared first. If it was not published or the date of writing has determined its position the date of writing is given. Where there is no mention of a periodical at the end of an article, it has never been published before. "Why I Write", written in 1946, has been placed at the beginning of Volume I, as it seems a suitable introduction to the whole collection. Where an article was reprinted in the major collections of his writing, this has been indicated and the following abbreviations used for the various books: CE, *Collected Essays*; CrE, *Critical Essays*; DD, *Dickens, Dali and Others*; EYE, *England Your England*; ITW, *Inside the Whale*; OR, *The Orwell Reader*; SE, *Shooting an Elephant*; SJ, *Such, Such Were the Joys*.

Any title in square brackets at the head of an article or review has been supplied by us. All the others are either Orwell's own or those of the editors of the publication in question. He certainly wrote his own titles for his *Tribune* pieces: some of the others read as if he had written them but with most it is hard to tell and there is no way of finally checking.

Only when the article has never been printed before have we had the manuscript to work from and none of these were revised by Orwell as they would have been had he published them. With everything else we have had to use the text as it appeared in print. As anyone who has ever done any journalism or book reviewing knows, this means the text which appears here may well be slightly, if not very, different from the text Orwell originally wrote. Editors cut, printers make errors which are not thought of as very important in journalism, and it is only when the writer wants to reprint his pieces in book form that he bothers to restore the cuts, correct the errors and generally prepare them to survive in more lasting form: the reader should bear in mind that they might well be very different if Orwell himself had revised them for re-publication. Both to these previously printed essays and journalism and to the hitherto unpublished articles and diaries we have given a uniform style in spelling, quotation marks and punctuation.

The letters were written, nearly always in haste, with scant attention to style and hardly any to punctuation; but throughout them we have corrected spelling mistakes, regularised the punctuation and have put book and periodical titles in italics. In a few cases postscripts of an unimportant nature have been omitted without indication. Otherwise cuts in both the letters and the journalism have been indicated by three dots, with a fourth dot to indicate a period. The same method was used by Orwell for indicating omissions when abridging excerpts he was quoting in reviews and essays, but as we have not made cuts in any of these excerpts there should be no confusion between our cuts and Orwell's own.

Orwell's "As I Please" column often consisted of two or more sections each devoted to a specific topic. Whenever one of the self-contained sections has been entirely omitted, this has not been indicated, but any cut made within a section is indicated by the usual three or four dots.

George Orwell never legally changed his name from Eric Blair and all the friends he made when young knew him and addressed him as Eric Blair. Later on new friends and acquaintances knew him and addressed him as George Orwell. In his letters he signs himself by the name his correspondent used. His earlier articles were signed E. A. Blair or Eric Blair and we have indicated these. From the moment this name is dropped in his published writing it is entirely signed George Orwell. Where a footnote deals with a period or a situation in which he would have looked upon himself primarily as Eric Blair we have referred to him by this name.

As this is an Anglo-American edition, many of the footnotes have been provided for the benefit of American readers and contain information we know to be familiar to English readers. We have put in the minimum of footnotes. This is largely because of the great difficulty of annotating the history of the period during which he wrote.

It is still too recent for standard histories of it to exist and the events
and people he discussed are often still the subjects of fierce polemic
making it difficult to give an "objective" footnote. We have only
footnoted the text in some detail where he talks about people or
events in his personal life or where there is a reference to some topic
about which the reader could find nothing in any existing book of
reference. The numbers in the cross-references in the footnotes refer
to items, not pages.

The Editors

1. The English People

In peace time, it is unusual for foreign visitors to this country to notice the existence of the English people. Even the accent referred to by Americans as "the English accent" is not in fact common to more than a quarter of the population. In cartoons in continental papers England is personified by an aristocrat with a monocle, a sinister capitalist in a top-hat, or a spinster in a Burberry. Hostile or friendly, nearly all the generalisations that are made about England base themselves on the property-owning class and ignore the other forty-five million.

But the chances of war brought to England, either as soldiers or as refugees, hundreds of thousands of foreigners who would not normally have come here, and forced them into intimate contact with ordinary people. Czechs, Poles, Germans and Frenchmen to whom "England" meant Piccadilly and the Derby found themselves quartered in sleepy East Anglian villages, in northern mining towns, or in the vast working-class areas of London whose names the world had never heard until they were blitzed. Those of them who had the gift of observation will have seen for themselves that the real England is not the England of the guide books. Blackpool is more typical than Ascot, the top-hat is a moth-eaten rarity, the language of the BBC is barely intelligible to the masses. Even the prevailing physical type does not agree with the caricatures, for the tall, lanky physique which is traditionally English is almost confined to the upper classes: the working classes, as a rule, are rather small, with short limbs and brisk movements, and with a tendency among the women to grow dumpy in early middle life.

It is worth trying for a moment to put oneself in the position of a foreign observer, new to England, but unprejudiced, and able because of his work to keep in touch with ordinary, useful, unspectacular people. Some of his generalisations would be wrong, because he would not make enough allowance for the temporary dislocations resulting from war. Never having seen England in normal times, he might underrate the power of class distinctions, or think English agriculture healthier than it is, or be too much impressed by the dinginess of the London streets or the prevalence of drunkenness. But with his fresh eyes he would see a great deal that a native observer misses, and his probable impressions are worth tabulating. Almost certainly he would find the salient characteristics of the English common people to be artistic insensibility, gentleness, respect for legality, suspicion of foreigners, sentimentality about animals, hypocrisy, exaggerated class distinctions, and an obsession with sport.

As for our artistic insensibility, ever-growing stretches of beautiful countryside are ruined by planless building, the heavy industries are allowed to convert whole counties into blackened deserts, ancient monuments are wantonly pulled down or swamped by seas of yellow brick, attractive vistas are blocked by hideous statues to nonentities— and all this without any *popular* protest whatever. When England's housing problem is discussed, its aesthetic aspect simply does not enter the mind of the average man. Nor is there any widespread interest in any of the arts, except perhaps music. Poetry, the art in which above all others England has excelled, has for more than a century had no appeal whatever for the common people. It is only acceptable when—as in some popular songs and mnemonic rhymes— it is masquerading as something else. Indeed the very word "poetry" arouses either derision or embarrassment in ninety-eight people out of a hundred.

Our imaginary foreign observer would certainly be struck by our gentleness: by the orderly behaviour of English crowds, the lack of pushing and quarrelling, the willingness to form queues, the good temper of harassed, overworked people like bus conductors. The manners of the English working class are not always very graceful, but they are extremely considerate. Great care is taken in showing a stranger the way, blind people can travel across London with the certainty that they will be helped on and off every bus and across every street. In war-time a few of the policemen carry revolvers, but England has nothing corresponding to the *gendarmerie*, the semi-military police living in barracks and armed with rifles (sometimes even with tanks and aeroplanes), who are the guardians of society all the way from Calais to Tokyo. And except for certain well-defined areas in half a dozen big towns there is very little crime or violence. The average of honesty is lower in the big towns than in the country, but even in London the news-vendor can safely leave his pile of pennies on the pavement while he goes for a drink. The prevailing gentleness of manners is a recent thing, however. Well within living memory it was impossible for a smartly dressed person to walk down Ratcliff Highway without being assaulted, and an eminent jurist, asked to name a typically English crime, could answer: "Kicking your wife to death".

There is no revolutionary tradition in England, and even in extremist political parties, it is only the middle-class membership that thinks in revolutionary terms. The masses still more or less assume that "against the law" is a synonym for "wrong". It is known that the criminal law is harsh and full of anomalies and that litigation is so expensive as always to favour the rich against the poor: but there is a general feeling that the law, such as it is, will be scrupulously administered, that a judge or magistrate cannot be bribed, that no one will be punished without trial. An Englishman does not believe in his bones, as a Spanish or Italian peasant does, that the law is simply a racket. It is precisely this general confidence in the law that has allowed a good deal of recent tampering with Habeas Corpus to escape public notice. But it also causes some ugly situations to end peacefully. During the worst of the London blitz the authorities tried to prevent the public from using the Tube stations as shelters. The people did not reply by storming the gates, they simply bought themselves penny-halfpenny tickets: they thus had legal status as passengers, and there was no thought of turning them out again.

The traditional English xenophobia is stronger among the working class than the middle class. It was partly the resistance of the trade unions that prevented a really large influx of refugees from the Fascist countries before the war, and when the German refugees were interned in 1940, it was not the working class that protested. The difference in habits, and especially in food and language, makes it very hard for English working people to get on with foreigners. Their diet differs a great deal from that of any European nation, and they are extremely conservative about it. As a rule they will refuse even to sample a foreign dish, they regard such things as garlic and olive oil with disgust, life is unliveable to them unless they have tea and puddings. And the peculiarities of the English language make it almost impossible for anyone who has left school at fourteen to learn a foreign language after he has grown up. In the French Foreign Legion, for instance, the British and American legionaries seldom rise out of the ranks, because they cannot learn French, whereas a German learns French in a few months. English working people, as a rule, think it effeminate even to pronounce a foreign word correctly. This is bound up with the fact that the upper classes learn foreign languages as a regular part of their education. Travelling abroad, speaking foreign tongues, enjoying foreign food, are vaguely felt to be upper-class habits, a species of snobbery, so that xenophobia is reinforced by class jealousy.

Perhaps the most horrible spectacles in England are the Dogs' Cemeteries in Kensington Gardens, at Stoke Poges (it actually adjoins the churchyard where Gray wrote his famous "Elegy") and at various other places. But there were also the Animals' ARP[1] Centres, with miniature stretchers for cats, and in the first year of the war there was the spectacle of Animal Day being celebrated with all its usual pomp in the middle of the Dunkirk evacuation. Although its worst follies are committed by the upper-class women, the animal cult runs right through the nation and is probably bound up with the decay of agriculture and the dwindled birthrate. Several years of stringent rationing have failed to reduce the dog and cat population, and even in poor quarters of big towns the bird-fanciers' shops display canary seed at prices ranging up to twenty-five shillings a pint.

Hypocrisy is so generally accepted as part of the English character that a foreign observer would be prepared to meet with it at every turn, but he would find especially ripe examples in the laws dealing with gambling, drinking, prostitution, and profanity. He would find it difficult to reconcile the anti-imperialistic sentiments which are commonly expressed in England with the size of the British Empire. If he were a continental European he would notice with ironical amusement that the English think it wicked to have a big army but see nothing wrong in having a big navy. This too he would set down as hypocrisy—not altogether fairly, for it is the fact of being an island, and therefore not needing a big army, that has allowed British democratic institutions to grow up, and the mass of the people are fairly well aware of this.

Exaggerated class distinctions have been diminishing over a period of about thirty years, and the war has probably speeded up the process, but newcomers to England are still astonished and sometimes horrified by the blatant differences between class and class.

[1] Air Raid Precautions.

The great majority of the people can still be "placed" in an instant by their manners, clothes, and general appearance. Even the physical type differs considerably, the upper classes being on an average several inches taller than the working class. But the most striking difference of all is in language and accent. The English working class, as Mr Wyndham Lewis has put it, are "branded on the tongue". And though class distinctions do not exactly coincide with economic distinctions, the contrast between wealth and poverty is very much more glaring, and more taken for granted, than in most countries.

The English were the inventors of several of the world's most popular games, and have spread them more widely than any other product of their culture. The word "football" is mispronounced by scores of millions who have never heard of Shakespeare or Magna Carta. The English themselves are not outstandingly good at all games, but they enjoy playing them, and to an extent that strikes foreigners as childish they enjoy reading about them and betting on them. During the between-war years the football pools did more than any other one thing to make life bearable for the unemployed. Professional footballers, boxers, jockeys, and even cricketers enjoy a popularity that no scientist or artist could hope to rival. Nevertheless sport worship is not carried to quite such imbecile lengths as one would imagine from reading the popular press. When the brilliant lightweight boxer, Kid Lewis, stood for Parliament in his native borough, he only scored a hundred and twenty-five votes.

These traits that we have enumerated are probably the ones that would strike an intelligent observer first. Out of them he might feel that he could construct a reliable picture of the English character. But then probably a thought would strike him: is there such a thing as "the English character"? Can one talk about nations as though they were individuals? And supposing that one can, is there any genuine continuity between the England of today and the England of the past?

As he wandered through the London streets, he would notice the old prints in the bookshop windows, and it would occur to him that if these things are representative, then England must have changed a great deal. It is not much more than a hundred years since the distinguishing mark of English life was its brutality. The common people, to judge by the prints, spent their time in an almost unending round of fighting, whoring, drunkenness and bull-baiting. Moreover, even the physical type appears to have changed. Where are they gone, the hulking draymen and low-browed prize-fighters, the brawny sailors with their buttocks bursting out of their white trousers, and the great overblown beauties with their swelling bosoms, like the figure-heads of Nelson's ships? What had these people in common with the gentle-mannered, undemonstrative, law-abiding English of today? Do such things as "national cultures" really exist?

This is one of those questions, like the freedom of the will or the identity of the individual, in which all the arguments are on one side and instinctive knowledge is on the other. It is not easy to discover the connecting thread that runs through English life from the sixteenth century onwards, but all English people who bother about such subjects feel that it exists. They feel that they understand the institutions that have come to them out of the past—Parliament, for instance, or sabbatarianism, or the subtle grading of the class system—with an inherited knowledge impossible to a foreigner. Individuals, too, are felt to conform to a national pattern. D. H. Lawrence is felt to be "very English", but so is Blake; Dr Johnson and G. K. Chesterton are somehow the same kind of person. The belief that we resemble our ancestors—that Shakespeare, say, is more like a modern Englishman than a modern Frenchman or German—may be unreasonable, but by existing it influences conduct. Myths which are believed in tend to become true, because they set up a type, or "persona", which the average person will do his best to resemble.

During the bad period of 1940 it became clear that in Britain national solidarity is stronger than class antagonism. If it were really true that "the proletarian has no country", 1940 was the time for him to show it. It was exactly then, however, that class feeling slipped into the background, only reappearing when the immediate danger had passed. Moreover, it is probable that the stolid behaviour of the British town populations under the bombing was partly due to the existence of the national "persona"—that is, to their preconceived idea of themselves. Traditionally the Englishman is phlegmatic, unimaginative, not easily rattled: and since that is what he thinks he ought to be, that is what he tends to become. Dislike of hysteria and "fuss", admiration for stubbornness, are all but universal in England, being shared by everyone except the intelligentsia. Millions of English people willingly accept as their national emblem the bulldog, an animal noted for its obstinacy, ugliness, and impenetrable stupidity. They have a remarkable readiness to admit that foreigners are more "clever" than themselves, and yet they feel that it would be an out-rage against the laws of God and Nature for England to be ruled by foreigners. Our imaginary observer would notice, perhaps, that Wordsworth's sonnets during the Napoleonic war might have been written during this one. He would know already that England has produced poets and scientists rather than philosophers, theologians, or pure theorists of any description. And he might end by deciding that a profound, almost unconscious patriotism and an inability to think logically are the abiding features of the English character, traceable in English literature from Shakespeare onwards.

THE MORAL OUTLOOK OF THE ENGLISH PEOPLE

For perhaps a hundred and fifty years organised religion, or con-scious religious belief of any kind, have had very little hold on the mass of the English people. Only about ten per cent of them ever go near a place of worship except to be married and buried. A vague theism and an intermittent belief in life after death are prob-ably fairly widespread, but the main Christian doctrines have been largely forgotten. Asked what he meant by "Christianity", the aver-age man would define it wholly in ethical terms ("unselfishness", or "loving your neighbour", would be the kind of definition he would give). This was probably much the same in the early days of the Industrial Revolution, when the old village life had been suddenly broken up and the Established Church had lost touch with its followers. But in recent times the Nonconformist sects have also lost much of their vigour, and within the last generation the Bible reading which used to be traditional in England has lapsed. It is quite common to meet with young people who do not know the Bible stories even as *stories*.

But there is one sense in which the English common people have remained more Christian than the upper classes, and probably than any other European nation. This is in their non-acceptance of the modern cult of power worship. While almost ignoring the spoken doctrines of the Church, they have held on to the one that the Church never formulated, because taking it for granted: namely, that might is not right. It is here that the gulf between the intelligentsia and the common people is widest. From Carlyle onwards, but especially in the last generation, the British intelligentsia have tended to take their ideas from Europe and have been infected by habits of thought

that derive ultimately from Machiavelli. All the cults that have been
fashionable in the last dozen years, Communism, Fascism, and
pacifism, are in the last analysis forms of power worship. It is significant that in this country, unlike most others, the Marxist version
of Socialism has found its warmest adherents in the middle class. Its
methods, if not its theories, obviously conflict with what is called
"bourgeois morality" (i.e. common decency), and in moral matters it
is the proletarians who are bourgeois.

One of the basic folk-tales of the English-speaking peoples is
Jack the Giant-Killer—the little man against the big man. Mickey
Mouse, Popeye the Sailor, and Charlie Chaplin are all essentially
the same figure. (Chaplin's films, it is worth noticing, were banned
in Germany as soon as Hitler came to power, and Chaplin has been
viciously attacked by English Fascist writers.) Not merely a hatred
of bullying, but a tendency to support the weaker side merely because
it is weaker, are almost general in England. Hence the admiration
for a "good loser" and the easy forgiveness of failures, either in
sport, politics, or war. Even in very serious matters the English
people do not feel that an unsuccessful action is necessarily futile.
An example in this war was the campaign in Greece. No one expected
it to succeed, but nearly everyone thought that it should be under-
taken. And the popular attitude to foreign politics is nearly always
coloured by the instinct to side with the underdog.

An obvious recent instance was pro-Finnish sentiment in the Russo-
Finnish war of 1940. This was genuine enough, as several by-elections
fought mainly on this issue showed. Popular feeling towards the
USSR had been increasingly friendly for some time past, but Finland
was a small country attacked by a big one, and that settled the issue
for most people. In the American civil war the British working
classes sided with the North—the side that stood for the abolition
of slavery—in spite of the fact that the Northern blockade of the
cotton ports was causing great hardship in Britain. In the Franco-
Prussian war, such pro-French sentiment as there was in England
was among the working class. The small nationalities oppressed by
the Turks found their sympathisers in the Liberal Party, at that time
the party of the working class and the lower middle class. And in so
far as it bothered with such issues at all, British mass sentiment was
for the Abyssinians against the Italians, for the Chinese against the
Japanese, and for the Spanish Republicans against Franco. It was
also friendly to Germany during the period when Germany was weak

and disarmed, and it would not be surprising to see a similar swing of sentiment after this war.

The feeling that one ought always to side with the weaker party probably derives from the balance-of-power policy which Britain has followed from the eighteenth century onwards. A European critic would add that it is humbug, pointing in proof to the fact that Britain herself holds down subject populations in India and elsewhere. We don't, in fact, know what settlement the English common people would make with India if the decision were theirs. All political parties and all newspapers of whatever colour have conspired to prevent them from seeing the issue clearly. We do know, however, that they have sometimes championed the weak against the strong when it was obviously not to their own advantage. The best example is the Irish civil war. The real weapon of the Irish rebels was British public opinion, which was substantially on their side and prevented the British Government from crushing the rebellion in the only way possible. Even in the Boer war there was a considerable volume of pro-Boer sentiment, though it was not strong enough to influence events. One must conclude that in this matter the English common people have lagged behind their century. They have failed to catch up with power politics, "realism", *sacro egoismo* and the doctrine that the end justifies the means.

The general English hatred of bullying and terrorism means that any kind of violent criminal gets very little sympathy. Gangsterism on American lines could not flourish in England, and it is significant that the American gangsters have never tried to transfer their activities to this country. At need, the whole nation would combine against people who kidnap babies and fire machine-guns in the street: but even the efficiency of the English police force really depends on the fact that the police have public opinion behind them. The bad side of this is the almost universal toleration of cruel and out-of-date punishments. It is not a thing to be proud of that England should still tolerate such punishments as flogging. It continues partly because of the widespread psychological ignorance, partly because men are only flogged for crimes that forfeit nearly everyone's sympathy. There would be an outcry if it were applied to non-violent crimes, or reinstituted for military offences. Military punishments are not taken for granted in England as they are in most countries. Public opinion is almost certainly opposed to the death penalty for cowardice and desertion, though there is no strong feeling against hanging murderers. In general the English attitude to crime is ignorant and old-fashioned, and humane treatment even of child offenders is a recent thing. Still, if Al Capone were in an English jail, it would not be for evasion of income tax.

A more complex question than the English attitude to crime and violence is the survival of puritanism and the world-famed English hypocrisy.

The English people proper, the working masses who make up seventy-five per cent of the population, are not puritanical. The dismal theology of Calvinism never popularised itself in England as it did for a while in Wales and Scotland. But puritanism in the looser sense in which the word is generally used (that is, prudishness, asceticism, the "kill-joy" spirit) is something that has been unsuccessfully forced upon the working class by the class of small traders and manufacturers immediately above them. In its origin it had a clear though unconscious economic motive behind it. If you could persuade the working man that every kind of recreation was sinful, you could get more work out of him for less money. In the early nineteenth century there was even a school of thought which maintained that the working man ought not to marry. But it would be unfair to suggest that the puritan moral code was mere humbug. Its exaggerated fear of sexual immorality, which extended to a disapproval of stage plays, dancing, and even bright-coloured clothes, was partly a protest against the real corruption of the later Middle Ages: there was also the new factor of syphilis, which appeared in England about the sixteenth century and worked frightful havoc for the next century or two. A little later there was another new factor in the introduction of distilled liquors—gin, brandy, and so forth—which were very much more intoxicating than the beer and mead which the English had been accustomed to. The "temperance" movement was a well-meant reaction against the frightful drunkenness of the nineteenth century, product of slum conditions and cheap gin. But it was necessarily led by fanatics who regarded not merely drunkenness but even the moderate drinking of alcohol as sinful. During the past fifty years or so there has even been a similar drive against tobacco. A hundred years ago, or two hundred years ago, tobacco-smoking was much disapproved of, but only on the ground that it was dirty, vulgar, and injurious to health: the idea that it is a wicked self-indulgence is modern.

This line of thought has never really appealed to the English masses. At most they have been sufficiently intimidated by middle-class puritanism to take some of their pleasures rather furtively. It is universally agreed that the working classes are far more moral than the upper classes, but the idea that sexuality is wicked in itself has no popular basis. Music-hall jokes, Blackpool postcards, and the songs the soldiers make up are anything but puritanical. On the other hand, almost no one in England approves of prostitution. There are several big towns where prostitution is extremely blatant, but it is completely unattractive and has never been really tolerated. It could not be regulated and humanised as it has been in some countries, because every English person feels in his bones that it is wrong. As for the general weakening of sex morals that has happened during the past twenty or thirty years, it is probably a temporary thing, resulting from the excess of women over men in the population.

In the matter of drink, the only result of a century of "temperance" agitation has been a slight increase in hypocrisy. The practical disappearance of drunkenness as an English vice has not been due to the anti-drink fanatics, but to competing amusements, education, the improvement in industrial conditions, and the expensiveness of drink itself. The fanatics have been able to see to it that the Englishman drinks his glass of beer under difficulties and with a faint feeling of wrong-doing, but have not actually been able to prevent him from drinking it. The pub, one of the basic institutions of English life, carries on in spite of the harassing tactics of Nonconformist local authorities. So also with gambling. Most forms of gambling are illegal according to the letter of the law, but they all happen on an enormous scale. The motto of the English people might be the chorus of Marie Lloyd's song, "A little of what you fancy does you good". They are not vicious, not even lazy, but they will have their bit of fun, whatever the higher-ups may say. And they seem to be gradually winning their battle against the kill-joy minorities. Even the horrors of the English Sunday have been much mitigated during the past dozen years. Some of the laws regulating pubs—designed in every case to discourage the publican and make drinking unattractive—have been relaxed during the war. And it is a very good sign that the stupid rule forbidding children to enter pubs, which tended to dehumanise the pub and turn it into a mere drinking-shop, is beginning to be disregarded in some parts of the country.

Traditionally, the Englishman's home is his castle. In an age of conscription and identity cards this cannot really be true. But the hatred of regimentation, the feeling that your spare time is your own and that a man must not be persecuted for his opinions, is deeply ingrained, and the centralising processes inevitable in wartime have not destroyed it.

It is a fact that the much-boasted freedom of the British press is theoretical rather than actual. To begin with the centralised ownership of the press means in practice that unpopular opinions can only be printed in books or in newspapers with small circulations. Moreover, the English people as a whole are not sufficiently interested in the printed word to be very vigilant about this aspect of their liberties, and during the last twenty years there has been much tampering with the freedom of the press, with no real popular protest. Even the demonstrations against the suppression of the *Daily Worker*[1] were probably stage-managed by a small minority. On the other hand, freedom of speech is a reality, and respect for it is almost general. Extremely few English people are afraid to utter their political opinions in public, and there are not even very many who want to silence the opinions of others. In peace time, when unemployment can be used as a weapon, there is a certain amount of petty persecution of "reds", but the real totalitarian atmosphere, in which the State endeavours to control people's thoughts as well as their words, is hardly imaginable.

The safeguard against it is partly the respect for integrity of conscience, and the willingness to hear both sides, which can be observed at any public meeting. But it is also partly the prevailing lack of intellectuality. The English are not sufficiently interested in intellectual matters to be intolerant about them. "Deviations" and "dangerous thoughts" do not seem very important to them. An ordinary Englishman, Conservative, Socialist, Catholic, Communist, or what not, almost never grasps the full logical implications of the creed he professes: almost always he utters heresies without noticing it. Orthodoxies, whether of the Right or the Left, flourish chiefly among the literary intelligentsia, the people who ought in theory to be the guardians of freedom of thought.

The English people are not good haters, their memory is very short, their patriotism is largely unconscious, they have no love of military glory and not much admiration for great men. They have the virtues and the vices of an old-fashioned people. To twentieth-

[1] The *Daily Worker*, now renamed the *Morning Star*, the Communist newspaper, was banned from 21 January 1941 to 26 August 1942.

century political theories they oppose not another theory of their own, but a moral quality which must be vaguely described as decency. On the day in 1936 when the Germans reoccupied the Rhineland I was in a northern mining town. I happened to go into a pub just after this piece of news, which quite obviously meant war, had come over the wireless, and I remarked to the others at the bar, "The German army has crossed the Rhine." With a vague air of capping a quotation someone answered, "Parley-voo." No more response than that! Nothing will ever wake these people up, I thought. But later in the evening, at the same pub, someone sang a song which had recently come out, with the chorus:

> For you can't do that there 'ere,
> No, you can't do that there 'ere;
> Anywhere else you can do that there,
> But you can't do that there 'ere!

And it struck me that perhaps this was the English answer to Fascism. At any rate it is true that it has not happened here, in spite of fairly favourable circumstances. The amount of liberty, intellectual or other, that we enjoy in England ought not to be exaggerated, but the fact that it has not markedly diminished in nearly five years of desperate war is a hopeful symptom.

THE POLITICAL OUTLOOK OF THE ENGLISH PEOPLE

The English people are not only indifferent to fine points of doctrine, but are remarkably ignorant politically. They are only now beginning to use the political terminology which has been current for years in continental countries. If you asked a random group of people from any stratum of the population to define capitalism, Socialism, Communism, Anarchism, Trotskyism, Fascism, you would get mostly vague answers, and some of them would be surprisingly stupid ones.

But they are also distinctly ignorant about their own political system. During recent years, for various reasons, there has been a revival of political activity, but over a longer period the interest in party politics has been dwindling. Great numbers of adult English people have never in their lives bothered to vote in an election. In big towns it is quite common for people not to know the name of their MP or what constituency they live in. During the war years owing to the failure to renew the registers, the young have no votes (at one time no one under twenty-nine had a vote), and do not seem much troubled by the fact. Nor does the anomalous electoral system, which usually favours the Conservative Party, arouse much protest. Attention focuses on policies and individuals (Chamberlain, Churchill, Cripps, Beveridge, Bevin) rather than on parties. The feeling that Parliament really controls events, and that sensational changes are to be expected when a new government comes in, has been gradually fading ever since the first Labour Government in 1923.

In spite of many subdivisions, Britain has in effect only two political parties, the Conservative Party and the Labour Party, which between them broadly represent the main interests of the nation. But during the last twenty years the tendency of these two parties has been to resemble one another more and more. Everyone knows in advance that any government, whatever its political principles may be, can be relied upon not to do certain things. Thus, no Conservative government will ever revert to what would have been called Conservatism in the nineteenth century. No Socialist government will massacre the propertied class, nor even expropriate them without compensation. A good recent example of the changing temper of politics was the reception given to the Beveridge Report. Thirty years ago any Conservative would have denounced this as State charity, while most Socialists would have rejected it as a capitalist bribe. In 1944 the only discussion that arises is about whether it will be adopted in whole or in part. This blurring of party distinctions is happening in almost all countries, partly because everywhere, except, perhaps, in the USA, the drift is towards a planned economy, partly because in an age of power politics national survival is felt to be more important than class warfare. But Britain has certain peculiarities resulting from its being both a small island and the centre of an empire. To begin with, given the present economic system, Britain's prosperity depends partly on the Empire, while all Left parties are theoretically anti-imperialist. Politicians of the Left are therefore aware—or have recently become aware—that once in power they choose between abandoning some of their principles or lowering the English standard of living. Secondly, it is impossible for Britain to go through the kind of revolutionary process that the USSR went through. It is too small, too highly organised, too dependent on imported food. Civil war in England would mean starvation or conquest by some foreign power, or both. Thirdly and most important of all, civil war is not *morally* possible in England. In any circumstances that we can foresee, the proletariat of Hammersmith will not arise and massacre the bourgeoisie of Kensington: they are not different enough. Even the most drastic changes will have to happen peacefully and with a show of legality, and everyone except the "lunatic fringes" of the various political parties is aware of this.

These facts make up the background of the English political outlook. The great mass of the people want profound changes, but they do not want violence. They want to preserve their own standard of living, and at the same time they want to feel that they are not exploiting less fortunate peoples. If you issued a questionnaire to the whole nation, asking, "What do you want from politics?" the answer would be much the same in the overwhelming majority of cases. Substantially it would be: "Economic security, a foreign policy which will ensure peace, more social equality, and a settlement with India". Of these, the first is by far the most important, unemployment being an even greater nightmare than war. But few people would think it necessary to mention either capitalism or Socialism. Neither word has much emotional appeal. No one's heart beats faster at the thought of nationalising the Bank of England: on the other hand, the old line of talk about sturdy individualism and the sacred rights of property is no longer swallowed by the masses. They know it is not true that "there's plenty of room at the top", and in any case most of them don't want to get to the top: they want steady jobs and a fair deal for their children.

During the last few years, owing to the social frictions arising out of the war, discontent with the obvious inefficiency of old-style capitalism and admiration for Soviet Russia, public opinion has moved considerably to the Left, but without growing more doctrinaire or markedly bitterer. None of the political parties which call themselves revolutionary have seriously increased their following. There are about half a dozen of these parties, but their combined membership, even if one counts the remnants of Mosley's Blackshirts,[1] would probably not amount to 150,000. The most important of them is the Communist Party, but even the Communist Party, after twenty-five years of existence, must be held to have failed. Although it has had considerable influence at moments when circumstances favoured it, it has never shown signs of growing into a mass

[1] The British Union of Fascists.

party of the kind that exists in France or used to exist in pre-Hitler Germany.

Over a long period of years, Communist Party membership has gone up or down in response to the changes in Russian foreign policy. When the USSR is on good terms with Britain, the British Communists follow a "moderate" line hardly distinguishable from that of the Labour Party, and their membership swells to some scores of thousands. When British and Russian policy diverge, the Communists revert to a "revolutionary" line and membership slumps again. They can, in fact, only get themselves a worth-while following by abandoning their essential objectives. The various other Marxist parties, all of them claiming to be the true and uncorrupted successors of Lenin, are in an even more hopeless position. The average Englishman is unable to grasp their doctrines and uninterested in their grievances. And in England the lack of the conspiratorial mentality which has been developed in police-ridden European countries is a great handicap. English people in large numbers will not accept any creed whose dominant notes are hatred and illegality. The ruthless ideologies of the Continent—not merely Communism and Fascism, but Anarchism, Trotskyism, and even ultramontane Catholicism—are accepted in their pure form only by the intelligentsia, who constitute a sort of island of bigotry amid the general vagueness. It is significant that English revolutionary writers are obliged to use a bastard vocabulary whose key phrases are mostly translations. There are no native English words for most of the concepts they are dealing with. Even the word "proletarian", for instance, is not English and the great majority of English people do not know what it means. It is generally used, if at all, to mean simply "poor". But even so it is given a social rather than an economic slant and most people would tell you that a blacksmith or a cobbler is a proletarian and that a bank clerk is not. As for the word "bourgeois", it is used almost exclusively by people who are of bourgeois origin themselves. The only genuinely popular use of the word is as a printer's term. It is then, as one might expect, anglicised and pronounced "boorjoyce".

But there is one abstract political term which is fairly widely used and has a loose but well-understood meaning attached to it. This is the word "democracy". In a way, the English people do feel that they live in a democratic country. Not that anyone is so stupid as to take this in a literal sense. If democracy means either popular rule or social equality, it is clear that Britain is not democratic. It is, however, democratic in the secondary sense which has attached itself to that word since the rise of Hitler. To begin with, minorities have some power of making themselves heard. But more than this, public opinion cannot be disregarded when it chooses to express itself. It may have to work in indirect ways, by strikes, demonstrations and letters to the newspapers, but it can and visibly does affect government policy. A British government may be unjust, but it cannot be quite arbitrary. It cannot do the kind of thing that a totalitarian government does as a matter of course. One example out of the thousands that might be chosen is the German attack on the USSR. The significant thing is not that this was made without a declaration of war—that was natural enough—but that it was made without any propaganda build-up beforehand. The German people woke up to find themselves at war with a country that they had been ostensibly on friendly terms with on the previous evening. Our own government would not dare to do such a thing, and the English people are fairly well aware of this. English political thinking is much governed by the word "They". "They" are the higher-ups, the mysterious powers who do things to you against your will. But there is a widespread feeling that "They", though tyrannical, are not omnipotent. "They" will respond to pressure if you take the trouble to apply it: "They" are even removable. And with all their political ignorance the English people will often show surprising sensitiveness when some small incident seems to show that "They" are overstepping the mark. Hence, in the midst of seeming apathy, the sudden fuss every now and then over a rigged by-election or a too-Cromwellian handling of Parliament.

One thing that is extremely difficult to be certain about is the persistence in England of monarchist sentiment. There cannot be much doubt that at any rate in the south of England it was strong and genuine until the death of King George V. The popular response to the Silver Jubilee in 1935 took the authorities by surprise, and the celebrations had to be prolonged for an extra week. At normal times it is only the richer classes who are overtly royalist: in the West End of London, for instance, people stand to attention for "God Save the King" at the end of a picture show, whereas in the poorer quarters they walk out. But the affection shown for George V at the Silver Jubilee was obviously genuine, and it was even possible to see in it the survival, or recrudescence, of an idea almost as old as history, the idea of the King and the common people being in a sort of alliance against the upper classes; for example, some of the London slum streets bore during the Jubilee the rather servile slogan "Poor but Loyal". Other slogans, however, coupled loyalty to the King with hostility to the landlord, such as "Long Live the King. Down with the Landlord", or more often, "No Landlords Wanted" or "Landlords Keep Away". It is too early to say whether royalist sentiment was killed outright by the Abdication, but unquestionably the Abdication dealt it a serious blow. Over the past four hundred years it has waxed or waned according to circumstances. Queen Victoria, for instance, was decidedly unpopular during part of her reign, and in the first quarter of the nineteenth century public interest in the Royal Family was not nearly as strong as it was a hundred years later. At this moment the mass of the English people are probably mildly republican. But it may well be that another long reign, similar to that of George V, would revive royalist feeling and make it—as it was between roughly 1880 and 1936—an appreciable factor in politics.

THE ENGLISH CLASS SYSTEM

In time of war the English class system is the enemy propagandist's best argument. To Dr Goebbels's charge that England is still "two nations", the only truthful answer would have been that she is in fact three nations. But the peculiarity of English class distinctions is not that they are unjust—for after all, wealth and poverty exist side by side in almost all countries—but that they are anachronistic. They do not exactly correspond to economic distinctions, and what is essentially an industrial and capitalist country is haunted by the ghost of a caste system.

It is usual to classify modern society under three headings: the upper class, or bourgeoisie, the middle class, or petty bourgeoisie, and the working class, or proletariat. This roughly fits the facts, but one can draw no useful inference from it unless one takes account of the subdivisions within the various classes and realises how deeply the whole English outlook is coloured by romanticism and sheer snobbishness.

England is one of the last remaining countries to cling to the outward forms of feudalism. Titles are maintained and new ones are constantly created, and the House of Lords, consisting mainly of hereditary peers, has real powers. At the same time England has no real aristocracy. The race difference on which aristocratic rule is usually founded was disappearing by the end of the Middle Ages, and the famous medieval families have almost completely vanished. The so-called old families are those that grew rich in the sixteenth, seventeenth and eighteenth centuries. Moreover, the notion that nobility exists in its own right, that you can be a nobleman even if you are poor, was already dying out in the age of Elizabeth, a fact commented on by Shakespeare. And yet, curiously enough, the English ruling class has never developed into a bourgeoisie plain and simple. It has never become purely urban or frankly commercial. The ambition to be a country gentleman, to own and administer land and draw at least a part of your income from rent, has survived every change. So it comes that each new wave of parvenus, instead of simply replacing the existing ruling class, has adopted its habits, intermarried with it, and, after a generation or two, become indistinguishable from it.

The basic reason for this may perhaps be that England is very small and has an equable climate and pleasantly varied scenery. It is almost impossible in England, and not easy even in Scotland, to be more than twenty miles from a town. Rural life is less inherently boorish than it is in bigger countries with colder winters. And the comparative integrity of the British ruling class—for when all is said and done they have not behaved so contemptibly as their European opposite numbers—is probably bound up with their idea of themselves as feudal landowners. This outlook is shared by considerable sections of the middle class. Nearly everyone who can afford to do so sets up as a country gentleman, or at least makes some effort in that direction. The manor house with its park and its walled gardens reappears in reduced form in the stockbroker's week-end cottage, in the suburban villa with its lawn and herbaceous border, perhaps even in the potted nasturtiums on the window-sill of the Bayswater flat. This widespread day-dream is undoubtedly snobbish, it has tended to stabilise class distinctions and has helped to prevent the modernisation of English agriculture: but it is mixed up with a kind of idealism, a feeling that style and tradition are more important than money.

Within the middle class there is a sharp division, cultural and not financial, between those who aim at gentility and those who do not. According to the usual classification, everyone between the capitalist and the weekly wage-earner can be lumped together as "petty bourgeoisie". This means that the Harley Street physician, the army officer, the grocer, the farmer, the senior civil servant, the solicitor, the clergyman, the schoolmaster, the bank manager, the speculative builder, and the fisherman who owns his own boat, are all in the same class. But no one in England feels them to belong to the same class, and the distinction between them is not a distinction of income but of accent, manners and, to some extent, outlook. Anyone who pays any attention to class differences at all would regard an army officer with £1,000 a year as socially superior to a shopkeeper with £2,000 a year. Even within the upper class a similar distinction holds good, the titled person being almost always more deferred to than an untitled person of larger income. Middle-class people are really graded according to their degree of resemblance to the aristocracy: professional men, senior officials, officers in the fighting services, university lecturers, clergymen, even the literary and scientific intelligentsia, rank higher than businessmen, though on the whole they earn less. It is a peculiarity of this class that their largest item of expenditure is education. Whereas a successful tradesman will send his son to the local grammar school, a clergyman with half his income will underfeed himself for years in order to send his son to a public school, although he knows that he will get no direct return for the money he spends.

There is, however, another noticeable division in the middle class. The old distinction was between the man who is "a gentleman" and the man who is "not a gentleman". In the last thirty years, however, the demands of modern industry, and the technical schools and provincial universities, have brought into being a new kind of man, middle class in income and to some extent in habits, but not much interested in his own social status. People like radio engineers and industrial chemists, whose education has not been of a kind to give them any reverence for the past, and who tend to live in blocks of flats or housing estates where the old social pattern has broken down, are the most nearly classless beings that England possesses. They are an important section of society, because their numbers are constantly growing. The war, for instance, made necessary the formation of an enormous air force, and so you got thousands of young men of working-class origin graduating into the technical middle class by way of the RAF. Any serious reorganisation of industry now will have similar effects. And the characteristic outlook of the technicians is already spreading among the older strata of the middle class. One symptom of this is that intermarriage within the middle class is freer than it used to be. Another is the increasing unwillingness of people below the £2,000 a year level to bankrupt themselves in the name of education.

Another series of changes, probably dating from the Education Act of 1870, is occurring in the working class. One cannot altogether acquit the English working class either of snobbishness or of servility. To begin with there is a fairly sharp distinction between the better-paid working class and the very poor. Even in Socialist literature it is common to find contemptuous references to slum-dwellers (the German word *Lumpenproletariat* is much used), and imported labourers with low standards of living, such as the Irish, are greatly looked down on. There is also, probably, more disposition to accept class distinctions as permanent, and even to accept the upper classes as natural leaders, than survives in most countries. It is significant that in the moment of disaster the man best able to unite the nation was Churchill, a Conservative of aristocratic origins. The word "Sir" is much used in England, and the man of obviously upper-class appearance can usually get more than his fair share of deference from commissionaires, ticket-collectors, policemen, and the like. It is this aspect of English life that seems most shocking to visitors from America and the Dominions. And the tendency towards servility probably did not decrease in the twenty years between the two wars: it may even have increased, owing chiefly to unemployment.

But snobbishness is never quite separable from idealism. The tendency to give the upper classes more than their due is mixed up with a respect for good manners and something vaguely describable as culture. In the south of England, at any rate, it is unquestionable that most working-class people want to resemble the upper classes in manners and habits. The traditional attitude of looking down on the upper classes as effeminate and "la-di-dah" survives best in the heavy-industry areas. Hostile nicknames like "toff" and "swell" have almost disappeared, and even the *Daily Worker* displays advertisements for "High-Class Gentleman's Tailor". Above all, throughout southern England there is almost general uneasiness about the cockney accent. In Scotland and northern England snobbishness about the local accents does exist, but it is not nearly so strong or widespread. Many a Yorkshireman definitely prides himself on his broad U's and narrow A's, and will defend them on linguistic grounds. In London there are still people who say "fice" instead of "face", but there is probably no one who regards "fice" as superior. Even a person who claims to despise the bourgeoisie and all its ways will still take care that his children grow up pronouncing their aitches.

But side by side with this there has gone a considerable growth of political consciousness and an increasing impatience with class privilege. Over a period of twenty or thirty years the working class has grown politically more hostile to the upper class, culturally less hostile. There is nothing incongruous in this: both tendencies are symptoms of the levelling of manners which results from machine civilisation and which makes the English class system more and more of an anachronism.

The obvious class differences still surviving in England astonish foreign observers, but they are far less marked, and far less real, than they were thirty years ago. People of different social origins, thrown together during the war in the armed forces, or in factories or offices, or as firewatchers and Home Guards, were able to mingle more easily than they did in the 1914–18 war. It is worth listing the various influences which—mechanically, as it were—tend to make Englishmen of all classes less and less different from one another.

First of all, the improvement in industrial technique. Every year less and less people are engaged in heavy manual labour which keeps them constantly tired and, by hypertrophying certain muscles, gives them a distinctive carriage. Secondly, improvements in housing. Between the two wars rehousing was done mostly by the local authorities, who have produced a type of house (the council house, with its bathroom, garden, separate kitchen, and indoor WC) which is nearer to the stockbroker's villa than it is to the labourer's cottage. Thirdly, the mass production of furniture which in ordinary times can be bought on the hire-purchase system. The effect of this is that the interior of a working-class house resembles that of a middle-class house very much more than it did a generation ago. Fourthly, and perhaps most important of all, the mass production of cheap clothes. Thirty years ago the social status of nearly everyone in England could be determined from his appearance, even at two hundred yards' distance. The working classes all wore ready-made clothes, and the ready-made clothes were not only ill-fitting but usually followed the upper-class fashions of ten or fifteen years earlier. The cloth cap was practically a badge of status. It was universal among the working class, while the upper classes only wore it for golf and shooting. This state of affairs is rapidly changing. Ready-made clothes now follow the fashions closely, they are made in many different fittings to suit every kind of figure, and even when they are of very cheap cloth they are superficially not very different from expensive clothes. The result is that it grows harder every year, especially in the case of women, to determine social status at a glance.

Mass-produced literature and amusements have the same effect. Radio programmes, for instance, are necessarily the same for everybody. Films, though often extremely reactionary in their implied outlook, have to appeal to a public of millions and therefore have to avoid stirring up class antagonisms. So also with some of the big-circulation newspapers. The *Daily Express*, for instance, draws its readers from all strata of the population. So also with some of the periodicals that have appeared in the past dozen years. *Punch* is obviously a middle- and upper-class paper, but *Picture Post* is not aimed at any particular class. And lending libraries and very cheap books, such as the Penguins, popularise the habit of reading and probably have a levelling effect on literary taste. Even taste in food tends to grow more uniform owing to the multiplication of cheap but fairly smart restaurants such as those of Messrs Lyons.

We are not justified in assuming that class distinctions are actually disappearing. The essential structure of England is still almost what it was in the nineteenth century. But real differences between man and man are obviously diminishing, and this fact is grasped and even welcomed by people who only a few years ago were clinging desperately to their social prestige.

Whatever may be the ultimate fate of the very rich, the tendency of the working class and the middle class is evidently to merge. It may happen quickly or slowly, according to circumstances. It has been accelerated by the war, and another ten years of all-round rationing, utility clothes, high income tax, and compulsory national service may finish the process once and for all. The final effects of this we cannot foresee. There are observers, both native and foreign, who believe that the fairly large amount of individual freedom that is enjoyed in England depends on having a well-defined class system. Liberty, according to some, is incompatible with equality. But at least it is certain that the present drift *is* towards greater social equality, and that this is what the great mass of the English people desire.

The English language has two outstanding characteristics to which most of its minor oddities can be finally traced. These characteristics are a very large vocabulary and simplicity of grammar.

If it is not the largest in the world, the English vocabulary is certainly among the largest. English is really two languages, Anglo-Saxon and Norman-French, and during the last three centuries it has been reinforced on an enormous scale by new words deliberately created from Latin and Greek roots. But in addition the vocabulary is made much larger than it appears by the practice of turning one part of speech into another. For example, almost any noun can be used as a verb: this in effect gives an extra range of verbs, so that you have *knife* as well as *stab*, *school* as well as *teach*, *fire* as well as *burn*, and so on. Then again, certain verbs can be given as many as twenty different meanings simply by adding prepositions to them. (Examples are *get out of*, *get up*, *give out*, *take over*.) Verbs can also change into nouns with considerable freedom, and by the use of affixes such as *-y*, *-ful*, *-like*, any noun can be turned into an adjective. More freely than in most languages, verbs and adjectives can be turned into their opposites by means of the prefix *un-*. And adjectives can be made more emphatic or given a new twist by tying a noun to them; for example, *lily-white*, *sky-blue*, *coal-black*, *iron-hard*, etc.

But English is also, and to an unnecessary extent, a borrowing language. It readily takes over any foreign word that seems to fill a need, often altering the meaning in doing so. A recent example is the word *blitz*. As a verb this word did not appear in print till late in 1940, but it has already become part of the language. Other examples from the vast armoury of borrowed words are *garage*, *charabanc*, *alias*, *alibi*, *steppe*, *thug*, *role*, *menu*, *lasso*, *rendezvous*, *chemise*. It will be noticed that in most cases an English equivalent exists already, so that borrowing adds to the already large stock of synonyms.

English grammar is simple. The language is almost completely uninflected, a peculiarity which marks it off from almost all languages west of China. Any regular English verb has only three inflections, the third person singular, the present participle, and the past participle. Thus, for instance, the verb *to kill* consists of *kill*, *kills*, *killing*, *killed*, and that is all. There is, of course, a great wealth of tenses, very much subtilised in meaning, but these are made by the use of auxiliaries which themselves barely inflect. *May, might, shall, will, should, would* do not inflect at all, except in the obsolete second person singular. The upshot is that every person in every tense of such a verb as *to kill* can be expressed in only about thirty words including the pronouns, or about forty if one includes the second person singular. The corresponding number in, for instance, French would be somewhere near two hundred. And in English there is the added advantage that the auxiliaries which are used to make the tenses are the same in every case.

There is no such thing in English as declension of nouns, and there is no gender. Nor are there many irregular plurals or comparatives. Moreover, the tendency is always towards greater simplicity, both in grammar and syntax. Long sentences with dependent clauses grow more and more unpopular, irregular but time-saving formations such as the "American subjunctive" (*it is necessary that you go* instead of *it is necessary that you should go*) gain ground, and difficult rules, such as the difference between *shall* and *will*, or *that* and *which*, are more and more ignored. If it continues to develop along its present lines English will ultimately have more in common with the uninflected languages of East Asia than with the languages of Europe.

The greatest quality of English is its enormous range not only of meaning but of *tone*. It is capable of endless subtleties, and of everything from the most high-flown rhetoric to the most brutal coarseness. On the other hand, its lack of grammar makes it easily compressible. It is the language of lyric poetry, and also of headlines. On its lower levels it is very easy to learn, in spite of its irrational spelling. It can also for international purposes be reduced to very simple pidgin dialects, ranging from Basic to the "Bêche-de-mer" English used in the South Pacific. It is therefore well suited to be a world lingua franca, and it has in fact spread more widely than any other language.

But there are also great disadvantages, or at least great dangers, in speaking English as one's native tongue. To begin with, as was pointed out earlier in this essay, the English are very poor linguists. Their own language is grammatically so simple that unless they have gone through the discipline of learning a foreign language in childhood, they are often quite unable to grasp what is meant by gender, person, and case. A completely illiterate Indian will pick up English far faster than a British soldier will pick up Hindustani. Nearly five million Indians are literate in English and millions more speak it in a debased form. There are some tens of thousands of Indians who

speak English as nearly as possible perfectly; yet the number of
Englishmen speaking any Indian language perfectly would not
amount to more than a few scores. But the great weakness of English
is its capacity for debasement. Just because it is so easy to use, it is
easy to use *badly*.

To write or even to speak English is not a science but an art. There
are no reliable rules: there is only the general principle that concrete
words are better than abstract ones, and that the shortest way of
saying anything is always the best. Mere correctness is no guarantee
whatever of good writing. A sentence like "an enjoyable time was
had by all present" is perfectly correct English, and so is the unintelligible mess of words on an income-tax return. Whoever writes
English is involved in a struggle that never lets up even for a sentence. He is struggling against vagueness, against obscurity, against
the lure of the decorative adjective, against the encroachment of
Latin and Greek, and, above all, against the worn-out phrases and
dead metaphors with which the language is cluttered up. In speaking,
these dangers are more easily avoided, but spoken English differs
from written English more sharply than is the case in most languages.
In the spoken tongue every word that can be omitted is omitted,
every possible abbreviation is used. Meaning is conveyed quite
largely by emphasis, though curiously enough the English do not
gesticulate, as one might reasonably expect them to do. A sentence
like *No, I don't mean that one, I mean that one* is perfectly intelligible
when spoken aloud, even without a gesture. But spoken English, when
it tries to be dignified and logical, usually takes on the vices of written
English, as you can see by spending half an hour either in the House
of Commons or at the Marble Arch.

English is peculiarly subject to jargons. Doctors, scientists, businessmen, officials, sportsmen, economists, and political theorists
all have their characteristic perversion of the language, which can
be studied in the appropriate magazines from the *Lancet* to the
Labour Monthly. But probably the deadliest enemy of good English
is what is called "standard English". This dreary dialect, the language
of leading articles, White Papers, political speeches, and BBC news
bulletins, is undoubtedly spreading: it is spreading downwards in
the social scale, and outwards into the spoken language. Its characteristic is its reliance on ready-made phrases—*in due course, take
the earliest opportunity, warm appreciation, deepest regret, explore
every avenue, ring the changes, take up the cudgels, legitimate assump-*

tion, the answer is in the affirmative, etc etc—which may once have been fresh and vivid, but have now become mere thought-saving devices, having the same relation to living English as a crutch has to a leg. Anyone preparing a broadcast or writing to *The Times* adopts this kind of language almost instinctively, and it infects the spoken tongue as well. So much has our language been weakened that the imbecile chatter in Swift's essay on polite conversation (a satire on the upper-class talk of Swift's own day) would actually be rather a good conversation by modern standards.

The temporary decadence of the English language is due, like so much else, to our anachronistic class system. "Educated" English has grown anaemic because for long past it has not been reinvigorated from below. The people likeliest to use simple concrete language, and to think of metaphors that really call up a visual image, are those who are in contact with physical reality. A useful word like *bottleneck*, for instance, would be most likely to occur to someone used to dealing with conveyor belts: or again, the expressive military phrase *to winkle out* implies acquaintance both with winkles and with machine-gun nests. And the vitality of English depends on a steady supply of images of this kind. It follows that language, at any rate the English language, suffers when the educated classes lose touch with the manual workers. As things are at present, nearly every Englishman, whatever his origins, feels the working-class manner of speech, and even working-class idioms, to be inferior. Cockney, the most widespread dialect, is the most despised of all. Any word or usage that is supposedly cockney is looked on as vulgar, even when, as is sometimes the case, it is merely an archaism. An example is *ain't*, which is now abandoned in favour of the much weaker form *aren't*. But *ain't* was good enough English eighty years ago, and Queen Victoria would have said *ain't*.

During the past forty years, and especially the past dozen years, English has borrowed largely from American, while American has shown no tendency to borrow from English. The reason for this is partly political. Anti-British feeling in the United States is far stronger than anti-American feeling in England, and most Americans dislike using a word or phrase which they know to be British. But American has gained a footing in England partly because of the vivid, almost poetic quality of its slang, partly because certain American usages (for instance, the formation of verbs by adding *ise* to a noun) save time, and most of all because one can adopt an American word without crossing a class barrier. From the English point of view American words have no class label. This applies even to thieves' slang. Words like *stooge* and *stool-pigeon* are considered much less vulgar than words like *nark* and *split*. Even a very snobbish English person would probably not mind calling a policeman a *cop*, which is American, but he would object to calling him a *copper*, which is working-class English. To the working classes, on the other hand, the use of Americanisms is a way of escaping from cockney without adopting the BBC dialect, which they instinctively dislike and cannot easily master. Hence, especially in the big towns, working-class children now use American slang from the moment that they learn to talk. And there is a noticeable tendency to use American words even when they are not slang and when an English equivalent already exists: for instance, *car* for *tram*, *escalator* for *moving stair-case*, *automobile* for *motor car*.

This process will probably continue for some time. One cannot check it simply by protesting against it, and in any case many American words and expressions are well worth adopting. Some are necessary neologisms, others (for instance, *fall* for *autumn*) are old words which we ought never to have dropped. But it ought to be realised that on the whole American is a bad influence and has already had a debasing effect.

To begin with, American has some of the vices of English in an exaggerated form. The interchangeability of different parts of speech has been carried further, the distinction between transitive and in-transitive verbs tends to break down, and many words are used which have no meaning whatever. For example, whereas English alters the meaning of a verb by tacking a preposition on to it, the American tendency is to burden every verb with a preposition that adds nothing to its meaning (*win out, lose out, face up to*, etc). On the other hand, American has broken more completely than English with the past and with literary traditions. It not only produces words like *beautician*, *moronic*, and *sexualise*, but often replaces strong primary words by feeble euphemisms. For instance, many Americans seem to regard the word *death* and various words that go with it (*corpse, coffin, shroud*) as almost unmentionable. But above all, to adopt the American language whole-heartedly would probably mean a huge loss of vocabulary. For though American produces vivid and witty turns of speech, it is terribly poor in names for natural objects and localities. Even the streets in American cities are usually known by numbers instead of names. If we really intended to model our language upon American we should have, for instance, to lump the lady-bird, the daddy-long-legs, the saw-fly, the water-boatman, the cockchafer, the cricket, the death-watch beetle and scores of other insects all together under the inexpressive name of *bug*. We should lose the poetic names of our wild flowers, and also, probably, our habit of giving individual names to every street, pub, field, lane, and hillock. In so far as American is adopted, that is the tendency. Those who take their language from the films, or from papers such as *Life* and *Time*, always prefer the slick time-saving word to the one with a history behind it. As to accent, it is doubtful whether the American accent has the superiority which it is now fashionable to claim for it. The "educated" English accent, a product of the last thirty years, is undoubtedly very bad and is likely to be abandoned, but the average English person probably speaks as clearly as the average American. Most English people blur their vowel sounds, but most Americans swallow their consonants. Many Americans pronounce, for instance, *water* as though it had no T in it, or even as though it had no consonant in it at all, except the W. On the whole we are justified in regarding the American language with suspicion. We ought to be ready to borrow its best words, but we ought not to let it modify the actual structure of our language.

However, there is no chance of resisting the American influence unless we can put new life into English itself. And it is difficult to do this while words and idioms are prevented from circulating freely among all sections of the population. English people of all classes now find it natural to express incredulity by the American slang phrase *sez you*. Many would even tell you in good faith that *sez you* has no English equivalent. Actually it has a whole string of them— for instance, *not half, I don't think, come off it, less of it, and then you wake up*, or simply *garn*. But most of these would be considered vulgar: you would never find an expression like *not half* in a *Times* leader, for instance. And on the other hand many necessary abstract words, especially words of Latin origin, are rejected by the working class because they sound public-schoolish, "tony" and effeminate. Language ought to be the joint creation of poets and manual workers, and in modern England it is difficult for these two classes to meet. When they can do so again—as, in a different way, they could in the feudal past—English may show more clearly than at present its kinship with the language of Shakespeare and Defoe.

THE FUTURE OF THE ENGLISH PEOPLE

This is not a book about foreign politics, but if one is to speak of the future of the English people, one must start by considering what kind of world they will probably be living in and what special part they can play in it.

Nations do not often die out, and the English people will still be in existence a hundred years hence, whatever has happened in the meantime. But if Britain is to survive as what is called a "great" nation, playing an important and useful part in the world's affairs, one must taken certain things as assured. One must assume that Britain will remain on good terms with Russia and Europe, will keep its special links with America and the Dominions, and will solve the problem of India in some amicable way. That is perhaps a great deal to assume, but without it there is not much hope for civilisation as a whole, and still less for Britain itself. If the savage international struggle of the last twenty years continues, there will only be room in the world for two or three great powers, and in the long run Britain will not be one of them. It has not either the population or the resources. In a world of power politics the English would ultimately dwindle to a satellite people, and the special thing that it is in their power to contribute might be lost.

But what is the special thing that they could contribute? The outstanding and—by contemporary standards—highly original quality of the English is their habit of *not killing one another*. Putting aside the "model" small states, which are in an exceptional position, England is the only European country where internal politics are conducted in a more or less humane and decent manner. It is—and this was true long before the rise of Fascism—the only country where armed men do not prowl the streets and no one is frightened of the secret police. And the whole British Empire, with all its crying abuses, its stagnation in one place and exploitation in another, at least has the merit of being internally peaceful. It has always been able to get along with a very small number of armed men, although it contains a quarter of the population of the earth. Between the wars its total armed forces amounted to about 600,000 men, of whom a third were Indians. At the outbreak of war the entire Empire was able to mobilise about a million trained men. Almost as many could have been mobilised by, say, Rumania. The English are probably more capable than most peoples of making revolutionary changes without bloodshed. In England, if anywhere, it would be possible to abolish poverty without destroying liberty. If the English took the trouble to make their own democracy work, they would become the political leaders of western Europe, and probably of some other parts of the world as well. They would provide the much-needed alternative to Russian authoritarianism on the one hand and American materialism on the other.

But to play a leading part the English have got to know what they are doing, and they have got to retain their vitality. For this, certain developments are needed within the next decade. These are a rising birthrate, more social equality, less centralisation and more respect for the intellect.

There has been a small rise in the birthrate during the war years, but that is probably of no significance, and the general curve is downwards. The position is not quite so desperate as it is sometimes said to be, but it can only be put right if the curve not only rises sharply, but does so within ten or at most twenty years. Otherwise the population will not only fall, but, what is worse, will consist predominantly of middle-aged people. If that point is reached, the decline may never be retrievable.

At bottom, the causes of the dwindled birthrate are economic. It is nonsense to say that it has happened because English people do not care for children. In the early nineteenth century they had an extremely high birthrate, and they also had an attitude towards children which now seems to us unbelievably callous. With very little public disapproval, children as young as six were sold into the mines and factories, and the death of a child, the most shocking event that modern people are able to imagine, was looked on as a very minor tragedy. In a sense it is true that modern English people have small families because they are too fond of children. They feel that it is wrong to bring a child into the world unless you are completely certain of being able to provide for him, and at a level not lower than your own. For the last fifty years, to have a big family has meant that your children must wear poorer clothes than others in the same group, must have less food and less attention, and probably must go to work earlier. This held good for all classes except the very rich and the unemployed. No doubt the dearth of babies is partly due to the competing attraction of cars and radios, but its main cause is a typically English mixture of snobbishness and altruism.

The philoprogenitive instinct will probably return when fairly large families are already the rule, but the first steps towards this must be economic ones. Half-hearted family allowances will not do the trick, especially when there is a severe housing shortage, as there is now. People should be better off for having children, just as they are in a peasant community, instead of being financially crippled, as they are in ours. Any government, by a few strokes of the pen, could make childlessness as unbearable an economic burden as a big family is now: but no government has chosen to do so, because of the ignorant idea that a bigger population means more unemployed. Far more drastically than anyone has proposed hitherto, taxation will have to be graded so as to encourage child-bearing and to save women with young children from being obliged to work outside the home. And this involves readjustment of rents, better public service in the matter of nursery schools and playing grounds, and the building of bigger and more convenient houses. It also probably involves the extension and improvement of free education, so that the middle-class family shall not, as at present, be crushed out of existence by impossibly high school fees.

The economic adjustments must come first, but a change of outlook is also needed. In the England of the last thirty years it has seemed all too natural that blocks of flats should refuse tenants with children, that parks and squares should be railed off to keep the children out of them, that abortion, theoretically illegal, should be looked on as a peccadillo, and that the main aim of commercial advertising should be to popularise the idea of "having a good time" and staying young as long as possible. Even the cult of animals, fostered by the newspapers, has probably done its bit towards reducing the birthrate. Nor have the public authorities seriously interested themselves in this question till very recently. Britain today has a million and a half less children than in 1914, and a million and a half more dogs. Yet even now, when the government designs a prefabricated house, it produces a house with only two bedrooms— with room, that is to say, for two children at the most. When one considers the history of the years between the wars, it is perhaps surprising that the birthrate has not dropped more catastrophically than it has. But it is not likely to rise to the replacement level until those in power, as well as the ordinary people in the street, come to feel that children matter more than money.

The English are probably less irked by class distinctions, more tolerant of privilege and of absurdities like titles, than most peoples.

There is nevertheless, as I have pointed out earlier, a growing wish for greater equality and a tendency, below the £2,000 a year level, for surface differences between class and class to disappear. At present this is happening only mechanically and quite largely as a result of the war. The question is how it can be speeded up. For even the change-over to a centralised economy, which, except, possibly, in the United States, is happening in all countries under one name or another, does of itself guarantee greater equality between man and man. Once civilisation has reached a fairly high technical level, class distinctions are an obvious evil. They not only lead great numbers of people to waste their lives in the pursuit of social prestige, but they also cause an immense wastage of talent. In England it is not merely the ownership of property that is concentrated in a few hands. It is also the case that all power, administrative as well as financial, belongs to a single class. Except for a handful of "self-made men" and Labour politicians, those who control our destinies are the product of about a dozen public schools and two universities. A nation is using its capacities to the full when any man can get any job that he is fit for. One has only to think of some of the people who have held vitally important jobs during the past twenty years, and to wonder what would have happened to them if they had been born into the working class, to see that this is not the case in England.

Moreover, class distinctions are a constant drain on morale, in peace as well as in war. And the more conscious, the better educated, the mass of the people become, the more this is so. The word "They", the universal feeling that "They" hold all the power and make all the decisions, and that "They" can only be influenced in indirect and uncertain ways, is a great handicap in England. In 1940 "They" showed a marked tendency to give place to "We", and it is time that it did so permanently. Three measures are obviously necessary, and they would begin to produce their effect within a few years.

The first is a scaling-up and scaling-down of incomes. The glaring inequality of wealth that existed in England before the war must not be allowed to recur. Above a certain point—which should bear a fixed relation to the lowest current wage—all income should be taxed out of existence. In theory, at any rate, this has happened already, with beneficial results. The second necessary measure is greater democracy in education. A completely unified system of education is probably not desirable. Some adolescents benefit by higher education, others do not, there is need to differentiate between

literary and technical education, and it is better that a few independent experimental schools should remain in existence. But it should
be the rule, as it is in some countries already, for all children to attend
the same schools up to the age of twelve or at least ten. After that
age it becomes necessary to separate the more gifted children from the
less gifted, but a uniform educational system for the early years
would cut away one of the deepest roots of snobbery.

The third thing that is needed is to remove the class labels from
the English language. It is not desirable that all the local accents
should disappear, but there should be a manner of speaking that is
definitely national and is not merely (like the accent of the BBC
announcers) a copy of the mannerisms of the upper classes. This
national accent—a modification of cockney, perhaps, or of one of
the northern accents—should be taught as a matter of course to all
children alike. After that they could, and in some parts of the country
they probably would, revert to the local accent, but they should be
able to speak standard English if they wished to. No one should be
"branded on the tongue". It should be impossible, as it is in the
United States and some European countries, to determine anyone's
status from his accent.

We need, too, to be less centralised. English agriculture has revived
during the war, and the revival may continue, but the English people
are still excessively urban in outlook. Culturally, moreover, the
country is very much over-centralised. Not only is the whole of
Britain in effect governed from London, but the sense of locality—
of being, say, an East Anglian or a West Countryman as well as an
Englishman—has been much weakened during the past century.
The ambition of the farm labourer is usually to get to a town, the
provincial intellectual always wants to get to London. In both
Scotland and Wales there are nationalist movements, but they are
founded on an economic grievance against England rather than on
genuine local pride. Nor is there any important literary or artistic
movement that is truly independent of London and the university
towns.

It is uncertain whether this centralising tendency is completely
reversible, but a good deal could be done to check it. Both Scotland
and Wales could and should be a great deal more autonomous than
they are at present. The provincial universities should be more
generously equipped and the provincial press subsidised. (At present
nearly the whole of England is "covered" by eight London news-

papers. No newspaper with a large circulation, and no first-class magazine, is published outside London.) The problem of getting people, and especially young, spirited people, to stay on the land would be partly solved if farm labourers had better cottages and if country towns were more civilised and cross-country bus services more efficient. Above all, local pride should be stimulated by teaching in the elementary schools. Every child ought as a matter of course to learn something of the history and topography of its own county. People ought to be proud of their own locality, they ought to feel that its scenery, its architecture and even its cookery are the best in the world. And such feelings, which do exist in some areas of the north but have lapsed throughout the greater part of England, would strengthen national unity rather than weaken it.

It has been suggested earlier that the survival of free speech in England is partly the result of stupidity. The people are not intellectual enough to be heresy-hunters. One does not wish them to grow less tolerant, nor, having seen the results, would one want them to develop the political sophistication that prevailed in pre-Hitler Germany or pre-Pétain France. But the instincts and traditions on which the English rely served them best when they were an exceptionally fortunate people, protected by geography from major disaster. In the twentieth century the narrow interests of the average man, the rather low level of English education, the contempt for "highbrows" and the almost general deadness to aesthetic issues, are serious liabilities.

What the upper classes think about "highbrows" can be judged from the Honours Lists. The upper classes feel titles to be important: yet almost never is any major honour bestowed on anyone describable as an intellectual. With very few exceptions, scientists do not get beyond baronetcies, or literary men beyond knighthoods. But the attitude of the man in the street is no better. He is not troubled by the reflection that England spends hundreds of millions every year on beer and the football pools while scientific research languishes for lack of funds; or that we can afford greyhound tracks innumerable but not even one National Theatre. Between the wars England tolerated newspapers, films and radio programmes of unheard-of silliness, and these produced further stupefaction in the public, blinding their eyes to vitally important problems. This silliness of the English press is partly artificial, since it arises from the fact that newspapers live off advertisements for consumption goods.

During the war the papers have grown very much more intelligent without losing their public, and millions of people read papers which they would have rejected as impossibly "highbrow" some years ago. There is, however, not only a low general level of taste, but a widespread unawareness that aesthetic considerations can possibly have any importance. Rehousing and town planning, for instance, are normally discussed without even a mention of beauty or ugliness. The English are great lovers of flowers, gardening and "nature", but this is merely a part of their vague aspiration towards an agricultural life. In the main they see no objection to "ribbon development" or to the filth and chaos of the industrial towns. They see nothing wrong in scattering the woods with paper bags and filling every pool and stream with tin cans and bicycle frames. And they are all too ready to listen to any journalist who tells them to trust their instincts and despise the "highbrow".

One result of this has been to increase the isolation of the British intelligentsia. English intellectuals, especially the younger ones, are markedly hostile to their own country. Exceptions can, of course, be found, but it is broadly true that anyone who would prefer T. S. Eliot to Alfred Noyes despises England, or thinks that he ought to do so. In "enlightened" circles, to express pro-British sentiments needs considerable moral courage. On the other hand, during the past dozen years there has been a strong tendency to develop a violent nationalistic loyalty to some foreign country, usually Soviet Russia. This must probably have happened in any case, because capitalism in its later phases pushes the literary and even the scientific intellectual into a position where he has security without much responsibility. But the philistinism of the English public alienates the intelligentsia still further. The loss to society is very great. It means that the people whose vision is acutest—the people, for instance, who grasped that Hitler was dangerous ten years before this was discovered by our public men—are hardly able to make contact with the masses and grow less and less interested in English problems.

The English will never develop into a nation of philosophers. They will always prefer instinct to logic, and character to intelligence. But they must get rid of their downright contempt for "cleverness". They cannot afford it any longer. They must grow less tolerant of ugliness, and mentally more adventurous. And they must stop despising foreigners. They are Europeans and ought to be aware of it. On the other hand they have special links with the other English-speakers overseas, and special imperial responsibilities, in which they ought to take more interest than they have done during these past twenty years. The intellectual atmosphere of England is already very much livelier than it was. The war scotched if it did not kill certain kinds of folly. But there is still need for a conscious effort at national re-education. The first step towards this is an improvement in elementary education, which involves not only raising the school-leaving age but spending enough money to ensure that elementary schools are adequately staffed and equipped. And there are immense educational possibilities in the radio, the film, and—if it could be freed once and for all from commercial interests—the press.

These, then, appear to be the immediate necessities of the English people. They must breed faster, work harder, and probably live more simply, think more deeply, get rid of their snobbishness and their anachronistic class distinctions, and pay more attention to the world and less to their own backyards. Nearly all of them already love their country, but they must learn to love it intelligently. They must have a clear notion of their own destiny and not listen either to those who tell them that England is finished or to those who tell them that the England of the past can return.

If they can do that they can keep their feet in the post-war world, and if they can keep their feet they can give the example that millions of human beings are waiting for. The world is sick of chaos and it is sick of dictatorship. Of all peoples the English are likeliest to find a way of avoiding both. Except for a small minority they are fully ready for the drastic economic changes that are needed, and at the same time they have no desire either for violent revolution or for foreign conquests. They have known for forty years, perhaps, something that the Germans and the Japanese have only recently learned, and that the Russians and the Americans have yet to learn: they know that it is not possible for any one nation to rule the earth. They want above all things to live at peace, internally and externally. And the great mass of them are probably prepared for the sacrifices that peace entails.

But they will have to take their destiny into their own hands. England can only fulfil its special mission if the ordinary English in the street can somehow get their hands on power. We have been told very frequently during this war that this time, when the danger is over, there should be no lost opportunities, no recurrence of the past. No more stagnation punctuated by wars, no more Rolls-Royces gliding past dole queues, no return to the England of the Distressed Areas, the endlessly stewing teapot, the empty pram, and the Giant Panda. We cannot be sure that this promise will be kept. Only we ourselves can make certain that it will come true, and if we do not, no further chance may be given us. The past thirty years have been a long series of cheques drawn upon the accumulated goodwill of the English people. That reserve may not be inexhaustible. By the end of another decade it will be finally clear whether England is to survive as a great nation or not. And if the answer is to be "Yes", it is the common people who must make it so.

["The English People" was commissioned by Collins in September 1943 for their series "Britain in Pictures" and written by May 1944, although it did not appear until August 1947. Because of the delay in publication some references were updated by the publisher in 1946. In the version printed here these have been altered back to the present tense. See IV, 92.

Because they deal with details of English life, five short pieces written in the 'forties have been printed here.]

2. In Defence of English Cooking

We have heard a good deal of talk in recent years about the desirability of attracting foreign tourists to this country. It is well known that England's two worst faults, from a foreign visitor's point of view, are the gloom of our Sundays and the difficulty of buying a drink.

Both of these are due to fanatical minorities who will need a lot of quelling, including extensive legislation. But there is one point on which public opinion could bring about a rapid change for the better: I mean cooking.

It is commonly said, even by the English themselves, that English cooking is the worst in the world. It is supposed to be not merely incompetent, but also imitative, and I even read quite recently, in a book by a French writer, the remark: "The best English cooking is, of course, simply French cooking".

Now that is simply not true. As anyone who has lived long abroad will know, there is a whole host of delicacies which it is quite impossible to obtain outside the English-speaking countries.

No doubt the list could be added to, but here are some of the things that I myself have sought for in foreign countries and failed to find.

First of all, kippers, Yorkshire pudding, Devonshire cream, muffins and crumpets. Then a list of puddings that would be interminable if I gave it in full: I will pick out for special mention Christmas pudding, treacle tart and apple dumplings. Then an almost equally long list of cakes: for instance, dark plum cake (such as you used to get at Buzzard's before the war), short-bread and saffron buns. Also innumerable kinds of biscuit, which exist, of course, elsewhere, but are generally admitted to be better and crisper in England.

Then there are the various ways of cooking potatoes that are peculiar to our own country. Where else do you see potatoes roasted under the joint, which is far and away the best way of cooking them? Or the delicious potato cakes that you get in the north of England? And it is far better to cook new potatoes in the English way—that is, boiled with mint and then served with a little melted butter or margarine—than to fry them as is done in most countries.

Then there are the various sauces peculiar to England. For instance, bread sauce, horse-radish sauce, mint sauce and apple sauce; not to mention redcurrant jelly, which is excellent with mutton as well as with hare, and various kinds of sweet pickle, which we seem to have in greater profusion than most countries.

What else? Outside these islands I have never seen a haggis, except one that came out of a tin, nor Dublin prawns, nor Oxford marmalade, nor several other kinds of jam (marrow jam and bramble jelly, for instance), nor sausages of quite the same kind as ours.

Then there are the English cheeses. There are not many of them but I fancy that Stilton is the best cheese of its type in the world, with Wensleydale not far behind. English apples are also outstandingly good, particularly the Cox's Orange Pippin.

And finally, I would like to put in a word for English bread. All the bread is good, from the enormous Jewish loaves flavoured with caraway seeds to the Russian rye bread which is the colour of black treacle. Still, if there is anything quite as good as the soft part of the crust from an English cottage loaf (how soon shall we be seeing cottage loaves again?) I do not know of it.

No doubt some of the things I have named above could be obtained in continental Europe, just as it is possible in London to obtain vodka or bird's nest soup. But they are all native to our shores, and over huge areas they are literally unheard of.

South of, say, Brussels, I do not imagine that you would succeed in getting hold of a suet pudding. In French there is not even a word that exactly translates "suet". The French, also, never use mint in cookery and do not use black currants except as a basis of a drink.

It will be seen that we have no cause to be ashamed of our cookery, so far as originality goes or so far as the ingredients go. And yet it must be admitted that there is a serious snag from the foreign visitor's point of view. This is, that you practically don't find good English cooking outside a private house. If you want, say, a good, rich slice of Yorkshire pudding you are more likely to get it in the poorest English home than in a restaurant, which is where the visitor necessarily eats most of his meals.

It is a fact that restaurants which are distinctively English and which also sell good food are very hard to find. Pubs, as a rule, sell no food at all, other than potato crisps and tasteless sandwiches. The expensive restaurants and hotels almost all imitate French cookery and write their menus in French, while if you want a good cheap meal you gravitate naturally towards a Greek, Italian or Chinese restaurant. We are not likely to succeed in attracting tourists while England is thought of as a country of bad food and unintelligible by-laws. At present one cannot do much about it, but sooner or later rationing will come to an end, and then will be the moment for our national cookery to revive. It is not a law of nature that every restaurant in England should be either foreign or bad, and the first step towards an improvement will be a less long-suffering attitude in the British public itself.

Evening Standard, 15 December 1945.

3. A Nice Cup of Tea

If you look up "tea" in the first cookery book that comes to hand you will probably find that it is unmentioned; or at most you will find a few lines of sketchy instructions which give no ruling on several of the most important points.

This is curious, not only because tea is one of the mainstays of civilisation in this country, as well as in Eire, Australia and New Zealand, but because the best manner of making it is the subject of violent disputes.

When I look through my own recipe for the perfect cup of tea, I find no fewer than eleven outstanding points. On perhaps two of them there would be pretty general agreement, but at least four others are acutely controversial. Here are my own eleven rules, every one of which I regard as golden:

First of all, one should use Indian or Ceylonese tea. China tea has virtues which are not to be despised nowadays—it is economical, and one can drink it without milk—but there is not much stimulation in it. One does not feel wiser, braver or more optimistic after drinking it. Anyone who uses that comforting phrase "a nice cup of tea" invariably means Indian tea. Secondly, tea should be made in small quantities—that is, in a teapot. Tea out of an urn is always tasteless, while army tea, made in a cauldron, tastes of grease and whitewash. The teapot should be made of china or earthenware. Silver or Britannia-ware pots produce inferior tea and enamel pots are worse: though curiously enough a pewter teapot (a rarity nowadays) is not so bad. Thirdly, the pot should be warmed beforehand. This is better done by placing it on the hob than by the usual method of swilling it out with hot water. Fourthly, the tea should be strong. For a pot holding a quart, if you are going to fill it nearly to the brim, six heaped teaspoons would be about right. In a time of rationing this is not an idea that can be realised on every day of the week, but I maintain that one strong cup of tea is better than 20 weak ones. All true tea-lovers not only like their tea strong, but like it a little stronger with each year that passes—a fact which is recognised in the extra ration issued to old-age pensioners. Fifthly, the tea should be put straight into the pot. No strainers, muslin bags or other devices to imprison the tea. In some countries teapots are fitted with little dangling baskets under the spout to catch the stray leaves, which are supposed to be harmful. Actually one can swallow tea-leaves in considerable quantities without ill effect, and if the tea is not loose in the pot it never infuses properly. Sixthly, one should take the teapot to the kettle and not the other way about. The water should be actually boiling at the moment of impact, which means that one should keep it on the flame while one pours. Some people add that one should only use water that has been freshly brought to the boil, but I have never noticed that this makes any difference. Seventhly, after making the tea, one should stir it, or better, give the pot a good shake, afterwards allowing the leaves to settle. Eighthly, one should drink out of a breakfast cup—that is the cylindrical type of cup, not the flat, shallow type. The breakfast cup holds more, and with the other kind one's tea is always half cold before one has well started on it. Ninthly, one should pour the cream off the milk before using it for tea. Milk that is too creamy always gives tea a sickly taste. Tenthly, one should pour tea into the cup first. This is one of the most controversial points of all; indeed in every family in Britain there are probably two schools of thought on the subject. The milk-first school can bring forward some fairly strong arguments, but I maintain that my own argument is unanswerable. This is that, by putting the tea in first and then stirring as one pours, one can exactly regulate the amount of milk whereas one is liable to put in too much milk if one does it the other way round.

Lastly, tea—unless one is drinking it in the Russian style—should be drunk *without sugar*. I know very well that I am in a minority here. But still, how can you call yourself a true tea-lover if you destroy the flavour of your tea by putting sugar in it? It would be equally reasonable to put pepper or salt. Tea is meant to be bitter, just as beer is meant to be bitter. If you sweeten it, you are no longer tasting the tea, you are merely tasting the sugar; you could make a very similar drink by dissolving sugar in plain hot water.

Some people would answer that they don't like tea in itself, that they only drink it in order to be warmed and stimulated, and they need sugar to take the taste away. To those misguided people I would say: Try drinking tea without sugar for, say, a fortnight and it is very unlikely that you will ever want to ruin your tea by sweetening it again.

These are not the only controversial points that arise in connection with tea-drinking, but they are sufficient to show how subtilised the whole business has become. There is also the mysterious social etiquette surrounding the teapot (why is it considered vulgar to drink out of your saucer, for instance?) and much might be written about the subsidiary uses of tea-leaves, such as telling fortunes, predicting the arrival of visitors, feeding rabbits, healing burns and sweeping the carpet. It is worth paying attention to such details as warming the pot and using water that is really boiling, so as to make quite sure of wringing out of one's ration the twenty good, strong cups that two ounces, properly handled, ought to represent.

Evening Standard, 12 January 1946

4. Review
The Pub and the People by Mass Observation

It is a pity that this large and careful survey could not have had a short appendix indicating what effect the war has had on our drinking habits. It seems to have been compiled just before the war, and even in that short period of time beer has doubled in price and been heavily diluted.

Writing at a time when "mild" was still fivepence a pint (between 1936 and 1941 rearmament only raised it by a penny), the Mass Observers found that in "Worktown" the regular pub-goer was putting away, on average, between fifteen and twenty pints a week. This sounds a good deal, but it is unquestionable that in the past seventy years the annual consumption of beer per head has decreased by nearly two-thirds, and it is the Mass Observers' conclusion that "the pub as a cultural institution is at present declining". This happens not merely because of persecution by Nonconformist town councils, nor even primarily because of the increased price of drink, but because the whole trend of the age is away from creative communal amusements and towards solitary mechanical ones. The pub, with its elaborate social ritual, its animated conversations and—at any rate in the North of England—its songs and week-end comedians, is gradually replaced by the passive, drug-like pleasures of the cinema and the radio. This is only a cause for rejoicing if one believes, as a few Temperance fanatics still do, that people go to pubs to get drunk. The Mass Observers, however, have no difficulty in showing that there was extraordinarily little drunkenness in the period they were studying: for every five thousand hours that the average pub stays open, only one of its clients is drunk and disorderly.

Working on the more old-fashioned provincial pubs where the various bars are still separate rooms and not, as in London, merely one long counter separated by partitions, the authors of this book have unearthed much curious information. In a short review it is impossible to dilate on the complex social code that differentiates the saloon bar from the public bar, or on the delicate ritual that centres round treating, or the cultural implications of the trend towards bottled beer, or the rivalry between church and pub and the consequent guilt-feelings associated with drinking; but the average reader is likely to find Chapters V, VI and VII the most interesting. At least one of the Observers seems to have taken the extreme step of being initiated into the Buffaloes, about which there are some surprising revelations. A questionnaire issued through the local press, asking people why they drank beer, elicited from more than half the answer that they drank it for their health—probably an echo of the brewers' advertisements which talk of beer as though it were a kind of medicine. There were some who answered more frankly, however: "A middle-aged man of about forty of labouring type says 'What the bloody hell dost tha tak it for?' I said for my health; he said 'Th'art a —— liar.' I paid for him a gill."

And one woman answered the questionnaire thus:

"My reason is, because I always liked to see my grandmother having a drink of beer at night. She did seem to enjoy it, and she could pick up a dry crust of bread and cheese, and it seemed like a feast. She said if you have a drink of beer you will live to be one hundred, she died at ninety-two. I shall never refuse a drink of beer. There is no bad ale, so Grandma said."

This little piece of prose, which impresses itself upon the memory like a poem, would in itself be a sufficient justification for beer, if indeed it needed justifying.

[Unsigned]

Listener, 21 January 1943

5. "The Moon under Water"

My favourite public house, "The Moon under Water", is only two minutes from a bus stop, but it is on a side-street, and drunks and rowdies never seem to find their way there, even on Saturday nights.

Its clientèle, though fairly large, consists mostly of "regulars" who occupy the same chair every evening and go there for conversation as much as for the beer.

If you are asked why you favour a particular public house, it would seem natural to put the beer first, but the thing that most appeals to me about "The Moon under Water" is what people call its "atmosphere".

To begin with, its whole architecture and fittings are uncompromisingly Victorian. It has no glass-topped tables or other modern miseries, and, on the other hand, no sham roof-beams, ingle-nooks or plastic panels masquerading as oak. The grained woodwork, the ornamental mirrors behind the bar, the cast-iron fireplaces, the florid ceiling stained dark yellow by tobacco-smoke, the stuffed bull's head over the mantelpiece—everything has the solid comfortable ugliness of the nineteenth century.

In winter there is generally a good fire burning in at least two of the bars, and the Victorian lay-out of the place gives one plenty of elbow-room. There are a public bar, a saloon bar, a ladies' bar, a bottle-and-jug for those who are too bashful to buy their supper beer publicly, and upstairs, a dining-room.

Games are only played in the public, so that in the other bars you can walk about without constantly ducking to avoid flying darts.

In "The Moon under Water" it is always quiet enough to talk. The house possesses neither a radio nor a piano, and even on Christmas Eve and such occasions the singing that happens is of a decorous kind.

The barmaids know most of their customers by name, and take a personal interest in everyone. They are all middle-aged women— two of them have their hair dyed in quite surprising shades—and they call everyone "dear", irrespective of age or sex. ("Dear", not "Ducky": pubs where the barmaid calls you "Ducky" always have a disagreeable raffish atmosphere.)

Unlike most pubs, "The Moon under Water" sells tobacco as well as cigarettes, and it also sells aspirins and stamps, and is obliging about letting you use the telephone.

You cannot get dinner at "The Moon under Water", but there is always the snack counter where you can get liver-sausage sandwiches, mussels (a speciality of the house), cheese, pickles and those large biscuits with caraway seeds in them which only seem to exist in public houses.

Upstairs, six days a week, you can get a good, solid lunch—for example, a cut off the joint, two vegetables and boiled jam roll— for about three shillings.

The special pleasure of this lunch is that you can have draught stout with it. I doubt whether as many as ten per cent of London pubs serve draught stout, but "The Moon under Water" is one of them. It is a soft, creamy sort of stout, and it goes better in a pewter pot.

They are particular about their drinking vessels at "The Moon under Water" and never, for example, make the mistake of serving a pint of beer in a handleless glass. Apart from glass and pewter mugs, they have some of those pleasant strawberry-pink china ones which are now seldom seen in London. China mugs went out about thirty years ago, because most people like their drink to be transparent, but in my opinion beer tastes better out of china.

The great surprise of "The Moon under Water" is its garden. You go through a narrow passage leading out of the saloon, and find yourself in a fairly large garden with plane trees under which there are little green tables with iron chairs round them. Up at one end of the garden there are swings and a chute for the children.

On summer evenings there are family parties, and you sit under the plane trees having beer or draught cider to the tune of delighted squeals from children going down the chute. The prams with the younger children are parked near the gate.

Many as are the virtues of "The Moon under Water" I think that the garden is its best feature, because it allows whole families to go there instead of Mum having to stay at home and mind the baby while Dad goes out alone.

And though, strictly speaking, they are only allowed in the garden, the children tend to seep into the pub and even to fetch drinks for their parents. This, I believe, is against the law, but it is a law that deserves to be broken, for it is the puritanical nonsense of excluding children—and therefore to some extent, women—from pubs that has turned these places into mere boozing-shops instead of the family gathering-places that they ought to be.

"The Moon under Water" is my ideal of what a pub should be— at any rate, in the London area. (The qualities one expects of a country pub are slightly different.)

But now is the time to reveal something which the discerning and disillusioned reader will probably have guessed already. There is no such place as "The Moon under Water".

That is to say, there may well be a pub of that name, but I don't know of it, nor do I know any pub with just that combination of qualities.

I know pubs where the beer is good but you can't get meals, others where you can get meals but which are noisy and crowded, and others which are quiet but where the beer is generally sour. As for gardens, offhand I can only think of three London pubs that possess them.

But, to be fair, I do know of a few pubs that almost come up to "The Moon under Water". I have mentioned above ten qualities that the perfect pub should have, and I know one pub that has eight of them. Even there, however, there is no draught stout and no china mugs.

And if anyone knows of a pub that has draught stout, open fires, cheap meals, a garden, motherly barmaids and no radio, I should be glad to hear of it, even though its name were something as prosaic as "The Red Lion" or "The Railway Arms".

Evening Standard, 9 February 1946

6. Review

Cricket Country by Edmund Blunden

Cricket arouses strong feelings, both "for" and "against", and during recent years it is the anti-cricket school that has been in the ascendant. Cricket has been labelled the sport of Blimps. It has been vaguely associated with top-hats, school prize-days, fox-hunting, and the poems of Sir Henry Newbolt. It has been denounced by left-wing writers, who imagine erroneously that it is played chiefly by the rich.

On the other hand, its two bitterest enemies of all are "Beachcomber" and "Timothy Shy",[1] who see in it an English institution which they feel it their duty to belittle, along with Wordsworth, William Blake and parliamentary government. But there are other reasons besides spite and ignorance for the partial decline in the popularity of cricket, and some of them can be read between the lines of Mr Blunden's apologia, eloquent though it is.

[1] "Beachcomber" and "Timothy Shy". For a fuller description of Orwell's attitude to them see 46.

Mr Blunden is a true cricketer. The test of a true cricketer is that he shall prefer village cricket to "good" cricket. Mr Blunden's own form, one guesses, is somewhere midway between the village green and the county ground, and he has due reverence for the famous figures of the cricketing world, whose names pepper his pages. He is old enough to have seen Ranjitsinhji play his famous leg-glide, and since then he has watched first-class matches regularly enough to have seen every well-known player, English or Australian. But it is obvious that all his friendliest memories are of village cricket; and not even cricket at the country-house level, where white trousers are almost universal and a pad on each leg is *de rigueur*, but the informal village game, where everyone plays in braces, where the blacksmith is liable to be called away in mid-innings on an urgent job, and sometimes, about the time when the light begins to fail, a ball driven for four kills a rabbit on the boundary.

In his love of cricket Mr Blunden is in good literary company. He could, he says, almost make up an eleven of poets and writers. It would include Byron (who played for Harrow), Keats, Cowper, Trollope, Francis Thompson, Gerard Manley Hopkins, Robert Bridges and Siegfried Sassoon. Mr Blunden might have included Blake, one of whose fragments mentions an incident all too common in village cricket, but he is perhaps wrong to number Dickens among the lovers of cricket, for Dickens's only reference to the game (in *Pickwick Papers*) shows that he was ignorant of its rules. But the essential thing in this book, as in nearly everything that Mr Blunden writes, is his nostalgia for the golden age before 1914, when the world was peaceful as it has never since been.

The well-known lines from one of his poems:

> I have been young and now am not too old.
> And I have seen the righteous man forsaken,
> His wealth, his honour, and his quality taken:
> This is not what we were formerly told,

sound as though they had been written after the dictators had swallowed Europe. Actually, however, they refer to the war of 1914–18, the great turning-point of Mr Blunden's life. The war shattered the leisurely world he had known, and, as he sadly perceives, cricket has never been quite the same since.

Several things have combined to make it less popular. To begin with, the increasing hurry and urbanisation of life are against a game which needs green fields and abundant spare time. Then there is the generally admitted dullness of first-class cricket. Like nearly everyone else, Mr Blunden abhors the kind of game in which twenty successive maiden overs are nothing unusual and a batsman may be in for an hour before he scores his first run. But they are the natural result of too-perfect grass and a too-solemn attitude towards batting averages. Then again cricket has been partly supplanted, at any rate among grown-up people, by golf and lawn tennis. There can no doubt that this is a disaster, for these games are not only far inferior aesthetically to cricket but they do not have the socially binding quality that cricket, at any rate, used to have.

Contrary to what its detractors say, cricket is not an inherently snobbish game, as Mr Blunden is careful to point out. Since it needs about twenty-five people to make up a game it necessarily leads to a good deal of social mixing. The inherently snobbish game is golf, which causes whole stretches of countryside to be turned into carefully guarded class preserves.

But there is another good reason for the decline in the popularity of cricket—a reason Mr Blunden does not point out, the extent to which it has been thrust down everybody's throat. For a long period cricket was treated as though it were a kind of religious ritual incumbent on every Englishman. Interminable test matches with their astronomical scores were given large headlines in most newspapers, and every summer tens of thousands of unwilling boys were— and still are—drilled in a game which merely bored them. For cricket has the peculiarity that either you like it or you don't, and either you have a gift for it, or you have not. Unlike most games, it cannot be learned if you have no talent to start with. In the circumstances there was bound to be a large-scale revolt against cricket.

Even by children it is now less played than it was. It was most truly rooted in the national life when it was voluntary and informal— as in the Rugby of Tom Brown's schooldays, or in the village matches on lumpy wickets, which are Mr Blunden's most cherished memory.

Will cricket survive? Mr Blunden believes so, in spite of the competition from other interests that it has to face, and we may hope that he is right. It is pleasant to find him, towards the end of his book, still finding time for a game or two during the war, against RAF teams. This book touches on much else besides cricket, for at the bottom of his heart it is perhaps less the game itself than the physical surroundings that appeals to Mr Blunden. He is the kind of cricketer who when his side is batting is liable to stroll away from the pavilion to have a look at the village church, and perhaps come across a quaint epitaph.

In places this book is a little over-written, because Mr Blunden is no more able to resist a quotation than some people are to refuse a drink. But it is pleasant reading, and a useful reminder that peace means something more than a temporary stoppage of the guns.

Manchester Evening News, 20 April 1944

1943

NATIONAL UNION OF JOURNALISTS

7 John Street, Bedford Row, London, W.C.1

'Phone:
HOLborn 2258

Telegrams:
Natujay Holb, London

This is to certify that

Mr. **GEORGE ORWELL**

of *The Tribune*

is a member of the *T. ± P.*
Branch of the National Union of Journalists.

Leslia R. Aldous Branch Sec.

(*Address*) *66, Priory Gans., N.6.*

.... Member's Sig.

George Orwell's National Union of Journalists'
membership card, 29 December 1943

7. Letter to Philip Rahv

10a Mortimer Crescent
London NW6
9 December 1943

Dear Rahv,[1]

Many thanks for your letter. You observe the date of the above. Your letter dated October 15 only reached me this morning. I don't know what to do about these posts. Some people actually say it is now quicker to send a letter by sea. Meanwhile the idea of my doing an extra bit for the December issue is finished. If you are going to become a quarterly and bring out the first number in December, I assume the next number will be in March 1944. That means any copy I send you should reach you by the end of February? So I'll post it about mid-January. I hope this is right, and if this letter gets to you in reasonable time you might be able to confirm this between now and then. It seems impossible to keep anywhere near up to date with these London Letters while the posts are as they are. However, so long as they're dated they have a certain interest as showing what was the state of opinion at the time when written.

You can certainly reprint the *Horizon* article.[2] Connolly won't object, but I'll let him know you are doing it. I don't know how things stand about payment. Better send it to Connolly and then if it is rightfully mine he'll send it on to me.

Dwight Macdonald has written telling me he is starting another review[3] and asking me to contribute. I don't know to what extent he will be in competition with *PR*, but I am writing telling him that I might do something "cultural" for him but can't do anything "political" while I have this arrangement with *PR*.

I have left the BBC after two wasted years in it and have become literary editor of the *Tribune*, a left-wing weekly which you may have seen. It leaves me a little spare time, which the BBC didn't, so I have got another book[4] under weigh which I hope to finish in a few months if nothing intervenes. I'll try to send *PR* a copy of the book of broadcasts which the Indian Section of the BBC recently published.[5] It

[1] Philip Rahv (1908–), American critic and editor, author of *Image and Idea*; a founder of *Partisan Review* which he has co-edited since its inception in 1934.

[2] Orwell's review of *Beggar My Neighbour* by Lionel Fielden. See II, 51.

[3] Dwight Macdonald (1906–), libertarian critic and pamphleteer, an associate of *Partisan Review*, sole founder and editor of *Politics*, 1944–9.

[4] *Animal Farm.*

[5] *Talking to India* edited by George Orwell.

might possibly be worth reviewing. In any case it has some interest
as a specimen of British propaganda (rather a favourable specimen,
however, as we in the Indian Section were regarded as very unimportant and therefore left a fairly free hand).

All the best.

Yours
Geo. Orwell

8. As I Please

[From 3 December 1943 until 16 February 1945 Orwell wrote a regular
weekly article for *Tribune* under the title of "As I Please".]

Scene in a tobacconist's shop. Two American soldiers sprawling
across the counter, one of them just sober enough to make unwanted
love to the two young women who run the shop, the other at the
stage known as "fighting drunk". Enter Orwell in search of matches.
The pugnacious one makes an effort and stands upright.

Soldier: "Wharrishay is, perfijious Albion. You heard that?
Perfijious Albion. Never trust a Britisher. You can't trust the b——s."

Orwell: "Can't trust them with what?"

Soldier: "Wharrishay is, down with Britain. Down with the
British. You wanna do anything 'bout that? Then you can ——
well do it." (Sticks his face out like a tomcat on a garden wall.)

Tobacconist: "He'll knock your block off if you don't shut up."

Soldier: "Wharrishay is, down with Britain." (Subsides across
the counter again. The tobacconist lifts his head delicately out of
the scales.)

This kind of thing is not exceptional. Even if you steer clear of
Piccadilly with its seething swarms of drunks and whores, it is
difficult to go anywhere in London without having the feeling that
Britain is now Occupied Territory. The general consensus of opinion
seems to be that the only American soldiers with decent manners
are the Negroes. On the other hand the Americans have their own
justifiable complaints—in particular, they complain of the children
who follow them night and day, cadging sweets.

Does this sort of thing matter? The answer is that it might matter
at some moment when Anglo-American relations were in the balance,
and when the still-powerful forces in this country which want an

understanding with Japan were able to show their faces again. At such moments popular prejudice can count for a great deal. Before the war there was no popular anti-American feeling in this country. It all dates from the arrival of the American troops, and it is made vastly worse by the tacit agreement never to discuss it in print.

Seemingly it is our fixed policy in this war not to criticise our allies, nor to answer their criticisms of us. As a result things have happened which are capable of causing the worst kind of trouble sooner or later. An example is the agreement by which American troops in this country are not liable to British courts for offences against British subjects—practically "extra-territorial rights". Not one English person in ten knows of the existence of this agreement; the newspapers barely reported it and refrained from commenting on it. Nor have people been made to realise the extent of anti-British feeling in the United States. Drawing their picture of America from films carefully edited for the British market, they have no notion of the kind of thing that Americans are brought up to believe about us. Suddenly to discover, for instance, that the average American thinks the USA had more casualties than Britain in the last war comes as a shock, and the kind of shock that can cause a violent quarrel. Even such a fundamental difficulty as the fact that an American soldier's pay is five times that of a British soldier has never been properly ventilated. No sensible person wants to whip up Anglo-American jealousy. On the contrary, it is just because one does want a good relationship between the two countries that one wants plain speaking. Our official soft-soaping policy does us no good in America, while in this country it allows dangerous resentments to fester just below the surface.

Since 1935, when pamphleteering revived, I have been a steady collector of pamphlets, political, religious and what-not. To anyone who happens to come across it and has a shilling to spare I recommend *The 1946 MS* by Robin Maugham, published by the War Facts Press. It is a good example of that small but growing school of literature, the non-party radical school. It purports to describe the establishment in Britain of a Fascist dictatorship, starting in 1944 and headed by a successful general who is (I think) drawn from a living model. I found it interesting because it gives you the average middle-class man's conception of what Fascism would be like, and more important, of the reasons why Fascism might succeed. Its appearance (along with other similar pamphlets I have in my collection) shows how far that average middle-class man has travelled since 1939, when Socialism still meant dividing the money up and what happened in Europe was none of our business.

Who wrote this?

> As we walked over the Drury Lane gratings of the cellars a most foul stench came up, and one in particular that I remember to this day. A man half dressed pushed open a broken window beneath us, just as we passed by, and there issued such a blast of corruption, made up of gases bred by filth, air breathed and re-breathed a hundred times, charged with the odours of unnamable personal uncleanliness and disease, that I staggered to the gutter with a qualm which I could scarcely conquer.... I did not know, until I came in actual contact with them, how far away the classes which lie at the bottom of great cities are from those above them; how completely they are inaccessible to motives which act upon ordinary human beings, and how deeply they are sunk beyond ray of sun or stars, immersed in the selfishness naturally begotten of their incessant struggle for existence and incessant warfare with society. It was an awful thought to me, ever present on those Sundays, and haunting me at other times; that men, women and children were living in brutish degradation, and that as they died others would take their place. Our civilisation seemed nothing but a thin film or crust lying over a bottomless pit and I often wondered whether some day the pit would not break up through it and destroy us all.

You would know, at any rate, that this comes from some nineteenth-century writer. Actually it is from a novel, *Mark Rutherford's Deliverance*. (Mark Rutherford, whose real name was Hale White, wrote this book as a pseudo-autobiography.) Apart from the prose, you could recognise this as coming from the nineteenth century because of that description of the unendurable filth of the slums. The London slums of that day *were* like that, and all honest writers so described them. But even more characteristic is that notion of a whole block of the population being so degraded as to be beyond contact and beyond redemption.

Almost all nineteenth-century English writers are agreed upon this, even Dickens. A large part of the town working class, ruined by industrialism, are simply savages. Revolution is not a thing to be hoped for: it simply means the swamping of civilisation by the sub-human. In this novel (it is one of the best novels in English) Mark Rutherford describes the opening of a sort of mission or settlement near Drury Lane. Its object was "gradually to attract Drury Lane to come and be saved". Needless to say this was a failure. Drury Lane not only did not want to be saved in the religious sense, it didn't even want to be civilised. All that Mark Rutherford and his friend succeeded in doing, all that one could do, indeed, at that time, was to provide a sort of refuge for the few people of the neighbourhood who did not belong to their surroundings. The general masses were outside the pale.

Mark Rutherford was writing of the 'seventies, and in a footnote dated 1884 he remarks that "socialism, nationalisation of the land and other projects" have now made their appearance, and may perhaps give a gleam of hope. Nevertheless, he assumes that the condition of the working class will grow worse and not better as time goes on. It was natural to believe this (even Marx seems to have believed it), because it was hard at that time to foresee the enormous increase in the productivity of labour. Actually, such an improvement in the standard of living has taken place as Mark Rutherford and his contemporaries would have considered quite impossible.

The London slums are still bad enough, but they are nothing to those of the nineteenth century. Gone are the days when a single room used to be inhabited by four families, one in each corner, and when incest and infanticide were taken almost for granted. Above all, gone are the days when it seemed natural to write off a whole stratum of the population as irredeemable savages. The most snobbish Tory alive would not now write of the London working class as Mark Rutherford does. And Mark Rutherford—like Dickens, who shared his attitude—was a Radical! Progress does happen, hard though it may be to believe it, in this age of concentration camps and big beautiful bombs.

Tribune, 3 December 1943

9. As I Please

So many letters have arrived, attacking me for my remarks about the American soldiers in this country, that I must return to the subject.

Contrary to what most of my correspondents seem to think, I was not trying to make trouble between ourselves and our Allies, nor am I consumed by hatred for the United States. I am much less anti-American than most English people are at this moment. What I say, and what I repeat, is that our policy of not criticising our Allies, and not answering their criticism of us (we don't answer the Russians either, nor even the Chinese) is a mistake, and is likely to defeat its own object in the long run. And so far as Anglo-American relations go, there are three difficulties which badly need dragging into the open and which simply don't get mentioned in the British press.

1. *Anti-American feeling in Britain.* Before the war, anti-American feeling was a middle-class, and perhaps upper-class thing, resulting from imperialist and business jealousy and disguising itself as dislike of the American accent etc. The working class, so far from being anti-American, were becoming rapidly Americanised in speech by means of the films and jazz songs. Now, in spite of what my correspondents may say, I can hear few good words for the Americans anywhere. This obviously results from the arrival of the American troops. It has been made worse by the fact that, for various reasons, the Mediterranean campaign had to be represented as an American show while most of the casualties had to be suffered by the British. (See Philip Jordan's remarks in his *Tunis Diary*.)[1] I am not saying that popular English prejudices are always justified: I am saying that they exist.

2. *Anti-British feeling in America.* We ought to face the fact that large numbers of Americans are brought up to dislike and despise us. There is a large section of the press whose main accent is anti-British, and countless other papers which attack Britain in a more sporadic way. In addition there is a systematic guying of what are supposed to be British habits and manners on the stage and in comic strips and cheap magazines. The typical Englishman is represented as a chinless ass with a title, a monocle and a habit of saying "Haw, haw". This legend is believed in by relatively responsible Americans, for example by the veteran novelist Theodore Dreiser, who remarks

[1] Philip Jordan, a well-known war-time correspondent for the *News Chronicle*, had been covering the North African campaign.

in a public speech that "the British are horse-riding aristocratic snobs". (Forty-six million horse-riding snobs!) It is a commonplace on the American stage that the Englishman is almost never allowed to play a favourable role, any more than the Negro is allowed to appear as anything more than a comic. Yet right up to Pearl Harbour the American movie industry had an agreement with the Japanese Government never to present a Japanese character in an unfavourable light!

I am not blaming the Americans for all this. The anti-British press has powerful business forces behind it, besides ancient quarrels in many of which Britain was in the wrong. As for popular anti-British feeling, we partly bring it on ourselves by exporting our worst specimens. But what I do want to emphasise is that these anti-British currents in the USA are very strong, and that the British press has consistently failed to draw attention to them. There has never been in England anything that one could call an anti-American press: and since the war there has been a steady refusal to answer criticism and a careful censorship of the radio to cut out anything that the Americans might object to. As a result, many English people don't realise how they are regarded, and get a shock when they find out.

3. *Soldiers' Pay.* It is now nearly two years since the first American troops reached this country, and I rarely see American and British soldiers together. Quite obviously the major cause of this is the difference of pay. You can't have really close and friendly relations with somebody whose income is five times your own. Financially, the whole American army is in the middle class. In the field this might not matter, but in the training period it makes it almost impossible for British and American soldiers to fraternise. If you don't want friendly relations between the British army and the American army, well and good. But if you do, you must either pay the British soldier ten shillings a day or make the American soldier bank the surplus of his pay in America. I don't profess to know which of these alternatives is the right one.

One way of feeling infallible is not to keep a diary. Looking back through the diary I kept in 1940 and 1941[1] I find that I was usually wrong when it was possible to be wrong. Yet I was not so wrong as the Military Experts. Experts of various schools were telling us in

[1] See II, 57.

1939 that the Maginot Line was impregnable, and that the Russo-German Pact had put an end to Hitler's eastward expansion; in early 1940 they were telling us that the days of tank warfare were over; in mid 1940 they were telling us that the Germans would invade Britain forthwith; in mid 1941 that the Red army would fold up in six weeks; in December, 1941, that Japan would collapse after 90 days; in July, 1942, that Egypt was lost—and so on, more or less indefinitely.

Where now are the men who told us those things? Still on the job, drawing fat salaries. Instead of the unsinkable battleship we have the unsinkable Military Expert. . . .

Books have gone up in price like everything else, but the other day I picked up a copy of Lemprière's *Classical Dictionary*, the *Who's Who* of the ancients, for only sixpence. Opening it at random, I came upon the biography of Laïs, the famous courtesan, daughter of the mistress of Alcibiades:

> She first began to sell her favours at Corinth for 10,000 drachmas, and the immense number of princes, noblemen, philosophers, orators and plebeians who courted her, bear witness to her personal charms. . . . Demosthenes visited Corinth for the sake of Laïs, but informed by the courtesan that admittance to her bed was to be bought at the enormous sum of about £200 English money, the orator departed, and observed that he would not buy repentance at so dear a price. . . . She ridiculed the austerity of philosophers, and the weakness of those who pretend to have gained a superiority over their passions, by observing that sages and philosophers were not above the rest of mankind, for she found them at her door as often as the rest of the Athenians.

There is more in the same vein. However, it ends on a good moral, for "the other women, jealous of her charms, assassinated her in the temple of Venus about 340 BC". That was 2,283 years ago. I wonder how many of the present denizens of *Who's Who* will seem worth reading about in AD 4226?

Tribune, 17 December 1943

10. Review

Collected Poems by W. H. Davies

Seen in bulk, W. H. Davies's work gives a somewhat different impression from that given by the handful of poems that have found their way into so many anthologies. So far as manner goes, indeed, almost any of his poems is representative. His great fault is lack of variation—a quality that one might, perhaps, call wateriness, since it gives one the feeling of drinking draught after draught of spring water, wonderfully pure and refreshing, but somehow turning one's mind in the direction of whisky after the first pint or two. On the other hand—and it is here that the anthologies have probably misrepresented him—his subject-matter is remarkably variegated. Not only did his years of vagabondage in common lodging houses supply a large part of it, but he shows a distinct tinge of morbidity. Behind the lambs and the wild flowers there is an almost Baudelairean background of harlots, drunkenness and corpses, and in poems like "The Rat" and "Down Underground" he does not flinch from the most horrible subjects that any writer could deal with. Yet his manner never varies, or barely varies: the clouds in the April sky and the dead girl rotting in her grave are spoken of in almost the same tone of voice.

One thing that emerges from this collection of over six hundred poems is the perfection of Davies's taste. If he lacks vitality, at least he has a sort of natural good breeding. None of his poems is perfect, there is not one in which one cannot find an unnecessary word or an annoyingly bad rhyme, and yet nothing is vulgar either. More than this, however empty he may seem, there is nothing that one can put one's finger on and say that it is silly. Like Blake, he appears to avoid silliness by not being afraid of it; and perhaps (like Blake again) this appearance is partly deceptive, and he is less artless than he seems. Davies's best qualities, as well as some of his faults, can be seen in the justly celebrated poem, "The Two Children":

> "Ah, little boy! I see
>   You have a wooden spade.
> Into this sand you dig
>   So deep—for what?" I said.
> "There's more rich gold", said he,
>   "Down under where I stand,
> Then twenty elephants
>   Could move across the land."

> "Ah, little girl with wool!—
>   What are you making now?"
> "Some stockings for a bird,
>   To keep his legs from snow."
> And there those children are,
>   So happy, small, and proud:
> The boy that digs his grave,
>   The girl that knits her shroud.

How near this comes to folly and sentimentality! But the point is that it doesn't get there. Whether Davies is being deliberately cunning it would be hard to say. The almost namby-pamby language in which the poem starts may or may not be intended to give force to the two magnificent lines at the end. But at any rate, whether it is consciously or not, Davies always does avoid the silliness and vulgarity which so often seem to be in wait for him.

On the blurb of this book Sir John Squire is quoted as preferring Davies to "the fashionable poets of today" (at the time of writing this probably meant Mr T. S. Eliot) and Mr Basil de Selincourt as seeing in Davies an upholder of "our English tradition". Davies has had much praise of this kind, and has been used as a stick to beat many another contemporary, basically because he does not force anyone to think. Not to be made to think—and therefore, if possible, to prevent literature from developing—is often the aim of the academic critic. But Davies is not, as Sir John Squire and Mr de Selincourt seem to claim, the restorer of an ancient tradition. Indeed, if there is one thing that he is not, it is traditional. He belongs in no line of descent; he does not derive from his immediate predecessors, and he has had no influence on his successors. According to his own account, he was brought up by a pious grandmother whose only books were *Paradise Lost*, *The Pilgrim's Progress*, Young's *Night Thoughts*, and (presumably) the Bible. He read Shelley, Marlowe and Shakespeare on the sly, as another boy might read Sexton Blake. At the age of thirty-four, when still living in a common lodging house and never having seen even the fringes of the literary world, he began to write poems. He gives the impression of having imitated chiefly the poets of the seventeenth century; there are frequent echoes, though probably no plagiarisms. Having completed his first batch of poems, Davies attempted to sell them from door to door at threepence a copy—needless to say, without success. . . .

Observer, 19 December 1943

11. As I Please

Reading Michael Roberts's book on T. E. Hulme, I was reminded once again of the dangerous mistake that the Socialist movement makes in ignoring what one might call the neo-reactionary school of writers. There is a considerable number of these writers: they are intellectually distinguished, they are influential in a quiet way and their criticisms of the Left are much more damaging than anything that issues from the Individualist League or the Conservative Central Office.

T. E. Hulme was killed in the last war and left little completed work behind him, but the ideas that he had roughly formulated had great influence, especially on the numerous writers who were grouped round the *Criterion* in the 'twenties and 'thirties. Wyndham Lewis, T. S. Eliot, Aldous Huxley, Malcolm Muggeridge, Evelyn Waugh and Graham Greene all probably owe something to him. But more important than the extent of his personal influence is the general intellectual movement to which he belonged, a movement which could fairly be described as the revival of pessimism. Perhaps its best-known living exponent is Marshal Pétain. But the new pessimism has queerer affiliations than that. It links up not only with Catholicism, Conservatism and Fascism, but also with pacifism (California brand especially), and Anarchism. It is worth noting that T. E. Hulme, the upper-middle-class English Conservative in a bowler hat, was an admirer and to some extent a follower of the Anarcho-Syndicalist, Georges Sorel.

The thing that is common to all these people, whether it is Pétain mournfully preaching "the discipline of defeat", or Sorel denouncing liberalism, or Berdyaev shaking his head over the Russian Revolution, or "Beachcomber" delivering side-kicks at Beveridge in the *Express*, or Huxley advocating non-resistance behind the guns of the American Fleet, is their refusal to believe that human society can be fundamentally improved. Man is non-perfectible, merely political changes can effect nothing, progress is an illusion. The connection between this belief and political reaction is, of course, obvious. Other-worldliness is the best alibi a rich man can have. "Men cannot be made better by act of Parliament; therefore I may as well go on drawing my dividends." No one puts it quite so coarsely as that, but the thought of all these people is along those lines: even of those who, like Michael Roberts and Hulme himself, admit that a little, just a *little*, improvement in earthly society may be thinkable.

The danger of ignoring the neo-pessimists lies in the fact that up to a point they are right. So long as one thinks in short periods it is wise not to be hopeful about the future. Plans for human betterment do normally come unstuck, and the pessimist has many more opportunities of saying "I told you so" than the optimist. By and large the prophets of doom have been righter than those who imagined that a real step forward would be achieved by universal education, female suffrage, the League of Nations, or what not.

The real answer is to dissociate Socialism from Utopianism. Nearly all neo-pessimist apologetics consist in putting up a man of straw and knocking him down again. The man of straw is called Human Perfectibility. Socialists are accused of believing that society can be—and indeed, after the establishment of Socialism, will be—completely perfect; also that progress is *inevitable*. Debunking such beliefs is money for jam, of course.

The answer, which ought to be uttered more loudly than it usually is, is that Socialism is not perfectionist, perhaps not even hedonistic. Socialists don't claim to be able to make the world perfect: they claim to be able to make it better. And any thinking Socialist will concede to the Catholic that when economic injustice has been righted, the fundamental problem of man's place in the universe will still remain. But what the Socialist does claim is that that problem cannot be dealt with while the average human being's pre-occupations are necessarily economic. It is all summed up in Marx's saying that after Socialism has arrived, human history can begin. Meanwhile the neo-pessimists are there, well entrenched in the press of every country in the world, and they have more influence and make more converts among the young than we sometimes care to admit.

From Philip Jordan's *Tunis Diary*:

> We discussed the future of Germany; and John [Strachey] said to an American present, "You surely don't want a Carthaginian peace, do you?" Our American friend with great slowness but solemnity said, "I don't recollect we've ever had much trouble from the Carthaginians since." Which delighted me.

It doesn't delight me. One answer to the American might have been, "No, but we've had a lot of trouble from the Romans". But there is more to it than that. What the people who talk about a

Carthaginian peace don't realise is that in our day such things are simply not practicable. Having defeated your enemy you have to choose (unless you want another war within a generation) between exterminating him and treating him generously. Conceivably the first alternative is desirable, but it isn't possible. It is quite true that Carthage was utterly destroyed, its buildings levelled to the ground, its inhabitants put to the sword. Such things were happening all the time in antiquity. But the populations involved were tiny. I wonder if that American knew how many people were found within the walls of Carthage when it was finally sacked? According to the nearest authority I can lay hands on, five thousand! What is the best way of killing off 70 million Germans? Rat poison? We might keep this in mind when "Make Germany Pay" becomes a battle-cry again.

Attacking me in the *Weekly Review* for attacking Douglas Reed, Mr A. K. Chesterton remarks: " 'My country—right or wrong' is a maxim which apparently has no place in Mr Orwell's philosophy." He also states that "all of us believe that whatever her condition Britain must win this war, or for that matter any other war in which she is engaged".

The operative phrase is *any other war*. There are plenty of us who would defend our own country, under no matter what government, if it seemed that we were in danger of actual invasion and conquest. But "any war" is a different matter. How about the Boer War, for instance? There is a neat little bit of historical irony here. Mr A. K. Chesterton is the nephew of G. K. Chesterton, who courageously opposed the Boer war, and once remarked that "My country, right or wrong" was on the same moral level as "My mother, drunk or sober".

Tribune, 24 December 1943

12. As I Please

Reading the discussions of "war guilt" which reverberate in the correspondence columns of the newspapers, I note the surprise with which many people seem to discover that war is not crime. Hitler, it appears, has not done anything actionable. He has not raped anybody, nor carried off any pieces of loot with his own hands, nor personally flogged any prisoners, buried any wounded men alive, thrown any babies into the air and spitted them on his bayonet, dipped any nuns in petrol and touched them off with church tapers—in fact he has not done any of the things which enemy nationals are usually credited with doing in war-time. He has merely precipitated a world war which will perhaps have cost twenty million lives before it ends. And there is nothing illegal in that. How could there be, when legality implies authority and there *is* no authority with the power to transcend national frontiers?

At the recent trials in Kharkov some attempt was made to fix on Hitler, Himmler and the rest the responsibility for their subordinates' crimes, but the mere fact that this had to be done shows that Hitler's guilt is not self-evident. His crime, it is implied, was not to build up an army for the purpose of aggressive war, but to instruct that army to torture its prisoners. So far as it goes, the distinction between an atrocity and an act of war is valid. An atrocity means an act of terrorism which has no genuine military purpose. One must accept such distinctions if one accepts war at all, which in practice everyone does. Nevertheless, a world in which it is wrong to murder an individual civilian and right to drop a thousand tons of high explosive on a residential area does sometimes make me wonder whether this earth of ours is not a loony-bin made use of by some other planet.

As the 53 bus carries me to and fro I never, at any rate when it is light enough to see, pass the little church of St John, just across the road from Lord's, without a pang. It is a Regency church, one of the very few of the period, and when you pass that way it is well worth going inside to have a look at its friendly interior and read the resounding epitaphs of the East India Nabobs who lie buried there. But its façade, one of the most charming in London, has been utterly ruined by a hideous war memorial which stands in front of it. That seems to be a fixed rule in London: whenever you do by some chance have a decent vista, block it up with the ugliest statue you can find. And, unfortunately, we have never been sufficiently short of bronze for these things to be melted down.

If you climb to the top of the hill in Greenwich Park, you can have the mild thrill of standing exactly on longitude 0°, and you can also examine the ugliest building in the world, Greenwich Observatory.

Then look down the hill towards the Thames. Spread out below you are Wren's masterpiece, Greenwich Hospital (now the Naval College) and another exquisite classical building known as the Queen's House. The architects responsible for that shapeless sprawling muddle at the top of the hill had those other two buildings under their eyes while every brick was laid.

As Mr Osbert Sitwell remarked at the time of the "Baedeker raids"[1]—how simple-minded of the Germans to imagine that we British could be cowed by the destruction of our ancient monuments! As though any havoc of the German bombs could possibly equal the things we have done ourselves!

I see that Mr Bernard Shaw, among others, wants to rewrite the second verse of the National Anthem. Mr Shaw's version retains references to God and the King, but is vaguely internationalist in sentiment. This seems to me ridiculous. Not to have a national anthem would be logical. But if you do have one, its function must necessarily be to point out that we are Good and our enemies are Bad. Besides, Mr Shaw wants to cut out the only worth-while lines the anthem contains. All the brass instruments and big drums in the world cannot turn "God Save the King" into a good tune, but on the very rare occasions when it is sung in full it does spring to life in the two lines:

> Confound their politics,
> Frustrate their knavish tricks!

And, in fact, I had always imagined that the second verse is habitually left out because of a vague suspicion on the part of the Tories that these lines refer to themselves.

Another ninepenny acquisition: *Chronological Tablets, exhibiting every Remarkable Occurrence from the Creation of the World down to the Present Time.* Printed by J. D. Dewick, Aldersgate Street, in the year 1801.

With some interest I looked up the date of the creation of the world, and found it was in 4004 BC, and "is supposed to have taken place in the autumn". Later in the book it is given more exactly as September, 4004.

[1] The German air raids on English towns where places of no possible military value but of historic or artistic interest were hit, e.g. the raid on Canterbury.

At the end there are a number of blank sheets in which the reader can carry on the chronicles for himself. Whoever possessed this book did not carry it very far, but one of the last entries is: "Tuesday 4 May. Peace proclaimed here. General Illumination." That was the Peace of Amiens. This might warn us not to be too previous with our own illuminations when the armistice comes.

Tribune, 31 December 1943

1944

10a Mortimer Crescent
London NW 6
17.2.44

Dear Mr Struve,

Please forgive me for not writing
earlier to thank you for the very kind gift of "25 Years of Soviet
Russian Literature", with its still more kind inscription. I am
afraid I know very little about Russian literature and I hope your
book will fill up some of the many gaps in my knowledge. It has
already roused my interest in Zamyatin's "We", which I had not heard
of before. I am interested in that kind of book, and even keep making
notes for one myself that may get written sooner or later. I wonder
whether you can tell if there is an adequate translation of Blok?
I saw some translated fragments about ten years ago in "Life and
Letters", but whether they were any good as a translation I do not
know.

I am writing a little squib which might amuse you when it
comes out, but it is so not O.K. politically that I don't feel
certain in advance that anyone will publish it. Perhaps that gives
you a hint of its subject.

Yours sincerely

Geo. Orwell

A letter from George Orwell to Gleb Struve, 17 February 1944

13. As I Please

Looking through the photographs in the New Year's Honours List, I am struck (as usual) by the quite exceptional ugliness and vulgarity of the faces displayed there. It seems to be almost the rule that the kind of person who earns the right to call himself Lord Percy de Falcontowers should look at best like an overfed publican and at worst like a tax-collector with a duodenal ulcer. But our country is not alone in this. Anyone who is a good hand with scissors and paste could compile an excellent book entitled *Our Rulers*, and consisting simply of published photographs of the great ones of the earth. The idea first occurred to me when I saw in *Picture Post* some "stills" of Beaverbrook delivering a speech and looking more like a monkey on a stick than you would think possible for anyone who was not doing it on purpose.

When you had got together your collection of fuehrers, actual and would-be, you would notice that several qualities recur throughout the list. To begin with, they are all old. In spite of the lip-service that is paid everywhere to youth, there is no such thing as a person in a truly commanding position who is less than fifty years old. Secondly, they are nearly all undersized. A dictator taller than five feet six inches is a very great rarity. And, thirdly, there is this almost general and sometimes quite fantastic ugliness. The collection would contain photographs of Streicher bursting a blood vessel, Japanese war-lords impersonating baboons, Mussolini with his scrubby dewlap, the chinless de Gaulle, the stumpy short-armed Churchill, Gandhi with his long sly nose and huge bat's ears, Tojo displaying thirty-two teeth with gold in every one of them. And opposite each, to make a contrast, there would be a photograph of an ordinary human being from the country concerned. Opposite Hitler a young sailor from a German submarine, opposite Tojo a Japanese peasant of the old type—and so on.

But to come back to the Honours List. When you remember that nearly the whole of the rest of the world has dropped it, it does seem strange to see this flummery still continuing in England, a country in which the very notion of aristocracy perished hundreds of years ago. The race-difference on which aristocratic rule is usually founded had disappeared from England by the end of the Middle Ages, and the concept of "blue blood" as something valuable in itself, and independent of money, was vanishing in the age of Elizabeth. Since then we have been a plutocracy plain and simple. Yet we still make spasmodic efforts to dress ourselves in the colours of medieval feudalism.

Think of the Heralds' Office solemnly faking pedigrees and inventing coats of arms with mermaids and unicorns couchant, regardant and what not, for company directors in bowler hats and striped trousers! What I like best is the careful grading by which honours are always dished out in direct proportion to the amount of mischief done—baronies for big business, baronetcies for fashionable surgeons, knighthoods for tame professors. But do these people imagine that by calling themselves lords, knights and so forth they somehow come to have something in common with the medieval aristocracy? Does Sir Walter Citrine, say, feel himself to be rather the same kind of person as Childe Roland (Childe Citrine to the dark tower came!), or is Lord Nuffield under the impression that we shall mistake him for a crusader in chain-armour?

However, this honours-list business has one severely practical aspect, and that is that a title is a first-class alias. Mr X can practically cancel his past by turning himself into Lord Y. Some of the ministerial appointments that have been made during this war would hardly have been possible without some such disguise. As Tom Paine put it: "These people change their names so often that it is as hard to know them as it is to know thieves."

I write this to the tune of an electric drill. They are drilling holes in the walls of a surface shelter, removing bricks at regular intervals. Why? Because the shelter is in danger of falling down and it is necessary to give it a cement facing.

It seems doubtful whether these surface shelters were ever of much use. They would give protection against splinters and blast, but not more than the walls of an ordinary house, and the only time I saw a bomb drop anywhere near one it sliced it off the ground as neatly as if it had been done with a knife. The real point is, however, that at the time when these shelters were built it was known that they would fall down in a year or two. Innumerable people pointed this out. But nothing happened; the slovenly building continued, and somebody scooped the contract. Sure enough, a year or two later, the prophets were justified. The mortar began to fall out of the walls, and it became necessary to case the shelters in cement. Once again somebody —perhaps it was the same somebody—scooped the contract.

I do not know whether, in any part of the country, these shelters are actually used in air raids. In my part of London there has never been any question of using them; in fact, they are kept permanently locked lest they should be used for "improper purposes". There is one thing, however, that they might conceivably be useful for, and that is as block-houses in street fighting. And on the whole they have been built in the poorer streets. It would amuse me if when the time came the higher-ups were unable to crush the populace because they had thoughtlessly provided them with thousands of machine-gun nests beforehand.

Tribune, 7 January 1944

14. As I Please

The old custom of binding up magazines and periodicals in book form seems to have gone out almost entirely, which is a pity, for a year's issue of even a very stupid magazine is more readable after a lapse of time than the majority of books. I do not believe I ever had a better bargain than the dozen volumes of the *Quarterly Review*, starting in 1809, which I once picked up for two shillings at a farmhouse auction; but a good sixpennyworth was a year's issue of the *Cornhill* when either Trollope or Thackeray, I forget which, was editing it, and another good buy was some odd volumes of the *Gentleman's Magazine* of the mid-sixties, at threepence each. I have also had some happy half-hours with Chambers's *Papers for the People*, which flourished in the 'fifties, the *Boy's Own Paper* in the days of the Boer war, the *Strand* in its great Sherlock Holmes days, and—a book I unfortunately only saw and didn't buy—a bound volume of the *Athenæum* in the early 'twenties, when Middleton Murry was editing it, and T. S. Eliot, E. M. Forster and various others were making their first impact on the big public. I do not know why no one bothers to do this nowadays, for to get a year's issue of a magazine bound costs less than buying a novel, and you can even do the job yourself if you have a spare evening and the right materials.

The great fascination of these old magazines is the completeness with which they "date". Absorbed in the affairs of the moment, they tell one about political fashions and tendencies which are hardly mentioned in the more general history books. It is interesting, for instance, to study in contemporary magazines the war scare of the early 'sixties, when it was assumed on all sides that Britain was about to be invaded, the Volunteers were formed, amateur strategists published maps showing the routes by which the French armies would converge on London, and peaceful citizens cowered in ditches while the bullets of the Rifle Clubs (the then equivalent of the Home Guard) ricochetted in all directions.

The mistake that nearly all British observers made at that time was not to notice that Germany was dangerous. The sole danger was supposed to come from France, which had shot its bolt as a military power and had in any case no reason for quarrelling with Britain. And I believe that casual readers in the future, dipping into our newspapers and magazines, will note a similar aberration in the turning-away from democracy and frank admiration for totalitarianism which overtook the British intelligentsia about 1940. Recently, turning up a back number of *Horizon*, I came upon a long article on James Burnham's *Managerial Revolution*, in which Burnham's main thesis was accepted almost without examination. It represented, many people would have claimed, the most intelligent forecast of our time. And yet—founded as it really was on a belief in the invincibility of the German army—events have already blown it to pieces.

Tribune, 14 January 1944

15. London Letter to *Partisan Review*

[15 January 1944]
Dear Editors,
I suppose by the time this is printed the Second Front will have opened. It is generally assumed that this will happen within the next few months, that the German part of the war will end this year; and that there will be a General Election turning on domestic issues soon afterwards. Meanwhile not much is happening politically. It has occurred to me that it might be useful if I gave you some background stuff about two contestants in the British political scene, Parliament and the Monarchy, which I have rather taken for granted in previous letters. But first of all something about current developments, in so far as there are any.

The Government's whole policy, internal and external, continues to move more and more openly to the Right, while public feeling continues to swing leftward as strongly, I should say, in a more disillusioned way, as it did in 1940. Fed-upness and disbelief in sunshine promises are general, and show themselves in sudden outbursts of indignation like the row that occurred over Mosley's release from internment. On the face of it this was a bad symptom amounting as it did to a popular protest against Habeas Corpus (incidentally there was far more clamour against Mosley's release than there had been in favour of locking him up in the beginning), and it is also true that most of the public demonstrations were stage-managed by Communists anxious to live down their own anti-war activities. But there was a great deal of genuine feeling, especially among working people, always on the ground that "They've only let him out because he's a rich man". Since 1940 we have suffered a long series of Thermidors, and people grasp the general drift, but only through events that influence their own lives. There is no authoritative voice on the Left to tell them that things like the AMG[1] policy in Italy, or the jailing of the Indian Congress leaders, also matter. By-elections show a big turnover of votes against the Government, and in some cases a big rise in the percentage of the electorate voting. Since I wrote to you last, the Government has only lost one election (out of about half a dozen), but might have lost others if the Opposition vote had not been split. There is a new crop of "independent" candidates, whose policy is usually of a kind to split the Opposition rather than the Government vote. Some people think that these "independents" are financed by the Conservative Party.

My own fear is that the moment the war is over the Conservatives will conduct a whirlwind campaign, present themselves as "the party that won the war", bring forward hundreds of handsome young RAF officers as candidates, promise everything under the sun, and then chuck it all down the drain as soon as they are back in office. However, more experienced observers than I think that they couldn't bring this off, the people have grown too wise to be fooled again, and the Government can only win the General Election by keeping on the Coalition. Theoretically, this puts the Labour Party in the strong position of being able to extort a high price for their support, or else to fight the election on their own with a good chance of winning. In practice the existing Labour leaders, who are terrified of power, will certainly keep on the Coalition and demand very little in return, unless very strongly prodded from below: in which case we shall get a Parliament similar to the present one but with a stronger

[1] Allied Military Government.

Opposition. There have been a few tentative moves towards some kind of Popular Front, but they don't get far in the face of official Labour disapproval and the hostility of the minor Left parties towards one another. The only organised opposition is still Common Wealth, which has made a little headway (they have won another by-election), but is suffering from mysterious internal dissensions. Control of it seems to have partly passed out of Acland's[1] hands into those of a rather sinister businessman who is helping to finance it and is thought by some to have entered the party with the object of neutralising it. Since Acland no leading figure has appeared on the Left except for Beveridge, who has won a kind of popular renown and probably has political ambitions. Though a professor rather than a politician, he is just conceivable as a popular leader—a lively, attractive little man, rather like Cripps in his willingness to talk to anybody, but much more genial. Nor has anyone worth bothering about appeared on the other side. The group of Disraelian "Young Tories", apart from having no definite policy, are a wretched crew, with not one really talented person among them.

Pro-Russian sentiment is still strong but is cooling off in my opinion. The Kharkov trials dismayed a lot of people. Even the distinctly doubtful public-opinion polls conducted by the russophile *News Chronicle* show that the mass of the people don't want reprisals or a vindictive peace, though they do want Germany disarmed. If they grasped what was happening I can imagine them turning anti-Russian quite rapidly if there were any question of forced labour or mass trials of war criminals; or even as the result of heavy casualties when the Second Front opens. Relations between the American troops and the locals are better, I think, though one could not call

---

[1] Sir Richard Acland (1906–   ), became a Liberal MP in 1935. At the beginning of the war he announced his conversion to Socialism and in July 1942 he founded a new political party, Common Wealth, of which he became President. Its views were those of Utopian Socialism but it supported the war effort and, apart from the anti-war Independent Labour Party, formed the only organised Socialist opposition to the political truce and the Churchill Government. Acland was one of the most brilliant and effective orators in the country and could fill a large provincial hall despite the black-out. Common Wealth was largely financed and organised by a businessman, Alan P. Good (1906–53), who mystified many of his colleagues. As he explained himself, he was not a Socialist but believed that Acland's doctrines were good for industrial relations. However, he certainly made no discernible attempt to influence the party's policies, and confined himself to organising and providing its finances.

them good. There is much jealousy between American white and coloured troops. The press shuts down on this subject to such an extent that when a rape or something like that happens, one can only discover by private inquiry whether the American involved is white or coloured. Discussion of inter-allied relations is still avoided in the press and utterly taboo on the air. The best example of this is the BBC celebrating the 25th anniversary of the Red army without mentioning Trotsky, but American susceptibilities are studied even more carefully than Russian. We are still not broadcasting in Russian —this at the request of the Russians themselves—though we are broadcasting in nearly fifty other languages.

Well, now a word or two about our ancient institutions.

PARLIAMENT

When I was working with the BBC I sometimes had to go and listen to a debate in the Commons. The last time I had been there was about ten years previously, and I was very much struck by the deterioration that seemed to have taken place. The whole thing now has a mangy, forgotten look. Even the ushers' shirt fronts are grimy. And it is noticeable now that, except from the places they sit in (the Opposition always sits on the Speaker's left), you can't tell one party from another. It is just a collection of mediocre-looking men in dingy, dark suits, nearly all speaking in the same accent and all laughing at the same jokes. I may say, however, that they don't look such a set of crooks as the French Deputies used to look. The most striking thing of all is the lack of attendance. It would be very rare indeed for 400 members out of the 640 to turn up. The House of Lords, where they are now sitting, only has seating accommodation for about 250, and the old House of Commons (it was blitzed) cannot have been much larger. I attended the big debate on India after Cripps came back. At the start there were a little over 200 members present, which rapidly shrank to about 45. It seems to be the custom to clear out, presumably to the bar, as soon as any important speech begins, but the House fills up again when there are questions or anything else that promises a bit of fun. There is a marked family atmosphere. Everyone shouts with laughter over jokes and allusions which are unintelligible to anyone not an MP, nicknames are used freely, violent political opponents pal up over drinks. Nearly any member of long standing is corrupted by this kind of thing sooner or later. Maxton, the ILP[1] MP, twenty years ago an inflammatory orator whom the ruling classes hated like poison, is now the pet of the House, and Gallacher, the Communist MP, is going the same road. Each time I have been in the House recently I have found myself thinking the same thought—that the Roman Senate still existed under the later Empire.

I don't need to indicate to you the various features of capitalism that make democracy unworkable. But apart from these, and apart from the dwindling prestige of representative institutions, there are special reasons why it is difficult for able men to find their way into Parliament. To begin with, the out-of-date electoral system grossly favours the Conservative Party. The rural areas, where, on the whole, people vote as the landlords tell them to, are so much over-represented, and the industrial areas so much under-represented that the Conservatives consistently win a far higher proportion of seats than their share in the total vote entitles them to. Secondly, the electorate seldom have a chance to vote for anyone except the nominees of the party machines. In the Conservative Party safe seats are peddled round to men rich enough to "keep up" the seat (contributions to local charities etc), and no doubt to pay an agreed sum into the party funds as well. Labour Party candidates are selected for their political docility, and a proportion of the Labour MPs are always elderly trade-union officials who have been allotted a seat as a kind of pension. Naturally, these men are even more slavishly obedient to the party machine than the Tories. To any MP who shows signs of independent thought the same threat is always applied—"We won't support you at the next election". In practice a candidate cannot win an election against the opposition of his own party machine, unless the inhabitants of that locality have some special reason for admiring him personally. But the party system has destroyed the territorial basis of politics. Few MPs have any connection with their constituency, even to the extent of living there: many have never seen it till they go down to fight their first election. At this moment Parliament is more than usually unrepresentative because, owing to the war, literally millions of people are disenfranchised. There has been no register of voters since 1939, which means that no one under twenty-five, and no one who has changed his place of residence, now has a vote; for practical purposes the men in the forces are disenfranchised as well. On the whole, the people who have lost their votes are those

[1] Independent Labour Party.

who would vote against the Government. It is fair to add that in the general mechanics of an election in England there is no dirty work— no intimidation, no miscounting of votes or direct bribery, and the ballot is genuinely secret.

The feeling that Parliament has lost its importance is very wide-spread. The electorate are conscious of having no control over their MPs; the MPs are conscious that it is not they who are directing affairs. All major decisions, whether to go to war, whether to open a Second Front, and where, which power to go into alliance with, and so forth, are taken by an Inner Cabinet which acts first and announces the *fait accompli* afterwards. Theoretically, Parliament has the power to overthrow the Government if it wishes, but the party machines can usually prevent this. The average MP, or even a minor member of the Government, has no more information about what is going on than any reader of *The Times*. There is an extra hurdle for any progressive policy in the House of Lords, which has supposedly been shorn of its powers but still has the power of obstruction. In all, only two or three bills thrown out by the Lords have ever been forced through by the Commons. Seeing all this, people of every political colour simply lose interest in Parliament, which they refer to as "the talking shop". One cannot judge from war-time, but for years before the war the percentage of the electorate voting had been going down. Sixty per cent was considered a high vote. In big towns many people do not know the name of their MP or which constituency they live in. A social survey at a recent election showed that many adults now don't know the first facts about British electoral procedure—e.g. don't know that the ballot is secret.

Nevertheless, I myself feel that Parliament has justified its existence during the war, and I even think that its prestige has risen slightly in the last two or three years. While losing most of its original powers it has retained its power of criticism, and it is the only remaining place in which one is free, theoretically as well as practically, to utter literally any opinion. Except for sheer personal abuse (and even that has to be something fairly extreme), any remark made in Parliament is privileged. The Government has, of course, devices for dodging awkward questions, but can't dodge all of them. However, the importance of Parliamentary criticism is not so much its direct effect on the Government as its effect on public opinion. For what is said in Parliament cannot go altogether unreported. The newspapers, even *The Times*, and the BBC probably do tend to play down the speeches of Opposition members, but cannot do so very grossly because of the existence of Hansard, which publishes the Parliamentary debates verbatim. The effective circulation of Hansard is small (2 or 3 thousand), but so long as it is available to anyone who wants it, a lot of things that the Government would like to suppress get across to the public. This critical function of Parliament is all the more noticeable because intellectually this must be one of the worst Parliaments we have ever had. Outside the Government, I do not think there can be thirty able men in the House, but that small handful have managed to give every subject from dive-bombers to 18b an airing. As a legislative body Parliament has become relatively unimportant, and it has even less control over the executive than over the Government. But it still functions as a kind of uncensored supplement to the radio —which, after all, is something worth preserving.

THE MONARCHY

Nothing is harder than to be sure whether royalist sentiment is still a reality in England. All that is said on either side is coloured by wish-thinking. My own opinion is that royalism, i.e. popular royalism, was a strong factor in English life up to the death of George V, who had been there so long that he was accepted as "the" King (as Victoria had been "the" Queen), a sort of father-figure and projection of the English domestic virtues. The 1935 Silver Jubilee, at any rate in the south of England, was a pathetic outburst of popular affection, genuinely spontaneous. The authorities were taken by surprise and the celebrations were prolonged for an extra week while the poor old man, patched up after pneumonia and in fact dying, was hauled to and fro through slum streets where the people had hung out flags of their own accord and chalked "Long Live the King. Down with the Landlord" across the roadway.

I think, however, that the Abdication of Edward VIII must have dealt royalism a blow from which it may not recover. The row over the Abdication, which was very violent while it lasted, cut across existing political divisions, as can be seen from the fact that Edward's loudest champions were Churchill, Mosley and H. G. Wells; but broadly speaking, the rich were anti-Edward and the working classes were sympathetic to him. He had promised the unemployed miners that he would do something on their behalf, which was an offence in the eyes of the rich; on the other hand, the miners and other unemployed probably felt that he had let them down by abdicating for the sake of a woman. Some continental observers believed that Edward had been got rid of because of his association with leading Nazis and were rather impressed by this exhibition of Cromwellism. But the net effect of the whole business was probably to weaken the feeling of royal sanctity which had been so carefully built up from 1880 onwards. It brought home to people the personal powerlessness of the King, and it showed that the much-advertised royalist sentiment of the upper classes was humbug. At the least I should say it would need another long reign, and a monarch with some kind of charm, to put the Royal Family back where it was in George V's day.

The function of the King in promoting stability and acting as a sort of keystone in a non-democratic society is, of course, obvious. But he also has, or can have, the function of acting as an escape-valve for dangerous emotions. A French journalist said to me once that the monarchy was one of the things that have saved Britain from Fascism. What he meant was that modern people can't, apparently, get along without drums, flags and loyalty parades, and that it is better that they should tie their leader-worship onto some figure who has no real power. In a dictatorship the power and the glory belong to the same person. In England the real power belongs to unprepossessing men in bowler hats: the creature who rides in a gilded coach behind soldiers in steel breast-plates is really a waxwork. It is at any rate possible that while this division of function exists a Hitler or a Stalin cannot come to power. On the whole the European countries which have most successfully avoided Fascism have been constitutional monarchies. The conditions seemingly are that the Royal Family shall be long-established and taken for granted, shall understand its own position and shall not produce strong characters with political ambitions. These have been fulfilled in Britain, the Low Countries and Scandinavia, but not in, say, Spain or Rumania. If you point these facts out to the average left-winger he gets very angry, but only because he has not examined the nature of his own feelings towards Stalin. I do not defend the institution of monarchy in an absolute sense, but I think that in an age like our own it may have an inoculating effect, and certainly it does far less harm than the existence of our so-called aristocracy. I have often advocated that a Labour government, i.e. one that meant business, would abolish titles while retaining the Royal Family. But such a move would only have meaning if royal sentiment exists, and so far as I can judge it is much weakened. I am told that the royal visits to war factories are looked on as time-wasting ballyhoo. Nor did the news that the King had caused a black line to be painted round all the baths in Buckingham Palace do much to popularise the five-inch bath.

Well, no more news. I am afraid I have written rather a lot already. It is a foul winter, not at all cold, but with endless fogs, almost like the famous "London fogs" of my childhood. The black-out seems to get less and not more tolerable as the war goes on. Food is much as usual, but wine has almost vanished and whisky can only be bought by the nip, unless you have influential pals. There are air-raid alarms almost every night, but hardly any bombs. There is much talk about the rocket guns with which the Germans are supposedly going to bombard London. A little while before the talk was of a four-hundred ton bomb which was to be made in the form of an enormous glider and towed across by fleets of German aeroplanes. Rumours of this kind have followed one another since the beginning of the war, and are always firmly believed in by numbers of people, evidently fulfilling some obscure psychological need.

Yours ever,
George Orwell

Partisan Review, Spring 1944

16. As I Please

A correspondent reproaches me with being "negative" and "always attacking things". The fact is that we live in a time when causes for rejoicing are not numerous. But I like praising things, when there is anything to praise, and I would like here to write a few lines—they have to be retrospective, unfortunately—in praise of the Woolworth's Rose.

In the good days when nothing in Woolworth's cost over sixpence, one of their best lines was their rose bushes. They were always very young plants, but they came into bloom in their second year, and I don't think I ever had one die on me. Their chief interest was that they were never, or very seldom, what they claimed to be on their labels. One that I bought for a Dorothy Perkins turned out to be a beautiful little white rose with a yellow heart, one of the finest ramblers I have ever seen. A polyantha rose labelled yellow turned out to be deep red. Another, bought for an Albertine, was like an Albertine, but more double, and gave astonishing masses of blossom. These roses had all the interest of a surprise packet, and there was always the chance that you might happen upon a new variety which you would have the right to name John Smithii or something of that kind.

Last summer I passed the cottage where I used to live before the war. The little white rose, no bigger than a boy's catapult when I put it in, had grown into a huge vigorous bush, the Albertine or near-Albertine was smothering half the fence in a cloud of pink blossom. I had planted both of those in 1936. And I thought, "All that for sixpence!" I do not know how long a rose bush lives; I suppose ten years might be an average life. And throughout that time a rambler will be in full bloom for a month or six weeks each year, while a bush rose will be blooming, on and off, for at least four months. All that for sixpence—the price, before the war, of ten Players, or a pint and a half of mild, or a week's subscription to the *Daily Mail*, or about twenty minutes of twice-breathed air in the movies!

Tribune, 21 January 1944

17. As I Please

I see that Mr Suresh Vaidya, an Indian journalist living in England, has been arrested for refusing military service. This is not the first case of its kind, and if it is the last it will probably be because no more Indians of military age are left to be victimised.

Everyone knows without being told them the juridical aspects of Mr Vaidya's case, and I have no wish to dwell on them. But I would like to draw attention to the common-sense aspect, which the British Government so steadily refuses to consider. Putting aside the seamen who come and go, and the handful of troops who are still here, there might perhaps be two thousand Indians in this country, of all kinds and ages. By applying conscription to them you may raise a few score extra soldiers; and by coercing the minority who "object" you may swell the British prison population by about a dozen. That is the net result from the military point of view.

But unfortunately that isn't all. By behaviour of this kind you antagonise the entire Indian community in Britain—for no Indian, whatever his views, admits that Britain had the right to declare war on India's behalf or has the right to impose compulsory service on Indians. Anything that happens in the Indian community here has prompt repercussions in India, and appreciable effects further afield. One Indian war resister victimised does us more harm than ten thousand British ones. It seems a high price to pay for the satisfaction the Blimps probably feel at having another "red" in their clutches. I don't expect the Blimps to see Mr Vaidya's point of view. But they really might see, after all their experience, that making martyrs does not pay.

A correspondent has sent us a letter in defence of Ezra Pound, the American poet who transferred his allegiance to Mussolini some years before the war and has been a lively propagandist on the Rome radio. The substance of his claim is (a) that Pound did not sell himself simply for money, and (b) that when you get hold of a true poet you can afford to ignore his political opinions.

Now, of course, Pound did not sell himself solely for money. No writer ever does that. Anyone who wanted money before all else would choose some more paying profession. But I think it probable that Pound did sell himself partly for prestige, flattery and a professorship. He had a most venomous hatred for both Britain and the USA, where he felt that his talents had not been fully appreciated, and obviously believed that there was a conspiracy against him throughout the English-speaking countries. Then there were several ignominious episodes in which Pound's phony erudition was shown up, and which he no doubt found it hard to forgive. By the mid-thirties Pound was singing the praises of "the Boss" (Mussolini) in a number of English papers, including Mosley's quarterly, *British Union* (to which Vidkun Quisling was also a contributor). At the time of the Abyssinian war Pound was vociferously anti-Abyssinian. In 1938 or thereabouts the Italians gave him a chair at one of their universities, and some time after war broke out he took Italian citizenship.

Whether a poet, as such, is to be forgiven his political opinions is a different question. Obviously one mustn't say "X agrees with me: therefore he is a good writer", and for the last ten years honest literary criticism has largely consisted in combating this outlook. Personally I admire several writers (Céline, for instance) who have gone over to

the Fascists, and many others whose political outlook I strongly
object to. But one has the right to expect ordinary decency even of a
poet. I never listened to Pound's broadcasts, but I often read them in
the BBC Monitoring Reports, and they were intellectually and morally
disgusting. Antisemitism, for instance, is simply not the doctrine of
a grown-up person. People who go in for that kind of thing must take
the consequences. But I do agree with our correspondent in hoping
that the American authorities do not catch Pound and shoot him,
as they have threatened to do. It would establish his reputation so
thoroughly that it might be a good hundred years before anyone
could determine dispassionately whether Pound's much-debated
poems are any good or not.

The other night a barmaid informed me that if you pour beer into
a damp glass it goes flat much more quickly. She added that to dip
your moustache into your beer also turns it flat. I immediately
accepted this without further inquiry; in fact, as soon as I got home
I clipped my moustache, which I had forgotten to do for some days.

Only later did it strike me that this was probably one of those
superstitions which are able to keep alive because they have the air
of being scientific truths. In my note-book I have a long list of fallacies
which were taught to me in my childhood, in each case not as an old
wives' tale but as a scientific fact. I can't give the whole list, but here
are a few hardy favourites:

That a swan can break your leg with a blow of its wing.

That if you cut yourself between the thumb and forefinger you
get lockjaw.

That powdered glass is poisonous.

That if you wash your hands in the water eggs have been boiled
in (why anyone should do this is a mystery) you will get warts.

That bulls become infuriated at the sight of red.

That sulphur in a dog's drinking water acts as a tonic.

And so on and so forth. Almost everyone carries some or other of
these beliefs into adult life. I have met someone of over thirty who
still retained the second of the beliefs I have listed above. As for
the third, it is so widespread that in India, for instance, people are
constantly trying to poison one another with powdered glass, with
disappointing results.

I wish now that I had read *Basic English versus the Artificial
Languages* before and not after reviewing the interesting little book

in which Professor Lancelot Hogben sets forth his own artificial language, Interglossa.[1] For in that case I should have realised how comparatively chivalrous Professor Hogben had been towards the inventors of rival international languages. Controversies on serious subjects are often far from polite. Followers of the Stalinist-Trotskyist controversy will have observed that an unfriendly note tends to creep into it, and when the *Tablet* and the *Church Times* are having a go at one another the blows are not always above the belt. But for sheer dirtiness of fighting the feuds between the inventors of various of the international languages would take a lot of beating.

Tribune may before long print one or more articles on Basic English. If any language is ever adopted as a world-wide "second" language it is immensely unlikely that it will be a manufactured one, and of the existing natural ones English has much the best chance, though not necessarily in the Basic form. Public opinion is beginning to wake up to the need for an international language, though fantastic misconceptions still exist. For example, many people imagine that the advocates of an international language aim at suppressing the natural languages, a thing no one has ever seriously suggested.

At present, in spite of the growing recognition of this need, the world is growing more and not less nationalistic in language. This is partly from conscious policy (about half a dozen of the existing languages are being pushed in an imperialistic way in various parts of the world), and partly owing to the dislocation caused by the war. And the difficulties of trade, travel and intercommunication between scientists, and the time-wasting labour of learning foreign languages, still continue. In my life I have learned seven foreign languages, including two dead ones, and out of those seven I retain only one, and that not brilliantly. This would be quite a normal case. A member of a small nationality, a Dane or a Dutchman, say, has to learn three foreign languages as a matter of course, if he wants to be educated at all. Clearly this position could be bettered, and the great difficulty is to decide which language is to be adopted as the international one. But there is going to be some ugly scrapping before that is settled, as anyone who has ever glanced into this subject knows.

Tribune, 28 January 1944

[1] Orwell reviewed Lancelot Hogben's *Interglossa* in the *Manchester Evening News*, 23 December 1943.

18. As I Please

When Sir Walter Raleigh was imprisoned in the Tower of London, he occupied himself with writing a history of the world. He had finished the first volume and was at work on the second when there was a scuffle between some workmen beneath the window of his cell, and one of the men was killed. In spite of diligent enquiries, and in spite of the fact that he had actually seen the thing happen, Sir Walter was never able to discover what the quarrel was about: whereupon, so it is said—and if the story is not true it certainly ought to be—he burned what he had written and abandoned his project.

This story has come into my head I do not know how many times during the past ten years, but always with the reflection that Raleigh was probably wrong. Allowing for all the difficulties of research at that date, and the special difficulty of conducting research in prison, he could probably have produced a world history which had some resemblance to the real course of events. Up to a fairly recent date, the major events recorded in the history books probably happened. It is probably true that the battle of Hastings was fought in 1066, that Columbus discovered America, that Henry VIII had six wives, and so on. A certain degree of truthfulness was possible so long as it was admitted that a fact may be true even if you don't like it. Even as late as the last war it was possible for the *Encyclopaedia Britannica*, for instance, to compile its articles on the various campaigns partly from German sources. Some of the facts—the casualty figures, for instance—were regarded as neutral and in substance accepted by everybody. No such thing would be possible now. A Nazi and a non-Nazi version of the present war would have no resemblance to one another, and which of them finally gets into the history books will be decided not by evidential methods but on the battlefield.

During the Spanish civil war I found myself feeling very strongly that a true history of this war never would or could be written. Accurate figures, objective accounts of what was happening, simply did not exist. And if I felt that even in 1937, when the Spanish Government was still in being, and the lies which the various Republican factions were telling about each other and about the enemy were relatively small ones, how does the case stand now? Even if Franco is overthrown, what kind of records will the future historian have to go upon? And if Franco or anyone at all resembling him remains in power, the history of the war will consist quite largely of "facts" which millions of people now living know to be lies. One of these "facts", for instance, is that there was a considerable Russian army in Spain. There exists the most abundant evidence that there was no such army. Yet if Franco remains in power, and if Fascism in general survives, that Russian army will go into the history books and future schoolchildren will believe in it. So for practical purposes the lie will have become truth.

This kind of thing is happening all the time. Out of the millions of instances which must be available, I will choose one which happens to be verifiable. During part of 1941 and 1942, when the Luftwaffe was busy in Russia, the German radio regaled its home audience with stories of devastating air raids on London. Now, we are aware that those raids did not happen. But what use would our knowledge be if the Germans conquered Britain? For the purposes of a future historian, did those raids happen, or didn't they? The answer is: If Hitler survives, they happened, and if he falls they didn't happen. So with innumerable other events of the past ten or twenty years. Is the Protocols of the Elders of Zion a genuine document? Did Trotsky plot with the Nazis? How many German aeroplanes were shot down in the Battle of Britain? Does Europe welcome the New Order? In no case do you get one answer which is universally accepted because it is true: in each case you get a number of totally incompatible answers, one of which is finally adopted as the result of a physical struggle. History is written by the winners.

In the last analysis our only claim to victory is that if we win the war we shall tell less lies about it than our adversaries. The really frightening thing about totalitarianism is not that it commits "atrocities" but that it attacks the concept of objective truth: it claims to control the past as well as the future. In spite of all the lying and self-righteousness that war encourages, I do not honestly think it can be said that that habit of mind is growing in Britain. Taking one thing with another, I should say that the press is slightly freer than it was before the war. I know out of my own experience that you can print things now which you couldn't print ten years ago. War resisters have probably been less maltreated in this war than in the last one, and the expression of unpopular opinions in public is certainly safer. There is some hope, therefore, that the liberal habit of mind, which thinks of truth as something outside yourself, something to be discovered, and not as something you can make up as you go along, will survive. But I still don't envy the future historian's job. Is it not a strange commentary on our time that even the casualties in the present war cannot be estimated within several millions?

Announcing that the Board of Trade is about to remove the ban on turned-up trouser-ends, a tailor's advertisement hails this as "a first instalment of the freedom for which we are fighting".

If we were really fighting for turned-up trouser-ends, I should be inclined to be pro-Axis. Turn-ups have no function except to collect dust, and no virtue except that when you clean them out you occasionally find a sixpence there. But beneath that tailor's jubilant cry there lies another thought: that in a little while Germany will be finished, the war will be half over, rationing will be relaxed, and clothes snobbery will be in full swing again. I don't share that hope. The sooner we are able to stop food rationing the better I shall be pleased, but I would like to see clothes rationing continue till the moths have devoured the last dinner-jacket and even the undertakers have shed their top-hats. I would not mind seeing the whole nation in dyed battledress for five years if by that means one of the main breeding points of snobbery and envy could be eliminated. Clothes rationing was not conceived in a democratic spirit, but all the same it has had a democratising effect. If the poor are not much better dressed, at least the rich are shabbier. And since no real structural change is occurring in our society, the mechanical levelling process that results from sheer scarcity is better than nothing.

Tribune, 4 February 1944

19. As I Please

There are two journalistic activities that will always bring you a come-back. One is to attack the Catholics and the other is to defend the Jews. Recently I happened to review some books dealing with the persecution of the Jews in medieval and modern Europe.[1] The review brought me the usual wad of antisemitic letters, which left me thinking for the thousandth time that this problem is being evaded even by the people whom it concerns most directly.

[1] Orwell reviewed *The Devil and the Jews* by Joshua Trachtenberg and *Why I Am a Jew* by Edmond Fleg in the *Observer*, 30 January 1944.

The disquieting thing about these letters is that they do not all come from lunatics. I don't greatly mind the person who believes in the Protocols of the Elders of Zion, nor even the discharged army officer who has been shabbily treated by the Government and is infuriated by seeing "aliens" given all the best jobs. But in addition to these types there is the small business or professional man who is firmly convinced that the Jews bring all their troubles upon themselves by underhand business methods and complete lack of public spirit. These people write reasonable, well-balanced letters, disclaim any belief in racialism, and back up everything they say with copious instances. They admit the existence of "good Jews", and usually declare (Hitler says just the same in *Mein Kampf*) that they did not start out with any anti-Jewish feeling but have been forced into it simply by observing how Jews behave.

The weakness of the left-wing attitude towards antisemitism is to approach it from a rationalistic angle. Obviously the charges made against Jews are not true. They cannot be true, partly because they cancel out, partly because no one people could have such a monopoly of wickedness. But simply by pointing this out one gets no further. The official left-wing view of antisemitism is that it is something "got up" by the ruling classes in order to divert attention away from the real evils of society. The Jews, in fact, are scapegoats. This is no doubt correct, but it is quite useless as an argument. One does not dispose of a belief by showing that it is irrational. Nor is it any use, in my experience, to talk about the persecution of the Jews in Germany. If a man has the slightest disposition towards antisemitism, such things bounce off his consciousness like peas off a steel helmet. The best argument of all, if rational arguments were ever of any use, would be to point out that the alleged crimes of the Jews are only possible because we live in a society which rewards crime. If all Jews are crooks, let us deal with them by so arranging our economic system that crooks cannot prosper. But what good is it to say that kind of thing to the man who believes as an article of faith that Jews dominate the Black Market, push their way to the front of queues and dodge military service?

We could do with a detailed enquiry into the causes of antisemitism, and it ought not to be vitiated in advance by the assumption that those causes are wholly economic. However true the "scapegoat" theory may be in general terms, it does not explain why the Jews rather than some other minority group are picked on, nor does it make clear what they are a scapegoat *for*. A thing like the Dreyfus Case, for instance, is not easily translated into economic terms. So far as Britain is concerned, the important things to find out are just what charges are made against the Jews, whether antisemitism is really on the increase (it may actually have decreased over the past thirty years), and to what extent it is aggravated by the influx of refugees since about 1938.

One not only ought not to assume that the causes of antisemitism are economic in a crude, direct way (unemployment, business jealousy, etc), one also ought not to assume that "sensible" people are immune to it. It flourishes especially among literary men, for instance. Without even getting up from this table to consult a book I can think of passages in Villon, Shakespeare, Smollett, Thackeray, H. G. Wells, Aldous Huxley, T. S. Eliot and many another which would be called antisemitic if they had been written since Hitler came to power. Both Belloc and Chesterton flirted, or something more than flirted, with antisemitism, and other writers whom it is possible to respect have swallowed it more or less in its Nazi form. Clearly the neurosis lies very deep, and just what it is that people hate when they say that they hate a non-existent entity called "the Jews" is still uncertain. And it is partly the fear of finding out how widespread antisemitism is that prevents it from being seriously investigated.

The following lines are quoted in Anthony Trollope's *Autobiography*:

> When Payne-Knight's *Taste* was issued on the town
> A few Greek verses in the text set down
> Were torn to pieces, mangled into hash,
> Hurled to the flames as execrable trash;
> In short, were butchered rather than dissected
> And several false quantities detected;
> Till, when the smoke had risen from the cinders
> It was discovered that—the lines were Pindar's!

Trollope does not make clear who is the author of these lines, and I should be very glad if any reader could let me know. But I also quote them for their own sake—that is, for the terrible warning to literary critics that they contain—and for the sake of drawing attention to Trollope's *Autobiography*, which is a most fascinating book, although or because it is largely concerned with money.

The dispute that has been going on in *Time and Tide* about Mr J. F. Horrabin's atlas of war geography[1] is a reminder that maps are tricky things, to be regarded with the same suspicion as photographs and statistics.

It is an interesting minor manifestation of nationalism that every nation colours itself red on the map. There is also a tendency to make yourself look bigger than you are, which is possible without actual forgery since every projection of the earth as a flat surface distorts some part or other. During the Empire Free Trade "crusade" there was a free distribution to schools of large coloured wall-maps which were made on a new projection and dwarfed the USSR while exaggerating the size of India and Africa. Then there are ethnological and political maps, a most rewarding material for propaganda. During the Spanish civil war, maps were pinned up in the Spanish villages which divided the world into Socialist, democratic and Fascist states. From these you could learn that India was a democracy, while Madagascar and Indo-China (this was the period of the Popular Front Government in France) were labelled "Socialist".

The war has probably done something towards improving our geography. People who five years ago thought that Croats rhymed with goats and drew only a very shadowy distinction between Minsk and Pinsk, could now tell you which sea the Volga flows into and indicate without much searching the whereabouts of Guadalcanal or Buthidaung. Hundreds of thousands, if not millions, of English people can nearly pronounce Dnepropetrovsk. But it takes a war to make map-reading popular. As late as the time of Wavell's Egyptian campaign I met a woman who thought that Italy was joined up with Africa, and in 1938, when I was leaving for Morocco, some of the people in my village—a very rustic village, certainly, but only 50 miles from London—asked whether it would be necessary to cross the sea to get there. If you ask any circle of people (I should particularly like to do this with the members of the House of Commons) to draw a map of Europe from memory, you get some surprising results. Any government which genuinely cared about education

[1] In a very unfavourable reference to his *Atlas of Post-War Problems*, an article in *Time and Tide*, 8 January 1944, had accused Horrabin, among other things, of implying that it had been unfortunate to dismember the Austro-Hungarian Empire after 1918 because of the excellence of its system of transport, and added "As an indictment of the Treaty of Versailles [Horrabin's] tendentious maps are a free gift to Goebbels".

would see to it that a globe map, at present an expensive rarity, was accessible to every schoolchild. Without some notion of which country is next to which, and which is the quickest route from one place to another, and where a ship can be bombed from shore, and where it can't, it is difficult to see what value the average citizen's views on foreign policy can have.

Tribune, 11 February 1944

20. A Hundred Up

It is now a hundred years since the final numbers of *Martin Chuzzlewit* were published, and though it came thus early in Dickens's career (it was his fourth novel, if one counts *Pickwick* as a novel), it has more the air of being a pot-boiler than any of his books except the *Sketches*. There cannot be many people living who could outline its plot from memory. Whereas books like *Oliver Twist*, or *Bleak House*, or *Great Expectations*, have a central theme which can in some cases be reduced to a single word, the various parts of *Martin Chuzzlewit* have not much more relationship to one another than the sounds produced by a cat walking across the piano. The best characters are "supers".

What do people remember when they think of *Martin Chuzzlewit*? The American interlude, Mrs Gamp, and Todgers's (especially Bailey). Martin Chuzzlewit himself is a stick, Mark Tapley a tedious paradox on two legs, Pecksniff a partial failure. It is ironical that Dickens should have tried, more or less unsuccessfully, to make Pecksniff into a monumental figure of a hypocrite, and at the same time, almost incidentally, should have painted such a devastating picture of hypocrisy in the American chapters. Dickens's comic genius is dependent on his moral sense. He is funniest when he is discovering new sins. To denounce Pecksniff did not call into play his special powers, because, after all, no one supposes that hypocrisy is desirable. But to see through the pretensions of American democracy, or even, at that date, to see that Mrs Gamp was a luxury that society might well do without, did need the eye of a Dickens. The book's lack of any real central theme can be seen in its fearful ending. It is as though Dickens were dissolving into lukewarm treacle, and —as so often when he says something that he does not really feel—whole paragraphs of the final chapter will go straight into blank verse:

> Thy life is tranquil, calm, and happy, Tom.
> In the soft strain which ever and again
> Comes stealing back upon the ear, the memory
> Of thine old love may find a voice perhaps;
> But it is a pleasant, softened, whispering memory,
> Like that in which we sometimes hold the dead,
> And does not pain or grieve thee, God be thanked!

Yet the man who could write this stuff could also record the conversations of Bailey, and could not only create Mrs Gamp but could throw in, just for good measure, the metaphysical puzzle, Mrs Harris.

The American chapters are a good example of Dickens's habit of telling small lies in order to emphasise what he regards as a big truth. No doubt many of the things he reports actually happened (other travellers of the time confirm him on some details) but his picture of American society as a whole cannot possibly be true: not only because no community is wholly bad, but because the chaos of real life has been deliberately left out. Every incident, every character, is simply an illustration of Dickens's thesis. Moreover, the strongest charge that he makes against the Americans, that they boast of being democratic while actually living on slave labour, is obviously unfair. It implies that American opinion as a whole acquiesced in slavery, whereas a bloody civil war was to be fought mainly on this issue only twenty years later. But Dickens says these things in order to hit at what he feels to be the real fault of the Americans, their ignorant contempt for Europe and unjustified belief in their own superiority. Perhaps there *were* a few Americans who did not edit libellous newspapers or emit sentences like "the libation of freedom must sometimes be quaffed in blood"; but to lay too much stress upon them would have been to spoil the picture. After all, the business of a caricaturist is to make his point, and these chapters have worn very much better than *American Notes*.

The mental atmosphere of the American interlude is one that has since become familiar to us in the books written by British travellers to Soviet Russia. Some of these report that everything is good, others that everything is bad, but nearly all share the same propagandist outlook. A hundred years ago America, "the land of the free", had rather the same place in the European imagination that Soviet Russia has now, and *Martin Chuzzlewit* is the 1844 equivalent of André Gide's *Retour de l'URSS*. But it is a sign of the changing temper of the world that Dickens's attack, so much more violent and unfair than Gide's, could be so quickly forgiven.

Martin Chuzzlewit stands somewhere near the turning-point of Dickens's literary development, when he was becoming less of a picaresque writer and more of a novelist. The times were changing with the rise of the new cautious middle class, and Dickens was too much alive not to be affected by the atmosphere he lived in. *Martin Chuzzlewit* is his last completely disorderly book. In spite of its frequent flashes of genius, it is difficult to feel that by following up this vein in himself Dickens could have given us anything to compensate for the loss of *Hard Times* and *Great Expectations*.

Observer, 13 February 1944

21. Letter to Gleb Struve

10a Mortimer Crescent
London NW6
17 February 1944

Dear Mr Struve,[1]

Please forgive me for not writing earlier to thank you for the very kind gift of *25 Years of Soviet Russian Literature*, with its still more kind inscription. I am afraid I know very little about Russian literature and I hope your book will fill up some of the many gaps in my knowledge. It has already roused my interest in Zamyatin's *We*, which I had not heard of before. I am interested in that kind of book, and even keep making notes for one myself that may get written sooner or later. I wonder whether you can tell [me] if there is an adequate translation of Blok? I saw some translated fragments about ten years ago in *Life and Letters*, but whether they were any good as a translation I do not know.

I am writing a little squib[2] which might amuse you when it comes

---

[1] Gleb Struve (1898–   ), born in St Petersburg. Taught at the School of Slavonic and East European Studies, London University 1932–47; Professor of Slavic Languages and Literature, University of California, Berkeley, 1947–65. Author of *Soviet Literature 1917–50* and *Russian Literature in Exile*.

[2] *Animal Farm*.

out, but it is so not OK politically that I don't feel certain in advance that anyone will publish it. Perhaps that gives you a hint of its subject.

Yours sincerely
Geo. Orwell

22. As I Please

A short story in the *Home Companion and Family Journal*, entitled "Hullo, Sweetheart", recounts the adventures of a young girl named Lucy Fallows who worked on the switchboard of a long-distance telephone exchange. She had "sacrificed her yearning to be in uniform" in order to take this job, but found it dull and uneventful. "So many silly people seemed to use long-distance just to blather to each other. . . . She felt fed up; she felt that she was a servant to selfish people"; and there was "a cloud in her hazel eyes". However, as you will readily guess, Lucy's job soon livened up, and before long she found herself in the middle of thrilling adventures which included the sinking of a U-boat, the capture of a German sabotage crew, and a long motor-ride with a handsome naval officer who had "a crisp voice". Such is life in the Telephone Exchange.

At the end of the story there is a little note: "Any of our young readers themselves interested in the work of the Long Distance Telephone Exchange (such work as Lucy Fallows was doing) should apply to the Staff Controller, LTR, London, who will inform them as to the opportunities open."

I do not know whether this is an advertisement likely to have much success. I should doubt whether even girls of the age aimed at would believe that capturing U-boats enters very largely into the lives of telephone operators. But I note with interest the direct correlation between a government recruiting advertisement and a piece of commercial fiction. Before the war the Admiralty, for instance, used to put its advertisements in the boys' adventure papers, which was a natural place to put them, but stories were not, so far as I know, written to order. Probably they are not definitely commissioned even now. It is more likely that the departments concerned keep their eye on the weekly papers (incidentally I like to think of some stripe-trousered personage in the GPO[1] reading "Hullo, Sweetheart" as part of his official duties) and push in an ad when any story seems likely to form an attractive bait. But from that to the actual commissioning of stories to be written round the ATS,[2] Women's Land Army, or any other body in need of recruits, is only a short step. One can almost hear the tired, cultured voices from the MOI[3] saying:

"Hullo! Hullo! Is that you, Tony? Oh, hullo. Look here, I've got another script for you, Tony, 'A Ticket to Paradise'. It's bus conductresses this time. They're not coming in. I believe the trousers don't fit, or something. Well, anyway, Peter says make it sexy, but kind of clean—*you* know. Nothing extra-marital. We want the stuff in by Tuesday. Fifteen thousand words. You can choose the hero. I rather favour the kind of outdoor man that dogs and kiddies all love—*you* know. Or very tall with a sensitive mouth, I don't mind, really. But pile on the sex, Peter says."

Something resembling this already happens with radio features and documentary films, but hitherto there has not been any very direct connection between fiction and propaganda. That half-inch ad in the *Home Companion* seems to mark another small stage in the process of "co-ordination" that is gradually happening to all the arts.

Looking through Chesterton's Introduction to *Hard Times* in the Everyman Edition (incidentally, Chesterton's Introductions to Dickens are about the best thing he ever wrote), I note the typically sweeping statement: "There are no new ideas". Chesterton is here claiming that the ideas which animated the French Revolution were not new ones but simply a revival of doctrines which had flourished earlier and then been abandoned. But the claim that "there is nothing new under the sun" is one of the stock arguments of intelligent reactionaries. Catholic apologists, in particular, use it almost automatically. Everything that you can say or think has been said or thought before. Every political theory from Liberalism to Trotskyism can be shown to be a development of some heresy in the early Church. Every system of philosophy springs ultimately from the

[1] General Post Office.
[2] Auxiliary Territorial Service: the women's forces attached to the army.
[3] Ministry of Information.

Greeks. Every scientific theory (if we are to believe the popular Catholic press) was anticipated by Roger Bacon and others in the thirteenth century. Some Hindu thinkers go even further and claim that not merely the scientific theories, but the products of applied science as well, aeroplanes, radio and the whole bag of tricks, were known to the ancient Hindus, who afterwards dropped them as being unworthy of their attention.

It is not very difficult to see that this idea is rooted in the fear of progress. If there is nothing new under the sun, if the past in some shape or another always returns, then the future when it comes will be something familiar. At any rate what will never come—since it has never come before—is that hated, dreaded thing, a world of free and equal human beings. Particularly comforting to reactionary thinkers is the idea of a cyclical universe, in which the same chain of events happens over and over again. In such a universe every seeming advance towards democracy simply means that the coming age of tyranny and privilege is a bit nearer. This belief, obviously superstitious though it is, is widely held nowadays, and is common among Fascists and near-Fascists.

In fact, there *are* new ideas. The idea that an advanced civilisation need not rest on slavery is a relatively new idea, for instance: it is a good deal younger than the Christian religion. But even if Chesterton's dictum were true, it would only be true in the sense that a statue is contained in every block of stone. Ideas may not change, but emphasis shifts constantly. It could be claimed, for example, that the most important part of Marx's theory is contained in the saying: "Where your treasure is, there will your heart be also". But before Marx developed it, what force had that saying had? Who had paid any attention to it? Who had inferred from it—what it certainly implies—that laws, religions and moral codes are all a superstructure built over existing property relations? It was Christ, according to the Gospel, who uttered the text, but it was Marx who brought it to life. And ever since he did so the motives of politicians, priests, judges, moralists and millionaires have been under the deepest suspicion—which, of course, is why they hate him so much.

Tribune, 25 February 1944

23. Review

The Edge of the Abyss by Alfred Noyes

Incoherent and, in places, silly though it is, this book raises a real problem and will set its readers thinking, even if their thinking only starts to be useful at about the place where Mr Noyes leaves off. His thesis is that western civilisation is in danger of actual destruction, and that it has been brought to this pass not by economic maladjustments but by the decay of the belief in absolute good and evil. The rules of behaviour on which any stable society has to rest are dissolving:

> What promise can we trust, what firm agreement can ever be made again, in a world where millions upon millions have been educated to believe that, if it seems in their interest to violate it, no pact or pledge, however solemnly drawn up, need be regarded by "realistic" minds, or "cold statesmanship", as more than a "scrap of paper", even though its violation involve the murder by night of sleeping and innocent millions?

There is much force in this question, which Mr Noyes repeats over and over again in various forms. In the chaos in which we are living, even the prudential reasons for common decency are being forgotten. Politics, internal or international, are probably no more immoral than they have always been, but what is new is the growing acquiescence of ordinary people in the doctrines of expediency, the callousness of public opinion in the face of the most atrocious crimes and sufferings, and the black-out memory which allows blood-stained murderers to turn into public benefactors overnight if "military necessity" demands it. Quite new, too, is the doubt cast by the various totalitarian systems on the very existence of objective truth, and the consequent large-scale falsification of history. Mr Noyes is quite right to cry out against all this, and he probably even under-emphasises the harm done to ordinary common sense by the cult of "realism", with its inherent tendency to assume that the dishonest course is always the profitable one. The loss of moral standards does, indeed, seem to undermine the sense of probability. Mr Noyes is also within his rights in saying that the intelligentsia are more infected by totalitarian ideas than the common people, and are partly to blame for the mess we are now in. But his diagnosis of the reasons for this is very shallow, and his suggested remedies are doubtful, even from the point of view of practicability.

To begin with it will not do to suggest, as Mr Noyes does throughout, that a decent society can only be founded on Christian principles. It amounts to saying that a good life can only be lived on the fringes of the Atlantic. About a quarter of the population of the world is nominally Christian, and the proportion is constantly diminishing. The vast block of Asia is not Christian, and without some unforeseeable miracle it never will be. Are we to say that a decent society cannot be established in Asia? If so, it cannot be established anywhere, and the whole attempt to regenerate society might as well be given up in advance. And Mr Noyes is probably wrong in imagining that the Christian faith, as it existed in the past, can be restored even in Europe. The real problem of our time is to restore the sense of absolute right and wrong when the belief that it used to rest on—that is, the belief in personal immortality—has been destroyed. This demands faith, which is a different thing from credulity. It seems doubtful whether Mr Noyes has fully grasped the distinction.

Then there is the question of the amount of blame attaching to "the highbrows" ("our pseudo-intellectuals" is Mr Noyes's favourite name for them) for the breakdown of moral standards. Mr Noyes writes on this subject in rather the same strain as the *London Mercury* of twenty years ago. "The highbrows" are gloomy, they are obscene, they attack religion, patriotism, the family, etc etc. But they are also, it appears, in some way responsible for the rise of Hitler. Now this contradicts the facts. During the crucial years it was precisely the "pseudo-intellectuals" whom Mr Noyes detests who cried out against the horrors of Fascism, while the Tory and clerical press did its best to hush them up. Mr Noyes condemns the policy of appeasement, but what was the attitude of his own Church and its press on that subject?

On the other hand, the intellectuals whom he *does* approve of are only very doubtfully on the side of the angels. One, of course, is Carlyle, who was one of the founders of the modern worship of power and success, and who applauded the third German war of aggression as vociferously as Pound did the fifth. The other is Kipling. Kipling was not totalitarian, but his moral outlook is equivocal at best. Mr Noyes remarks at the beginning of his book that one cannot cast out devils with the aid of Beelzebub, but he is also extremely angry because anti-British books can still be published in England and praised in British newspapers. Does it not occur to

him that if we stopped doing this kind of thing the main difference
between ourselves and our enemies would have disappeared?

Observer, 27 February 1944

24. As I Please

Some weeks ago a Catholic reader of *Tribune* wrote to protest against
a review by Mr Charles Hamblett. She objected to his remarks about
St Teresa and about St Joseph of Copertino, the saint who once
flew round a cathedral carrying a bishop on his back. I answered,
defending Mr Hamblett, and got a still more indignant letter in
return. This letter raises a number of very important points, and at
least one of them seems to me to deserve discussion. The relevance
of flying saints to the Socialist movement may not at first sight be
very clear, but I think I can show that the present nebulous state of
Christian doctrine has serious implications which neither Christians
nor Socialists have faced.

The substance of my correspondent's letter is that it doesn't
matter whether St Teresa and the rest of them flew through the air or
not: what matters is that St Teresa's "vision of the world changed the
course of history". I would concede this. Having lived in an oriental
country I have developed a certain indifference to miracles, and I
well know that having delusions, or even being an outright lunatic,
is quite compatible with what is loosely called genius. William Blake,
for instance, was a lunatic in my opinion. Joan of Arc was probably
a lunatic. Newton believed in astrology, Strindberg believed in
magic. However, the miracles of the saints are a minor matter. It also
appears from my correspondent's letter that even the most central
doctrines of the Christian religion don't have to be accepted in a
literal sense. It doesn't matter, for instance, whether Jesus Christ
ever existed. "The figure of Christ (myth, or man, or god, it does not
matter) so transcends all the rest that I only wish that everyone would
look, before rejecting that version of life." Christ, therefore, may be
a myth, or he may have been merely a human being, or the account
given of him in the Creeds may be true. So we arrive at this position:
Tribune must not poke fun at the Christian religion, but the existence
of Christ, which innumerable people have been burnt for denying, is
a matter of indifference.

Now, is this orthodox Catholic doctrine? My impression is that it is not. I can think of passages in the writing of popular Catholic apologists such as Father Woodlock and Father Ronald Knox in which it is stated in the clearest terms that Christian doctrine means what it appears to mean, and is not to be accepted in some wishy-washy metaphorical sense. Father Knox refers specifically to the idea that it doesn't matter whether Christ actually existed as a "horrible" idea. But what my correspondent says would be echoed by many Catholic intellectuals. If you talk to a thoughtful Christian, Catholic or Anglican, you often find yourself laughed at for being so ignorant as to suppose that anyone ever took the doctrines of the Church literally. These doctrines have, you are told, a quite other meaning which you are too crude to understand. Immortality of the soul doesn't "mean" that you, John Smith, will remain conscious after you are dead. Resurrection of the body doesn't mean that John Smith's body will actually be resurrected—and so on and so on. Thus the Catholic intellectual is able, for controversial purposes, to play a sort of handy-pandy game, repeating the articles of the Creed in exactly the same terms as his forefathers, while defending himself from the charge of superstition by explaining that he is speaking in parables. Substantially his claim is that though he himself doesn't believe in any very definite way in life after death, there has been no change in Christian belief, since our ancestors didn't really believe in it either. Meanwhile a vitally important fact—that one of the props of western civilisation has been knocked away—is obscured.

I do not know whether, officially, there has been any alteration in Christian doctrine. Father Knox and my correspondent would seem to be in disagreement about this. But what I do know is that belief in survival after death—the individual survival of John Smith, still conscious of himself as John Smith—is enormously less widespread than it was. Even among professing Christians it is probably decaying: other people, as a rule, don't even entertain the possibility that it might be true. But our forefathers, so far as we know, did believe in it. Unless all that they wrote about it was intended to mislead us, they believed it in an exceedingly literal, concrete way. Life on earth, as they saw it, was simply a short period of preparation for an infinitely more important life beyond the grave. But that notion has disappeared, or is disappearing, and the consequences have not really been faced.

Western civilisation, unlike some oriental civilisations, was founded partly on the belief in individual immortality. If one looks at the Christian religion from the outside, this belief appears far more important than the belief in God. The western conception of good and evil is very difficult to separate from it. There is little doubt that the modern cult of power worship is bound up with the modern man's feeling that life here and now is the only life there is. If death ends everything, it becomes much harder to believe that you can be in the right even if you are defeated. Statesmen, nations, theories, causes are judged almost inevitably by the test of material success. Supposing that one can separate the two phenomena, I would say that the decay of the belief in personal immortality has been as important as the rise of machine civilisation. Machine civilisation has terrible possibilities, as you probably reflected the other night when the ack-ack guns started up: but the other thing has terrible possibilities too, and it cannot be said that the Socialist movement has given much thought to them.

I do not want the belief in life after death to return, and in any case it is not likely to return. What I do point out is that its disappearance has left a big hole, and that we ought to take notice of that fact. Reared for thousands of years on the notion that the individual survives, man has got to make a considerable psychological effort to get used to the notion that the individual perishes. He is not likely to salvage civilisation unless he can evolve a system of good and evil which is independent of heaven and hell. Marxism, indeed, does supply this, but it has never really been popularised. Most Socialists are content to point out that once Socialism has been established we shall be happier in a material sense, and to assume that all problems lapse when one's belly is full. But the truth is the opposite: when one's belly is empty, one's only problem is an empty belly. It is when we have got away from drudgery and exploitation that we shall really start wondering about man's destiny and the reason for his existence. One cannot have any worth-while picture of the future unless one realises how much we have lost by the decay of Christianity. Few Socialists seem to be aware of this. And the Catholic intellectuals who cling to the letter of the Creeds while reading into them meanings they were never meant to have, and who snigger at anyone simple enough to suppose that the Fathers of the Church meant what they said, are simply raising smoke-screens to conceal their own disbelief from themselves.

I have very great pleasure in welcoming the reappearance of the *Cornhill Magazine* after its four years' absence. Apart from the articles—there is a good one on Mayakovsky by Maurice Bowra, and another good one by Raymond Mortimer on Brougham and Macaulay—there are some interesting notes by the editor on the earlier history of the *Cornhill*. One fact that these bring out is the size and wealth of the Victorian reading public, and the vast sums earned by literary men in those days. The first number of the *Cornhill* sold 120,000 copies. It paid Trollope £2,000 for a serial—he had demanded £3,000—and commissioned another from George Eliot at £10,000. Except for the tiny few who manage to crash into the film world, these sums would be quite unthinkable nowadays. You would have to be a top-notcher even to get into the £2,000 class. As for £10,000, to get that for a single book you would have to be someone like Edgar Rice Burroughs. A novel nowadays is considered to have done very well if it brings its author £500—a sum which a successful lawyer can earn in a single day. The book ramp is not so new as "Beachcomber" and other enemies of the literary race imagine.

Tribune, 3 March 1944

25. Letter to Roy Fuller

> 10a Mortimer Crescent
> London NW6
> 7 March 1944

Dear Mr Fuller,[1]
Since receiving your letter I have procured a copy of the *Little Reviews Anthology*[2] and read your story, "Fletcher". I must say that I myself cannot see anything antisemitic in it. I imagine that what Cedric Dover[3] meant was that the central character was a Jew and also a not very admirable character, and perhaps that counts as antisemitism nowadays. I am sorry about this, but you will under-

---

[1] Roy Fuller (1912–   ), poet and novelist.

[2] Edited by Denys Val Baker, 1943.

[3] Cedric Dover (d. 1951), born in Calcutta of Eurasian parents. An entomologist and a writer on history, sociology and politics. His book *Half Caste*, 1937 about the Eurasian community in India, caused much discussion. He reviewed *Little Reviews Anthology* in *Tribune*, 18 February 1944.

stand that as Literary Editor[1] I cannot read all the books sent out for review and have to take the reviewers' judgement for granted. Of course if he had made a bald-headed attack on you as an antisemite I should have checked up on it before printing, but I think he only said "subtly antisemitic" or words to that effect. I am sorry that you should have had this annoyance. I must add, however, that by my own experience it is almost impossible to mention Jews in print, either favourably or unfavourably, without getting into trouble.

Yours truly
Geo. Orwell

26. As I Please

Reading as nearly as possible simultaneously Mr Derrick Leon's *Life of Tolstoy*, Miss Gladys Storey's book on Dickens, Harry Levin's book on James Joyce, and the autobiography (not yet published in this country) of Salvador Dali, the surrealist painter, I was struck even more forcibly than usual by the advantage that an artist derives from being born into a relatively healthy society.

When I first read *War and Peace* I must have been twenty, an age at which one is not intimidated by long novels, and my sole quarrel with this book (three stout volumes—the length of perhaps four modern novels) was that it did not go on long enough. It seemed to me that Nicholas and Natasha Rostov, Pierre Bezukhov, Denisov and all the rest of them, were people about whom one would gladly go on reading for ever. The fact is that the minor Russian aristocracy of that date, with their boldness and simplicity, their countrified pleasures, their stormy love affairs and enormous families, were very charming people. Such a society could not possibly be called just or progressive. It was founded on serfdom, a fact that made Tolstoy uneasy even in his boyhood, and even the "enlightened" aristocrat would have found it difficult to think of the peasant as the same species of animal as himself. Tolstoy himself did not give up beating his servants till he was well on into adult life.

The landowner exercised a sort of *droit de seigneur* over the peasants on his estate. Tolstoy had at least one bastard, and his morganatic half-brother was the family coachman. And yet one

[1] Of *Tribune*.

cannot feel for these simple-minded, prolific Russians the same
contempt as one feels for the sophisticated cosmopolitan scum who
gave Dali his livelihood. Their saving grace is that they are rustics,
they have never heard of benzedrine or gilded toenails, and though
Tolstoy was later to repent of the sins of his youth more vociferously
than most people, he must have known that he drew his strength—
his creative power as well as the strength of his vast muscles—from
that rude, healthy background where one shot woodcocks on the
marshes and girls thought themselves lucky if they went to three
dances in a year.

One of the big gaps in Dickens is that he writes nothing, even in
a burlesque spirit, about country life. Of agriculture he does not
even pretend to know anything. There are some farcical descriptions
of shooting in the *Pickwick Papers*, but Dickens, as a middle-class
radical, would be incapable of describing such amusements sympa-
thetically. He sees field-sports as primarily an exercise in snobbishness, which they already were in the England of that date. The
enclosures, industrialism, the vast differentiation of wealth, and the
cult of the pheasant and the red deer had all combined to drive the
mass of the English people off the land and make the hunting instinct,
which is probably almost universal in human beings, seem merely a
fetish of the aristocracy. Perhaps the best thing in *War and Peace* is
the description of the wolf hunt. In the end it is the peasant's dog
that outstrips those of the nobles and gets the wolf; and afterwards
Natasha finds it quite natural to dance in the peasant's hut.

To see such scenes in England you would have had to go back a
hundred or two hundred years, to a time when difference in status
did not mean any very great difference in habits. Dickens's England
was already dominated by the "Trespassers will be Prosecuted"
board. When one thinks of the accepted left-wing attitude towards
hunting, shooting and the like, it is queer to reflect that Lenin,
Stalin and Trotsky were all of them keen sportsmen in their day.
But then they belonged to a large empty country where there was
no necessary connection between sport and snobbishness, and the
divorce between country and town was never complete. The society
which almost any modern novelist has as his material is very much
meaner, less comely and less carefree than Tolstoy's, and to grasp
this has been one of the signs of talent. Joyce would have been
falsifying the facts if he had made the people in *Dubliners* less disgusting than they are. But the natural advantage lay with Tolstoy:

for, other things being equal, who would not rather write about Pierre and Natasha than about furtive seductions in boarding-houses or drunken Catholic businessmen celebrating a "retreat"?

In his book on Joyce Mr Harry Levin gives a few biographical details, but is unable to tell us much about Joyce's last year of life. All we know is that when the Nazis entered France he escaped over the border into Switzerland, to die about a year later in his old home in Zurich. Even the whereabouts of Joyce's children is not, it seems, known for certain.

The academic critics could not resist the opportunity to kick Joyce's corpse. *The Times* gave him a mean, cagey little obituary, and then—though *The Times* has never lacked space for letters about batting averages or the first cuckoo—refused to print the letter of protest that T. S. Eliot wrote. This was in accordance with the grand old English tradition that the dead must always be flattered unless they happen to be artists. Let a politician die, and his worst enemies will stand up on the floor of the House and utter pious lies in his honour, but a writer or artist must be sniffed at, at least if he is any good. The entire British press united to insult D. H. Lawrence ("pornographer" was the usual description) as soon as he was dead. But the snooty obituaries were merely what Joyce would have expected. The collapse of France, and the need to flee from the Gestapo like a common political suspect, were a different matter, and when the war is over it will be very interesting to find out what Joyce thought about it.

Joyce was a conscious exile from Anglo-Irish philistinism. Ireland would have none of him, England and America barely tolerated him. His books were refused publication, destroyed when in type by timid publishers, banned when they came out, pirated with the tacit connivance of the authorities, and, in any case, largely ignored until the publication of *Ulysses*. He had a genuine grievance, and was extremely conscious of it. But it was also his aim to be a "pure" artist, "above the battle" and indifferent to politics. He had written *Ulysses* in Switzerland, with an Austrian passport and a British pension, during the 1914–18 war, to which he paid as nearly as possible no attention. But the present war, as Joyce found out, is not of a kind to be ignored, and I think it must have left him reflecting that a political choice *is* necessary and that even stupidity is better than totalitarianism.

One thing that Hitler and his friends have demonstrated is what a relatively good time the intellectual has had during the past hundred years. After all, how does the persecution of Joyce, Lawrence, Whitman, Baudelaire, even Oscar Wilde, compare with the kind of thing that has been happening to liberal intellectuals all over Europe since Hitler came to power? Joyce left Ireland in disgust: he did not have to run for his life, as he did when the panzers rolled into Paris. The British Government duly banned *Ulysses* when it appeared, but it took the ban off fifteen years later, and what is probably more important, it helped Joyce to stay alive while the book was written. And thereafter, thanks to the generosity of an anonymous admirer, Joyce was able to live a civilised life in Paris for nearly twenty years, working away at *Finnegans Wake* and surrounded by a circle of disciples, while industrious teams of experts translated *Ulysses* not only into various European languages but even into Japanese. Between 1900 and 1920 he had known hunger and neglect: but take it for all in all, his life would appear a pretty good one if one were viewing it from inside a German concentration camp.

What would the Nazis have done with Joyce if they could have laid hands on him? We don't know. They might even have made efforts to win him over and add him to their bag of "converted" literary men. But he must have seen that they had not only broken up the society that he was used to, but were the deadly enemies of everything that he valued. The battle which he had wanted to be "above" did, after all, concern him fairly directly, and I like to think that before the end he brought himself to utter some non-neutral comment on Hitler—and coming from Joyce it might be quite a stinger—which is lying in Zurich and will be accessible after the war.

Tribune, 10 March 1944

27. As I Please

With no power to put my decrees into operation, but with as much authority as most of the exile "governments" now sheltering in various parts of the world, I pronounce sentence of death on the following words and expressions:

Achilles' heel, jackboot, hydra-headed, ride roughshod over, stab in the back, petty-bourgeois, stinking corpse, liquidate, iron heel, blood-stained oppressor, cynical betrayal, lackey, flunkey, mad dog, jackal, hyena, blood-bath.

No doubt this list will have to be added to from time to time, but it will do to go on with. It contains a fair selection of the dead metaphors and ill-translated foreign phrases which have been current in Marxist literature for years past.

There are, of course, many other perversions of the English language besides this one. There is official English, or Stripetrouser, the language of White Papers, Parliamentary debates (in their more decorous moments) and BBC news bulletins. There are the scientists and the economists, with their instinctive preference for words like "contraindicate" and "deregionalisation". There is American slang, which for all its attractiveness probably tends to impoverish the language in the long run. And there is the general slovenliness of modern English speech with its decadent vowel sounds (throughout the London area you have to use sign language to distinguish between "threepence" and "three-halfpence") and its tendency to make verbs and nouns interchangeable. But here I am concerned only with one kind of bad English, Marxist English, or Pamphletese, which can be studied in the *Daily Worker*, the *Labour Monthly*, *Plebs*, the *New Leader*, and similar papers.

Many of the expressions used in political literature are simply euphemisms or rhetorical tricks. "Liquidate" for instance (or "eliminate") is a polite word for "to kill", while "realism" normally means "dishonesty". But Marxist phraseology is peculiar in that it consists largely of translations. Its characteristic vocabulary comes ultimately from German or Russian phrases which have been adopted in one country after another with no attempt to find suitable equivalents. Here, for instance, is a piece of Marxist writing—it happens to be an address delivered to the Allied armies by the citizens of Pantelleria. The citizens of Pantelleria

pay grateful homage to the Anglo-American forces for the promptness with which they have liberated them from the evil yoke of a megalomaniac and satanic régime which, not content with having sucked like a monstrous octopus the best energies of true Italians for twenty years, is now reducing Italy to a mass of ruins and misery for one motive only—the insane personal profit of its chiefs, who, under an ill-concealed mask of hollow, so-called patriotism, hide the basest passions, and, plotting together with the German pirates, hatch the lowest egoism and blackest treatment while all the time, with revolting cynicism, they tread on the blood of thousands of Italians.

This filthy stew of words is presumably a translation from the Italian, but the point is that one would not recognise it as such. It might be a translation from any other European language, or it might come straight out of the *Daily Worker*; so truly international is this style of writing. Its characteristic is the endless use of ready-made metaphors. In the same spirit, when Italian submarines were sinking the ships that took arms to Republican Spain, the *Daily Worker* urged the British Admiralty to "sweep the mad dogs from the seas". Clearly, people capable of using such phrases have ceased to remember that words have meanings.

A Russian friend tells me that the Russian language is richer than English in terms of abuse, so that Russian invective cannot always be accurately translated. Thus when Molotov referred to the Germans as "cannibals", he was perhaps using some word which sounded natural in Russian, but to which "cannibal" was only a rough approximation. But our local Communists have taken over, from the defunct *Inprecor* and similar sources, a whole series of these crudely translated phrases, and from force of habit have come to think of them as actual English expressions. The Communist vocabulary of abuse (applied to Fascists or Socialists according to the "line" of the moment) includes such terms as hyena, corpse, lackey, pirate, hangman, bloodsucker, mad dog, criminal, assassin. Whether at first, second or third hand, these are all translations, and by no means the kind of word that an English person naturally uses to express disapproval. And language of this kind is used with an astonishing indifference as to its meaning. Ask a journalist what a jackboot is, and you will find that he does not know. Yet he goes on talking about jackboots. Or what is meant by "to ride roughshod"? Very few people know that either. For that matter, in my experience, very few Socialists know the meaning of the word "proletariat".

You can see a good example of Marxist language at its worst in the words "lackey" and "flunkey". Pre-revolutionary Russia was still a feudal country in which hordes of idle men-servants were part of the social set-up; in that context "lackey", as a word of abuse, had a meaning. In England, the social landscape is quite different.

Except at public functions, the last time I saw a footman in livery was in 1921. And, in fact, in ordinary speech, the word "flunkey" has been obsolete since the 'nineties, and the word "lackey" for about a century. Yet they and other equally inappropriate words are dug up for pamphleteering purposes. The result is a style of writing that bears the same relation to writing real English as doing a jigsaw puzzle bears to painting a picture. It is just a question of fitting together a number of ready-made pieces. Just talk about hydra-headed jackboots riding roughshod over blood-stained hyenas, and you are all right. For confirmation of which, see almost any pamphlet issued by the Communist Party—or by any other political party, for that matter.

Tribune, 17 March 1944

28. As I Please

Of all the unanswered questions of our time, perhaps the most important is: "What is Fascism?"

One of the social survey organisations in America recently asked this question of a hundred different people, and got answers ranging from "pure democracy" to "pure diabolism". In this country if you ask the average thinking person to define Fascism, he usually answers by pointing to the German and Italian régimes. But this is very unsatisfactory, because even the major Fascist states differ from one another a good deal in structure and ideology.

It is not easy, for instance, to fit Germany and Japan into the same framework, and it is even harder with some of the small states which are describable as Fascist. It is usually assumed, for instance, that Fascism is inherently warlike, that it thrives in an atmosphere of war hysteria and can only solve its economic problems by means of war preparation or foreign conquests. But clearly this is not true of, say, Portugal or the various South American dictatorships. Or again, antisemitism is supposed to be one of the distinguishing marks of Fascism; but some Fascist movements are not antisemitic. Learned controversies, reverberating for years on end in American magazines, have not even been able to determine whether or not Fascism is a form of capitalism. But still, when we apply the terms "Fascism" to Germany or Japan or Mussolini's Italy, we know broadly what we mean. It is in internal politics that this word has lost the last vestige of meaning. For if you examine the press you will find that there is almost no set of people—certainly no political party or organised body of any kind—which has not been denounced as Fascist during the past ten years.

Here I am not speaking of the verbal use of the term "Fascist". I am speaking of what I have seen in print. I have seen the words "Fascist in sympathy", or "of Fascist tendency", or just plain "Fascist", applied in all seriousness to the following bodies of people:

Conservatives: All Conservatives, appeasers or anti-appeasers, are held to be subjectively pro-Fascist. British rule in India and the Colonies is held to be indistinguishable from Nazism. Organisations of what one might call a patriotic and traditional type are labelled crypto-Fascist or "Fascist-minded". Examples are the Boy Scouts, the Metropolitan Police, MI.5,[1] the British Legion. Key phrase: "The public schools are breeding-grounds of Fascism".

Socialists: Defenders of old-style capitalism (example, Sir Ernest Benn) maintain that Socialism and Fascism are the same thing. Some Catholic journalists maintain that Socialists have been the principal collaborators in the Nazi-occupied countries. The same accusation is made from a different angle by the Communist Party during its ultra-Left phases. In the period 1930-5 the *Daily Worker* habitually referred to the Labour Party as the Labour Fascists. This is echoed by other Left extremists such as Anarchists. Some Indian Nationalists consider the British trade unions to be Fascist organisations.

Communists: A considerable school of thought (examples, Rauschning, Peter Drucker, James Burnham, F. A. Voigt) refuses to recognise a difference between the Nazi and Soviet régimes, and holds that all Fascists and Communists are aiming at approximately the same thing and are even to some extent the same people. Leaders in *The Times* (pre-war) have referred to the USSR as a "Fascist country". Again from a different angle this is echoed by Anarchists and Trotskyists.

Trotskyists: Communists charge the Trotskyists proper, i.e. Trotsky's own organisation, with being a crypto-Fascist organisation in Nazi pay. This was widely believed on the Left during the Popular

[1] Military Intelligence 5: the security service whose task it is to observe and render harmless foreign espionage networks operating on British soil.

Front period. In their ultra-Right phases the Communists tend to apply the same accusation to all fractions to the Left of themselves, e.g. Common Wealth or the ILP.

Catholics: Outside its own ranks, the Catholic Church is almost universally regarded as pro-Fascist, both objectively and subjectively.

War resisters: Pacifists and others who are anti-war are frequently accused not only of making things easier for the Axis, but of becoming tinged with pro-Fascist feeling.

Supporters of the war: War resisters usually base their case on the claim that British imperialism is worse than Nazism, and tend to apply the term "Fascist" to anyone who wishes for a military victory. The supporters of the People's Convention came near to claiming that willingness to resist a Nazi invasion was a sign of Fascist sympathies. The Home Guard was denounced as a Fascist organisation as soon as it appeared. In addition, the whole of the Left tends to equate militarism with Fascism. Politically conscious private soldiers nearly always refer to their officers as "Fascist-minded" or "natural Fascists". Battle-schools, spit and polish, saluting of officers are all considered conducive to Fascism. Before the war, joining the Territorials was regarded as a sign of Fascist tendencies. Conscription and a professional army are both denounced as Fascist phenomena.

Nationalists: Nationalism is universally regarded as inherently Fascist, but this is held only to apply to such national movements as the speaker happens to disapprove of. Arab nationalism, Polish nationalism, Finnish nationalism, the Indian Congress Party, the Muslim League, Zionism, and the IRA[1] are all described as Fascist—but not by the same people.

It will be seen that, as used, the word "Fascism" is almost entirely meaningless. In conversation, of course, it is used even more wildly than in print. I have heard it applied to farmers, shopkeepers, Social Credit, corporal punishment, fox-hunting, bull-fighting, the 1922 Committee, the 1941 Committee, Kipling, Gandhi, Chiang Kai-Shek, homosexuality, Priestley's broadcasts, Youth Hostels, astrology, women, dogs and I do not know what else.

Yet underneath all this mess there does lie a kind of buried meaning. To begin with, it is clear that there are very great differences, some of them easy to point out and not easy to explain away,

[1] Irish Republican Army.

between the régimes called Fascist and those called democratic. Secondly, if "Fascist" means "in sympathy with Hitler", some of the accusations I have listed above are obviously very much more justified than others. Thirdly, even the people who recklessly fling the word "Fascist" in every direction attach at any rate an emotional significance to it. By "Fascism" they mean, roughly speaking, something cruel, unscrupulous, arrogant, obscurantist, anti-liberal and anti-working-class. Except for the relatively small number of Fascist sympathisers, almost any English person would accept "bully" as a synonym for "Fascist". That is about as near to a definition as this much-abused word has come.

But Fascism is also a political and economic system. Why, then, cannot we have a clear and generally accepted definition of it? Alas! we shall not get one—not yet, anyway. To say why would take too long, but basically it is because it is impossible to define Fascism satisfactorily without making admissions which neither the Fascists themselves, nor the Conservatives, nor Socialists of any colour, are willing to make. All one can do for the moment is to use the word with a certain amount of circumspection and not, as is usually done, degrade it to the level of a swearword.

Tribune, 24 March 1944

29. As I Please

The other day I attended a press conference at which a newly arrived Frenchman, who was described as an "eminent jurist"—he could not give his name or other specifications because of his family in France—set forth the French point of view on the recent execution of Pucheu. I was surprised to note that he was distinctly on the defensive, and seemed to think that the shooting of Pucheu was a deed that would want a good deal of justification in British and American eyes. His main point was that Pucheu was not shot for political reasons, but for the ordinary crime of "collaborating with the enemy", which has always been punishable by death under French law.

An American correspondent asked the question: "Would collaborating with the enemy be equally a crime in the case of some petty official—an inspector of police, for example?" "Absolutely the same," answered the Frenchman. As he had just come from France he was presumably voicing French opinion, but one can assume that in practice only the most active collaborators will be put to death. Any really big-scale massacre, if it really happened, would be quite largely the punishment of the guilty by the guilty. For there is much evidence that large sections of the French population were more or less pro-German in 1940 and only changed their minds when they found out what the Germans were like.

I do not want people like Pucheu to escape, but a few very obscure quislings, including one or two Arabs, have been shot as well, and this whole business of taking vengeance on traitors and captured enemies raises questions which are strategic as well as moral. The point is that if we shoot too many of the small rats now we may have no stomach for dealing with the big ones when the time comes. It is difficult to believe that the Fascist régimes can be throughly crushed without the killing of the responsible individuals, to the number of some hundreds or even thousands in each country. But it could well happen that all the truly guilty people will escape in the end, simply because public opinion has been sickened beforehand by hypocritical trials and cold-blooded executions.

In effect this was what happened in the last war. Who that was alive in those years does not remember the maniacal hatred of the Kaiser that was fostered in this country? Like Hitler in this war, he was supposed to be the cause of all our ills. No one doubted that he would be executed as soon as caught, and the only question was what method would be adopted. Magazine articles were written in which the rival merits of boiling in oil, drawing and quartering and breaking on the wheel were carefully examined. The Royal Academy exhibitions were full of allegorical pictures of incredible vulgarity, showing the Kaiser being thrown into Hell. And what came of it in the end? The Kaiser retired to Holland and (though he had been "dying of cancer" in 1915) lived another twenty-two years, one of the richest men in Europe.

So also with all the other "war criminals". After all the threats and promises that had been made, no war criminals were tried: to be exact, a dozen people or so were put on trial, given sentences of imprisonment and soon released. And though, of course, the failure to crush the German military caste was due to the conscious policy of the Allied leaders, who were terrified of revolution in Germany, the revulsion of feeling in ordinary people helped to make it possible. They did not want revenge when it was in their power. The Belgian atrocities, Miss Cavell, the U-boat captains who had sunk passenger ships without warning and machine-gunned the survivors—somehow it was all forgotten. Ten million innocent men had been killed, and no one wanted to follow it up by killing a few thousand guilty ones.

Whether we do or don't shoot the Fascists and quislings who happen to fall into our hands is probably not very important in itself. What is important is that revenge and "punishment" should have no part in our policy or even in our day-dreams. Up to date, one of the mitigating features of this war is that in this country there has been very little hatred. There has been none of the nonsensical racialism that there was last time—no pretence that all Germans have faces like pigs, for instance. Even the word "Hun" has not really popularised itself. The Germans in this country, mostly refugees, have not been well treated, but they have not been meanly persecuted as they were last time. In the last war it would have been very unsafe, for instance, to speak German in a London street. Wretched little German bakers and hairdressers had their shops sacked by the mob, German music fell out of favour, even the breed of dachshunds almost disappeared because no one wanted to have a "German dog". And the weak British attitude in the early period of German rearmament had a direct connection with those follies of the war years.

Hatred is an impossible basis for policy, and curiously enough it can lead to over-softness as well as to over-toughness. In the war of 1914-18 the British people were whipped up into a hideous frenzy of hatred, they were fed on preposterous lies about crucified Belgian babies and German factories where corpses were made into margarine: and then as soon as the war stopped they suffered the natural revulsion, which was all the stronger because the troops came home, as British troops usually do, with a warm admiration for the enemy. The result was an exaggerated pro-German reaction which set in about 1920 and lasted till Hitler was well in the saddle. Throughout those years all "enlightened" opinion (see any number of the *Daily Herald* before 1929, for instance) held it as an article of faith that Germany bore no responsibility for the war. Treitschke, Bernhardi, the Pan-Germans, the "nordic" myth, the open boasts about "Der Tag" which the Germans had been making from 1900 onwards—all this went for nothing. The Versailles Treaty was the greatest infamy the world had ever seen: few people had even heard of Brest-Litovsk. All this was the price of that four years' orgy of lying and hatred.

Anyone who tried to awaken public opinion during the years of Fascist aggression from 1933 onwards knows what the after-effects of that hate propaganda were like. "Atrocities" had come to be looked on as synonymous with "lies". But the stories about the German concentration camps were atrocity stories: therefore they were lies—so reasoned the average man. The left-wingers who tried to make the public see that Fascism was an unspeakable horror were fighting against their own propaganda of the past fifteen years.

That is why—though I would not save creatures like Pucheu even if I could—I am not happy when I see trials of "war criminals", especially when they are very petty criminals and when witnesses are allowed to make inflammatory political speeches. Still less am I happy to see the Left associating itself with schemes to partition Germany, enrol millions of Germans in forced-labour gangs and impose reparations which will make the Versailles reparations look like a bus fare. All these vindictive day-dreams, like those of 1914–18, will simply make it harder to have a realistic post-war policy. If you think *now* in terms of "making Germany pay", you will quite likely find yourself praising Hitler in 1950. Results are what matter, and one of the results we want from this war is to be quite sure that Germany will not make war again. Whether this is best achieved by ruthlessness or generosity I am not certain: but I am quite certain that either of these will be more difficult if we allow ourselves to be influenced by hatred.

Tribune, 31 March 1944

30. Review

The Road to Serfdom by F. A. Hayek, *The Mirror of the Past* by K. Zilliacus

Taken together, these two books give grounds for dismay. The first of them is an eloquent defence of *laissez-faire* capitalism, the other is an even more vehement denunciation of it. They cover to some extent the same ground, they frequently quote the same authorities, and they even start out with the same premise, since each of them assumes that western civilisation depends on the sanctity of the individual. Yet each writer is convinced that the other's policy leads directly to slavery, and the alarming thing is that they may both be right.

Of the two, Professor Hayek's book is perhaps the more valuable, because the views it puts forward are less fashionable at the moment than those of Mr Zilliacus. Shortly, Professor Hayek's thesis is that Socialism inevitably leads to despotism, and that in Germany the Nazis were able to succeed because the Socialists had already done most of their work for them, especially the intellectual work of weakening the desire for liberty. By bringing the whole of life under the control of the State, Socialism necessarily gives power to an inner ring of bureaucrats, who in almost every case will be men who want power for its own sake and will stick at nothing in order to retain it. Britain, he says, is now going the same road as Germany, with the left-wing intelligentsia in the van and the Tory Party a good second. The only salvation lies in returning to an unplanned economy, free competition, and emphasis on liberty rather than on security.

In the negative part of Professor Hayek's thesis there is a great deal of truth. It cannot be said too often—at any rate, it is not being said nearly often enough—that collectivism is not inherently democratic, but, on the contrary, gives to a tyrannical minority such powers as the Spanish Inquisitors never dreamed of.

Professor Hayek is also probably right in saying that in this country the intellectuals are more totalitarian-minded than the common people. But he does not see, or will not admit, that a return to "free" competition means for the great mass of people a tyranny probably worse, because more irresponsible, than that of the State. The trouble with competitions is that somebody wins them. Professor Hayek denies that free capitalism necessarily leads to monopoly, but in practice that is where it has led, and since the vast majority of people would far rather have State regimentation than slumps and unemployment, the drift towards collectivism is bound to continue if popular opinion has any say in the matter.

Mr Zilliacus's able and well-documented attack on imperialism and power politics consists largely of an exposure of the events leading up to the two world wars. Unfortunately the enthusiasm with which he debunks the war of 1914 makes one wonder on what grounds he is supporting this one. After retelling the sordid story of the secret treaties and commercial rivalries which led up to 1914, he concludes that our declared war aims were lies and that "we declared war on Germany because if she won her war against France and Russia she would become master of all Europe, and strong enough to help herself to British colonies". Why else did we go to war this time? It seems that it was equally wicked to oppose Germany in the decade before 1914 and to appease her in the nineteen-thirties, and that we ought to have made a compromise peace in 1917, whereas it would be treachery to make one now. It was even wicked, in 1915, to agree to Germany being partitioned and Poland being regarded as "an internal affair of Russia": so do the same actions change their moral colour with the passage of time.

The thing Mr Zilliacus leaves out of account is that wars have results, irrespective of the motives of those who precipitate them. No one can question the dirtiness of international politics from 1870 onwards: it does not follow that it would have been a good thing to allow the German army to rule Europe. It is just possible that some rather sordid transactions are going on behind the scenes now, and that current propaganda "against Nazism" (cf "against Prussian militarism") will look pretty thin in 1970, but Europe will certainly be a better place if Hitler and his followers are removed from it.

Between them these two books sum up our present predicament. Capitalism leads to dole queues, the scramble for markets, and war. Collectivism leads to concentration camps, leader worship, and war. There is no way out of this unless a planned economy can be somehow combined with the freedom of the intellect, which can only happen if the concept of right and wrong is restored to politics.

Both of these writers are aware of this, more or less: but since they can show no practicable way of bringing it about the combined effect of their books is a depressing one.

Observer, 9 April 1944

31. As I Please

The April issue of *Common Wealth* devotes several paragraphs to the problem of the falling British birthrate. A good deal of what it says is true, but it also lets drop the following remarks:

> The know-alls are quick to point to contraceptives, nutritional errors, infertility, selfishness, economic insecurity, etc as basic causes of decline. But facts do not support them. In Nazi

Germany, where contraceptives are illegal, the birthrate has reached a record low ebb, whereas in the Soviet Union, where there are no such restrictions, population is healthily on the up and up. . . . Reproduction, as the Peckham experiment has helped to prove, is stimulated in an environment marked by fellowship and co-operation. . . . Once meaning and purpose are restored to life, the wheels of production are kept humming, and life is again an adventure instead of just an endurance, we shall hear no more of the baby shortage.

It is not fair to the public to treat all-important subjects in this slapdash way. To begin with, you would gather from the passage quoted above that Hitler lowered the German birthrate. On the contrary, he raised it to levels unheard-of during the Weimar Republic. Before the war it was above replacement level, for the first time in many years. The catastrophic drop in the German birthrate began in 1942, and must have been partly caused by so many German males being away from home. Figures cannot be available yet, but the Russian birthrate must almost certainly have dropped over the same period.

You would also gather that the high Russian birthrate dates from the Revolution. But it was also high in Czarist times. Nor is there any mention of the countries where the birthrate is highest of all, that is, India, China, and (only a little way behind) Japan. Would it be accurate to say, for instance, that a South Indian peasant's life is "an adventure instead of just an endurance"?

The one thing that can be said with almost complete certainty on this subject is that a high birthrate goes with a low standard of living, and vice versa. There are few if any real exceptions to this. Otherwise the question is exceedingly complex. It is, all the same, vitally important to learn as much about it as we can, because there will be a calamitous drop in our own population unless the present trend is reversed within ten or, at most, twenty years. One ought not to assume, as some people do, that this is impossible, for such changes of trend have often happened before. The experts are proving now that our population will be only a few millions by the end of this century, but they were also proving in 1870 that by 1940 it would be 100 millions. To reach replacement level again, our birthrate would not have to take such a sensational upward turn as, for instance, the Turkish birthrate did after Mustapha Kemal took over.

But the first necessity is to find out *why* populations rise and fall, and it is just as unscientific to assume that a high birthrate is a by-product of Socialism as to swallow everything that is said on the subject by childless Roman Catholic priests.

When I read of the goings-on in the House of Commons the week before last, I could not help being reminded of a little incident that I witnessed twenty years ago and more.

It was at a village cricket match. The captain of one side was the local squire, who, besides being exceedingly rich, was a vain, childish man to whom the winning of this match seemed extremely important. Those playing on his side were all or nearly all his own tenants.

The squire's side were batting, and he himself was out and was sitting in the pavilion. One of the batsmen accidentally hit his own wicket at about the same moment as the ball entered the wicket-keeper's hands. "That's not out," said the squire promptly, and went on talking to the person beside him. The umpire, however, gave a verdict of "out", and the batsman was half-way back to the pavilion before the squire realised what was happening. Suddenly he caught sight of the returning batsman, and his face turned several shades redder.

"What!" he cried, "he's given him out? Nonsense! Of course he's not out!" And then, standing up, he cupped his hands and shouted to the umpire: "Hi, what did you give that man out for? He wasn't out at all!"

The batsman had halted. The umpire hesitated, then recalled the batsman to the wicket and the game went on.

I was only a boy at the time, and this incident seemed to me about the most shocking thing I had ever seen. Now, so much do we coarsen with the passage of time, my reaction would merely be to inquire whether the umpire was the squire's tenant as well.

Attacking Mr C. A. Smith and myself in the *Malvern Torch* for various remarks about the Christian religion, Mr Sidney Dark grows very angry because I have suggested that the belief in personal immortality is decaying. "I would wager," he says, "that if a Gallup poll were taken seventy-five per cent (of the British population) would confess to a vague belief in survival." Writing elsewhere during the same week, Mr Dark puts it at eighty-five per cent.

Now, I find it very rare to meet anyone, of whatever background, who admits to believing in personal immortality. Still, I think it quite likely that if you asked everyone the question and put pencil and paper in his hands, a fairly large number (I am not so free with my percentages as Mr Dark) would admit the possibility that after death there might be "something". The point Mr Dark has missed is that the belief, such as it is, hasn't the actuality it had for our forefathers. Never, literally never in recent years, have I met anyone who gave me the impression of believing in the next world as firmly as he believed in the existence of, for instance, Australia. Belief in the next world does not influence conduct as it would if it were genuine. With that endless existence beyond death to look forward to, how trivial our lives here would seem! Most Christians profess to believe in Hell. Yet have you ever met a Christian who seemed as afraid of Hell as he was of cancer? Even very devout Christians will make jokes about Hell. They wouldn't make jokes about leprosy, or RAF pilots with their faces burnt away: the subject is too painful. Here there springs into my mind a little triolet by the late G. K. Chesterton:[1]

> It's a pity that Poppa has sold his soul,
> It makes him sizzle at breakfast so.
> The money was useful, but still on the whole
> It's a pity that Poppa has sold his soul
> When he might have held on like the Baron de Coal,
> And not cleared out when the price was low.
> It's a pity that Poppa has sold his soul,
> It makes him sizzle at breakfast so.

Chesterton, a Catholic, would presumably have said that he believed in Hell. If his next-door neighbour had been burnt to death he would not have written a comic poem about it, yet he can make jokes about somebody being fried for millions of years. I say that such belief has no reality. It is a sham currency, like the money in Samuel Butler's Musical Banks.

Tribune, 14 April 1944

[1] Orwell acknowledged later that he was mistaken in attributing these verses to G. K. Chesterton and that they were by A. M. Currie and had appeared in G. K. Chesterton's paper, *G.K.'s Weekly*.

32. London Letter to *Partisan Review*

[17 April 1944]

Dear Editors,

Spring is here, a late spring after a mild winter, and there is universal expectation that "It" (I don't have to tell you what "It" is) will begin some time next month. The streets swarm with American troops. In the expensive quarters of the town British soldiers, who are not allowed to spend their leave in London unless they have their homes there, are hardly to be seen. The air raids began to hot up about the beginning of February and there have been one or two biggish ones—nothing like 1940 but still very trying because of the deafening noise of the ack-ack. On the other hand, the scenic effects are terrific. The orange-coloured flares dropped by the German planes drift slowly down, making everything almost as light as day, and carmine-coloured tracer shells sail up to meet them: and as the flares get lower the shadows on the window pane move slowly upwards. The food situation is as always. I am ashamed to say that only very recently I had my first meal in a British Restaurant and was amazed to find that the food was quite good and very cheap. (These places are run by the public authorities on a non-profit basis.) Various kinds of manufactured goods are now almost unprocurable. It is almost impossible to buy a watch or clock, new or second-hand. A typewriter which before the war would have cost twelve pounds now costs at least thirty pounds second-hand, supposing that you can get hold of one at all. Cars are scarcer than ever on the roads. On the other hand the bourgeoisie are coming more and more out of their holes, as one can see by the advertisements for servants quite in the old style, e.g. this one from *The Times*: "Countess of Shrewsbury requires experienced Head Housemaid of three". There were several years during which one did not see advertisements of that kind. Evening dress (for men) is said to be reappearing though I haven't seen anyone wearing it yet.

There isn't a great deal of political news. Churchill, if one can judge by his voice, is ageing a good deal but grows more and more intolerant of opposition. It is assumed on all sides that if anything should happen to Churchill, Eden will automatically become PM. Those who know Eden say he is such a weakling that the right-wing Tories would find it more convenient to keep him in office as a figurehead than to put in a strong man after their own hearts. The Labour Party has sunk a few feet deeper in everyone's estimation after the vote of confidence business—the Government were outvoted on a minor issue, Churchill told the Members to take their votes back, and nearly everyone did so. Common Wealth is still making some headway but constantly rumbles with internal dissensions which I can't get the hang of. It came out recently that, up to date, three-fifths of its expenses have been paid by Acland (who has now come to the end of his money) and a rather doubtful person named Alan Good, a wealthy businessman (light industries) who has been in the Party since almost the beginning. The Communists have been taking a slightly more anti-Government line and on one occasion have supported an opposition candidate at a by-election.

The big event of the last few months has been the large-scale coal strikes, which are the culmination of a long period during which coal production has been behind schedule and—coming on the eve of the Second Front—obviously indicate very serious grievances. The immediate trouble is over money, but the root cause is the unbearable conditions in the British mines, which naturally seem worse in war-time when unemployment hardly enters into the picture. I don't know a great deal about the technical side of mining, but I have been down a number of mines and I know that the conditions are such that human beings simply will not stand them except under some kind of compulsion. (I described all this years ago in a book called *The Road to Wigan Pier*.) Most of the British mines are very old, and they belong to a multitude of comparatively small owners who often haven't the capital to modernise them even if they wanted to. This means not only that they often lack up-to-date machinery, but that the "travelling" may be almost more exhausting than the work itself. In the older mines it may be more than three miles from the shaft to the coal face (a mile would be a normal distance) and most of the way the galleries will be only four feet high or less. This means that the miner has to do the whole journey bent double, sometimes crawling on all fours for a hundred yards or so, and then on top of this do his day's work, which may have to be done kneeling down if it is a shallow seam. The exertion is so great that men who come back to work after a long go of unemployment sometimes fall by the wayside, unable even to get as far as the coal face. Added to this there are the ghastly hovels that most of the miners have to live in, built in the worst period of the Industrial Revolution, the general lack of pit-head baths, the dullness of the mining towns compared with the newer towns that have sprung up round the light industries, and, of course, very poor wages. In peace time, when the dole is the alternative, people will just put up with this, but now every miner is aware that if he could only get out of the mines (which he isn't allowed to, of course) he could be earning twice the money for easy work in some hygienic factory. It has been found impossible to recruit enough miners and for some time past they have had to be conscripted. This is done by ballot, and it is an index of how mining is regarded that to be drawn as a miner (instead of, say, being put in a submarine) is looked on as a disaster. The conscripted youths, who include public-school boys, have been to the fore in the strikes. On top of all the other causes for discontent, it is said that the coal owners, while reading the miners sermons on patriotism, are doing jiggery-pokery by working uneconomic seams, saving up the good seams for after the war when the demand for coal will have dropped again.

Everyone except the interested minority is aware that these conditions can't be cured without nationalisation of the mines, and public opinion is entirely ready for this step. Even the left-wing Tories, though not facing up to nationalisation, talk of compelling the coal owners to amalgamate into larger units. It is, in fact, obvious that without centralising the industry it would be impossible to raise the enormous sums needed to bring the mines up to date. But nationalisation would solve the short-term problem as well, for it would give the miners something to look forward to, and in return they would certainly undertake to refrain from striking for the duration of the war. Needless to say there is no sign of any such thing happening. Instead there has been a hue and cry after the Trotskyists, who are alleged to be responsible for the strikes. Trotskyism, which not one English person in a hundred had heard of before the war, actually got the big headlines for several days. In reality the English Trotskyists only number, I believe, about five hundred, and it is unlikely they have a footing among the full-time miners, who are very suspicious of anyone outside their own community.

As this end of the war approaches its climax, the extraordinary contradictions in the attitude of the intelligentsia become more apparent. Even now large numbers of pinks claim to believe that no Second Front is intended, in spite of the vast American armies that have been brought here. But at the same time as they cry out for the Second Front to be opened immediately they protest against the bombing of Germany and Italy, not merely because of the loss of life but because of the material destruction. I have also heard people say almost in the same breath (a) that we must open a Second Front at once, (b) that it is no longer necessary because the Russians can defeat the Germans singlehanded, and (c) that it is bound to be a failure. Simultaneously with the desire to finish this war quickly there is quite frank rejoicing when something goes wrong, e.g. the stalemate in Italy, and a readiness to believe any rumour without examination so long as it is a rumour of disaster. Almost simultaneously, again, people approve the Russian proposals to partition Germany and exact enormous reparations, and tell you what a lot Hitler has done for Europe and how much preferable he is to the British Tories. Again—I notice this every day in the short stories and poems sent in to the *Tribune*—numbers of left-wingers have a definitely schizophrenic attitude towards war and militarism. What one might call the official left-wing view is that war is a meaningless massacre brought about by capitalists, no war can ever lead to any good result, in battle no one has any thought except to run away, and the soldier is a downtrodden slave who hates his officer like poison and looks on the enemy as a comrade. But as soon as the Red army is involved the whole of this conception is turned upside down. Not only does war become glorious and purposeful, but the soldier becomes a happy warrior who positively enjoys military discipline, loves his officer like a dog, hates the enemy like the Devil (a phrase that occurs frequently in these stories that are sent in to me is "his heart was fired with passionate hatred") and utters edifying slogans while in the act of slinging a hand-grenade. There is further schizophrenia on the subject of atrocities: any atrocity story reported by the Russians is true, anything reported by the British or Americans untrue. Ditto with the Asiatic quislings. Wang Ching-Wei is a contemptible traitor, Subhas Chandra Bose a heroic liberator. Emotionally, what the Left intelligentsia wish for is that Germany and Japan should be defeated but that Britain and America should not be victorious. Once the Second Front has started it would not surprise me to see them change their attitude, become defeatist about the whole business and disclaim the demands for a Second Front which they have been making for more than two years.

Russophile feeling is on the surface stronger than ever. It is now next door to impossible to get anything overtly anti-Russian printed. Anti-Russian books do appear, but mostly from Catholic publishing firms and always from a religious or frankly reactionary angle. "Trotskyism", using the word in a wide sense, is even more effectively silenced than in the 1935–9 period. The Stalinists themselves don't seem to have regained their influence in the press, but apart from the general russophile feeling of the intelligentsia, all the appeasers, e.g. Professor E. H. Carr, have switched their allegiance from Hitler to Stalin. The servility of the so-called intellectuals is astonishing. The *Mission to Moscow* film, which I gather raised something of a storm in the USA, was accepted here with hardly a murmur. It is interesting too that pacifists almost never say anything anti-Russian, though temperamentally they are not always russophile. Their implied line is that it is wrong for us to defend ourselves by violence, but is all right for the Russians. This is sheer cowardice: they dare not flout prevailing left-wing opinion, which, of course, they are more afraid of than public opinion in the wider sense.

I suspect, however, that Russian and pro-Russian propaganda will in the long run defeat itself simply by being overdone. Lately I have several times been surprised to hear ordinary working-class or middle-class people say, "Oh, I'm fed up with the Russians! They're too good to live", or words to that effect. One must remember that the USSR means different things to the working class and the Left intelligentsia. The former are russophile because they feel Russia to be the working-class country where the common man is in control, whereas the intellectuals are influenced at least partly by power worship. The affection they feel for the USSR is still vaguely bound up with the idea of the meek inheriting the earth, and the tone of latter-day Soviet propaganda obviously contradicts this. In any case, English people usually react in the end against too-blatant propaganda. A good illustration of this is General Montgomery, idolised a year or two ago and now thoroughly unpopular because over-publicised.[1]

---

[1] Here is a sample of the kind of story now told about Montgomery. General Eisenhower is having lunch with the King. "How do you get on with Montgomery?" asks the King. "Very well," replies Eisenhower, "except that I have a kind of feeling that he's after my job." "Oh," says the King, "I was afraid he was after mine."

Other similar stories are told of Eisenhower or Montgomery interchangeably. For example:

Three doctors who had just died arrived at the gates of Heaven. The first two, a physician and a surgeon, were refused admittance. The third described himself as a psychiatrist. "Come in!" said St Peter immediately. "We should like your professional advice. God has been behaving in a very peculiar way lately. He thinks He's General Eisenhower (or Montgomery)." [Author's footnote.]

I don't think I have any more news. You will be interested to hear that several American soldiers have rung me up, introducing themselves as readers of *PR*. These are still the only contacts I have made with American soldiers. The troops and the public, other than girls, are still very stand-offish. I notice that Negroes do not seem to pick up girls so easily as the whites, though everyone says they like the Negroes better. A little while back a young American soldier had rung up and I asked him to stay the night at our flat. He was quite interested and said it was the first time he had been inside an English home. I said, "How long have you been in this country?" and he said, "two months." He went on to tell me that the previous day a girl had come up to him on the pavement and seized hold of his penis with the words, "Hullo, Yank!" Yet he had not seen the interior of an ordinary English home. This makes me sad. Even at their best English people are not very hospitable to strangers, but I would like the Americans to know that the cold welcome they have had in this country is partly due to the fact that the rations are not easy to stretch and that after years of war people are ashamed of the shabby interiors of their houses, while the films have taught them to believe or half-believe that every American lives in a palace with a chromium-plated cocktail bar.

I am going to send two copies of this, one air mail and one sea mail, hoping that the latter may get there a bit sooner. The time that letters take to cross the Atlantic nowadays has made some people wonder whether the air mail travels in balloons.

George Orwell

Partisan Review, Summer 1944

33. As I Please

In a letter published in this week's *Tribune*, someone attacks me rather violently for saying that the BBC is a better source of news than the daily papers, and is so regarded by the public. I have never, he suggests, heard ordinary working men shouting "Turn that dope off!" when the news bulletin comes on.

On the contrary, I have heard this frequently. Still more frequently I have seen the customers in a pub go straight on with their darts, music and so forth without the slightest slackening of noise when the news bulletin began. But it was not my claim that anyone likes the BBC, or thinks it interesting, or grown-up, or democratic, or progressive. I said only that people regard it as a relatively sound source of news. Again and again I have known people, when they see some doubtful item of news, wait to have it confirmed by the radio before they believe it. Social surveys show the same thing— i.e. that as against the radio the prestige of newspapers has declined.

And I repeat what I said before—that in my experience the BBC *is* relatively truthful and, above all, has a responsible attitude towards news and does not disseminate lies simply because they are "newsy". Of course, untrue statements are constantly being broadcast and anyone can tell you of instances. But in most cases this is due to genuine error, and the BBC sins much more by simply avoiding anything controversial than by direct propaganda. And after all—a point not met by our correspondent—its reputation abroad is comparatively high. Ask any refugee from Europe which of the belligerent radios is considered to be the most truthful. So also in Asia. Even in India, where the population are so hostile that they will not listen to British propaganda and will hardly listen to a British entertainment programme, they listen to BBC news because they believe that it approximates to the truth.

Even if the BBC passes on the British official lies, it does make some effort to sift the others. Most of the newspapers, for instance, have continued to publish without any query as to their truthfulness the American claims to have sunk the entire Japanese fleet several times over. The BBC, to my knowledge, developed quite early on an attitude of suspicion towards this and certain other unreliable sources. On more than one occasion I have known a newspaper to print a piece of news—and news unfavourable to Britain—on no other authority than the German radio, because it was "newsy" and made a good "para".

If you see something obviously untruthful in a newspaper and ring up to ask "Where did you get that from?" you are usually put off with the formula: "I'm afraid Mr So-and-So is not in the office." If you persist, you generally find that the story has no basis whatever but that it looked like a good bit of news, so in it went. Except where libel is involved, the average journalist is astonished and even contemptuous if anyone bothers about accuracy with regard to names, dates, figures and other details. And any daily journalist will tell you that one of the most important secrets of his trade is the trick of making it appear that there is news when there is no news.

Towards the end of May 1940, newspaper posters were prohibited in order to save paper. Several newspapers, however, continued to display posters for some time afterwards. On inquiry it was found that they were using old ones. Such headlines as "Panzer Divisions Hurled Back" or "French Army Standing Firm" could be used over and over again. Then came the period when the paper-sellers supplied their own posters with a slate and a bit of chalk, and in their hands the poster became a comparatively sober and truthful thing. It referred to something that was actually in the paper you were going to buy, and it usually picked out the real news and not some piece of sensational nonsense. The paper-sellers, who frequently did not know which way round a capital S goes, had a better idea of what is news, and more sense of responsibility towards the public, than their millionaire employers.

Our correspondent considers that the public and the journalists rather than the proprietors are to blame for the silliness of English newspapers. You could not, he implies, make an intelligent newspaper pay because the public wants tripe. I am not certain whether this is so. For the time being most of the tripe has vanished and newspaper circulations have not declined. But I do agree—and I said so—that the journalists share the blame. In allowing their profession to be degraded they have largely acted with their eyes open, whereas, I suppose, to blame somebody like Northcliffe for making money in the quickest way is like blaming a skunk for stinking.

One mystery about the English language is why, with the biggest vocabulary in existence, it has to be constantly borrowing foreign words and phrases. Where is the sense, for instance, of saying *cul de sac* when you mean blind alley? Other totally unnecessary French phrases are *joie de vivre, amour propre, reculer pour mieux sauter, raison d'être, vis-à-vis, tête-à-tête, au pied de la lettre, esprit de corps.* There are dozens more of them. Other needless borrowings come from Latin (though there is a case for "i.e." and "e.g.", which are useful abbreviations), and since the war we have been much infested by German words, *Gleichschaltung, Lebensraum, Weltanschauung, Wehrmacht, Panzerdivisionen* and others being flung about with great freedom. In nearly every case an English equivalent already exists or could easily be improvised. There is also a tendency to take over American slang phrases without understanding their meaning. For example, the expression "barking up the wrong tree" is fairly widely used, but enquiry shows that most people don't know its origin nor exactly what it means.

Sometimes it is necessary to take over a foreign word, but in that case we should anglicise its pronunciation, as our ancestors used to do. If we really need the word "café" (we got on well enough with "coffee house" for two hundred years), it should either be spelled "caffay" or pronounced "cayfe". "Garage" should be pronounced "garridge". For what point is there in littering our speech with fragments of foreign pronunciation, very tiresome to anyone who does not happen to have learned that particular language?

And why is it that most of us never use a word of English origin if we can find a manufactured Greek one? One sees a good example of this in the rapid disappearance of English flower names. What until twenty years ago was universally called a snapdragon is now called an antirrhinum, a word no one can spell without consulting a dictionary. Forget-me-nots are coming more and more to be called myosotis. Many other names, Red Hot Poker, Mind Your Own Business, Love Lies Bleeding, London Pride, are disappearing in favour of colourless Greek names out of botany textbooks. I had better not continue too long on this subject, because last time I mentioned flowers in this column an indignant lady wrote in to say that flowers are bourgeois. But I don't think it a good augury for the future of the English language that "marigold" should be dropped in favour of "calendula", while the pleasant little Cheddar Pink loses its name and becomes merely Dianthus Caesius.

Tribune, 21 April 1944

34. As I Please

On the night in 1940 when the big ack-ack barrage was fired over London for the first time, I was in Piccadilly Circus when the guns opened up, and I fled into the Café Royal to take cover. Among the crowd inside a good-looking, well-made youth of about twenty-five was making somewhat of a nuisance of himself with a copy of *Peace News*, which he was forcing upon the attention of everyone at the neighbouring tables. I got into conversation with him, and the conversation went something like this:

The youth: "I tell you, it'll all be over by Christmas. There's obviously going to be a compromise peace. I'm pinning my faith to Sir Samuel Hoare. It's degrading company to be in, I admit, but still Hoare is on our side. So long as Hoare's in Madrid, there's always hope of a sell-out."

Orwell: "What about all these preparations that they're making against invasion—the pill-boxes that they're building everywhere, the LDVs,[1] and so forth?"

The youth: "Oh, that merely means that they're getting ready to crush the working class when the Germans get here. I suppose some of them might be fools enough to try to resist, but Churchill and the Germans between them won't take long to settle them. Don't worry, it'll soon be over."

Orwell: "Do you really want to see your children grow up Nazis?"

The youth: "Nonsense! You don't suppose the Germans are going to encourage Fascism in this country, do you? They don't want to breed up a race of warriors to fight against them. Their object will be to turn us into slaves. They'll encourage every pacifist movement they can lay hands on. That's why I'm a pacifist. They'll encourage people like me."

Orwell: "And shoot people like me?"

The youth: "That would be just too bad."

Orwell: "But why are you so anxious to remain alive?"

The youth: "So that I can get on with my work, of course."

It had come out in the conversation that the youth was a painter —whether good or bad I do not know; but, at any rate, sincerely interested in painting and quite ready to face poverty in pursuit of it. As a painter, he would probably have been somewhat better off under a German occupation than a writer or journalist would be. But still, what he said contained a very dangerous fallacy, now very widespread in the countries where totalitarianism has not actually established itself.

The fallacy is to believe that under a dictatorial government you can be free *inside*. Quite a number of people console themselves with this thought, now that totalitarianism in one form or another is visibly on the up-grade in every part of the world. Out in the street

[1] The Local Defence Volunteers, which later became the Home Guard, consisting of civilians armed and organised to resist invasion.

the loudspeakers bellow, the flags flutter from the rooftops, the police with their tommy-guns prowl to and fro, the face of the Leader, four feet wide, glares from every hoarding; but up in the attics the secret enemies of the régime can record their thoughts in perfect freedom—that is the idea, more or less. And many people are under the impression that this is going on now in Germany and other dictatorial countries.

Why is this idea false? I pass over the fact that modern dictatorships don't, in fact, leave the loopholes that the old-fashioned despotisms did; and also the probable weakening of the *desire* for intellectual liberty owing to totalitarian methods of education. The greatest mistake is to imagine that the human being is an autonomous individual. The secret freedom which you can supposedly enjoy under a despotic government is nonsense, because your thoughts are never entirely your own. Philosophers, writers, artists, even scientists, not only need encouragement and an audience, they need constant stimulation from other people. It is almost impossible to think without talking. If Defoe had really lived on a desert island he could not have written *Robinson Crusoe*, nor would he have wanted to. Take away freedom of speech, and the creative faculties dry up. Had the Germans really got to England my acquaintance of the Café Royal would soon have found his painting deteriorating, even if the Gestapo had let him alone. And when the lid is taken off Europe, I believe one of the things that will surprise us will be to find how little worth-while writing of any kind—even such things as diaries, for instance—has been produced in secret under the dictators.

Mr Basil Henriques, chairman of the East London Juvenile Court, has just been letting himself go on the subject of the Modern Girl. English boys, he says, are "just grand", but it is a different story with girls:

> One seldom comes across a really bad boy. The war seems to have affected girls more than boys. . . . Children now went to the pictures several times a week and saw what they imagined was the high life of America, when actually it was a great libel on that country. They also suffer from the effects of listening through the microphone to wild raucous jitterbugging noises called music. . . . Girls of 14 now dress and talk like those of 18 and 19, and put the same filth and muck on their faces.

I wonder whether Mr Henriques knows (a) that well before the other war it was already usual to attribute juvenile crime to the evil example of the cinematograph, and (b) that the Modern Girl has been just the same for quite 2,000 years?

One of the big failures in human history has been the age-long attempt to stop women painting their faces. The philosophers of the Roman Empire denounced the frivolity of the modern woman in almost the same terms as she is denounced today. In the fifteenth century the Church denounced the damnable habit of plucking the eyebrows. The English Puritans, the Bolsheviks and the Nazis all attempted to discourage cosmetics, without success. In Victorian England rouge was considered so disgraceful that it was usually sold under some other name, but it continued to be used.

Many styles of dress, from the Elizabethan ruff to the Edwardian hobble skirt, have been denounced from the pulpit, without effect. In the nineteen-twenties, when skirts were at their shortest, the Pope decreed that women improperly dressed were not to be admitted to Catholic churches; but somehow feminine fashions remained unaffected. Hitler's "ideal woman", an exceedingly plain specimen in a mackintosh, was exhibited all over Germany and much of the rest of the world, but inspired few imitators. I prophesy that English girls will continue to "put filth and muck on their faces" in spite of Mr Henriques. Even in jail, it is said, the female prisoners redden their lips with the dye from the Post Office mail bags.

Just why women use cosmetics is a different question, but it seems doubtful whether sex attraction is the main object. It is very unusual to meet a man who does not think painting your fingernails scarlet is a disgusting habit, but hundreds of thousands of women go on doing it all the same. Meanwhile it might console Mr Henriques to know that though make-up persists, it is far less elaborate than it used to be in the days when Victorian beauties had their faces "enamelled", or when it was usual to alter the contour of your cheeks by means of "plumpers", as described in Swift's poem, "On a Beautiful Young Nymph Going to Bed".

Tribune, 28 April 1944

35. Propaganda and Demotic Speech

... When you examine Government leaflets and White Papers, or leading articles in the newspapers, or the speeches and broadcasts of politicians, or the pamphlets and manifestos of any political party whatever, the thing that nearly always strikes you is their remoteness from the average man. It is not merely that they assume non-existent knowledge: often it is right and necessary to do that. It is also that clear, popular, everyday language seems to be instinctively avoided. The bloodless dialect of government spokesmen (characteristic phrases are: in due course, no stone unturned, take the earliest opportunity, the answer is in the affirmative) is too well known to be worth dwelling on. Newspaper leaders are written either in this same dialect or in an inflated bombastic style with a tendency to fall back on archaic words (peril, valour, might, foe, succour, vengeance, dastardly, rampart, bulwark, bastion) which no normal person would ever think of using. Left-wing political parties specialise in a bastard vocabulary made up of Russian and German phrases translated with the maximum of clumsiness. And even posters, leaflets and broadcasts which are intended to give instructions, to tell people what to do in certain circumstances, often fail in their effect. For example, during the first air raids on London, it was found that innumerable people did not know which siren meant the Alert and which the All Clear. This was after months or years of gazing at ARP posters. These posters had described the Alert as a "warbling note": a phrase which made no impression, since air-raid sirens don't warble, and few people attach any definite meaning to the word.

When Sir Richard Acland, in the early months of the war, was drawing up a manifesto to be presented to the Government, he engaged a squad of Mass Observers to find out what meaning, if any, the ordinary man attaches to the high-sounding abstract words which are flung to and fro in politics. The most fantastic misunderstandings came to light. It was found, for instance, that most people don't know that "immorality" means anything besides sexual immorality.[1] One man thought that "movement" had something to do with constipation. And it is a nightly experience in any pub to see broadcast speeches and news bulletins make no impression on the average listener, because they are uttered in stilted bookish language

[1] In spite of this, Common Wealth has adopted the astonishingly feeble slogan: "What is morally wrong cannot be politically right". [Author's footnote.]

and, incidentally, in an upper-class accent. At the time of Dunkirk I watched a gang of navvies eating their bread and cheese in a pub while the one o'clock news came over. Nothing registered: they just went on stolidly eating. Then, just for an instant, reporting the words of some soldier who had been hauled aboard a boat, the announcer dropped into spoken English, with the phrase, "Well, I've learned to swim this trip, anyway!" Promptly you could see ears being pricked up: it was ordinary language, and so it got across. A few weeks later, the day after Italy entered the war, Duff Cooper announced that Mussolini's rash act would "add to the ruins for which Italy has been famous". It was neat enough, and a true prophecy, but how much impression does that kind of language make on nine people out of ten? The colloquial version of it would have been: "Italy has always been famous for ruins. Well, there are going to be a damn' sight more of them now." But that is not how Cabinet Ministers speak, at any rate in public.

Examples of futile slogans, obviously incapable of stirring strong feelings or being circulated by word of mouth, are: "Deserve Victory", "Freedom is in Peril. Defend it with all your Might", "Socialism the only Solution", "Expropriate the Expropriators", "Austerity", "Evolution not Revolution", "Peace is Indivisible". Examples of slogans phrased in spoken English are: "Hands off Russia", "Make Germany Pay", "Stop Hitler", "No Stomach Taxes", "Buy a Spitfire", "Votes for Women". Examples about mid-way between these two classes are: "Go to it", "Dig for Victory", "It all depends on ME", and some of Churchill's phrases, such as "the end of the beginning", "soft underbelly", "blood, toil, tears and sweat" and "never was so much owed by so many to so few". (Significantly, in so far as this last saying has been repeated by word of mouth, the bookish phrase *in the field of human conflict* has dropped out of it.) One has to take into account the fact that nearly all English people dislike anything that sounds high-flown and boastful. Slogans like "They shall not pass", or "Better to die on your feet than live on your knees", which have thrilled continental nations, seem slightly embarrassing to an Englishman, especially a workingman. But the main weakness of propagandists and popularisers is their failure to notice that spoken and written English are two different things.

When recently I protested in print against the Marxist dialect which makes use of phrases like "objectively counter-revolutionary left-deviationism" or "drastic liquidation of petty-bourgeois elements", I received indignant letters from lifelong Socialists who told me that I was "insulting the language of the proletariat". In rather the same spirit, Professor Harold Laski devotes a long passage in his last book, *Faith, Reason and Civilisation*, to an attack on Mr T. S. Eliot, whom he accuses of "writing only for the few". Now Eliot, as it happens, is one of the few writers of our time who have tried seriously to write English as it is spoken. Lines like:

> And nobody came, and nobody went,
> But he took in the milk and he paid the rent

are about as near to spoken English as print can come. On the other hand, here is an entirely typical sentence from Laski's own writing:

> As a whole, our system was a compromise between democracy in the political realm—itself a very recent development in our history—and an economic power oligarchically organised which was in its turn related to a certain aristocratic vestigia still able to influence profoundly the habits of our society.

This sentence, incidentally, comes from a reprinted lecture; so one must assume that Professor Laski actually stood up on a platform and spouted it forth, parenthesis and all. It is clear that people capable of speaking or writing in such a way have simply forgotten what everyday language is like. But this is nothing to some of the other passages I could dig out of Professor Laski's writings, or better still, from Communist literature, or best of all, from Trotskyist pamphlets. Indeed, from reading the left-wing press you get the impression that the louder people yap about the proletariat, the more they despise its language.

I have said already that spoken English and written English are two different things. This variation exists in all languages, but is probably greater in English than in most. Spoken English is full of slang, it is abbreviated wherever possible, and people of all social classes treat its grammar and syntax in a slovenly way. Extremely few English people ever button up a sentence if they are speaking extempore. Above all, the vast English vocabulary contains thousands of words which everyone uses when writing, but which have no real currency in speech: and it also contains thousands more which are really obsolete but which are dragged forth by anyone who wants to sound clever or uplifting. If one keeps this in mind, one can think of ways of ensuring that propaganda, spoken or written, shall reach the audience it is aimed at.

So far as writing goes, all one can attempt is a process of simplification. The first step—and any social survey organisation could do this for a few hundreds or thousands of pounds—is to find out which of the abstract words habitually used by politicians are really understood by large numbers of people. If phrases like "unprincipled violation of declared pledges" or "insidious threat to the basic principles of democracy" don't mean anything to the average man, then it is stupid to use them. Secondly, in writing one can keep the spoken word constantly in mind. To get genuine spoken English on to paper is a complicated matter, as I shall show in a moment. But if you habitually say to yourself, "Could I simplify this? Could I make it more like speech?" you are not likely to produce sentences like the one quoted from Professor Laski above: nor are you likely to say "eliminate" when you mean kill, or "static water" when you mean fire tank.

Spoken propaganda, however, offers greater possibilities of improvement. It is here that the problem of writing in spoken English really arises.

Speeches, broadcasts, lectures and even sermons are normally written down beforehand. The most effective orators, like Hitler or Lloyd George, usually speak extempore, but they are very great rarities. As a rule—you can test this by listening at Hyde Park Corner—the so-called extempore speaker only keeps going by endlessly tacking one cliché on to another. In any case, he is probably delivering a speech which he has delivered dozens of times before. Only a few exceptionally gifted speakers can achieve the simplicity and intelligibility which even the most tongue-tied person achieves in ordinary conversation. On the air extempore speaking is seldom even attempted. Except for a few programmes, like the Brains Trust, which in any case are carefully rehearsed beforehand, every word that comes from the BBC has been written down, and is delivered exactly as written. This is not only for censorship reasons: it is also because many speakers are liable to dry up at the microphone if they have no script to follow. The result is the heavy, dull, bookish lingo which causes most radio users to switch off as soon as a talk is announced. It might be thought that one could get nearer to colloquial speech by dictating than by writing; but actually, it is the other way about. Dictating, at any rate to a human being, is always slightly embarrassing. One's impulse is to avoid long pauses, and one necessarily does so by clutching at the ready-made phrases and the dead and stinking metaphors (ring the changes on, ride rough-shod over, cross swords with, take up the cudgels for) with which the English language is littered. A dictated script is usually less life-like than a written one. What is wanted, evidently, is some way of getting ordinary, slipshod, colloquial English on to paper.

But is this possible? I think it is, and by a quite simple method which so far as I know has never been tried. It is this: Set a fairly ready speaker down at the microphone and let him just talk, either continuously or intermittently, on any subject he chooses. Do this with a dozen different speakers, recording it every time. Vary it with a few dialogues or conversations between three or four people. Then play your recordings back and let a stenographer reduce them to writing: not in the shortened, rationalised version that stenographers usually produce, but word for word, with such punctuation as seems appropriate. You would then—for the first time, I believe— have on paper some authentic specimens of spoken English. Probably they would not be readable as a book or a newspaper article is readable, but then spoken English is not meant to be read, it is meant to be listened to. From these specimens you could, I believe, formulate the rules of spoken English and find out how it differs from the written language. And when writing in spoken English had become practicable, the average speaker or lecturer who has to write his material down beforehand could bring it far closer to his natural diction, make it more essentially speakable, than he can at present.

Of course, demotic speech is not solely a matter of being colloquial and avoiding ill-understood words. There is also the question of accent. It seems certain that in modern England the "educated", upper-class accent is deadly to any speaker who is aiming at a large audience. All effective speakers in recent times have had either cockney or provincial accents. The success of Priestley's broadcasts in 1940 was largely due to his Yorkshire accent, which he probably broadened a little for the occasion. Churchill is only a seeming exception to this rule. Too old to have acquired the modern "educated" accent he speaks with the Edwardian upper-class twang which to the average man's ear sounds like cockney. The "educated" accent, of which the accent of the BBC announcers is a sort of parody, has no asset except its intelligibility to English-speaking foreigners.

In England the minority to whom it is natural don't particularly like it, while in the other three-quarters of the population it arouses an immediate class antagonism. It is also noticeable that where there is doubt about the pronunciation of a name, successful speakers will stick to the working-class pronunciation even if they know it to be wrong. Churchill, for instance, mispronounced "Nazi" and "Gestapo" as long as the common people continued to do so. Lloyd George during the last war rendered "Kaiser" as "Kayser", which was the popular version of the word.

In the early days of the war the Government had the greatest difficulty in inducing people to bother to collect their ration books. At parliamentary elections, even when there is an up-to-date register, it often happens that less than half of the electorate use their votes. Things like these are symptoms of the intellectual gulf between the rulers and the ruled. But the same gulf lies always between the intelligentsia and the common man. Journalists, as we can see by their election forecasts, never know what the public is thinking. Revolutionary propaganda is incredibly ineffective. Churches are empty all over the country. The whole idea of trying to find out what the average man thinks, instead of assuming that he thinks what he ought to think, is novel and unwelcome. Social surveys are viciously attacked from Left and Right alike. Yet some mechanism for testing public opinion is an obvious necessity of modern government, and more so in a democratic country than in a totalitarian one. Its complement is the ability to speak to the ordinary man in words that he will understand and respond to.

At present propaganda only seems to succeed when it coincides with what people are inclined to do in any case. During the present war, for instance, the Government has done extraordinarily little to preserve morale: it has merely drawn on the existing reserves of goodwill. And all political parties alike have failed to interest the public in vitally important questions—in the problem of India, to name only one. But some day we may have a genuinely democratic government, a government which will want to tell people what is happening, and what must be done next, and what sacrifices are necessary, and why. It will need the mechanisms for doing so, of which the first are the right words, the right tone of voice. The fact that when you suggest finding out what the common man is like, and approaching him accordingly, you are either accused of being an intellectual snob who wants to "talk down to" the masses, or else suspected of plotting to establish an English Gestapo, shows how sluggishly nineteenth-century our notion of democracy has remained.

Written [late April 1944]; *Persuasion*, Summer 1944

36. Letter to Philip Rahv

10a Mortimer Crescent
London NW6
1 May 1944

Dear Rahv,

Thanks so much for your letter dated April 17th. It got here today, so the air mail is definitely looking up. I sent off my London Letter on about April 17th, so that should certainly reach you before the end of May unless held up in the censorship. After I had sent it off it struck me there were several things in it the censorship might object to (on policy grounds, not security of course), but I haven't had any note from them to say they were stopping it, so I suppose it's all right. Your letter hadn't been opened by the censor, by the way.

I dare say the Dial people will have got my MS[1] by about now. As you say you're in touch with them, I wonder if you could ask them to let you have a look at it. I think you will agree it deserves to be printed, but its "message" is hardly a popular one nowadays. I am having hell and all to find a publisher for it here though normally I have no difficulty in publishing my stuff and in any case all publishers are now clamouring for manuscripts. A few weeks back a newspaper I write for regularly refused to print a book review of mine because it was anti-Stalin in tone.[2] Comically enough the Stalinists

---

[1] Orwell had sent the manuscript of *Animal Farm* to the Dial Press, New York.

[2] Orwell's review of Harold Laski's *Faith, Reason and Civilisation*, which should have appeared in the *Manchester Evening News*, 16 March 1944, was rejected by the editor. Dwight Macdonald, in an editorial comment in *Politics*, November 1944, wrote:

"A letter that came in the other day from George Orwell in London gives some interesting evidence of the 'russification' of English political thought in the last two years. 'I was interested to see,' he writes, 'that the May number of *Politics* reviews Laski's *Faith, Reason and Civilisation*, and I thought it might amuse you to see the review I wrote of it when first published. This review was written for the *Manchester Evening News*, the evening paper of the *Manchester*

themselves haven't much influence in the press, but Stalin seems to be becoming a figure rather similar to what Franco used to be, a Christian gent whom it is not done to criticise. By some arrangement the Soviet government have made, most of the Russian propaganda books are published by ——, a big octopus publisher who puts out not only very cheap tripe-novels but vicious anti-Left pamphlets and semi-Fascist stuff from Vansittart's[1] followers.

As to the Dial publishing other books of mine. Several have actually been published in the USA (they never sold much). The one that *ought* to be reprinted is my one about the Spanish civil war, but of course that's the most hopeless of all subjects now. I don't know whether the Penguin books are sold in the USA. My Burma novel[2] which Harper's published in 1934 is being penguinised, but if the Penguins don't get across the Atlantic it seems to me it is a book

---

Guardian (generally looked on as the only truthful paper in England), for which I write once a fortnight. The editor refused to print it, evidently because of its anti-Stalin implications. If you look through it, you will see that I have gone about as far as was consistent with ordinary honesty *not* to say what pernicious tripe the book is, and yet my remarks were too strong even for the *Manchester Evening News*. This will give you an idea of the kind of thing you can't print in England nowadays. Yet this isn't due to Stalinists, who aren't much regarded nowadays. Editors will print nothing anti-Russian because of the supposed russomania of the general public and also because of the complaints which the Soviet government is constantly raising about the British press.'

Orwell's rejected review terms Russia 'a state definitely describable as Socialist' and praises Laski because 'he is aware that the USSR is the real dynamo of the Socialist movement in this country and everywhere else'. ('Therefore, the USSR must be safeguarded at all costs,' the reviewer adds.) His quarrel with Laski is that Laski shuts his eyes to 'purges, liquidations, the dictatorship of a minority, suppression of criticism and so forth'. Orwell also takes to pieces Laski's phony analogy of Stalin's Russia with the early Christian church. That such a review, agreeing with Laski on the main point—the Socialist nature of the USSR today—and merely venturing to make the criticism any honest and intelligent reviewer would have to make of Laski's book—that such a review should be too hot for a paper like the *Manchester Evening News* shows how seriously the feats of the Red army have misled English public opinion about Russia. (It will be recalled that the *Manchester Guardian*—and the English liberal press in general —was much more honest and critical about the Moscow Trials than our own liberal journals; the *Guardian* in particular threw its columns open to Trotsky himself.)"

¹ Lord Vansittart (1881–1957), diplomat and writer. Chief diplomatic adviser to the Foreign Secretary 1938–41. Well known before and during the early part of the war for his outspoken criticism of Germany and the Germans.

² *Burmese] Days.*

someone might reprint over there as Burma is a bit more in the news now. I believe the copyright is mine but could find out any way. There are others that I think are worth reprinting as books, but the trouble is that they're too local to be of much interest in America. However, this autumn I intend to publish a book of reprinted literary essays. I would have done it before, but there are several more I want to write before issuing the book, and I haven't been able to do so because of being smothered under other work. However I should get them all done by the end of July, and perhaps the Dial would be interested in that book. I suppose it won't hurt if it's done here simultaneously as well.

Yours
Geo. Orwell

37. As I Please

For anyone who wants a good laugh I recommend a book which was published about a dozen years ago, but which I only recently succeeded in getting hold of. This is I. A. Richards's *Practical Criticism*.

Although mostly concerned with the general principles of literary criticism, it also describes an experiment that Mr Richards made with, or one should perhaps say *on*, his English students at Cambridge. Various volunteers, not actually students but presumably interested in English literature, also took part. Thirteen poems were presented to them, and they were asked to criticise them. The authorship of the poems was not revealed, and none of them was well enough known to be recognised at sight by the average reader. You are getting, therefore, specimens of literary criticism not complicated by snobbishness of the ordinary kind.

One ought not to be too superior, and there is no need to be, because the book is so arranged that you can try the experiment on yourself. The poems, unsigned, are all together at the end, and the authors' names are on a fold-over page which you need not look at till afterwards. I will say at once that I only spotted the authorship of two, one of which I knew already, and though I could date most of the others within a few decades, I made two bad bloomers, in one case attributing to Shelley a poem written in the nineteen-twenties. But still, some of the comments recorded by Dr Richards are startling. They go to show that many people who would describe themselves as lovers of poetry have no more notion of distinguishing between a good poem and a bad one than a dog has of arithmetic.

For example, a piece of completely spurious bombast by Alfred Noyes gets quite a lot of praise. One critic compares it to Keats. A sentimental ballad from *Rough Rhymes of a Padre*, by "Woodbine Willie", also gets quite a good press. On the other hand, a magnificent sonnet by John Donne gets a distinctly chilly reception. Dr Richards records only three favourable criticisms and about a dozen cold or hostile ones. One writer says contemptuously that the poem "would make a good hymn," while another remarks, "I can find no other reaction except disgust." Donne was at that time at the top of his reputation and no doubt most of the people taking part in this experiment would have fallen on their faces at his name. D. H. Lawrence's poem "The Piano" gets many sneers, though it is praised by a minority. So also with a short poem by Gerard Manley Hopkins. "The worst poem I have ever read," declares one writer, while another's criticism is simply "Pish-posh!"

However, before blaming these youthful students for their bad judgement, let it be remembered that when some time ago somebody published a not very convincing fake of an eighteenth-century diary, the aged critic, Sir Edmund Gosse, librarian of the House of Lords, fell for it immediately. And there was also the case of the Parisian art critics, of I forget which "school", who went into rhapsodies over a picture which was afterwards discovered to have been painted by a donkey with a paint-brush tied to its tail.

Under the heading "We Are Destroying Birds that Save Us", the *News Chronicle* notes that "beneficial birds suffer from human ignorance. There is senseless persecution of the kestrel and barn owl. No two species of birds do better work for us."

Unfortunately it isn't even from ignorance. Most of the birds of prey are killed off for the sake of that enemy of England, the pheasant. Unlike the partridge, the pheasant does not thrive in England, and apart from the neglected woodlands and the vicious game laws that it has been responsible for, all birds or animals that are suspected of eating its eggs or chicks are systematically wiped out. Before the war, near my village in Hertfordshire, I used to pass a stretch of fence where the gamekeeper kept his "larder". Dangling from the wires were the corpses of stoats, weasels, rats, hedgehogs, jays, owls, kestrels and sparrow-hawks. Except for the rats and perhaps the jays, all of these creatures are beneficial to agriculture. The stoats keep down the rabbits, the weasels eat mice, and so do the kestrels and sparrow-hawks, while the owls eat rats as well. It has been calculated that a barn owl destroys between 1,000 and 2,000 rats and mice in a year. Yet it has to be killed off for the sake of this useless bird which Rudyard Kipling correctly described as "lord of many a shire".

Tribune, 5 May 1944

38. As I Please

Reading recently a batch of rather shallowly optimistic "progressive" books, I was struck by the automatic way in which people go on repeating certain phrases which were fashionable before 1914. Two great favourites are "the abolition of distance" and "the disappearance of frontiers". I do not know how often I have met with the statements that "the aeroplane and the radio have abolished distance" and "all parts of the world are now interdependent".

Actually, the effect of modern inventions has been to increase nationalism, to make travel enormously more difficult, to cut down the means of communication between one country and another, and to make the various parts of the world *less*, not more dependent on one another for food and manufactured goods. This is not the result of the war. The same tendencies had been at work ever since 1918, though they were intensified after the World Depression.

Take simply the instance of travel. In the nineteenth century some parts of the world were unexplored, but there was almost no restriction on travel. Up to 1914 you did not need a passport for any country except Russia. The European emigrant, if he could scrape together a few pounds for the passage, simply set sail for America or Australia, and when he got there no questions were asked. In the eighteenth century it had been quite normal and safe to travel in a country with which your own country was at war.

In our own time, however, travel has been becoming steadily more difficult. It is worth listing the parts of the world which were already inaccessible before the war started.

First of all, the whole of central Asia. Except perhaps for a very few tried Communists, no foreigner has entered Soviet Asia for many years past. Tibet, thanks to Anglo-Russian jealousy, has been a closed country since about 1912. Sinkiang, theoretically part of China, was equally un-get-atable. Then the whole of the Japanese Empire, except Japan itself, was practically barred to foreigners. Even India has been none too accessible since 1918. Passports were often refused even to British subjects—sometimes even to Indians!

Even in Europe the limits of travel were constantly narrowing. Except for a short visit it was very difficult to enter Britain, as many a wretched anti-Fascist refugee discovered. Visas for the USSR were issued very grudgingly from about 1935 onwards. All the Fascist countries were barred to anyone with a known anti-Fascist record. Various areas could only be crossed if you undertook not to get out of the train. And along all the frontiers were barbed wire, machine-guns and prowling sentries, frequently wearing gas-masks.

As to migration, it had practically dried up since the nineteen-twenties. All the countries of the New World did their best to keep the immigrant out unless he brought considerable sums of money with him. Japanese and Chinese immigration into the Americas had been completely stopped. Europe's Jews had to stay and be slaughtered because there was nowhere for them to go, whereas in the case of the Czarist pogroms forty years earlier they had been able to flee in all directions. How, in the face of all this, anyone can say that modern methods of travel promote intercommunication between different countries defeats me.

Intellectual contacts have also been diminishing for a long time past. It is nonsense to say that the radio puts people in touch with foreign countries. If anything, it does the opposite. No ordinary person ever listens in to a foreign radio; but if in any country large numbers of people show signs of doing so, the government prevents it either by ferocious penalties, or by confiscating short-wave sets, or by setting up jamming stations. The result is that each national radio is a sort of totalitarian world of its own, braying propaganda night and day to people who can listen to nothing else. Meanwhile, literature grows less and less international. Most totalitarian countries bar foreign newspapers and let in only a small number of foreign books, which they subject to careful censorship and sometimes issue in garbled versions. Letters going from one country to another are habitually tampered with on the way. And in many countries, over the past dozen years, history books have been rewritten in far more nationalistic terms than before, so that children may grow up with as false a picture as possible of the world outside.

The trend towards economic self-sufficiency ("autarchy") which has been going on since about 1930 and has been intensified by the war, may or may not be reversible. The industrialisation of countries like India and South America increases their purchasing power and therefore ought, in theory, to help world trade. But what is not grasped by those who say cheerfully that "all parts of the world are interdependent" is that they don't any longer *have* to be interdependent. In an age when wool can be made out of milk and rubber out of oil, when wheat can be grown almost on the Arctic Circle, when atebrin will do instead of quinine and vitamin C tablets are a tolerable substitute for fruit, imports don't matter very greatly. Any big area can seal itself off much more completely than in the days when Napoleon's Grand Army, in spite of the embargo, marched to Moscow wearing British overcoats. So long as the world tendency is towards nationalism and totalitarianism, scientific progress simply helps it along.

Here are some current prices.

Small Swiss-made alarm clock, price before the war, 5/- or 10/-: present price, £3 15s. Second-hand portable typewriter, price before the war, £12 new: present price, £30. Small, very bad quality coconut fibre scrubbing-brush, price before the war, 3d: present price, 1/9d. Gas lighter, price before the war, about a 1/-: present price, 5/9d.

I could quote other similar prices. It is worth noticing that, for instance, the clock mentioned above must have been manufactured before the war at the old price. But, on the whole, the worst racket seems to be in second-hand goods—for instance, chairs, tables, clothes, watches, prams, bicycles and bed linen. On enquiry, I find that there is now a law against overcharging on second-hand goods. This comforts me a great deal, just as it must comfort the 18b-ers to hear about Habeas Corpus, or Indian coolies to learn that all British subjects are equal before the law.

In Hooper's *Campaign of Sedan* there is an account of the interview in which General de Wympffen tried to obtain the best possible terms for the defeated French army. "It is to your interest," he said, "from a political standpoint, to grant us honourable conditions. . . . A peace based on conditions which would flatter the *amour-propre* of the army would be durable, whereas rigorous measures would awaken bad passions, and, perhaps bring on an endless war between France and Prussia."

Here Bismarck, the Iron Chancellor, chipped in, and his words are recorded from his memoirs:

> I said to him that we might build on the gratitude of a prince, but certainly not on the gratitude of a people—least of all on the gratitude of the French. That in France neither institutions nor circumstances were enduring; that governments and dynasties were constantly changing, and one need not carry out what the other had bound itself to do. . . . As things stood it would be folly if we did not make full use of our success.

The modern cult of "realism" is generally held to have started with Bismarck. That imbecile speech was considered magnificently "realistic" then, and so it would be now. Yet what Wympffen said, though he was only trying to bargain for terms, was perfectly true. If the Germans had behaved with ordinary generosity (i.e. by the standards of the time) it might have been impossible to whip up the *revanchiste* spirit in France. What would Bismarck have said if he had been told that harsh terms now would mean a terrible defeat forty-eight years later? There is not much doubt of the answer: he would have said that the terms ought to have been harsher still. Such is "realism"—and on the same principle, when the medicine makes the patient sick, the doctor responds by doubling the dose.

Tribune, 12 May 1944

39. Letter to H. J. Willmett

> 10a Mortimer Crescent
> London NW6
> 18 May 1944

Dear Mr Willmett,[1]

Many thanks for your letter. You ask whether totalitarianism, leader worship, etc are really on the up-grade and instance the fact that they are not apparently growing in this country and the USA.

I must say I believe, or fear, that taking the world as a whole

[1] Not identified.

these things are on the increase. Hitler, no doubt, will soon disappear, but only at the expense of strengthening (a) Stalin, (b) the Anglo-American millionaires and (c) all sorts of petty fuehrers of the type of de Gaulle. All the national movements everywhere, even those that originate in resistance to German domination, seem to take non-democratic forms, to group themselves round some superhuman fuehrer (Hitler, Stalin, Salazar, Franco, Gandhi, De Valera are all varying examples) and to adopt the theory that the end justifies the means. Everywhere the world movement seems to be in the direction of centralised economies which can be made to "work" in an economic sense but which are not democratically organised and which tend to establish a caste system. With this go the horrors of emotional nationalism and a tendency to disbelieve in the existence of objective truth because all the facts have to fit in with the words and prophecies of some infallible fuehrer. Already history has in a sense ceased to exist, i.e. there is no such thing as a history of our own times which could be universally accepted, and the exact sciences are endangered as soon as military necessity ceases to keep people up to the mark. Hitler can say that the Jews started the war, and if he survives that will become official history. He can't say that two and two are five, because for the purposes of, say, ballistics they have to make four. But if the sort of world that I am afraid of arrives, a world of two or three great superstates which are unable to conquer one another, two and two could become five if the fuehrer wished it. That, so far as I can see, is the direction in which we are actually moving, though, of course, the process is reversible.

As to the comparative immunity of Britain and the USA. Whatever the pacifists etc may say, we have *not* gone totalitarian yet and this is a very hopeful symptom. I believe very deeply, as I explained in my book *The Lion and the Unicorn*,[1] in the English *people* and in their capacity to centralise their economy without destroying freedom in doing so. But one must remember that Britain and the USA haven't been really tried, they haven't known defeat or severe suffering, and there are some bad symptoms to balance the good ones. To begin with there is the general indifference to the decay of democracy. Do you realise, for instance, that no one in England under 26 now has a vote and that so far as one can see the great mass of people of that age don't give a damn for this? Secondly there is the fact that the intellectuals are more totalitarian in outlook than the common

[1] See II, 17.

people. On the whole the English intelligentsia have opposed Hitler, but only at the price of accepting Stalin. Most of them are perfectly ready for dictatorial methods, secret police, systematic falsification of history, etc so long as they feel that it is on "our" side. Indeed the statement that we haven't a Fascist movement in England largely means that the young, at this moment, look for their fuehrer elsewhere. One can't be sure that that won't change, nor can one be sure that the common people won't think ten years hence as the intellectuals do now. I *hope* they won't, I even trust they won't, but if so it will be at the cost of a struggle. If one simply proclaims that all is for the best and doesn't point to the sinister symptoms, one is merely helping to bring totalitarianism nearer.

You also ask, if I think the world tendency is towards Fascism, why do I support the war. It is a choice of evils—I fancy nearly every war is that. I know enough of British imperialism not to like it, but I would support it against Nazism or Japanese imperialism, as the lesser evil. Similarly I would support the USSR against Germany because I think the USSR cannot altogether escape its past and retains enough of the original ideas of the Revolution to make it a more hopeful phenomenon than Nazi Germany. I think and have thought ever since the war began, in 1936 or thereabouts, that our cause is the better, but we have to keep on making it the better, which involves constant criticism.

Yours sincerely
Geo. Orwell

40. As I Please

Miss Vera Brittain's pamphlet, *Seed of Chaos*, is an eloquent attack on indiscriminate or "obliteration" bombing. "Owing to the RAF raids," she says, "thousands of helpless and innocent people in German, Italian and German-occupied cities are being subjected to agonising forms of death and injury comparable to the worst tortures of the Middle Ages." Various well-known opponents of bombing, such as General Franco and Major-General Fuller, are brought out in support of this. Miss Brittain is not, however, taking the pacifist standpoint. She is willing and anxious to win the war, apparently. She merely wishes us to stick to "legitimate" methods of war and abandon civilian bombing, which she fears will blacken our reputation in the eyes of posterity. Her pamphlet is issued by the Bombing Restriction Committee, which has issued others with similar titles.

Now, no one in his senses regards bombing, or any other operation of war, with anything but disgust. On the other hand, no decent person cares tuppence for the opinion of posterity. And there is something very distasteful in accepting war as an instrument and at the same time wanting to dodge responsibility for its more obviously barbarous features. Pacifism is a tenable position, provided that you are willing to take the consequences. But all talk of "limiting" or "humanising" war is sheer humbug, based on the fact that the average human being never bothers to examine catchwords.

The catchwords used in this connection are "killing civilians", "massacre of women and children" and "destruction of our cultural heritage". It is tacitly assumed that air bombing does more of this kind of thing than ground warfare.

When you look a bit closer, the first question that strikes you is: Why is it worse to kill civilians than soldiers? Obviously one must not kill children if it is in any way avoidable, but it is only in propaganda pamphlets that every bomb drops on a school or an orphanage. A bomb kills a cross-section of the population; but not quite a representative selection, because the children and expectant mothers are usually the first to be evacuated, and some of the young men will be away in the army. Probably a disproportionately large number of bomb victims will be middle-aged. (Up to date, German bombs have killed between six and seven thousand children in this country. This is, I believe, less than the number killed in road accidents in the same period.) On the other hand, "normal" or "legitimate" warfare picks out and slaughters all the healthiest and bravest of the young male population. Every time a German submarine goes to the bottom about fifty young men of fine physique and good nerve are suffocated. Yet people who would hold up their hands at the very words "civilian bombing" will repeat with satisfaction such phrases as "We are winning the Battle of the Atlantic". Heaven knows how many people our blitz on Germany and the occupied countries has killed and will kill, but you can be quite certain it will never come anywhere near the slaughter that has happened on the Russian front.

War is not avoidable at this stage of history, and since it has to happen it does not seem to me a bad thing that others should be killed besides young men. I wrote in 1937: "Sometimes it is a comfort

to me to think that the aeroplane is altering the conditions of war.
Perhaps when the next great war comes we may see that sight
unprecedented in all history, a jingo with a bullet hole in him."
We haven't yet seen that (it is perhaps a contradiction in terms), but
at any rate the suffering of this war has been shared out more evenly
than the last one was. The immunity of the civilian, one of the things
that have made war possible, has been shattered. Unlike Miss Brittain,
I don't regret that. I can't feel that war is "humanised" by being
confined to the slaughter of the young and becomes "barbarous"
when the old get killed as well.

As to international agreements to "limit" war, they are never
kept when it pays to break them. Long before the last war the nations
had agreed not to use gas, but they used it all the same. This time they
have refrained, merely because gas is comparatively ineffective in a
war of movement, while its use against civilian populations would be
sure to provoke reprisals in kind. Against an enemy who can't hit
back, e.g. the Abyssinians, it is used readily enough. War is of its
nature barbarous, it is better to admit that. If we see ourselves as the
savages we are, some improvement is possible, or at least thinkable.

A specimen of *Tribune's* correspondence:

TO THE JEW-PAID EDITOR,
TRIBUNE,
LONDON.
JEWS IN THE POLISH ARMY.
YOU ARE CONSTANTLY ATTACKING OUR GALLANT POLISH ALLY
BECAUSE THEY KNOW HOW TO TREAT THE JEW PEST. THEY ALSO KNOW
HOW TO TREAT ALL JEW-PAID EDITORS AND COMMUNIST PAPERS.
WE KNOW YOU ARE IN THE PAY OF THE YIDS AND SOVIETS.

YOU ARE A FRIEND OF THE ENEMIES OF BRITAIN. THE DAY OF RECKON-
ING IS AT HAND. BEWARE. ALL JEW PIGS WILL BE EXTERMINATED THE
HITLER WAY—THE ONLY WAY TO GET RID OF THE YIDS.
PERISH JUDAH.

Typed on a Remington typewriter (postmark S.W.), and, what is
to my mind an interesting detail, this is a carbon copy.

Anyone acquainted with the type will know that no assurance, no
demonstration, no proof of the most solid kind would ever con-
vince the writer of this that *Tribune* is *not* a Communist paper and
not in the pay of the Soviet Government. One very curious charac-

teristic of Fascists—I am speaking of amateur Fascists: I assume that the Gestapo are cleverer—is their failure to recognise that the parties of the Left are distinct from one another and by no means aiming at the same thing. It is always assumed that they are all one gang, whatever the outward appearances may be. In the first number of Mosley's *British Union Quarterly*, which I have by me (incidentally, it contains an article by no less a person than Major Vidkun Quisling), I note that even Wyndham Lewis speaks of Stalin and Trotsky as though they were equivalent persons. Arnold Lunn, in his *Spanish Rehearsal*, actually seems to suggest that Trotsky started the Fourth International on Stalin's instructions.

In just the same way, very few Communists, in my experience, will believe that the Trotskyists are not in the pay of Hitler. I have sometimes tried the experiment of pointing out that if the Trotskyists were in the pay of Hitler, or of anybody, they would occasionally have some money. But it is no use, it doesn't register. So also with the belief in the machinations of the Jews, or the belief, widespread among Indian nationalists, that all Englishmen, of whatever political colour, are in secret conspiracy with one another. The belief in the Freemasons as a revolutionary organisation is the strangest of all. In this country it would be just as reasonable to believe such a thing of the Buffaloes. Less than a generation ago, if not now, there were Catholic nuns who believed that at Masonic gatherings the Devil appeared in person, wearing full evening dress with a hole in the trousers for his tail to come through. In one form or another this kind of thing seems to attack nearly everybody, apparently answering to some obscure psychological need of our time.

Tribune, 19 May 1944

41. As I Please

I was talking the other day to a young American soldier, who told me—as quite a number of others have done—that anti-British feeling is completely general in the American army. He had only recently landed in this country, and as he came off the boat he asked the Military Policeman on the dock, "How's England?"

"The girls here walk out with niggers," answered the MP. "They call them American Indians."

That was the salient fact about England, from the MP's point of view. At the same time my friend told me that anti-British feeling is not violent and there is no very clearly-defined cause of complaint. A good deal of it is probably a rationalisation of the discomfort most people feel at being away from home. But the whole subject of anti-British feeling in the United States badly needs investigation. Like antisemitism, it is given a whole series of contradictory explanations, and again like antisemitism, it is probably a psychological substitute for something else. *What* else is the question that needs investigating.

Meanwhile, there is one department of Anglo-American relations that seems to be going well. It was announced some months ago that no less than 20,000 English girls had already married American soldiers and sailors, and the number will have increased since. Some of these girls are being educated for their life in a new country at the "Schools for Brides of US Servicemen" organised by the American Red Cross. Here they are taught practical details about American manners, customs and traditions—and also, perhaps, cured of the widespread illusion that every American owns a motor car and every American house contains a bathroom, a refrigerator and an electric washing-machine.

The May number of the *Matrimonial Post and Fashionable Marriage Advertiser* contains advertisements from 191 men seeking brides and over 200 women seeking husbands. Advertisements of this type have been running in a whole series of magazines since the 'sixties or earlier, and they are nearly always very much alike. For example:

> Bachelor, age 25, height 6 ft 1 in, slim, fond of horticulture, animals, children, cinema, etc would like to meet lady, age 27 to 35, with love of flowers, nature, children, must be tall, medium build, Church of England.

The general run of them are just like that, though occasionally a more unusual note is struck. For instance:

> I'm 29, single, 5 ft 10 in, English, large build, kind, quiet, varied intellectual interests, firm moral background (registered unconditionally as absolute CO), progressive, creative, literary inclinations. A dealer in rare stamps, income variable but quite adequate. Strong swimmer, cyclist, slight stammer occasionally.

Looking for the following rarity, amiable, adaptable, educated girl, easy on eye and ear, under 30, secretary type or similar, mentally adventurous, immune to mercenary and social incentives, bright sense of genuine humour, a reliable working partner. Capital unimportant, character vital.

The thing that is and always has been striking in these advertisements is that nearly all the applicants are remarkably eligible. It is not only that most of them are broad-minded, intelligent, home-loving, musical, loyal, sincere and affectionate, with a keen sense of humour and, in the case of women, a good figure: in the majority of cases they are financially OK as well. When you consider how fatally easy it is to get married, you would not imagine that a 36-year-old bachelor, "dark hair, fair complexion, slim build, height 6 ft, well educated and of considerate, jolly and intelligent disposition, income £1,000 per annum and capital", would need to find himself a bride through the columns of a newspaper. And ditto with "Adventurous young woman, left-wing opinions, modern outlook" with "fairly full but shapely figure, medium colour curly hair, grey-blue eyes, fair skin, natural colouring, health exceptionally good, interested in music, art, literature, cinema, theatre, fond of walking, cycling, tennis, skating and rowing". Why does such a paragon have to advertise?

It should be noted that the *Matrimonial Post* is entirely above-board and checks up carefully on its advertisers.

What these things really demonstrate is the atrocious loneliness of people living in big towns. People meet for work and then scatter to widely separated homes. Anywhere in inner London it is probably exceptional to know even the names of the people who live next door.

Years ago I lodged for a while in the Portobello Road. This is hardly a fashionable quarter, but the landlady had been lady's maid to some woman of title and had a good opinion of herself. One day something went wrong with the front door and my landlady, her husband and myself were all locked out of the house. It was evident that we should have to get in by an upper window, and as there was a jobbing builder next door I suggested borrowing a ladder from him. My landlady looked somewhat uncomfortable.

"I wouldn't like to do that," she said finally. "You see we don't know him. We've been here fourteen years, and we've always taken care not to know the people on either side of us. It *wouldn't do*, not in a neighbourhood like this. If you once begin talking to them they get familiar, you see."

So we had to borrow a ladder from a relative of her husband's, and carry it nearly a mile with great labour and discomfort.

Tribune, 26 May 1944

42. Benefit of Clergy: Some Notes on Salvador Dali

Autobiography is only to be trusted when it reveals something disgraceful. A man who gives a good account of himself is probably lying, since any life when viewed from the inside is simply a series of defeats. However, even the most flagrantly dishonest book (Frank Harris's autobiographical writings are an example) can without intending it give a true picture of its author. Dali's recently published *Life*[1] comes under this heading. Some of the incidents in it are flatly incredible, others have been rearranged and romanticised, and not merely the humiliation but the persistent *ordinariness* of everyday life has been cut out. Dali is even by his own diagnosis narcissistic, and his autobiography is simply a strip-tease act conducted in pink limelight. But as a record of fantasy, of the perversion of instinct that has been made possible by the machine age, it has great value.

Here, then, are some of the episodes in Dali's life, from his earliest years onward. Which of them are true and which are imaginary hardly matters: the point is that this is the kind of thing that Dali would have *liked* to do.

When he is six years old there is some excitement over the appearance of Halley's comet:

> Suddenly one of my father's office clerks appeared in the drawing-room doorway and announced that the comet could be seen from the terrace. . . . While crossing the hall I caught sight of my little three-year-old sister crawling unobtrusively through a doorway. I stopped, hesitated a second, then gave her a terrible kick in the head as though it had been a ball, and continued running, carried away with a "delirious joy" induced by this savage act. But my father, who was behind me, caught me and led me down into his office, where I remained as a punishment till dinner-time.

[1] *The Secret Life of Salvador Dali*, Dial Press, New York.

A year earlier than this Dali had "suddenly, as most of my ideas occur" flung another little boy off a suspension bridge. Several other incidents of the same kind are recorded, including (*this was when he was twenty-nine years old*) knocking down and trampling on a girl "until they had to tear her, bleeding, out of my reach".

When he is about five he gets hold of a wounded bat which he puts into a tin pail. Next morning he finds that the bat is almost dead and is covered with ants which are devouring it. He puts it in his mouth, ants and all, and bites it almost in half.

When he is adolescent a girl falls desperately in love with him. He kisses and caresses her so as to excite her as much as possible, but refuses to go further. He resolves to keep this up for five years (he calls it his "five year plan"), enjoying her humiliation and the sense of power it gives him. He frequently tells her that at the end of five years he will desert her, and when the time comes he does so.

Till well into adult life he keeps up the practice of masturbation, and likes to do this, apparently, in front of a looking-glass. For ordinary purposes he is impotent, it appears, till the age of thirty or so. When he first meets his future wife, Gala, he is greatly tempted to push her off a precipice. He is aware that there is something that she wants him to do to her, and after their first kiss the confession is made:

> I threw back Gala's head, pulling it by the hair, and trembling with complete hysteria, I commanded:
> "Now tell me what you want me to do with you! But tell me slowly, looking me in the eye, with the crudest, the most ferociously erotic words that can make both of us feel the greatest shame!"
> . . . Then Gala, transforming the last glimmer of her expression of pleasure into the hard light of her own tyranny, answered:
> "I want you to kill me"!

He is somewhat disappointed by this demand, since it is merely what he wanted to do already. He contemplates throwing her off the bell-tower of the cathedral of Toledo, but refrains from doing so.

During the Spanish civil war he astutely avoids taking sides, and makes a trip to Italy. He feels himself more and more drawn towards the aristocracy, frequents smart *salons*, finds himself wealthy patrons, and is photographed with the plump Vicomte de Noailles, whom he describes as his "Maecenas". When the European war approaches he has one preoccupation only: how to find a place which has good cookery and from which he can make a quick bolt if danger comes too near. He fixes on Bordeaux, and duly flees to Spain during the Battle of France. He stays in Spain long enough to pick up a few anti-red atrocity stories, then makes for America. The story ends in a blaze of respectability. Dali, at thirty-seven, has become a devoted husband, is cured of his aberrations, or some of them, and is completely reconciled to the Catholic Church. He is also, one gathers, making a good deal of money.

However, he has by no means ceased to take pride in the pictures of his Surrealist period, with titles like "The Great Masturbator", "Sodomy of a Skull with a Grand Piano", etc. There are reproductions of these all the way through the book. Many of Dali's drawings are simply representational and have a characteristic to be noted later. But from his Surrealist paintings and photographs the two things that stand out are sexual perversity and necrophilia. Sexual objects and symbols—some of them well known, like our old friend the high-heeled slipper, others, like the crutch and the cup of warm milk, patented by Dali himself—recur over and over again, and there is a fairly well-marked excretory motif as well. Of his painting, "Le Jeu Lugubre", he says, "the drawers bespattered with excrement were painted with such minute and realistic complacency that the whole little Surrealist group was anguished by the question: Is he coprophagic or not?" Dali adds firmly that he is *not*, and that he regards this aberration as "repulsive", but it seems to be only at that point that his interest in excrement stops. Even when he recounts the experience of watching a woman urinate standing up, he has to add the detail that she misses her aim and dirties her shoes. It is not given to any one person to have all the vices, and Dali also boasts that he is not homosexual, but otherwise he seems to have as good an outfit of perversions as anyone could wish for.

However, his most notable characteristic is his necrophilia. He himself freely admits to this, and claims to have been cured of it. Dead faces, skulls, corpses of animals occur fairly frequently in his pictures, and the ants which devoured the dying bat make countless reappearances. One photograph shows an exhumed corpse, far gone in decomposition. Another shows the dead donkeys putrefying on top of grand pianos which formed part of the Surrealist film, "Le Chien Andalou". Dali still looks back on these donkeys with great enthusiasm.

I "made up" the putrefaction of the donkeys with great pots of sticky glue which I poured over them. Also I emptied their eye-sockets and made them larger by hacking them out with scissors. In the same way I furiously cut their mouths open to make the rows of their teeth show to better advantage, and I added several jaws to each mouth, so that it would appear that although the donkeys were already rotting they were vomiting up a little more of their own death, above those other rows of teeth formed by the keys of the black pianos.

And finally there is the picture—apparently some kind of faked photograph—of "Mannequin rotting in a taxi-cab". Over the already somewhat bloated face and breast of an apparently dead girl, huge snails are crawling. In the caption below the picture Dali notes that these are Burgundy snails—that is, the edible kind.

Of course, in this long book of 400 quarto pages there is more than I have indicated, but I do not think that I have given an unfair account of its moral atmosphere and mental scenery. It is a book that stinks. If it were possible for a book to give a physical stink off its pages, this one would—a thought that might please Dali, who before wooing his future wife for the first time rubbed himself all over with an ointment made of goat's dung boiled up in fish glue. But against this has to be set the fact that Dali is a draughtsman of very exceptional gifts. He is also, to judge by the minuteness and the sureness of his drawings, a very hard worker. He is an exhibitionist and a careerist, but he is not a fraud. He has fifty times more talent than most of the people who would denounce his morals and jeer at his paintings. And these two sets of facts, taken together, raise a question which for lack of any basis of agreement seldom gets a real discussion.

The point is that you have here a direct, unmistakable assault on sanity and decency; and even—since some of Dali's pictures would tend to poison the imagination like a pornographic postcard—on life itself. What Dali has done and what he has imagined is debatable, but in his outlook, his character, the bedrock decency of a human being does not exist. He is as antisocial as a flea. Clearly, such people are undesirable, and a society in which they can flourish has something wrong with it.

Now, if you showed this book, with its illustrations, to Lord Elton, to Mr Alfred Noyes, to *The Times* leader-writers who exult over the "eclipse of the highbrow"—in fact, to any "sensible" art-hating English person—it is easy to imagine what kind of response you would get. They would flatly refuse to see any merit in Dali whatever. Such people are not only unable to admit that what is morally degraded can be aesthetically right, but their real demand of every artist is that he shall pat them on the back and tell them that thought is unnecessary. And they can be especially dangerous at a time like the present, when the Ministry of Information and the British Council put power into their hands. For their impulse is not not only to crush every new talent as it appears, but to castrate the past as well. Witness the renewed highbrow-baiting that is now going on in this country and America, with its outcry not only against Joyce, Proust and Lawrence, but even against T. S. Eliot.

But if you talk to the kind of person who *can* see Dali's merits, the response that you get is not as a rule very much better. If you say that Dali, though a brilliant draughtsman, is a dirty little scoundrel, you are looked upon as a savage. If you say that you don't like rotting corpses, and that people who do like rotting corpses are mentally diseased, it is assumed that you lack the aesthetic sense. Since "Mannequin rotting in a taxi-cab" is a good composition (as it undoubtedly is), it cannot be a disgusting, degrading picture; whereas Noyes, Elton, etc would tell you that because it is disgusting it cannot be a good composition. And between these two fallacies there is no middle position; or, rather, there is a middle position, but we seldom hear much about it. On the one side *Kulturbolschewismus*: on the other (though the phrase itself is out of fashion) "Art for Art's sake". Obscenity is a very difficult question to discuss honestly. People are too frightened either of seeming to be shocked or of seeming not to be shocked, to be able to define the relationship between art and morals.

It will be seen that what the defenders of Dali are claiming is a kind of *benefit of clergy*. The artist is to be exempt from the moral laws that are binding on ordinary people. Just pronounce the magic word "art", and everything is OK. Rotting corpses with snails crawling over them are OK; kicking little girls on the head is OK; even a film like "L'Age d'Or" is OK.[1] It is also OK that Dali should batten

---

[1] Dali mentions "L'Age d'Or" and adds that its first public showing was broken up by hooligans, but he does not say in detail what it was about. According to Henry Miller's account of it, it showed among other things some fairly detailed shots of a woman defecating. [Author's footnote.]

on France for years and then scuttle off like a rat as soon as France is in danger. So long as you can paint well enough to pass the test, all shall be forgiven you.

One can see how false this is if one extends it to cover ordinary crime. In an age like our own, when the artist is an altogether exceptional person, he must be allowed a certain amount of irresponbility, just as a pregnant woman is. Still, no one would say that a pregnant woman should be allowed to commit murder, nor would anyone make such a claim for the artist, however gifted. If Shakespeare returned to the earth tomorrow, and if it were found that his favourite recreation was raping little girls in railway carriages, we should not tell him to go ahead with it on the ground that he might write another *King Lear*. And, after all, the worst crimes are not always the punishable ones. By encouraging necrophilic reveries one probably does quite as much harm as by, say, picking pockets at the races. One ought to be able to hold in one's head simultaneously the two facts that Dali is a good draughtsman and a disgusting human being. The one does not invalidate or, in a sense, affect the other. The first thing that we demand of a wall is that it shall stand up. If it stands up, it is a good wall, and the question of what purpose it serves is separable from that. And yet even the best wall in the world deserves to be pulled down if it surrounds a concentration camp. In the same way it should be possible to say, "This is a good book or a good picture, and it ought to be burned by the public hangman". Unless one can say that, at least in imagination, one is shirking the implications of the fact that an artist is also a citizen and a human being.

Not, of course, that Dali's autobiography, or his pictures, ought to be suppressed. Short of the dirty postcards that used to be sold in Mediterranean seaport towns, it is doubtful policy to suppress anything, and Dali's fantasies probably cast useful light on the decay of capitalist civilisation. But what he clearly needs is diagnosis. The question is not so much *what* he is, as *why* he is like that. It ought not to be in doubt that he is a diseased intelligence, probably not much altered by his alleged conversion, since genuine penitents, or people who have returned to sanity, do not flaunt their past vices in that complacent way. He is a symptom of the world's illness. The important thing is not to denounce him as a cad who ought to be horse-whipped or to defend him as a genius who ought not to be questioned, but to find out *why* he exhibits that particular set of aberrations.

The answer is probably discoverable in his pictures, and those I myself am not competent to examine. But I can point to one clue which perhaps takes one part of the distance. This is the old-fashioned, over-ornate, Edwardian style of drawing to which Dali tends to revert when he is not being Surrealist. Some of Dali's drawings are reminiscent of Dürer, one (p. 113) seems to show the influence of Beardsley, another (p. 269) seems to borrow something from Blake. But the most persistent strain is the Edwardian one. When I opened the book for the first time and looked at its innumerable marginal illustrations, I was haunted by a resemblance which I could not immediately pin down. I fetched up at the ornamental candlestick at the beginning of Part I (p. 7). What did this remind me of? Finally I tracked it down. It reminded me of a large, vulgar, expensively got-up edition of Anatole France (in translation) which must have been published about 1914. That had ornamental chapter headings and tailpieces after this style. Dali's candlestick displays at one end a curly fish-like creature that looks curiously familiar (it seems to be based on the conventional dolphin), and at the other is the burning candle. This candle, which recurs in one picture after another, is a very old friend. You will find it, with the same picturesque gouts of wax arranged on its sides, in those phony electric lights done up as candlesticks which are popular in sham-Tudor country hotels. This candle, and the design beneath it, convey at once an intense feeling of sentimentality. As though to counteract this, Dali has spattered a quill-ful of ink all over the page, but without avail. The same impression keeps popping up on page after page. The design at the bottom of page 62, for instance, would nearly go into *Peter Pan*. The figure on page 224, in spite of having her cranium elongated into an immense sausage-like shape, is the witch of the fairy-tale books. The horse on page 234 and the unicorn on page 218 might be illustrations to James Branch Cabell. The rather pansified drawings of youths on page 97, 100 and elsewhere convey the same impression. Picturesqueness keeps breaking in. Take away the skulls, ants, lobsters, telephones and other paraphernalia, and every now and again you are back in the world of Barrie, Rackham, Dunsany and *Where the Rainbow Ends*.

Curiously enough, some of the naughty-naughty touches in Dali's autobiography tie up with the same period. When I read the passage I quoted at the beginning, about the kicking of the little sister's head, I was aware of another phantom resemblance. What was it? Of

course! *Ruthless Rhymes for Heartless Homes* by Harry Graham.
Such rhymes were very popular round about 1912, and one that ran:

> Poor little Willy is crying so sore,
> A sad little boy is he,
> For he's broken his little sister's neck
> And he'll have no jam for tea.

might almost have been founded on Dali's anecdote. Dali, of course,
is aware of his Edwardian leanings, and makes capital out of them,
more or less in a spirit of pastiche. He professes an especial affection
for the year 1900, and claims that every ornamental object of 1900
is full of mystery, poetry, eroticism, madness, perversity, etc. Pastiche,
however, usually implies a real affection for the thing parodied. It
seems to be, if not the rule, at any rate distinctly common for an
intellectual bent to be accompanied by a non-rational, even childish
urge in the same direction. A sculptor, for instance, is interested in
planes and curves, but he is also a person who enjoys the physical
act of mucking about with clay or stone. An engineer is a person who
enjoys the feel of tools, the noise of dynamos and the smell of oil.
A psychiatrist usually has a leaning towards some sexual aberration
himself. Darwin became a biologist partly because he was a country
gentleman and fond of animals. It may be, therefore, that Dali's
seemingly perverse cult of Edwardian things (for example, his
"discovery" of the 1900 subway-entrances) is merely the symptom
of a much deeper, less conscious affection. The innumerable,
beautifully executed copies of text-book illustrations, solemnly
labelled *le rossignol, une montre* and so on, which he scatters all
over his margins, may be meant partly as a joke. The little boy in
knickerbockers playing with a diabolo on page 103 is a perfect period
piece. But perhaps these things are also there because Dali can't help
drawing that kind of thing, because it is to that period and that style
of drawing that he really belongs.

If so, his aberrations are partly explicable. Perhaps they are a
way of assuring himself that he is not commonplace. The two qualities
that Dali unquestionably possesses are a gift for drawing and an
atrocious egoism. "At seven," he says in the first paragraph of his
book, "I wanted to be Napoleon. And my ambition has been growing
steadily ever since." This is worded in a deliberately startling way,
but no doubt it is substantially true. Such feelings are common
enough. "I knew I was a genius," somebody once said to me, "long

before I knew what I was going to be a genius *about*." And suppose that you have nothing in you except your egoism and a dexterity that goes no higher than the elbow; suppose that your real gift is for a detailed, academic, representational style of drawing, your real *métier* to be an illustrator of scientific textbooks. How then do you become Napoleon?

There is always one escape: *into wickedness*. Always do the thing that will shock and wound people. At five, throw a little boy off a bridge, strike an old doctor across the face with a whip and break his spectacles—or, at any rate, dream about doing such things. Twenty years later, gouge the eyes out of dead donkeys with a pair of scissors. Along those lines you can always feel yourself original. And after all, it pays! It is much less dangerous than crime. Making all allowance for the probable suppressions in Dali's autobiography, it is clear that he has not had to suffer for his eccentricities as he would have done in an earlier age. He grew up in the corrupt world of the nineteen-twenties, when sophistication was immensely widespread and every European capital swarmed with aristocrats and *rentiers* who had given up sport and politics and taken to patronising the arts. If you threw dead donkeys at people, they threw money back. A phobia for grasshoppers—which a few decades back would merely have provoked a snigger—was now an interesting "complex" which could be profitably exploited. And when that particular world collapsed before the German army, America was waiting. You could even top it all up with religious conversion, moving at one hop and without a shadow of repentance from the fashionable *salons* of Paris to Abraham's bosom.

That, perhaps, is the essential outline of Dali's history. But why his aberrations should be the particular ones they were, and why it should be so easy to "sell" such horrors as rotting corpses to a sophisticated public—those are questions for the psychologist and the sociological critic. Marxist criticism has a short way with such phenomena as Surrealism. They are "bourgeois decadence" (much play is made with the phrases "corpse poisons" and "decaying *rentier* class"), and that is that. But though this probably states a fact, it does not establish a connection. One would still like to know *why* Dali's leaning was towards necrophilia (and not, say, homosexuality), and *why* the *rentiers* and the aristocrats should buy his pictures instead of hunting and making love like their grandfathers. Mere moral disapproval does not get one any further. But neither ought one to pretend, in the name of "detachment", that such pictures as "Manne-quin rotting in a taxi-cab" are morally neutral. They are diseased and disgusting, and any investigation ought to start out from that fact.

[Written [June] 1944. " 'Benefit of Clergy' made a sort of phantom appear-ance in the *Saturday Book* for 1944. The book was in print when its pub-lishers, Messrs Hutchinson, decided that this essay must be suppressed on grounds of obscenity. It was accordingly cut out of each copy, though for technical reasons it was impossible to remove its title from the table of contents." Author's note to CTE and DD; CE.]

43. As I Please

An extract from the Italian radio, about the middle of 1942, describ-ing life in London:

> Five shillings were given for one egg yesterday, and one pound sterling for a kilogram of potatoes. Rice has disappeared, even from the Black Market, and peas have become the prerogative of millionaires. There is no sugar on the market, although small quantities.are still to be found at prohibitive prices.

One day there will be a big, careful, scientific enquiry into the extent to which propaganda is believed. For instance, what is the effect of an item like the one above, which is fairly typical of the Fascist radio? Any Italian who took it seriously would have to assume that Britain was due to collapse within a few weeks. When the collapse failed to happen, one would expect him to lose confidence in the authorities who had deceived him. But it is not certain that that is the reaction. For quite long periods, at any rate, people can remain undisturbed by obvious lies, either because they simply forget what is said from day to day or because they are under such a constant propaganda bombardment that they become anaesthet-ised to the whole business.

It seems clear that it pays to tell the truth when things are going badly, but it is by no means certain that it pays to be consistent in your propaganda. British propaganda is a good deal hampered by its efforts not to be self-contradictory. It is almost impossible, for instance, to discuss the colour question in a way that will please both the Boers and the Indians. The Germans are not troubled by a little thing like that. They just tell everyone what they think he will want to hear, assuming, probably rightly, that no one is interested in anyone else's problems. On occasion their various radio stations have even attacked one another.

One which aimed at middle-class Fascists used sometimes to warn its listeners against the pseudo-Left Worker's Challenge, on the ground that the latter was "financed by Moscow".

Another thing that that enquiry, if it ever takes place, will have to deal with is the magical properties of names. Nearly all human beings feel that a thing becomes different if you call it by a different name. Thus when the Spanish civil war broke out the BBC produced the name "Insurgents" for Franco's followers. This covered the fact that they were rebels while making rebellion sound respectable. During the Abyssinian war Haile Selassie was called the Emperor by his friends and the Negus by his enemies. Catholics strongly resent being called Roman Catholics. The Trotskyists call themselves Bolshevik-Leninists but are refused this name by their opponents. Countries which have liberated themselves from a foreign conqueror or gone through a nationalist revolution almost invariably change their names, and some countries have a whole series of names, each with a different implication. Thus the USSR is called Russia or USSR (neutral or for short), Soviet Russia (friendly) and Soviet Union (very friendly). And it is a curious fact that of the six names by which our own country is called, the only one that does not tread on somebody or other's toes is the archaic and slightly ridiculous name "Albion".

Wading through the entries for the Short Story Competition,[1] I was struck once again by the disability that English short stories suffer in being all cut to a uniform length. The great short stories of the past are of all lengths from perhaps 1,500 words to 20,000. Most of Maupassant's stories, for instance, are very short, but his two masterpieces, "Boule de Suif" and "La Maison de Madame Tellier", are decidedly long. Poe's stories vary similarly. D. H. Lawrence's "England, My England", Joyce's "The Dead", Conrad's "Youth", and many stories by Henry James, would probably be considered too long for any modern English periodical. So, certainly, would a story like Mérimée's *Carmen*. This belongs to the class of "long short" stories which have almost died out in this country, because

[1] Organised by Orwell for *Tribune*.

there is no place for them. They are too long for the magazines and too short to be published as books. You can, of course, publish a book containing several short stories, but this is not often done because at normal times these books never sell.

It would almost certainly help to rehabilitate the short story if we could get back to the bulky nineteenth-century magazine, which had room in it for stories of almost any length. But the trouble is that in modern England monthly and quarterly magazines of any intellectual pretensions don't pay. Even the *Criterion*, perhaps the best literary paper we have ever had, lost money for sixteen years before expiring.

Why? Because people were not willing to fork out the seven and sixpence that it cost. People won't pay that much for a mere magazine. But why then will they pay the same sum for a novel, which is no bulkier than the *Criterion*, and much less worth keeping? Because they don't pay for the novel directly. The average person never buys a new book, except perhaps a Penguin. But he does, without knowing it, buy quite a lot of books by paying twopences into lending libraries. If you could take a literary magazine out of the library just as you take a book, these magazines would become commercial propositions and would be able to enlarge their bulk as well as paying their contributors better. It is book-borrowing and not book-buying that keeps authors and publishers alive, and there seems no good reason why the lending library system should not be extended to magazines. Restore the monthly magazine—or make the weekly paper about a quarter of an inch fatter—and you might be able to restore the short story. And incidentally the book review, which for lack of elbow room has dwindled to a perfunctory summary, might become a work of art again, as it was in the days of the *Edinburgh* and the *Quarterly*.

After reading the *Matrimonial Post* last week I looked in the Penguin Herodotus for a passage I vaguely remembered about the marriage customs of the Babylonians. Here it is:

> Once a year in each village the maidens of an age to marry were collected altogether into one place, while the men stood round them in a circle. Then a herald called up the damsels one by one and offered them for sale. He began with the most beautiful. When she was sold for no small sum of money, he

offered for sale the one who came next to her in beauty. .... The custom was that when the herald had gone through the whole number of the beautiful damsels, he should then call up the ugliest and offer her to the men, asking who would agree to take her with the smallest marriage portion. And the man who offered to take the smallest sum had her assigned to him. The marriage portions were furnished by the money paid for the beautiful damsels, and thus the fairer maidens portioned out the uglier.

This custom seems to have worked very well and Herodotus is full of enthusiasm for it. He adds, however, that, like other good customs, it was already going out round about 450 BC.

Tribune, 2 June 1944

44. As I Please

Arthur Koestler's recent article in *Tribune*[1] set me wondering whether the book racket will start up again in its old vigour after the war, when paper is plentiful and there are other things to spend your money on.

Publishers have got to live, like anyone else, and you cannot blame them for advertising their wares, but the truly shameful feature of literary life before the war was the blurring of the distinction between advertisement and criticism. A number of the so-called reviewers, and especially the best-known ones, were simply blurb writers. The "screaming" advertisement started some time in the nineteen-twenties, and as the competition to take up as much space and use as many superlatives as possible became fiercer, publishers' advertisements grew to be an important source of revenue to a number of papers. The literary pages of several well-known papers were practically owned by a handful of publishers, who had their quislings planted in all the important jobs. These wretches churned forth

---

[1] In *Tribune*, 28 April 1944, Koestler had written an article in the form of a letter to a young Corporal who had written to ask for advice as to which book reviewers could be taken as reliable guides. Koestler pointed out the dismal standards of criticism prevailing in most of the press.

their praise—"masterpiece", "brilliant", "unforgettable" and so forth—like so many mechanical pianos. A book coming from the right publishers could be absolutely certain not only of favourable reviews, but of being placed on the "recommended" list which industrious book borrowers would cut out and take to the library the next day.

If you published books at several different houses you soon learned how strong the pressure of advertisement was. A book coming from a big publisher, who habitually spent large sums on advertisement, might get fifty or seventy-five reviews: a book from a small publisher might get only twenty. I knew of one case where a theological publisher, for some reason, took it into his head to publish a novel. He spent a great deal of money on advertising it. It got exactly four reviews in the whole of England, and the only full-length one was in a motoring paper, which seized the opportunity to point out that the part of the country described in the novel would be a good place for a motoring tour. This man was not in the racket, his advertisements were not likely to become a regular source of revenue to the literary papers, and so they just ignored him.

Even reputable literary papers could not afford to disregard their advertisers altogether. It was quite usual to send a book to a reviewer with some such formula as, "Review this book if it seems any good. If not, send it back. We don't think it's worth while to print simply damning reviews."

Naturally, a person to whom the guinea or so that he gets for the review means next week's rent is not going to send the book back. He can be counted on to find something to praise, whatever his private opinion of the book may be.

In America even the pretence that hack reviewers read the books they are paid to criticise has been partially abandoned. Publishers, or some publishers, send out with review copies a short synopsis telling the reviewer what to say. Once, in the case of a novel of my own, they mis-spelt the name of one of the characters. The same mis-spelling turned up in review after review. The so-called critics had not even glanced into the book—which, nevertheless, most of them were boosting to the skies.

A phrase much used in political circles in this country is "playing into the hands of". It is a sort of charm or incantation to silence uncomfortable truths. When you are told that by saying this, that or the other you are "playing into the hands of" some sinister enemy, you know that it is your duty to shut up immediately.

For example, if you say anything damaging about British imperialism, you are playing into the hands of Dr Goebbels. If you criticise Stalin you are playing into the hands of the *Tablet* and the *Daily Telegraph*. If you criticise Chiang Kai-Shek you are playing into the hands of Wang Ching-Wei—and so on, indefinitely.

Objectively this charge is often true. It is always difficult to attack one party to a dispute without temporarily helping the other. Some of Gandhi's remarks have been very useful to the Japanese. The extreme Tories will seize on anything anti-Russian, and don't necessarily mind if it comes from Trotskyist instead of right-wing sources. The American imperialists, advancing to the attack behind a smoke-screen of novelists, are always on the look-out for any disreputable detail about the British Empire. And if you write anything truthful about the London slums, you are liable to hear it repeated on the Nazi radio a week later. But what, then, are you expected to do? Pretend there are no slums?

Everyone who has ever had anything to do with publicity or propaganda can think of occasons when he was urged to tell lies about some vitally important matter, because to tell the truth would give ammunition to the enemy. During the Spanish civil war, for instance, the dissensions on the Government side were never properly thrashed out in the left-wing press, although they involved fundamental points of principle. To discuss the struggle between the Communists and the Anarchists, you were told, would simply give the *Daily Mail* the chance to say that the Reds were all murdering one another. The only result was that the left-wing cause as a whole was weakened. The *Daily Mail* may have missed a few horror stories because people held their tongues, but some all-important lessons were not learned, and we are suffering from the fact to this day.

Tribune, 9 June 1944

45. As I Please

Several times, by word of mouth and in writing, I have been asked why I do not make use of this column for an onslaught on the Brains

Trust.[1] "For Christ's sake take a crack at Joad," one reader put it. Now, I would not deny that the Brains Trust is a very dismal thing. I am objectively anti-Brains Trust, in the sense that I always switch off any radio from which it begins to emerge. The phony pretence that the whole thing is spontaneous and uncensored, the steady avoidance of any serious topic and concentration on questions of the "Why do children's ears stick out" type, the muscular-curate heartiness of the question-master, the frequently irritating voices, and the thought of incompetent amateur broadcasters being paid ten or fifteen shillings a minute to say "Er—er—er", are very hard to bear. But I cannot feel the same indignation against this programme as many of my acquaintances seem to do, and it is worth explaining why.

By this time the big public is probably growing rather tired of the Brains Trust, but over a long period it was a genuinely popular programme. It was listened to not only in England, but in various other parts of the world, and its technique has been adopted by countless discussion groups in the Forces and Civil Defence. It was an idea that "took on", as the saying goes. And it is not difficult to see why. By the standards of newspaper and radio discussion prevailing in this country up to about 1940, the Brains Trust was a great step forward. It did at least make some show of aiming at free speech and at intellectual seriousness, and though latterly it has had to keep silent about "politics and religion", you could pick up from it interesting facts about birds' nest soup or the habits of porpoises, scraps of history and a smattering of philosophy. It was less obviously frivolous than the average radio programme. By and large it stood for enlightenment, and that was why millions of listeners welcomed it, at any rate for a year or two.

It was also why the Blimps loathed it, and still do. The Brains Trust is the object of endless attacks by right-wing intellectuals of the G. M. Young-A. P. Herbert type (also Mr Douglas Reed), and when a rival brains trust under a squad of clergymen was set up, all the Blimps went about saying how much better it was than Joad and company. These people see the Brains Trust as a symbol of freedom of thought, and they realise that, however silly its programmes may be in themselves, their tendency is to start people thinking. You or I,

[1] The Brains Trust was a popular BBC programme, led by Dr Joad, head of the Department of Psychology and Philosophy at Birkbeck College, London, with a panel of "experts" which answered questions sent in by listeners.

perhaps, would not think of the BBC as a dangerously subversive organisation, but that is how it is regarded in some quarters, and there are perpetual attempts to interfere with its programmes. To a certain extent a man may be known by his enemies, and the dislike with which all right-thinking people have regarded the Brains Trust—and also the whole idea of discussion groups, public or private—from the very start, is a sign that there must be something good in it. That is why I feel no strong impulse to take a crack at Dr Joad, who gets his fair share of cracks anyway. I say rather: just think what the Brains Trust would have been like if its permanent members had been (as they might so well have been) Lord Elton, Mr Harold Nicolson and Mr Alfred Noyes.

One cannot buy magazines from abroad nowadays, but I recommend anyone who has a friend in New York to try and cadge a copy of *Politics*, the new monthly magazine, edited by the Marxist literary critic, Dwight Macdonald. I don't agree with the policy of this paper, which is anti-war (not from a pacifist angle), but I admire its combination of highbrow political analysis with intelligent literary criticism. It is sad to have to admit it, but we have no monthly or quarterly magazines in England to come up to the American ones—for there are several others of rather the same stamp as *Politics*. We are still haunted by a half-conscious idea that to have aesthetic sensibilities you must be a Tory. But of course the present superiority of American magazines is partly due to the war. Politically, the paper in this country most nearly corresponding to *Politics* would be, I suppose, the *New Leader*. You have only to compare the get-up, the style of writing, the range of subjects and the intellectual level of the two papers, to see what it means to live in a country where there are still leisure and wood-pulp.

Tribune, 16 June 1944

46. As I Please

The week before last *Tribune* printed a centenary article on Gerard Manley Hopkins, and it was only after this that the chance of running across an April number of the American *Nation* reminded me that

1944 is also the centenary of a much better-known writer—Anatole France.

When Anatole France died, twenty years ago, his reputation suffered one of those sudden slumps to which highbrow writers who have lived long enough to become popular are especially liable. In France, according to the charming French custom, vicious personal attacks were made upon him while he lay dying and when he was freshly dead. A particularly venomous one was written by Pierre Drieu la Rochelle, afterwards to become a collaborator of the Nazis. In England, also, it was discovered that Anatole France was no good. A few years later than this a young man attached to a weekly paper (I met him afterwards in Paris and found that he could not buy a tram ticket without assistance) solemnly assured me that Anatole France "wrote very bad French." France was, it seemed, a vulgar, spurious and derivative writer whom everyone could now "see through". Round about the same time, similar discoveries were being made about Bernard Shaw and Lytton Strachey: but curiously enough all three writers have remained very readable, while most of their detractors are forgotten.

How far the revulsion against Anatole France was genuinely literary I do not know. Certainly he had been overpraised, and one must at times get tired of a writer so mannered and so indefatigably pornographic. But it is unquestionable that he was attacked partly from political motives. He may or may not have been a great writer, but he was one of the symbolic figures in the politico-literary dog-fight which has been raging for a hundred years or more. The clericals and reactionaries hated him in just the same way as they hated Zola. Anatole France had championed Dreyfus, which needed considerable courage, he had debunked Joan of Arc, he had written a comic history of France; above all, he had lost no opportunity of poking fun at the Church. He was everything that the clericals and *revanchistes*, the people who first preached that the Boche must never be allowed to recover and afterwards sucked the blacking off Hitler's boots, most detested.

I do not know whether Anatole France's most characteristic books, for instance, *La Rotisserie de la Reine Pédauque*, are worth rereading at this date. Whatever is in them is really in Voltaire. But it is a different story with the four novels dealing with Monsieur Bergeret. Besides being extremely amusing these give a most valuable picture of French society in the 'nineties and the background of the

Dreyfus case. There is also "Crainquebille", one of the best short stories I have ever read, and incidentally a devastating attack on "law and order".

But though Anatole France could speak up for the working class in a story like "Crainquebille", and though cheap editions of his works were advertised in Communist papers, one ought not really to class him as a Socialist. He was willing to work for Socialism, even to deliver lectures on it in draughty halls, and he knew that it was both necessary and inevitable, but it is doubtful whether he subjectively wanted it. The world, he once said, would get about as much relief from the coming of Socialism as a sick man gets from turning over in bed. In a crisis he was ready to identify himself with the working class, but the thought of a Utopian future depressed him, as can be seen from his book, *La Pierre Blanche*. There is an even deeper pessimism in *Les Dieux Ont Soif*, his novel about the French Revolution. Temperamentally he was not a Socialist but a Radical. At this date that is probably the rarer animal of the two, and it is his Radicalism, his passion for liberty and intellectual honesty, that give their special colour to the four novels about Monsieur Bergeret.

I have never understood why the *News Chronicle*, whose politics are certainly a very pale pink—about the colour of shrimp paste, I should say, but still pink—allows the professional Roman Catholic "Timothy Shy" (D. B. Wyndham Lewis) to do daily sabotage in his comic column. In Lord Beaverbrook's *Express* his fellow-Catholic "Beachcomber" (J. B. Morton) is, of course, more at home.

Looking back over the twenty years or so that these two have been on the job, it would be difficult to find a reactionary cause that they have not championed—Pilsudski, Mussolini, appeasement, flogging, Franco, literary censorship; between them they have found good words for everything that any decent person instinctively objects to. They have conducted endless propaganda against Socialism, the League of Nations and scientific research. They have kept up a campaign of abuse against every writer worth reading, from Joyce onwards. They were viciously anti-German until Hitler appeared, when their anti-Germanism cooled off in a remarkable manner. At this moment, needless to say, the especial target of their hatred is Beveridge.

It is a mistake to regard these two as comics pure and simple. Every word they write is intended as Catholic propaganda, and some at least of their co-religionists think very highly of their work in this direction. Their general "line" will be familar to anyone who has read Chesterton and kindred writers. Its essential note is denigration of England and of the Protestant countries generally. From the Catholic point of view this is necessary. A Catholic, at least an apologist, feels that he *must* claim superiority for the Catholic countries, and for the Middle Ages as against the present, just as a Communist feels that he must in all circumstances support the USSR. Hence the endless jibing of "Beachcomber" and "Timothy Shy" at every English institution—tea, cricket, Wordsworth, Charlie Chaplin, kindness to animals, Nelson, Cromwell and what not. Hence also "Timothy Shy's" attempts to rewrite English history and the snarls of hatred that escape him when he thinks of the defeat of the Spanish Armada. (How it sticks in his gizzard, that Spanish Armada! As though anyone cared, at this date!) Hence, even, the endless jeering at novelists, the novel being essentially a post-Reformation form of literature at which on the whole Catholics have not excelled.

From either a literary or a political point of view these two are simply the leavings on Chesterton's plate. Chesterton's vision of life was false in some ways, and he was hampered by enormous ignorance, but at least he had courage. He was ready to attack the rich and powerful, and he damaged his career by doing so. But it is the peculiarity of both "Beachcomber" and "Timothy Shy" that they take no risks with their own popularity. Their strategy is always indirect. Thus, if you want to attack the principle of freedom of speech, do it by sneering at the Brains Trust, as if it were a typical example. Dr Joad won't retaliate! Even their deepest convictions go into cold storage when they become dangerous. Earlier in the war, when it was safe to do so, "Beachcomber" wrote viciously anti-Russian pamphlets, but no anti-Russian remarks appear in his column these days. They will again, however, if popular pro-Russian feeling dies down. I shall be interested to see whether either "Beachcomber" or "Timothy Shy" reacts to these remarks of mine. If so, it will be the first recorded instance of either of them attacking anyone likely to hit back.[1]

Tribune, 23 June 1944

---

[1] They never did.

47. Letter to T. S. Eliot

10a Mortimer Crescent
NW6
(Or "Tribune" CEN 2572)
28 June 1944

Dear Eliot,
This MS[1] has been blitzed which accounts for my delay in delivering it and its slightly crumpled condition, but it is not damaged in any way.

I wonder if you could be kind enough to let me have Messrs Fabers' decision fairly soon. If they are interested in seeing more of my work, I could let you have the facts abt my existing contract with Gollancz, which is not an onerous one nor likely to last long.

If you read this MS yourself you will see its meaning which is not an acceptable one at this moment, but I could not agree to make any alterations except a small one at the end which I intended making anyway. Cape[2] or the MOI,[3] I am not certain which from the wording of his letter,[4] made the imbecile suggestion that some other animal than pigs might be made to represent the Bolsheviks. I could not of course make any change of that description.

Yours sincerely
Geo. Orwell

Could you have lunch with me one of the days when you are in town?

48. As I Please

I notice that apart from the widespread complaint that the German pilotless planes "seem so unnatural" (a bomb dropped by a live airman is quite natural, apparently), some journalists are denouncing them as barbarous, inhumane, and "an indiscriminate attack on civilians".

After what we have been doing to the Germans over the past two years, this seems a bit thick, but it is the normal human response to

[1] Of *Animal Farm*.
[2] Jonathan Cape Ltd, Publishers.
[3] Ministry of Information.
[4] Presumably from Leonard Moore of Christy & Moore Ltd, literary agents for Orwell until his death.

every new weapon. Poison gas, the machine-gun, the submarine, gunpowder, and even the crossbow were similarly denounced in their day. Every weapon seems unfair until you have adopted it yourself. But I would not deny that the pilotless plane, flying bomb, or whatever its correct name may be, is an exceptionally unpleasant thing, because, unlike most other projectiles, it gives you time to think. What is your first reaction when you hear that droning, zooming noise? Inevitably, it is a hope that the noise *won't stop*. You want to hear the bomb pass safely overhead and die away into the distance before the engine cuts out. In other words, you are hoping that it will fall on somebody else. So also when you dodge a shell or an ordinary bomb—but in that case you have only about five seconds to take cover and no time to speculate on the bottomless selfishness of the human being.

It cannot be altogether an accident that nationalists of the more extreme and romantic kind tend not to belong to the nation that they idealise. Leaders who base their appeal on *la patrie*, or "the fatherland", are sometimes outright foreigners, or else come from the border countries of great empires. Obvious examples are Hitler, an Austrian, and Napoleon, a Corsican, but there are many others. The man who may be said to have been the founder of British jingoism was Disraeli, a Spanish Jew, and it was Lord Beaverbrook, a Canadian, who tried to induce the unwilling English to describe themselves as Britons. The British Empire was largely built up by Irishmen and Scotsmen, and our most obstinate nationalists and imperialists have frequently been Ulstermen. Even Churchill, the leading exponent of romantic patriotism in our own day, is half an American. But not merely the men of action, but even the theorists of nationalism are frequently foreigners. Pan-Germanism, for instance, from which the Nazis later took many of their ideas, was largely the product of men who were not Germans: for instance, Houston Chamberlain, an Englishman, and Gobineau, a Frenchman. Rudyard Kipling was an Englishman, but of a rather doubtful kind. He came from an unusual Anglo-Indian background (his father was curator of the Bombay Museum), he had spent his early childhood in India, and he was of small stature and very dark complexion which caused him to be wrongly suspected of having Asiatic blood. I have always held that if we ever have a Hitler in this country he will be, perhaps, an Ulsterman, a South African, a Maltese, a

Eurasian, or perhaps an American—but, at any rate, not an English-man.

Six million books, it is said, perished in the blitz of 1940, including a thousand irreplaceable titles. Most of them were probably no loss, but it is dismaying to find how many standard works are now com-pletely out of print. Paper is forthcoming for the most ghastly tripe, as you can see by glancing into any bookshop window, while all the reprint editions, such as the Everyman Library, have huge gaps in their lists. Even so well-known a work of reference as Web-ster's dictionary is no longer obtainable unless you run across a copy second-hand. About a year ago I had to do a broadcast on Jack London. When I started to collect the material I found that those of his books that I most wanted had vanished so completely that even the London Library could not produce them. To get hold of them I should have had to go to the British Museum reading-room, which in these days is not at all easy of access. And this seems to me a disaster, for Jack London is one of those border-line writers whose works might be forgotten altogether unless somebody takes the trouble to revive them. Even *The Iron Heel* was distinctly a rarity for some years, and was only reprinted because Hitler's rise to power made it topical. . . .

Tribune, 30 June 1944

49. As I Please

When the Caliph Omar destroyed the libraries of Alexandria he is supposed to have kept the public baths warm for eighteen days with burning manuscripts, and great numbers of tragedies by Euripides and others are said to have perished, quite irrecoverably. I remember that when I read about this as a boy it simply filled me with en-thusiastic approval. It was so many less words to look up in the dictionary—that was how I saw it. For, though I am only forty-one, I am old enough to have been educated at a time when Latin and Greek were only escapable with great difficulty, while "English" was hardly regarded as a school subject at all.

Classical education is going down the drain at last, but even now there must be far more adults who have been flogged through the entire extant works of Aeschylus, Sophocles, Euripides, Aristophanes, Vergil, Horace and various other Latin and Greek authors than have read the English masterpieces of the eighteenth century. People pay lip service to Fielding and the rest of them, of course, but they don't read them, as you can discover by making a few enquiries among your friends. How many people have ever read *Tom Jones*, for instance? Not so many have even read the later books of *Gulliver's Travels*. *Robinson Crusoe* has a sort of popularity in nursery versions, but the book as a whole is so little known that few people are even aware that the second part (the journey through Tartary) exists. Smollett, I imagine, is the least read of all. The central plot of Shaw's play, *Pygmalion*, is lifted out of *Peregrine Pickle*, and I believe that no one has ever pointed this out in print, which suggests that few people can have read the book. But what is strangest of all is that Smollett, so far as I know, has never been boosted by the Scottish Nationalists, who are so careful to claim Byron for their own. Yet Smollett, besides being one of the best novelists the English-speaking races have produced, *was* a Scotsman, and proclaimed it openly at a time when being so was anything but helpful to one's career.

Life in the civilised world.
(The family are at tea.)
Zoom-zoom-zoom!
"Is there an alert on?"
"No, it's all clear."
"I thought there was an alert on."
Zoom-zoom-zoom!
"There's another of those things coming!"
"It's all right, it's miles away."
Zoom-zoom-ZOOM!
"Look out, here it comes! Under the table, quick!"
Zoom-zoom-zoom!
"It's all right, it's getting fainter."
Zoom-zoom-ZOOM!
"It's coming back!"
"They seem to kind of circle round and come back again. They've got something on their tails that makes them do it. Like a torpedo."
ZOOM-ZOOM-ZOOM!
"Christ! It's bang overhead!"

Dead silence.

"Now get *right* underneath. Keep your head well down. What a mercy baby isn't here!"

"Look at the cat! He's frightened too."

"Of course animals *know*. They can feel the vibrations."

BOOM!

"It's all right, I told you it was miles away."

(Tea continues.)

I see that Lord Winterton, writing in the *Evening Standard*, speaks of the "remarkable reticence (by no means entirely imposed by rule or regulation) which Parliament and press alike have displayed in this war to avoid endangering national security" and adds that it has "earned the admiration of the civilised world".

It is not only in war-time that the British press observes this voluntary reticence. One of the most extraordinary things about England is that there is almost no official censorship, and yet nothing that is actually offensive to the governing class gets into print, at least in any place where large numbers of people are likely to read it. If it is "not done" to mention something or other, it just doesn't get mentioned. The position is summed up in the lines by (I think) Hilaire Belloc[1]:

> You cannot hope to bribe or twist
> Thank God! the British journalist.
> But, seeing what the man will do
> Unbribed, there's no occasion to.

No bribes, no threats, no penalties—just a nod and a wink and the thing is done. A well-known example was the business of the Abdication. Weeks before the scandal officially broke, tens or hundreds of thousands of people had heard all about Mrs Simpson, and yet not a word got into the press, not even into the *Daily Worker*, although the American and European papers were having the time of their lives with the story. Yet I believe there was no definite official ban: just an official "request" and a general agreement that to break the news prematurely "would not do". And I can think of other instances of good news stories failing to see the light although there would have been no penalty for printing them.

Nowadays this kind of veiled censorship even extends to books. The MOI does not, of course, dictate a party line or issue an *index*

[1] It is in fact from *The Uncelestial City* by Humbert Wolfe.

expurgatorius. It merely "advises". Publishers take manuscripts to the MOI, and the MOI "suggests" that this or that is undesirable, or premature, or "would serve no good purpose". And though there is no definite prohibition, no clear statement that this or that must not be printed, official policy is never flouted. Circus dogs jump when the trainer cracks his whip, but the really well-trained dog is the one that turns his somersault when there is no whip. And that is the state we have reached in this country, thanks to three hundred years of living together without a civil war.

Here is a little problem sometimes used as an intelligence test.

A man walked four miles due south from his house and shot a bear. He then walked two miles due west, then walked another four miles due north and was back at his home again. What was the colour of the bear?

The interesting point is that—so far as my own observations go—men usually see the answer to this problem and women do not.

Tribune, 7 July 1944

50. As I Please

I have received a number of letters, some of them quite violent ones, attacking me for my remarks on Miss Vera Brittain's anti-bombing pamphlet. There are two points that seem to need further comment.

First of all there is the charge, which is becoming quite a common one, that "we started it", i.e. that Britain was the first country to practise systematic bombing of civilians. How anyone can make this claim, with the history of the past dozen years in mind, is almost beyond me. The first act in the present war—some hours, if I remember rightly, before any declaration of war passed—was the German bombing of Warsaw. The Germans bombed and shelled the city so intensively that, according to the Poles, at one time 700 fires were raging simultaneously. They made a film of the destruction of Warsaw, which they entitled "Baptism of Fire" and sent all round the world with the object of terrorising neutrals.

Several years earlier than this the Condor Legion, sent to Spain by Hitler, had bombed one Spanish city after another. The "silent raids" on Barcelona in 1938 killed several thousand people in a couple of days. Earlier than this the Italians had bombed entirely defenceless Abyssinians and boasted of their exploits as something screamingly funny. Bruno Mussolini wrote newspaper articles in which he described bombed Abyssinians "bursting open like a rose", which, he said, was "most amusing". And the Japanese ever since 1931, and intensively since 1937, have been bombing crowded Chinese cities where there are not even any ARP arrangements, let alone any AA guns or fighter aircraft.

I am not arguing that two blacks make a white, nor that Britain's record is a particularly good one. In a number of "little wars" from about 1920 onwards the RAF has dropped its bombs on Afghans, Indians and Arabs who had little or no power of hitting back. But it is simply untruthful to say that large-scale bombing of crowded town areas, with the object of causing panic, is a British invention. It was the Fascist states who started this practice, and so long as the air war went in their favour they avowed their aims quite clearly.

The other thing that needs dealing with is the parrot cry "killing women and children". I pointed out before, but evidently it needs repeating, that it is probably somewhat better to kill a cross-section of the population than to kill only the young men. If the figures published by the Germans are true, and we have really killed 1,200,000 civilians in our raids, that loss of life has probably harmed the German race somewhat less than a corresponding loss on the Russian front or in Africa and Italy.

Any nation at war will do its best to protect its children, and the number of children killed in raids probably does not correspond to their percentage of the general population. Women cannot be protected to the same extent, but the outcry against killing women, if you accept killing at all, is sheer sentimentality. Why is it worse to kill a woman than a man? The argument usually advanced is that in killing women you are killing the breeders, whereas men can be more easily spared. But this is a fallacy based on the notion that human beings can be bred like animals. The idea behind it is that since one man is capable of fertilising a very large number of women, just as a prize ram fertilises thousands of ewes, the loss of male lives is comparatively unimportant. Human beings, however, are not cattle. When the slaughter caused by a war leaves a surplus of women, the enormous majority of those women bear no children. Male lives are very nearly as important, biologically, as female ones.

In the last war the British Empire lost nearly a million men killed, of whom about three-quarters came from these islands. Most of them will have been under thirty. If all those young men had had only one child each we should now have an extra 750,000 people round about the age of twenty. France, which lost much more heavily, never recovered from the slaughter of the last war, and it is doubtful whether Britain has fully recovered, either. We can't yet calculate the casualties of the present war, but the last one killed between ten and twenty million young men. Had it been conducted, as the next one will perhaps be, with flying bombs, rockets and other long-range weapons which kill old and young, healthy and unhealthy, male and female impartially, it would probably have damaged European civilisation somewhat less than it did.

Contrary to what some of my correspondents seem to think, I have no enthusiasm for air raids, either ours or the enemy's. Like a lot of other people in this country, I am growing definitely tired of bombs. But I do object to the hypocrisy of accepting force as an instrument while squealing against this or that individual weapon, or of denouncing war while wanting to preserve the kind of society that makes war inevitable.

I note in my diary for 1940 an expectation that commercial advertisements will have disappeared from the walls within a year. This seemed likely enough at the time, and a year or even two years later the disappearance seemed to be actually happening, though more slowly than I had expected. Advertisements were shrinking both in numbers and size, and the announcements of the various Ministries were more and more taking their place both on the walls and in the newspapers. Judging from this symptom alone, one would have said that commercialism was definitely on the downgrade.

In the last two years, however, the commercial ad, in all its silliness and snobbishness, has made a steady come-back. In recent years I consider that the most offensive of all British advertisements are the ones for Rose's Lime Juice, with their "young squire" motif and their P. G. Wodehouse dialogue.

"I fear you do not see me at my best this morning, Jenkins. There were jollifications last night. Your young master looked upon the wine when it was red and also upon the whisky when it was yellow. To use the vulgar phrase, I have a thick head. What do you think the doctor would prescribe, Jenkins?"

"If I might make so bold, sir, a glass of soda water with a

dash of Rose's Lime Juice would probably have the desired effect."

"Go to it, Jenkins! You were always my guide, philosopher and friend," etc etc etc.

When you reflect that this advertisement appears, for instance, in every theatre programme, so that every theatre-goer is at any rate assumed to have a secret fantasy life in which he thinks of himself as a young man of fashion with faithful old retainers, the prospect of any drastic social change recedes perceptibly.

There are also the hair-tonic adverts which tell you how Daphne got promotion in the WAAFS[1] thanks to the neatness and glossiness of her hair. But these are misleading as well as whorish, for I seldom or never pass a group of officers in the WAAFS, ATS or WRENS[2] without having cause to reflect that, at any rate, promotion in the women's services has nothing to do with looks.

Tribune, 14 July 1944

51. Letter to John Middleton Murry

The Tribune
222 Strand
London WC2
14 July 1944

Dear Murry,[3]
Thanks for your letter.[4] I have not the text by me, but you wrote in an article in the *Adelphi* something that ran more or less as follows:

"We are in the habit of describing the war between Japan and China as though it were a war in the European sense. But it is nothing of the kind, because the average Chinese expects to be conquered.

[1] Women's Auxiliary Air Force.

[2] Women's Royal Naval Service.

[3] John Middleton Murry (1889–1957), prolific writer, critic and polemicist; founded the *Adelphi* in 1923 and controlled it for the next twenty-five years. Successively a fervent disciple of D. H. Lawrence, unorthodox Marxist, unorthodox Christian, pacifist and "back to the land" farmer. From July 1940 to April 1946 he was editor of *Peace News*.

[4] Murry's letter to Orwell does not survive nor can the correspondent referred to be identified, but this letter is included because it is the first of a sequence of letters to Murry about pacifism and the Soviet Union.

That is what the history of thousands of years has taught him to expect. China will absorb Japan, and Japan will energise China. And so also with India."

If this is not praise and encouragement of the Japanese invasion of China, and an invitation to the Japanese to go on and invade India, I don't know what it is. It takes no account of what has been happening in China since 1912 and uses exactly the same argument ("these people are used to being conquered") that was always brought forward to justify our own rule in India. In any case its moral is, "don't help the Chinese."

As to the general charge of "praising violence" which your correspondent refers to. Many remarks you have made in recent years seem to me to imply that you don't object to violence if it is violent enough. And you certainly seem or seemed to me to prefer the Nazis to ourselves, at least so long as they appeared to be winning.

If you'll send the book[1] along I'll naturally be glad to give it a notice, but I *might* have to turn it over to someone else, though I'll do it myself if possible. I am smothered under work, and also I've been bombed out and we have a very young baby,[2] all of which adds to one's work.

Yours,
Geo. Orwell

52. Letter to Rayner Heppenstall

The Tribune
222 Strand
London, WC2
17 July 1944

Dear Rayner,[3]

Thanks for the alterations in the review.[4] I finally sent the Scottish books to someone else (they didn't look much good) but am sending

---

[1] Probably Murry's *Adam and Eve*.

[2] In June 1944 Orwell and his wife had adopted a three-week-old boy who was christened Richard Horatio Blair. (Both Richard and Horatio were Blair family names, but the Richard also referred to Richard Rees.)

[3] Rayner Heppenstall (1911–), novelist, poet and critic, whose works include *The Blaze of Noon* and *Four Absentees*, met Orwell in the spring of 1935 through Richard Rees and had remained friends with him.

[4] Of Jacques Barzun's *Romanticism and the Modern Ego, Tribune,* 17 October 1944.

you something which *may* be interesting, though I haven't examined it. It is a printing of the first draft of *Portrait of the Artist* which I suppose someone rescued from the w.p.b.

I thought you would have seen the answers to your anti-Scotland review[1], but they were so damn silly they weren't worth answering any way. The only bright remark was "I spit in Mr Heppenstall's eye," which I suppose the writer hasn't actually done, up to date.

Eliot has been working for the British Council for a couple of years. He has also written at least once for *British Ally*, the British propaganda paper published in Moscow. To judge by his private conversation he has definitely changed some of his political views though he hasn't made any public pronouncement yet. Roy Campbell (I don't know him but I have mutual friends) stayed on in Spain after Franco won and was so disgusted by the resulting régime that he has become definitely anti-Fascist. He was acting as a paid fire-watcher for some time, then he joined the army where I think he still is. Arthur Bryant is one of the big guns of the Conservative intelligentsia. He was the one who said during the Spanish war that "the sawing off of a Conservative tradesman's legs is a commonplace in Republican Spain", a phrase which stuck in my memory.

I'd like very much to get down and see you, but it's difficult to get out of town. What with my work, our flat being blitzed, and a very young baby, life is pretty full now. Look me up (*Tribune* is the best address) any time you're in town.

Yours
Eric

53. Letter to Leonard Moore

Care of "Tribune"
222 Strand WC2
18 July 1944

Dear Mr Moore,
Thanks for your letter. . . .

Meanwhile could you send me the copy of the MS that you have. Faber's replied in much the same sense as Cape's.[2] Warburg again

[1] Of *Poetry Scotland No. 1* edited by Maurice Lindsay, *Tribune*, 7 April 1944.

[2] Jonathan Cape and Faber & Faber were among the publishers who had rejected *Animal Farm* on the grounds that it was an inopportune moment politically to publish such a work. For the text of T. S. Eliot's letter of rejection see *The Times*, 6 January 1969, p. 9.

says he wants to see it & would publish it if he can see his way to getting the paper, but that is a big "if". If that falls through I am not going to tout it round further publishers, which wastes time & may lead to nothing, but shall publish it myself as a pamphlet at 2/–. I have already half-arranged to do so & have got the necessary financial backing. With the demand for books there is now, and the strings I can pull in one or two papers, I have no doubt we should get our money back, though probably not make much profit. You understand that it is important to get this book into print, & this year if possible.

I think I told you I have been bombed out, so *Tribune* is the safest address.

Yours sincerely
E. A. Blair

54. As I Please

I have just found my copy of Samuel Butler's *Note-Books*, the full edition of the first series, published by Jonathan Cape in 1921. It is twenty years old and none the better for having gone through several rainy seasons in Burma, but at any rate it exists, which is all to the good, for this is another of those well-known books which have now ceased to be procurable. Cape's later produced an abridged version in the Traveller's Library, but it is an unsatisfactory abridgement, and the second series which was published about 1934 does not contain much that is of value. It is in the first series that you will find the story of Butler's interview with a Turkish official at the Dardanelles, the description of his method of buying new-laid eggs and his endeavours to photograph a seasick bishop, and other similar trifles which in a way are worth more than his major works.

Butler's main ideas now seem either to be unimportant, or to suffer from wrong emphasis. Biologists apart, who now cares whether the Darwinian theory of evolution, or the Lamarckian version which Butler supported, is the correct one? The whole question of evolution seems less momentous than it did, because, unlike the Victorians, we do not feel that to be descended from animals is degrading to human dignity. On the other hand, Butler often makes a mere joke out of something that now seems to us vitally important. For example:

> The principal varieties and sub-varieties of the human race are not now to be looked for among the Negroes, the Circassians, the Malays or the American aborigines, but among the rich and the poor. The difference in physical organisation between these two species of man is far greater than that between the so-called types of humanity. The rich man can go from (New Zealand) to England whenever he feels inclined. The legs of the other are by an invisible fatality prevented from carrying him beyond certain narrow limits. Neither rich nor poor can yet see the philosophy of the thing, or admit that he who can tack a portion of one of the P & O boats on to his identity is a much more highly organised being than he who cannot.

There are innumerable similar passages in Butler's work. You could easily interpret them in a Marxist sense, but the point is that Butler himself does not do so. Finally his outlook is that of a Conservative, in spite of his successful assaults on Christian belief and the institution of the family. Poverty is degrading: therefore, take care not to be poor—that is his reaction. Hence the improbable and unsatisfying ending of *The Way of All Flesh*, which contrasts so strangely with the realism of the earlier parts.

Yet Butler's books have worn well, far better than those of more earnest contemporaries like Meredith and Carlyle, partly because he never lost the power to use his eyes and to be pleased by small things, partly because in the narrow technical sense he wrote so well. When one compares Butler's prose with the contortions of Meredith or the affectations of Stevenson, one sees what a tremendous advantage is gained simply by not trying to be clever. Butler's own ideas on the subject are worth quoting:

> I never knew a writer yet who took the smallest pains with his style and was at the same time readable. Plato's having had seventy shies at one sentence is quite enough to explain to me why I dislike him. A man may, and ought to, take a great deal of pains to write clearly, tersely and euphoniously: he will write many a sentence three or four times over—to do much more than this is worse than not rewriting at all: he will be at great pains to see that he does not repeat himself, to arrange his matter in

the way that shall best enable the reader to master it, to cut out superfluous words and, even more, to eschew irrelevant matter: but in each case he will be thinking not of his own style but of his reader's convenience. . . . I should like to put it on record that I never took the smallest pains with my style, have never thought about it, and do not know or want to know whether it is a style at all or whether it is not, as I believe and hope, just common, simple straightforwardness. I cannot conceive how any man can take thought for his style without loss to himself and his readers.

Butler adds characteristically, however, that he has made considerable efforts to improve his handwriting.

An argument that Socialists ought to be prepared to meet, since it is brought up constantly both by Christian apologists and by neo-pessimists such as James Burnham, is the alleged immutability of "human nature". Socialists are accused—I think without justification —of assuming that Man is perfectible, and it is then pointed out that human history is in fact one long tale of greed, robbery and oppression. Man, it is said, will always try to get the better of his neighbour, he will always hog as much property as possible for himself and his family. Man is of his nature sinful, and cannot be made virtuous by Act of Parliament. Therefore, though economic exploitation can be controlled to some extent, the classless society is for ever impossible.

The proper answer, it seems to me, is that this argument belongs to the Stone Age. It presupposes that material goods will always be desperately scarce. The power hunger of human beings does indeed present a serious problem, but there is no reason for thinking that the greed for mere wealth is a permanent human characteristic. We are selfish in economic matters because we all live in terror of poverty. But when a commodity is not scarce, no one tries to grab more than his fair share of it. No one tries to make a corner in air, for instance. The millionaire as well as the beggar is content with just so much air as he can breathe. Or, again, water. In this country we are not troubled by lack of water. If anything we have too much of it, especially on Bank Holidays. As a result water hardly enters into our consciousness. Yet in dried-up countries like North Africa, what jealousies, what hatreds, what appalling crimes the lack of water can cause! So also with any other kind of goods. If they were made plentiful, as they so easily might be, there is no reason to think that the supposed acquisitive instincts of the human being could not be bred out in a couple of generations. And after all, if human nature never changes, why is it that we not only don't practise cannibalism any longer, but don't even want to?

Another brain-tickler.

A businessman was in the habit of going home by a suburban train which left London at seven-thirty. One evening the night-watchman, who had just come on duty, stopped him and said:

"Excuse me, sir, but I'd advise you not to go by your usual train tonight. I dreamed last night that the train was smashed up and half the people in it were killed. Maybe you'll think I'm superstitious, but it was all so vivid that I can't help thinking it was meant as a warning."

The businessman was sufficiently impressed to wait and take a later train. When he opened the newspaper the next morning he saw that, sure enough, the train *had* been wrecked and many people killed. That evening he sent for the night-watchman and said to him:

"I want to thank you for your warning yesterday. I consider that you saved my life, and in return I should like to make you a present of thirty pounds. In addition, I have to inform you that you are sacked. Take a week's notice from today."

This was an ungrateful act, but the businessman was strictly within his rights. Why?

Tribune, 21 July 1944

55. Letter to John Middleton Murry

The Tribune
222 Strand
London, WC2
21 July 1944

Dear Murry,
I am sorry I did not return your correspondent's letter, which is herewith.

I haven't the reference (all my papers are in store), but you will find it if you look through the files of the *Adelphi,* and I do not think it will be found to differ much from what I quoted. Nor can I agree that such a statement is not pro-Japanese both objectively and, to all appearances, subjectively. Ditto with many other statements of yours, e.g. your remarks about Hess [1] soon after his arrival. You are wrong, however, in thinking that I have made use of you as a scapegoat. I think I have only mentioned you in print twice, once in this article in *Horizon,* [2] the other time in the *Adelphi* [3] in the review I did for you of Alex Comfort's novel. You are wrong also in thinking that I dislike wholehearted pacifism, though I do think it mistaken. What I object to is the circumspect kind of pacifism which denounces one kind of violence while endorsing or avoiding mention of another. Your own failure to make a clear statement about the Russo-German war is the kind of thing I mean. I can respect anyone who is willing to face unpopularity, however much I may disagree with him.

Yours sincerely
Geo. Orwell

56. London Letter to *Partisan Review*

[24 July 1944]

Dear Editors,
There is very little political news. All the currents seem to be moving in the same directions as when I wrote to you last—public opinion moving leftward, the Right nevertheless consolidating its power owing to the weakness of the Labour leaders, and the minor left-wing parties quarrelling among themselves. It seems to be taken for granted that there will be a General Election before the end of the year, and most people assume that the Labour Party is going to fight the election independently, which I cannot believe: at least I cannot believe that they will make a serious effort to win it. The Conservatives, though continuing to disillusion the public by their

---

[1] Rudolf Hess (1894–), Nazi official, second to Goering as Hitler's successor, flew to Scotland on 10 May 1941, allegedly bearing peace proposals. He was interned in Britain and sentenced to life imprisonment by the international war crimes tribunal at Nuremberg in 1946.

[2] Orwell's review of Lionel Fielden's *Beggar My Neighbour.* See II, 51.

[3] Orwell's review of Alex Comfort's *No Such Liberty.* See II, 28.

every act, now feel strong enough to disclaim responsibility for their past mistakes. Many books and articles partially rehabilitating Chamberlain are being published, and a section of the Conservative Party, probably financed by Beaverbrook, has started a new paper which appears three times a week (in theory one is not allowed to start new periodicals but there are ways of evading this) and is taking a militantly anti-Socialist line.

There is violent competition by all parties to cash in on the popularity of the USSR. The pinks deprecate any criticism of the USSR on the ground that it "plays into the hands of the Tories", but on the other hand the Tories seem to be the most pro-Russian of the lot. From the point of view of the MOI and the BBC the only two people who are completely sacrosanct are Stalin and Franco. I imagine that the Russians themselves regard the Tories as their real friends in this country. It may possibly be of some significance that the Soviet press recently made a sharp attack on a group of very russophile left-wing MPs who had made the suggestion that the flying bombs were manufactured in Spain. These MPs included D. N. Pritt, the alleged "underground" Communist who has been perhaps the most effective pro-Soviet publicist in this country.

Common Wealth continues to score impressive votes at by-elections but is not gaining much in membership and seems to be less and less definite in its policy. It is not even certain whether it intends, as previously advertised, to fight 150 seats at the forthcoming General Election, or simply to make local arrangements with acceptable Labour candidates. People inside the party complain that it is infested by middling businessmen of the "managerial" type who are resigned to a centralised economy and foresee good pickings in it for themselves. The Communists, who for a short period were opposing the Government and even collaborated with Common Wealth at one or two elections, seem to be swinging to the support of the Conservatives. There have been some faint indications that attempts may be made to revive the almost extinct Liberal Party. Otherwise there are no political developments, i.e. in the narrower sense, that I can discern.

Domestic issues continue to occupy most people's attention. India, for instance, has almost dropped out of the news. The chief subjects of discussion are demobilisation, rehousing and, for those who are a little longer-sighted, the birthrate. The housing shortage, already serious, is going to be appalling as soon as the troops come home,

and the Government proposes to cope with it by means of prefabricated steel houses which are reasonably convenient but so small
as only to have room for one-child families. In theory these temporary shacks are to be scrapped after three years, but everyone
assumes that in practice the new houses will not be forthcoming.
It is widely recognised that our birthrate cannot be expected to rise
significantly unless people have houses to live in and that rehousing
on a big scale is impossible while private property rights are respected. It would be impossible to rebuild London, for instance,
without buying out tens of thousands of ground-landlords at fantastic prices. The Conservatives, who are on the whole more concerned about the birthrate situation than the Left, are at the same
time fighting the landlord's battles for him, and try to solve the
problem by preaching to the working class the duty of self-sacrifice
and the wickedness of birth control. The Left tends to evade this
problem, partly because small families are still vaguely associated
with enlightenment, partly because of a certain unwillingness to
recognise, or at any rate to say publicly, that a sudden rise in the
birthrate (it has got to rise drastically within ten or twenty years if
our population is to be kept up) would mean a drop in the standard
of living. There is a vague belief that "Socialism" would somehow
make people philoprogenitive again, and much praise of the high
Russian birthrate, without, however, any serious examination of the
Russian vital statistics. This is only one of the basic questions that
the Left habitually ignores, others being the relation between ourselves and the coloured peoples of the Empire, and the dependence
of British prosperity on trade and foreign investments. The Tories
are far more willing to admit that these problems exist, though
unable to produce any real solution. Very nearly all English left-
wingers, from Labourites to Anarchists, have the outlook of people
who neither want nor expect power. The Tories are not only more
courageous, but they don't make extravagant promises and have no
scruples about breaking the promises they do make.

Other highly unpopular subjects are post-war mobility of labour,
post-war continuation of food rationing, etc and the war against
Japan. People will, I have no doubt, be ready to go on fighting until
Japan is beaten, but their capacity for simply *forgetting* these years
of warfare that lie ahead is surprising. In conversation, "When the
war stops" invariably means when Germany packs up. The last

Mass Observation report shows a considerable recrudescence of 1918 habits of thought. Everyone expects not only that there will be a ghastly muddle over demobilisation, but that mass unemployment will promptly return. No one wants to remember that we shall have to keep living for years on a war-time basis and that the switchover to peace-time production and the recapture of lost markets may entail as great an effort as the war itself. Everyone wants, above all things, a rest. I overhear very little discussion of the wider issues of the war, and I can't discern much popular interest in the kind of peace we should impose on Germany. The newspapers of the Right and Left are outdoing one another in demanding a vindictive peace. Vansittart is now a back number; indeed the more extreme of his one-time followers have brought out a pamphlet denouncing him as pro-German.

The Communists are using the slogan "Make Germany Pay" (the diehard Tory slogan of 1918) and branding as pro-Nazi anyone who says either that we should make a generous peace or that publication of reasonable peace terms would hasten the German collapse. The peace terms that they and other russophiles advocate are indeed simply a worse version of the Versailles Treaty against which they yapped for twenty years. Thus the dog returns to his vomit, or more exactly to somebody else's vomit. But once again, I can't see that ordinary people want anything of the kind, and if past wars are any guide the troops will all come home pro-German. The implications of the fact that the common people are russophile but don't want the sort of peace that the Russians are demanding haven't yet sunk in, and left-wing journalists avoid discussing them. The Soviet Government now makes direct efforts to interfere with the British press. I suppose that from sheer weariness and the instinct to support Russia at all costs the man in the street might be brought to approve of an unjust peace, but there would be a rapid pro-German reaction, as last time.

There are a few social developments, which again take the same directions as I reported before. Evening dress (i.e. for men) is gradually reappearing. The distinction between first class and third class on the railways is being enforced again. Two years ago it had practically lapsed. Commercial advertisements, which I told you a year or so back were rapidly disappearing, are definitely on the up-grade again, and make use of the snobbery motif more boldly. The Home Guard still exists in as great numbers as before, but is employed largely on the AA guns and seems now to have no political colour of one kind or the other. It now consists to a great extent of youths who are conscripted at 16 or 17. For boys younger than this there are various cadet corps and the Air Training Corps, and even for young girls a uniformed formation named vaguely the Girls' Training Corps. All this is something quite new in English life, pre-military training having been practically confined to the middle and upper classes before the war. Everything grows shabbier and more rickety. Sixteen people in a railway carriage designed for ten is quite common. The countryside has quite changed its face, the once green meadows having changed into cornfields, and in the remotest places one cannot get away from the roar of aeroplanes, which has become the normal background noise, drowning the larks.

There are very few literary developments to report. After nine months as a literary editor I am startled and frightened by the lack of talent and vitality. The crowd who are grouped about *New Road*, *Now* and *Poetry London*—and I suppose these are "the movement" in so far as there is one—give me the impression of fleas hopping among the ruins of a civilisation. There are endless anthologies and other scissors-and-paste books, and an enormous output of unreadable pamphlets from every kind of political party and religious body, in spite of the paper shortage. On the other hand innumerable standard books are out of print and unobtainable. Attempts are constantly being made in short-lived reviews to revivify the various regional literatures, Scottish, Welsh, Irish and Northern Irish. These movements always have a strong nationalist and separatist tinge, sometimes bitterly anti-English, and will print anything however bad which is politically OK. But the various nationalisms are so to speak interchangeable. The leading anglophobes all contribute to one another's papers, and the London pacifist intellectuals pop up in all of them. There are also signs, which I haven't been able to investigate yet, that Australian literature is at last getting on its own feet.

No more news to speak of. This has been a foul summer, everything happening at the wrong time and hardly any fruit. I have been tied so tight to this beastly town that for the first time in my life I have not heard a cuckoo this year. After the wail of the siren comes the zoom-zoom-zoom of the bomb, and as it draws nearer you get up from your table and squeeze yourself into some corner that flying glass is not likely to reach. Then BOOM! the windows rattle in their sockets, and you go back to work. There are disgusting scenes in the Tube stations at night, sordid piles of bedding cluttering up the passage-ways and hordes of dirty-faced children playing round the platforms at all hours. Two nights ago, about midnight, I came on a little girl of five "minding" her younger sister, aged about two. The tiny child had got hold of a scrubbing brush with which she was scrubbing the filthy stones of the platform, and then sucking the bristles. I took it away from her and told the elder girl not to let her have it. But I had to catch my train, and no doubt the poor little brat would again be eating filth in another couple of minutes. This kind of thing is happening everywhere. However, the disorganisation and consequent neglect of children hasn't been serious compared with 1940.

George Orwell

Partisan Review, Fall 1944

57. As I Please

Some years ago, in the course of an article about boys' weekly papers,[1] I made some passing remarks about women's papers—I mean the twopenny ones of the type of *Peg's Paper*, often called "love books". This brought me, among much other correspondence, a long letter from a woman who had contributed to and worked for the *Lucky Star*, the *Golden Star*, *Peg's Paper*, *Secrets*, the *Oracle*, and a number of kindred papers. Her main point was that I had been wrong in saying that these papers aim at creating wealth fantasy. Their stories are "in no sense Cinderella stories" and do not exploit the "she married her boss" motif. My correspondent adds:

> Unemployment *is* mentioned—quite frequently. . . . The dole and the trade union are certainly never mentioned. The latter may be influenced by the fact that the largest publishers of these women's magazines are a non-union house. One is never allowed to criticise the system, or to show up the class struggle for what it really is, and the word Socialist is *never* mentioned—all this is perfectly true. But it might be interesting to add that class feeling is not altogether absent. The rich are often shown as

[1] See I, 163.

mean, and as cruel and crooked money-makers. The rich and idle beau is nearly always planning marriage without a ring, and the lass is rescued by her strong, hard-working garage hand. Men with cars are generally "bad" and men in well-cut expensive suits are nearly always crooks. The ideal of most of these stories is *not* an income worthy of a bank manager's wife, but a life that is "good". A life with an upright, kind husband, however poor, with babies and a "little cottage". The stories are conditioned to show that the meagre life is not so bad really, as you are at least honest and happy, and that riches bring trouble and false friends. The poor are given moral values to aspire to as something within their reach.

There are many comments I could make here, but I choose to take up the point of the moral superiority of the poor being combined with the non-mention of trade unions and Socialism. There is no doubt that this is deliberate policy. In one woman's paper I actually read a story dealing with a strike in a coal mine, and even in that connection trade unionism was not mentioned. When the USSR entered the war one of these papers promptly cashed in with a serial entitled "Her Soviet Lover", but we may be sure that Marxism did not enter into it very largely.

The fact is that this business about the moral superiority of the poor is one of the deadliest forms of escapism the ruling class have evolved. You may be downtrodden and swindled, but in the eyes of God you are superior to your oppressors, and by means of films and magazines you can enjoy a fantasy existence in which you constantly triumph over the people who defeat you in real life. In any form of art designed to appeal to large numbers of people, it is an almost un-heard-of thing for a rich man to get the better of a poor man. The rich man is usually "bad", and his machinations are invariably frustrated. "Good poor man defeats bad rich man" is an accepted formula, whereas if it were the other way about we should feel that there was something very wrong somewhere. This is as noticeable in films as in the cheap magazines, and it was perhaps most noticeable of all in the old silent films, which travelled from country to country and had to appeal to a very varied audience. The vast majority of the people who will see a film are poor, and so it is politic to make a poor man the hero. Film magnates, press lords and the like amass quite a lot of their wealth by pointing out that wealth is wicked.

The formula "good poor man defeats bad rich man" is simply a subtler version of "pie in the sky". It is a sublimation of the class struggle. So long as you can dream of yourself as a "strong, hard-working garage hand" giving some moneyed crook a sock on the jaw, the *real* facts can be forgotten. That is a cleverer dodge than wealth fantasy. But, curiously enough, reality does enter into these women's magazines, not through the stories but through the correspondence columns, especially in those papers that give free medical advice. Here you can read harrowing tales of "bad legs" and hemorrhoids, written by middle-aged women who give themselves such pseudonyms as "A Sufferer", "Mother of Nine" and "Always Constipated". To compare these letters with the love stories that lie cheek by jowl with them is to see how vast a part mere day-dreaming plays in modern life.

I have just been reading Arthur Koestler's novel *The Gladiators*, which describes the slave rebellion under Spartacus, about 70 BC. It is not one of his best books, and, in any case, any novel describing a slave rebellion in antiquity suffers by having to stand comparison with *Salammbô*, Flaubert's great novel about the revolt of the Carthaginian mercenaries. But it reminded me of how tiny is the number of slaves of whom anything whatever is known. I myself know the names of just three slaves—Spartacus himself, the fabulous Aesop, who is supposed to have been a slave, and the philosopher Epictetus, who was one of those learned slaves whom the Roman plutocrats liked to have among their retinue. All the others are not even names. We don't, for instance—or at least I don't—know the name of a single one of the myriads of human beings who built the Pyramids. Spartacus, I suppose, is much the most widely known slave there ever was. For five thousand years or more civilisation rested upon slavery. Yet when even so much as the name of a slave survives, it is because he did not obey the injunction "resist not evil", but raised violent rebellion. I think there is a moral in this for pacifists.

We published last week part of a very truculent letter about the anti-war poem entitled "The Little Apocalypse of Obadiah Horn-brook",[1] with the comment, "I am surprised that you publish it." Other letters and private comments took the same line.

---

[1] "The Little Apocalypse of Obadiah Hornbrook", pseudonym of Alex Comfort, appeared in *Tribune*, 30 June 1944. "Letter to an American Visitor", another poem by Alex Comfort, under the pseudonym of Obadiah Hornbooke [sic], appeared in *Tribune*, 4 June 1943. See II, 48.

I do not, any more than our correspondent, agree with "Obadiah Hornbrook", but that is not a sufficient reason for not publishing what he writes. Every paper has a policy, and in its political sections it will press that policy, more or less to the exclusion of all others. To do anything else would be stupid. But the literary end of a paper is another matter. Even there, of course, no paper will give space to direct attacks on the things it stands for. We wouldn't print an article in praise of antisemitism, for instance. But granted the necessary minimum of agreement, literary merit is the only thing that matters.

Besides, if this war is about anything at all, it is a war in favour of freedom of thought. I should be the last to claim that we are morally superior to our enemies, and there is quite a strong case for saying that British imperialism is actually worse than Nazism. But there does remain the difference, not to be explained away, that in Britain you are relatively free to say and print what you like. Even in the blackest patches of the British Empire, in India, say, there is very much more freedom of expression than in a totalitarian country. I want that to remain true, and by sometimes giving a hearing to unpopular opinions, I think we help it to do so.

Tribune, 28 July 1944

58. As I Please

Apropos of saturation bombing, a correspondent who disagreed with me very strongly added that he was by no means a pacifist. He recognised, he said, that "the Hun had got to be beaten". He merely objected to the barbarous methods that we are now using.

Now, it seems to me that you do less harm by dropping bombs on people than by calling them "Huns". Obviously one does not want to inflict death and wounds if it can be avoided, but I cannot feel that mere killing is all-important. We shall all be dead in less than a hundred years, and most of us by the sordid horror known as "natural death". The truly evil thing is to act in such a way that peaceful life becomes impossible. War damages the fabric of civilisation not by the destruction it causes (the net effect of a war may even be to increase the productive capacity of the world as a whole), nor even by the slaughter of human beings, but by stimulating hatred and dishonesty. By shooting at your enemy you are not in the deepest sense wronging him. But by hating him, by inventing lies about him and bringing children up to believe them, by clamouring for unjust peace terms which make further wars inevitable, you are striking not at one perishable generation, but at humanity itself.

It is a matter of observation that the people least infected by war hysteria are the fighting soldiers. Of all people they are the least inclined to hate the enemy, to swallow lying propaganda or to demand a vindictive peace. Nearly all soldiers—and this applies even to professional soldiers in peace time—have a sane attitude towards war. They realise that it is disgusting, and that it may often be necessary. This is harder for a civilian, because the soldier's detached attitude is partly due to sheer exhaustion, to the sobering effects of danger, and to continuous friction with his own military machine. The safe and well-fed civilian has more surplus emotion, and he is apt to use it up in hating somebody or other—the enemy if he is a patriot, his own side if he is a pacifist. But the war mentality is something that can be struggled against and overcome, just as the fear of bullets can be overcome. The trouble is that neither the Peace Pledge Union nor the Never Again Society know the war mentality when they see it. Meanwhile, the fact that in this war offensive nicknames like "Hun" have not caught on with the big public seems to me a good omen.

What has always seemed to me one of the most shocking deeds of the last war was one that did not aim at killing anyone—on the contrary, it probably saved a great many lives. Before launching their big attack at Caporetto, the Germans flooded the Italian army with faked Socialist propaganda leaflets in which it was alleged that the German soldiers were ready to shoot their officers and fraternise with their Italian comrades, etc etc. Numbers of Italians were taken in, came over to fraternise with the Germans, and were made prisoner— and, I believe, jeered at for their simple-mindedness. I have heard this defended as a highly intelligent and humane way of making war—which it is, if your sole aim is to save as many skins as possible. And yet a trick like that damages the very roots of human solidarity in a way that no mere act of violence could do.

I see that the railings are returning—only wooden ones, it is true, but still railings—in one London square after another. So the lawful denizens of the squares can make use of their treasured keys again, and the children of the poor can be kept out.

When the railings round the parks and squares were removed, the object was partly to accumulate scrap-iron, but the removal was also felt to be a democratic gesture. Many more green spaces were now open to the public, and you could stay in the parks till all hours instead of being hounded out at closing time by grim-faced keepers. It was also discovered that these railings were not only unnecessary but hideously ugly. The parks were improved out of recognition by being laid open, acquiring a friendly, almost rural look that they had never had before. And had the railings vanished permanently, another improvement would probably have followed. The dreary shrubberies of laurel and privet—plants not suited to England and always dusty, at any rate in London—would probably have been grubbed up and replaced by flower beds. Like the railings, they were merely put there to keep the populace out. However, the higher-ups managed to avert this reform, like so many others, and everywhere the wooden palisades are going up, regardless of the wastage of labour and timber.

When I was in the Home Guard we used to say that the bad sign would be when flogging was introduced. That has not happened yet, I believe, but all minor social symptoms point in the same direction. The worst sign of all—and I should expect this to happen almost immediately if the Tories win the General Election—will be the reappearance in the London streets of top-hats not worn by either undertakers or bank messengers.

We hope to review before long—and meanwhile I take the opportunity of drawing attention to it—an unusual book called *Branch Street*, by Marie Paneth. The author is or was a voluntary worker at a children's club, and her book reveals the almost savage conditions in which some London children still grow up. It is not quite clear, however, whether these conditions are to any extent worse as a result of the war. I should like to read—I suppose some such thing must exist somewhere, but I don't know of it—an authoritative account of the effect of the war on children. Hundreds of thousands of town children have been evacuated to country districts, many have had their schooling interrupted for months at a time, others have had terrifying experiences with bombs (earlier in the war, a little girl of eight, evacuated to a Hertfordshire village, assured me that she had been bombed out seven times), others have been sleeping in Tube shelters, sometimes for a year or so at a stretch. I would like to know to what extent the town children have adapted themselves to country life—whether they have grown interested in birds and animals, or whether they simply pine to be back among the picture houses—and whether there has been any significant increase in juvenile crime. The children described by Mrs Paneth sound almost like the gangs of "wild children" who were a by-product of the Russian Revolution.

Back in the eighteenth century, when the India muslins were one of the wonders of the world, an Indian king sent envoys to the court of Louis XV to negotiate a trade agreement. He was aware that in Europe women wield great political influence, and the envoys brought with them a bale of costly muslins, which they had been instructed to present to Louis's mistress. Unfortunately their information was not up to date: Louis's not very stable affections had veered, and the muslins were presented to a mistress who had already been discarded. The mission was a failure, and the envoys were decapitated when they got home.

I don't know whether this story has a moral, but when I see the kind of people that our Foreign Office likes to get together with, I am often reminded of it.

Tribune, 4 August 1944

59. Letter to John Middleton Murry

> Care of the "Tribune"
> The Outer Temple
> 222 Strand WC2
> 5 August 1944

Dear Murry,

Thanks for your letter of the 2nd. What I meant by not making "a clear statement about the Russo-German war" is that while advocating pacifism you have never, so far as I know, stated that the *Russians* ought not to defend themselves, and in such of your writings as I have read you have distinctly avoided the whole subject of the Russo-German war altogether. If I remember correctly, the next five or the next six numbers of the *Adelphi* following on the German invasion of the USSR did not even mention that Germany and Russia were at war. You also wrote in a tone of what I could only interpret as approval when the Russians invaded Poland in the early weeks of the war. The impression left by all that you have written about this—and I am by no means alone in inferring this—is that war is all right for Russians and perhaps for Germans and Japanese, but all wrong for us and the Americans. I simply do not see how you square this with pacifism. If it is wrong for one nation to defend its national sovereignty, then it is wrong for all nations. If it is right for any nation, then pacifism is nonsense.

As to "circumspect kind of pacifism". The issue of Russia comes in here again. You say to me, in a letter, that you are not even certain that the USSR is a less horrible phenomenon than Nazi Germany, and that which defeats the other is almost a matter of indifference to you. But in your published writings, so far as I know, you have written in a consistently approving tone of the USSR and invariably compared it with this country to our own disadvantage. You described the USSR as "the only *inherently* peaceful country", and you have even defended its intellectual totalitarianism on the ground that the same thing exists here in veiled forms. You also never raised your voice against such horrors as the purges of 1936–9, and you have used quite unnecessarily euphemistic terms about mass deportations of kulaks, etc. Judging by what I have read of them, I cannot reconcile your published statements with what you have written to me personally. And I cannot escape the impression that you avoid or gloze over the whole subject of Russian militarism and internal totalitarianism because it not only conflicts with your declared pacifism but because to speak clearly about it would also involve you in the only kind of unpopularity an intellectual cares about.

Of course, fanatical Communists and Russophiles generally can be respected, even if they are mistaken. But for people like ourselves, who suspect that something has gone very wrong with the Soviet Union, I consider that willingness to criticise Russia and Stalin is *the* test of intellectual honesty. It is the only thing that from a literary intellectual's point of view is really dangerous. If one is over military age or physically unfit, and if one lives one's life inside the intelligentsia, it seems to me nonsense to say that it needs any courage to refuse military service or to express any kind of antinomian opinions. To do so only gets one into trouble with the Blimps, and who cares what they say? In any case the Blimps hardly interfere. The thing that needs courage is to attack Russia, the only thing that the greater part of the British intelligentsia now believe in. The very tender way in which you have handled Stalin and his régime, compared with your denunciations of, say, Churchill, seems to me to justify the word "circumspect". If you are genuinely anti-violence you ought to be anti-Russian at least as much as you are anti-British. But to be anti-Russian makes enemies, whereas the other doesn't— i.e. not such enemies as people like us would care about.

I don't agree with pacifism, but I judge the sincerity of pacifists by the subjects they avoid. Most pacifists talk as though the war were a meaningless bombing match between Britain and Germany with no other countries involved. A courageous pacifist would not simply say "Britain ought not to bomb Germany." Anyone can say that. He would say, "The Russians should let the Germans have the Ukraine, the Chinese should not defend themselves against Japan, the European peoples should submit to the Nazis, the Indians should not try to drive out the British." Real pacifism would involve all of that: but one can't say that kind of thing and also keep on good terms with the rest of the intelligentsia. It is because they consistently avoid mentioning such issues as these, while continuing to squeal against obliteration bombing etc, that I find the majority of English pacifists so difficult to respect.

Yours sincerely
Geo. Orwell

60. As I Please

A few days ago a West African wrote to inform us that a certain London dance hall had recently erected a "colour bar", presumably in order to please the American soldiers who formed an important part of its clientele. Telephone conversations with the management of the dance hall brought us the answers: (a) that the "colour bar" had been cancelled, and (b) that it had never been imposed in the first place; but I think one can take it that our informant's charge had some kind of basis. There have been other similar incidents recently. For instance, during last week a case in a magistrate's court brought out the fact that a West Indian Negro working in this country had been refused admission to a place of entertainment when he was wearing Home Guard uniform. And there have been many instances of Indians, Negroes and others being turned away from hotels on the ground that "we don't take coloured people".

It is immensely important to be vigilant against this kind of thing, and to make as much public fuss as possible whenever it happens. For this is one of those matters in which making a fuss can achieve something. There is no kind of legal disability against coloured people in this country, and, what is more, there is very little popular colour feeling. (This is not due to any inherent virtue in the British people, as our behaviour in India shows. It is due to the fact that in Britain itself there is no colour problem.)

The trouble always arises in the same way. A hotel, restaurant or what not is frequented by people who have money to spend who object to mixing with Indians or Negroes. They tell the proprietor that unless he imposes a colour bar they will go elsewhere. They may be a very small minority, and the proprietor may not be in agreement with them, but it is difficult for him to lose good customers; so he imposes the colour bar. This kind of thing cannot happen when public opinion is on the alert and disagreeable publicity is given to any establishment where coloured people are insulted. Anyone who knows of a provable instance of colour discrimination ought always to expose it. Otherwise the tiny percentage of colour-snobs who exist among us can make endless mischief, and the British people are given a bad name which, as a whole, they do not deserve.

In the nineteen-twenties, when American tourists were as much a part of the scenery of Paris as tobacco kiosks and tin urinals, the beginnings of a colour bar began to appear even in France. The Americans spent money like water, and restaurant proprietors and the like could not afford to disregard them. One evening, at a dance in a very well-known café, some Americans objected to the presence of a Negro who was there with an Egyptian woman. After making some feeble protests, the proprietor gave in, and the Negro was turned out.

Next morning there was a terrible hullabaloo and the café proprietor was hauled up before a Minister of the Government and threatened with prosecution. It had turned out that the offended Negro was the Ambassador of Haiti. People of that kind can usually get satisfaction, but most of us do not have the good fortune to be ambassadors, and the ordinary Indian, Negro or Chinese can only be protected against petty insult if other ordinary people are willing to exert themselves on his behalf.

Tribune, 11 August 1944

61. Letter to John Middleton Murry

Care of the "Tribune"
The Outer Temple
222 Strand WC2
11 August 1944

Dear Murry,

Thanks for the copy of *Peace News,* and your letter. I must apologise very deeply for attacking you on the score of your attitude to the USSR. I seldom see *Peace News* and did not know that you had taken this line, and I was going on what you used to say earlier on, e.g. at the time of the Russian invasion of Poland and before the war. It is also unquestionable—as you yourself point out in this issue—that many pacifists regard Russia as sacrosanct and keep silent on this issue while denouncing the rest of the allied war effort, and I wrongly assumed that you would be doing so too. I ought to have kept up with your utterances and I am very sorry that I should have written you an almost abusive letter founded on out-of-date information. I know only too well what sort of trouble it gets one into to write anything anti-Stalin at this date, and I admire your courage in doing so. Fortunately I had not accused you in print of doing this particular thing—i.e. attacking militarism but making an exception of the Red Army. As to my remarks about pacifism in general, I don't think I can withdraw anything. I hold to my opinion that it acts objectively in favour of violence and tends to turn into power worship. But even here I may perhaps have been attributing to you too much of the outlook of the younger intellectual pacifists, some of whom seem to me completely corrupted. I wonder if you would send me a copy of your new book, *Adam and Eve,* when it comes out, and I could do something about it in my column in the *Tribune.* In that way I could get over the difficulty of finding time to do it. Meanwhile please accept my apologies for misjudging your attitude.

Yours sincerely
Geo. Orwell

PS. Do you ever see my column in the *Tribune*? You must not think that because I "support" the war and don't disapprove of bombing I am in favour of reprisals, making Germany pay, etc. You may not understand this, but I don't think it matters killing people so long as you do not hate them. I also think that there are times when you can only show your feeling of brotherhood for somebody else by killing him, or trying to. I believe most ordinary people feel this and would make a peace in that sense if they had any say in the matter. There has been very little popular resistance to this war, and also very little hatred. It is a job that has to be done.

62. As I Please

Apropos of my remarks on the railings round London squares, a correspondent writes:

> Are the squares to which you refer public or private properties? If private, I suggest that your comments in plain language advocate nothing less than theft and should be classed as such.

If giving the land of England back to the people of England is theft, I am quite happy to call it theft. In his zeal to defend private property, my correspondent does not stop to consider how the so-called owners of the land got hold of it. They simply seized it by force, afterwards hiring lawyers to provide them with title-deeds. In the case of the enclosure of the common lands, which was going on from about 1600 to 1850, the land-grabbers did not even have the excuse of being foreign conquerors; they were quite frankly taking the heritage of their own countrymen, upon no sort of pretext except that they had the power to do so.

Except for the few surviving commons, the high roads, the lands of the National Trust, a certain number of parks, and the sea shore below high-tide mark, every square inch of England is "owned" by a few thousand families. These people are just about as useful as so many tapeworms. It is desirable that people should own their own dwelling houses, and it is probably desirable that a farmer should own as much land as he can actually farm. But the ground-landlord in a town area has no function and no excuse for existence. He is merely a person who has found out a way of milking the public while giving nothing in return. He causes rents to be higher, he makes town planning more difficult, and he excludes children from green spaces: that is literally all that he does, except to draw his income. The removal of the railings in the squares was a first step against him. It was a very small step, and yet an appreciable one, as the present move to restore the railings shows. For three years or so the squares lay open, and their sacred turf was trodden by the feet of working-class children, a sight to make dividend-drawers gnash their false teeth. If that is theft, all I can say is, so much the better for theft.

I note that once again there is serious talk of trying to attract tourists to this country after the war. This, it is said, will bring in a welcome trickle of foreign currency. But it is quite safe to prophesy that the attempt will be a failure. Apart from the many other difficulties, our licensing laws and the artificial price of drink are quite enough to keep foreigners away. Why should people who are used to paying sixpence for a bottle of wine visit a country where a pint of beer costs a shilling? But even these prices are less dismaying to foreigners than the lunatic laws which permit you to buy a glass of beer at half past ten while forbidding you to buy it at twenty-five past, and which have done their best to turn the pubs into mere boozing shops by excluding children from them.

How downtrodden we are in comparison with most other peoples is shown by the fact that even people who are far from being "temperance" don't seriously imagine that our licensing laws could be altered. Whenever I suggest that pubs might be allowed to open in the afternoon, or to stay open till midnight, I always get the same answer: "The first people to object would be the publicans. *They* don't want to have to stay open twelve hours a day." People assume, you see, that opening hours, whether long or short, must be regulated by the law, even for one-man businesses. In France, and in various other countries, a café proprietor opens or shuts just as it suits him. He can keep open the whole twenty-four hours if he wants to; and, on the other hand, if he feels like shutting his café and going away for a week, he can do that too. In England we have had no such liberty for about a hundred years, and people are hardly able to imagine it.

England is a country that *ought* to be able to attract tourists. It has much beautiful scenery, an equable climate, innumerable attractive villages and medieval churches, good beer, and food-stuffs of excellent natural taste. If you could walk where you chose instead of being fenced in by barbed wire and "Trespassers will be Prosecuted" boards, if speculative builders had not been allowed to ruin every pleasant view within ten miles of a big town, if you could get a drink when you wanted it at a normal price, if an eatable meal in a country inn were a normal experience, and if Sunday were not artificially made into a day of misery, then foreign visitors might be expected to come here. But if those things were true England would no longer be England, and I fancy that we shall have to find some way of acquiring foreign currency that is more in accord with our national character.

In spite of my campaign against the jackboot—in which I am not operating single-handed—I notice that jackboots are as common as ever in the columns of the newspapers. Even in the leading articles in the *Evening Standard*, I have come upon several of them lately. But I am still without any clear information as to what a jackboot is. It is a kind of boot that you put on when you want to behave tyrannically: that is as much as anyone seems to know.

Others besides myself have noted that war, when it gets into the leading articles, is apt to be waged with remarkably old-fashioned weapons. Planes and tanks do make occasional appearances, but as soon as an heroic attitude has to be struck, the only armaments mentioned are the sword ("We shall not sheathe the sword until" etc etc), the spear, the shield, the buckler, the trident, the chariot and the clarion. All of these are hopelessly out of date (the chariot, for instance, has not been in effective use since about AD 50), and even the purpose of some of them has been forgotten. What is a buckler, for instance? One school of thought holds that it is a small round shield, but another school believes it to be a kind of belt. A clarion, I believe, is a trumpet, but most people imagine that a "clarion call" merely means a loud noise.

One of the early Mass Observation reports, dealing with the coronation of George VI, pointed out that what are called "national occasions" always seem to cause a lapse into archaic language. The "ship of state", for instance, when it makes one of its official appearances, has a prow and a helm instead of having a bow and a wheel, like modern ships. So far as it is applied to war, the motive for using this kind of language is probably a desire for euphemism.

"We will not sheathe the sword" sounds a lot more gentlemanly than "We will keep on dropping block-busters", though in effect it means the same.

One argument for Basic English is that by existing side by side with Standard English it can act as a sort of corrective to the oratory of statesmen and publicists. High-sounding phrases, when translated into Basic, are often deflated in a surprising way. For example, I presented to a Basic expert the sentence, "He little knew the fate that lay in store for him"—to be told that in Basic this would become "He was far from certain what was going to happen". It sounds decidedly less impressive, but it means the same. In Basic, I am told, you cannot make a meaningless statement without its being apparent that it is meaningless—which is quite enough to explain why so many schoolmasters, editors, politicians and literary critics object to it.

Tribune, 18 August 1944

63. As I Please

A certain amount of material dealing with Burma and the Burma campaign has been passed on to me by the India-Burma Association, which is an unofficial body representing the European communities in those countries, and standing for a "moderate" policy based on the Cripps proposals.

The India-Burma Association complains with justice that Burma has been extraordinarily ill-served in the way of publicity. Not only has the general public no interest in Burma, in spite of its obvious importance from many points of view, but the authorities have not even succeeded in producing an attractive booklet which would tell people what the problems of Burma are and how they are related to our own. Newspaper reports of the fighting in Burma, from 1942 onwards, have been consistently uninformative, especially from a political point of view. As soon as the Japanese attack began the newspapers and the BBC adopted the practice of referring to all the inhabitants of Burma as "Burmans", even applying this name to the quite distinct and semi-savage peoples of the far north. This is not only about as accurate as calling a Swede an Italian, but masks the fact that the Japanese find their support mostly among the Burmese proper, the minorities being largely pro-British. In the present campaign, when prisoners are taken, the newspaper reports never state whether they are Japanese or whether they are Burmese and Indian partisans—a point of very great importance.

Almost all the books that have been published about the campaign of 1942 are misleading. I know what I am talking about, because I have had most of them to review. They have either been written by American journalists with no background knowledge and a considerable anti-British bias, or by British officials who are on the defensive and anxious to cover up everything discreditable. Actually, the British officials and military men have been blamed for much that was not their fault, and the view of the Burma campaign held by left-wingers in this country was almost as distorted as that held by the Blimps. But this trouble arises because there is no official effort to publicise the truth. For to my knowledge manuscripts do exist which give valuable information, but which, for commercial reasons, cannot find publishers.

I can give three examples. In 1942 a young Burman who had been a member of the Thakin (extreme Nationalist) party and had intrigued with the Japanese fled to India, having changed his mind about the Japanese when he saw what their rule was like. He wrote a short book which was published in India under the title of *What Happened in Burma* and which was obviously authentic in the main. The Indian Government in its negligent way sent exactly two copies to England. I tried to induce various publishers to reissue it, but failed every time: they all gave the same reason—it was not worth wasting paper on a subject which the big public was not interested in. Later a Major Enriquez, who has published various travel books dealing with Burma, brought to England a diary covering the Burma campaign and the retreat into India. It was an extremely revealing— in places a disgracefully revealing—document, but it suffered the same fate as the other book. At the moment I am reading another manuscript which gives valuable background material about Burma's history, its economic conditions, its systems of land tenure, and so forth. But I would bet a small sum that it won't be published either, at any rate until the paper shortage lets up.

If paper and money are not forthcoming for books of this kind— books which may spill a lot of beans but do help to counteract the lies put about by Axis sympathisers—then the Government must not be surprised if the public knows nothing about Burma and cares less. And what applies to Burma applies to scores of other important but neglected subjects.

Meanwhile here is a suggestion. Whenever a document appears which is not commercially saleable but which is likely to be useful to future historians, it should be submitted to a committee set up by, for instance, the British Museum. If they consider it historically valuable they should have the power to print off a few copies and store them for the use of scholars. At present a manuscript rejected by the commercial publishers almost always ends up in the dustbin. How many possible correctives to accepted lies must have perished in this way!

Tribune, 25 August 1944

64. Raffles and Miss Blandish

Nearly half a century after his first appearance, Raffles, "the amateur cracksman", is still one of the best-known characters in English fiction. Very few people would need telling that he played cricket for England, had bachelor chambers in Albany and burgled the Mayfair houses which he also entered as a guest. Just for that reason he and his exploits make a suitable background against which to examine a more modern crime story such as *No Orchids for Miss Blandish*. Any such choice is necessarily arbitrary—I might equally well have chosen *Arsène Lupin*, for instance—but at any rate *No Orchids* and the Raffles books[1] have the common quality of being crime stories which play the limelight on the criminal rather than the policeman. For sociological purposes they can be compared. *No Orchids* is the 1939 version of glamorised crime, *Raffles* the 1900 version. What I am concerned with here is the immense difference in moral atmosphere between the two books, and the change in the popular attitude that this probably implies.

At this date, the charm of *Raffles* is partly in the period atmosphere and partly in the technical excellence of the stories. Hornung was a very conscientious and on his level a very able writer. Anyone who

[1] *Raffles, A Thief in the Night* and *Mr Justice Raffles* by E. W. Hornung. The third of these is definitely a failure, and only the first has the true Raffles atmosphere. Hornung wrote a number of crime stories, usually with a tendency to take the side of the criminal. A successful book in rather the same vein as *Raffles* is *Stingaree*. [Author's footnote.]

cares for sheer efficiency must admire his work. However, the truly dramatic thing about Raffles, the thing that makes him a sort of by-word even to this day (only a few weeks ago, in a burglary case, a magistrate referred to the prisoner as "a Raffles in real life"), is the fact that he is a *gentleman*. Raffles is presented to us—and this is rubbed home in countless scraps of dialogue and casual remarks—not as an honest man who has gone astray, but as a public-school man who has gone astray. His remorse, when he feels any, is almost purely social; he has disgraced "the old school", he has lost his right to enter "decent society", he has forfeited his amateur status and become a cad. Neither Raffles nor Bunny appears to feel at all strongly that stealing is wrong in itself, though Raffles does once justify himself by the casual remark that "the distribution of property is all wrong anyway". They think of themselves not as sinners but as renegades, or simply as outcasts. And the moral code of most of us is still so close to Raffles's own that we do feel his situation to be an especially ironical one. A West End club man who is really a burglar! That is almost a story in itself, is it not? But how if it were a plumber or a greengrocer who was really a burglar? Would there be anything inherently dramatic in that? No—although the theme of the "double life", of respectability covering crime, is still there. Even Charles Peace in his clergyman's dog-collar seems somewhat less of a hypocrite than Raffles in his I Zingari blazer.

Raffles, of course, is good at all games, but it is peculiarly fitting that his chosen game should be cricket. This allows not only of endless analogies between his cunning as a slow bowler and his cunning as a burglar, but also helps to define the exact nature of his crime. Cricket is not in reality a very popular game in England—it is nowhere near so popular as football, for instance—but it gives expression to a well-marked trait in the English character, the tendency to value "form" or "style" more highly than success. In the eyes of any true cricket-lover it is possible for an innings of ten runs to be "better" (i.e. more elegant) than an innings of a hundred runs: cricket is also one of the very few games in which the amateur can excel the professional. It is a game full of forlorn hopes and sudden dramatic changes of fortune, and its rules are so ill-defined that their interpretation is partly an ethical business. When Larwood, for instance, practised body-line bowling in Australia he was not actually breaking any rule: he was merely doing something that was "not cricket". Since cricket takes up a lot of time and is rather an expensive game to play, it is predominantly an upper-class game, but for the whole nation it is bound up with such concepts as "good form", "playing the game", etc, and it has declined in popularity just as the tradition of "don't hit a man when he's down" has declined. It is not a twentieth-century game, and nearly all modern-minded people dislike it. The Nazis, for instance, were at pains to discourage cricket, which had gained a certain footing in Germany before and after the last war. In making Raffles a cricketer as well as a burglar, Hornung was not merely providing him with a plausible disguise; he was also drawing the sharpest moral contrast that he was able to imagine.

Raffles, no less than *Great Expectations* or *Le Rouge et le Noir*, is a story of snobbery, and it gains a great deal from the precariousness of Raffles's social position. A cruder writer would have made the "gentleman burglar" a member of the peerage, or at least a baronet. Raffles, however, is of upper-middle-class origin and is only accepted by the aristocracy because of his personal charm. "We were in Society but not of it," he says to Bunny towards the end of the book; and "I was asked about for my cricket." Both he and Bunny accept the values of "society" unquestioningly, and would settle down in it for good if only they could get away with a big enough haul. The ruin that constantly threatens them is all the blacker because they only doubtfully "belong". A duke who has served a prison sentence is still a duke, whereas a mere man about town, if once disgraced, ceases to be "about town" for evermore. The closing chapters of the book, when Raffles has been exposed and is living under an assumed name, have a "twilight of the gods" feeling, a mental atmosphere rather similar to that of Kipling's poem, "Gentleman Rankers":

> Yes, a trooper of the forces—
> Who has run his own six horses! etc

Raffles now belongs irrevocably to the "cohorts of the damned". He can still commit successful burglaries, but there is no way back into Paradise, which means Piccadilly and the MCC[1]. According to the public-school code there is only one means of rehabilitation: death in battle. Raffles dies fighting against the Boers (a practised reader would foresee this from the start), and in the eyes of both Bunny and his creator this cancels his crimes.

Both Raffles and Bunny, of course, are devoid of religious belief,

[1] Marylebone Cricket Club.

and they have no real ethical code, merely certain rules of behaviour which they observe semi-instinctively. But it is just here that the deep moral difference between *Raffles* and *No Orchids* becomes apparent. Raffles and Bunny, after all, are gentlemen, and such standards as they do have are not to be violated. Certain things are "not done", and the idea of doing them hardly arises. Raffles will not, for example, abuse hospitality. He will commit a burglary in a house where he is staying as a guest, but the victim must be a fellow guest and not the host. He will not commit murder,[1] and he avoids violence wherever possible and prefers to carry out his robberies unarmed. He regards friendship as sacred, and is chivalrous though not moral in his relations with women. He will take extra risks in the name of "sportsmanship", and sometimes even for aesthetic reasons. And above all, he is intensely patriotic. He celebrates the Diamond Jubilee ("For sixty years, Bunny, we've been ruled over by absolutely the finest sovereign the world has ever seen") by despatching to the Queen through the post, an antique gold cup which he has stolen from the British Museum. He steals, from partly political motives, a pearl which the German Emperor is sending to one of the enemies of Britain, and when the Boer war begins to go badly his one thought is to find his way into the fighting line. At the front he unmasks a spy at the cost of revealing his own identity, and then dies gloriously by a Boer bullet. In this combination of crime and patriotism he resembles his near-contemporary Arsène Lupin, who also scores off the German Emperor and wipes out his very dirty past by enlisting in the Foreign Legion.

It is important to note that by modern standards Raffles's crimes are very petty ones. Four hundred pounds' worth of jewellery seems to him an excellent haul. And though the stories are convincing in their physical detail, they contain very little sensationalism—very few corpses, hardly any blood, no sex crimes, no sadism, no perversions of any kind. It seems to be the case that the crime story, at any rate on its higher levels, has greatly increased in blood-thirstiness during the past twenty years. Some of the early detective stories do not even contain a murder. The Sherlock Holmes stories, for instance, are not

---

[1] Actually Raffles does kill one man and is more or less consciously responsible for the death of two others. But all three of them are foreigners and have behaved in a very reprehensible manner. He also, on one occasion, contemplates murdering a blackmailer. It is, however, a fairly well-established convention in crime stories that murdering a blackmailer "doesn't count". [Author's footnote, 1945.]

all murders, and some of them do not even deal with an indictable crime. So also with the John Thorndyke stories, while of the Max Carrados stories only a minority are murders. Since 1918, however, a detective story not containing a murder has been a great rarity, and the most disgusting details of dismemberment and exhumation are commonly exploited. Some of the Peter Wimsey stories, for instance, display an extremely morbid interest in corpses. The Raffles stories, written from the angle of the criminal, are much less antisocial than many modern stories written from the angle of the detective. The main impression that they leave behind is of boyishness. They belong to a time when people had standards, though they happened to be foolish standards. Their key-phrase is "not done". The line that they draw between good and evil is as senseless as a Polynesian taboo, but at least, like the taboo, it has the advantage that everyone accepts it.

So much for *Raffles*. Now for a header into the cesspool. *No Orchids for Miss Blandish*, by James Hadley Chase, was published in 1939, but seems to have enjoyed its greatest popularity in 1940, during the Battle of Britain and the blitz. In its main outlines its story is this:

Miss Blandish, the daughter of a millionaire, is kidnapped by some gangsters who are almost immediately surprised and killed off by a larger and better organised gang. They hold her to ransom and extract half a million dollars from her father. Their original plan had been to kill her as soon as the ransom-money was received, but a chance keeps her alive. One of the gang is a young man named Slim, whose sole pleasure in life consists in driving knives into other people's bellies. In childhood he had graduated by cutting up living animals with a pair of rusty scissors. Slim is sexually impotent, but takes a kind of fancy to Miss Blandish. Slim's mother, who is the real brains of the gang, sees in this the chance of curing Slim's impotence, and decides to keep Miss Blandish in custody till Slim shall have succeeded in raping her. After many efforts and much persuasion, including the flogging of Miss Blandish with a length of rubber hosepipe, the rape is achieved. Meanwhile Miss Blandish's father has hired a private detective, and by means of bribery and torture the detective and the police manage to round up and exterminate the whole gang. Slim escapes with Miss Blandish and is killed after a final rape, and the detective prepares to restore Miss Blandish to her family. By this time, however, she has developed such a taste for Slim's caresses[1] that she feels unable to live without him, and she jumps out of the window of a sky-scraper.

Several other points need noticing before one can grasp the full implications of this book. To begin with, its central story bears a very marked resemblance to William Faulkner's novel *Sanctuary*. Secondly, it is not, as one might expect, the product of an illiterate hack, but a brilliant piece of writing, with hardly a wasted word or a jarring note anywhere. Thirdly, the whole book, *récit* as well as dialogue, is written in the American language; the author, an Englishman who has (I believe) never been in the United States, seems to have made a complete mental transference to the American underworld. Fourthly, the book sold, according to its publishers, no less than half a million copies.

I have already outlined the plot, but the subject-matter is much more sordid and brutal than this suggests. The book contains eight full-dress murders, an unassessable number of casual killings and woundings, an exhumation (with a careful reminder of the stench), the flogging of Miss Blandish, the torture of another woman with red-hot cigarette-ends, a strip-tease act, a third-degree scene of unheard-of cruelty and much else of the same kind. It assumes great sexual sophistication in its readers (there is a scene, for instance, in which a gangster, presumably of masochistic tendency, has an orgasm in the moment of being knifed), and it takes for granted the most complete corruption and self-seeking as the norm of human behaviour. The detective, for instance, is almost as great a rogue as the gangsters, and actuated by nearly the same motives. Like them, he is in pursuit of "five hundred grand". It is necessary to the machinery of the story that Mr Blandish should be anxious to get his daughter back, but apart from this, such things as affection, friendship, good nature or even ordinary politeness simply do not enter. Nor, to any great extent, does normal sexuality. Ultimately only one motive is at work throughout the whole story: the pursuit of power.

It should be noticed that the book is not in the ordinary sense pornography. Unlike most books that deal in sexual sadism, it lays the emphasis on the cruelty and not on the pleasure. Slim, the ravisher of Miss Blandish, has "wet, slobbering lips": this is dis-

---

[1] Another reading of the final episode is possible. It may mean merely that Miss Blandish is pregnant. But the interpretation I have given above seems more in keeping with the general brutality of the book. [Author's footnote, 1945.]

gusting, and it is meant to be disgusting. But the scenes describing cruelty to women are comparatively perfunctory. The real high-spots of the book are cruelties committed by men upon other men: above all, the third-degreeing of the gangster, Eddie Schultz, who is lashed into a chair and flogged on the windpipe with truncheons, his arms broken by fresh blows as he breaks loose. In another of Mr Chase's books, *He Won't Need It Now*, the hero, who is intended to be a sympathetic and perhaps even noble character, is described as stamping on somebody's face, and then, having crushed the man's mouth in, grinding his heel round and round in it. Even when physical incidents of this kind are not occurring, the mental atmo-sphere of these books is always the same. Their whole theme is the struggle for power and the triumph of the strong over the weak. The big gangsters wipe out the little ones as mercilessly as a pike gobbling up the little fish in a pond; the police kill off the criminals as cruelly as the angler kills the pike. If ultimately one sides with the police against the gangsters, it is merely because they are better organised and more powerful, because, in fact, the law is a bigger racket than crime. Might is right: *vae victis*.

As I have mentioned already, *No Orchids* enjoyed its greatest vogue in 1940, though it was successfully running as a play till some time later. It was, in fact, one of the things that helped to console people for the boredom of being bombed. Early in the war the *New Yorker* had a picture of a little man approaching a news-stall littered with papers with such headlines as "Great Tank Battles in Northern France", "Big Naval Battle in the North Sea", "Huge Air Battles over the Channel", etc etc. The little man is saying "*Action Stories*, please". That little man stood for all the drugged millions to whom the world of the gangsters and the prize-ring is more "real", more "tough", than such things as wars, revolutions, earthquakes, famines and pestilences. From the point of view of a reader of *Action Stories*, a description of the London blitz, or of the struggles of the European underground parties, would be "sissy stuff". On the other hand, some puny gun-battle in Chicago, resulting in perhaps half a dozen deaths, would seem genuinely "tough". This habit of mind is now extremely widespread. A soldier sprawls in a muddy trench, with the machine-gun bullets crackling a foot or two overhead, and whiles away his intolerable boredom by reading an American gangster story. And what is it that makes that story so exciting? Precisely the fact that people are shooting at each other with machine-guns!

Neither the soldier nor anyone else sees anything curious in this. It is taken for granted that an imaginary bullet is more thrilling than a real one.

The obvious explanation is that in real life one is usually a passive victim, whereas in the adventure story one can think of oneself as being at the centre of events. But there is more to it than that. Here it is necessary to refer again to the curious fact of *No Orchids* being written—with technical errors, perhaps, but certainly with considerable skill—in the American language.

There exists in America an enormous literature of more or less the same stamp as *No Orchids*. Quite apart from books, there is the huge array of "pulp magazines", graded so as to cater for different kinds of fantasy, but nearly all having much the same mental atmosphere. A few of them go in for straight pornography, but the great majority are quite plainly aimed at sadists and masochists. Sold at threepence a copy under the title of Yank Mags,[1] these things used to enjoy considerable popularity in England, but when the supply dried up owing to the war, no satisfactory substitute was forthcoming. English imitations of the "pulp magazine" do now exist, but they are poor things compared with the original. English crook films, again, never approach the American crook film in brutality. And yet the career of Mr Chase shows how deep the American influence has already gone. Not only is he himself living a continuous fantasy-life in the Chicago underworld, but he can count on hundreds of thousands of readers who know what is meant by a "clipshop" or the "hotsquat", do not have to do mental arithmetic when confronted by "fifty grand", and understand at sight a sentence like "Johnnie was a rummy and only two jumps ahead of the nut-factory." Evidently there are great numbers of English people who are partly Americanised in language and, one ought to add, in moral outlook. For there was no popular protest against *No Orchids*. In the end it was withdrawn, but only retrospectively, when a later work, *Miss Callaghan Comes to Grief*, brought Mr Chase's books to the attention of the authorities. Judging by casual conversations at the time, ordinary readers got a mild thrill out of the obscenities of *No Orchids*, but saw nothing undesirable in the book as a whole. Many people,

[1] They are said to have been imported into this country as ballast, which accounted for their low price and crumpled appearance. Since the war the ships have been ballasted with something more useful, probably gravel. [Author's footnote.]

incidentally, were under the impression that it was an American book reissued in England.

The thing that the ordinary reader *ought* to have objected to— almost certainly would have objected to, a few decades earlier—was the equivocal attitude towards crime. It is implied throughout *No Orchids* that being a criminal is only reprehensible in the sense that it does not pay. Being a policeman pays better, but there is no moral difference, since the police use essentially criminal methods. In a book like *He Won't Need It Now* the distinction between crime and crime prevention practically disappears. This is a new departure for English sensational fiction, in which till recently there has always been a sharp distinction between right and wrong and a general agreement that virtue must triumph in the last chapter. English books glorifying crime (modern crime, that is—pirates and highway-men are different) are very rare. Even a book like *Raffles*, as I have pointed out, is governed by powerful taboos, and it is clearly under-stood that Raffles's crimes must be expiated sooner or later. In America, both in life and fiction, the tendency to tolerate crime, even to admire the criminal so long as he is successful, is very much more marked. It is, indeed, ultimately this attitude that has made it possible for crime to flourish upon so huge a scale. Books have been written about Al Capone that are hardly different in tone from the books written about Henry Ford, Stalin, Lord Northcliffe and all the rest of the "log cabin to White House" brigade. And switching back eighty years, one finds Mark Twain adopting much the same attitude towards the disgusting bandit Slade, hero of twenty-eight murders, and towards the Western desperadoes generally. They were success-ful, they "made good", therefore he admired them.

In a book like *No Orchids* one is not, as in the old-style crime story, simply escaping from dull reality into an imaginary world of action. One's escape is essentially into cruelty and sexual perversion. *No Orchids* is aimed at the power instinct, which *Raffles* or the Sher-lock Holmes stories are not. At the same time the English attitude towards crime is not so superior to the American as I may have seemed to imply. It too is mixed up with power worship, and has become more noticeably so in the last twenty years. A writer who is worth examining is Edgar Wallace, especially in such typical books as *The Orator* and the Mr J. G. Reeder stories. Wallace was one of the first crime-story writers to break away from the old tradition of the private detective and make his central figure a Scotland Yard

official. Sherlock Holmes is an amateur, solving his problems without
the help and even, in the earlier stories, against the opposition of the
police. Moreover, like Lupin, he is essentially an intellectual, even
a scientist. He reasons logically from observed fact, and his intellectuality is constantly contrasted with the routine methods of the police.
Wallace objected strongly to this slur, as he considered it, on Scotland
Yard, and in several newspaper articles he went out of his way to
denounce Holmes by name. His own ideal was the detective inspector
who catches criminals not because he is intellectually brilliant but
because he is part of an all-powerful organisation. Hence the curious
fact that in Wallace's most characteristic stories the "clue" and the
"deduction" play no part. The criminal is always defeated either by
an incredible coincidence, or because in some unexplained manner
the police know all about the crime beforehand. The tone of the stories
makes it quite clear that Wallace's admiration for the police is pure
bully-worship. A Scotland Yard detective is the most powerful kind
of being that he can imagine, while the criminal figures in his mind as
an outlaw against whom anything is permissible, like the condemned slaves in the Roman arena. His policemen behave much
more brutally than British policemen do in real life—they hit people
without provocation, fire revolvers past their ears to terrify them and
so on—and some of the stories exhibit a fearful intellectual sadism.
(For instance, Wallace likes to arrange things so that the villain
is hanged on the same day as the heroine is married.) But it is sadism
after the English fashion: that is to say, it is unconscious, there is
not overtly any sex in it, and it keeps within the bounds of the law.
The British public tolerates a harsh criminal law and gets a kick out
of monstrously unfair murder trials: but still that is better, on any
count, than tolerating or admiring crime. If one must worship a bully,
it is better that he should be a policeman than a gangster. Wallace
is still governed to some extent by the concept of "not done". In
No Orchids anything is "done" so long as it leads on to power. All
the barriers are down, all the motives are out in the open. Chase is a
worse symptom than Wallace, to the extent that all-in wrestling is
worse than boxing, or Fascism is worse than capitalist democracy.

In borrowing from William Faulkner's *Sanctuary*, Chase only
took the plot; the mental atmosphere of the two books is not similar.
Chase really derives from other sources, and this particular bit of
borrowing is only symbolic. What it symbolises is the vulgarisation
of ideas which is constantly happening, and which probably happens

faster in an age of print. Chase has been described as "Faulkner for the masses", but it would be more accurate to describe him as Carlyle for the masses. He is a popular writer—there are many such in America, but they are still rarities in England—who has caught up with what it is now fashionable to call "realism", meaning the doctrine that might is right. The growth of "realism" has been the great feature of the intellectual history of our own age. Why this should be so is a complicated question. The interconnection between sadism, masochism, success worship, power worship, nationalism and totalitarianism is a huge subject whose edges have barely been scratched, and even to mention it is considered somewhat indelicate. To take merely the first example that comes to mind, I believe no one has ever pointed out the sadistic element in Bernard Shaw's work, still less suggested that this probably has some connection with Shaw's admiration for dictators. Fascism is often loosely equated with sadism, but nearly always by people who see nothing wrong in the most slavish worship of Stalin. The truth is, of course, that the countless English intellectuals who kiss the arse of Stalin are not different from the minority who give their allegiance to Hitler or Mussolini, nor from the efficiency experts who preached "punch", "drive", "personality" and "learn to be a Tiger man" in the nineteen-twenties, nor from the older generation of intellectuals, Carlyle, Creasy and the rest of them, who bowed down before German militarism. All of them are worshipping power and successful cruelty. It is important to notice that the cult of power tends to be mixed up with a love of cruelty and wickedness *for their own sakes*. A tyrant is all the more admired if he happens to be a blood-stained crook as well, and "the end justifies the means" often becomes, in effect, "the means justify themselves provided they are dirty enough". This idea colours the outlook of all sympathisers with totalitarianism, and accounts, for instance, for the positive delight with which many English intellectuals greeted the Nazi-Soviet Pact. It was a step only doubtfully useful to the USSR, but it was entirely unmoral, and for that reason to be admired; the explanations of it, which were numerous and self-contradictory, could come afterwards.

Until recently the characteristic adventure stories of the English-speaking peoples have been stories in which the hero fights *against odds*. This is true all the way from Robin Hood to Popeye the Sailor. Perhaps the basic myth of the western world is Jack the Giant-Killer, but to be brought up to date this should be renamed Jack the

Dwarf-Killer, and there already exists a considerable literature which teaches, either overtly or implicitly, that one should side with the big man against the little man. Most of what is now written about foreign policy is simply an embroidery on this theme, and for several decades such phrases as "Play the game", "Don't hit a man when he's down" and "It's not cricket" have never failed to draw a snigger from anyone of intellectual pretensions. What is comparatively new is to find the accepted pattern according to which (a) right is right and wrong is wrong, whoever wins, and (b) weakness must be respected, disappearing from popular literature as well. When I first read D. H. Lawrence's novels, at the age of about twenty, I was puzzled by the fact that there did not seem to be any classification of the characters into "good" and "bad". Lawrence seemed to sympathise with all of them about equally, and this was so unusual as to give me the feeling of having lost my bearings. Today no one would think of looking for heroes and villains in a serious novel, but in lowbrow fiction one still expects to find a sharp distinction between right and wrong and between legality and illegality. The common people, on the whole, are still living in the world of absolute good and evil from which the intellectuals have long since escaped. But the popularity of *No Orchids* and the American books and magazines to which it is akin shows how rapidly the doctrine of "realism" is gaining ground.

Several people, after reading *No Orchids*, have remarked to me, "It's pure Fascism". This is a correct description, although the book has not the smallest connection with politics and very little with social or economic problems. It has merely the same relation to Fascism as, say, Trollope's novels have to nineteenth-century capitalism. It is a day-dream appropriate to a totalitarian age. In his imagined world of gangsters Chase is presenting, as it were, a distilled version of the modern political scene, in which such things as mass bombing of civilians, the use of hostages, torture to obtain confessions, secret prisons, execution without trial, floggings with rubber truncheons, drownings in cesspools, systematic falsification of records and statistics, treachery, bribery and quislingism are normal and morally neutral, even admirable when they are done in a large and bold way. The average man is not directly interested in politics and, when he reads, he wants the current struggles of the world to be translated into a simple story about individuals. He can take an interest in Slim and Fenner as he could not in the GPU and the Gestapo. People worship power in the form in which they are able to understand it. A twelve-year-old boy worships Jack Dempsey. An adolescent in a Glasgow slum worships Al Capone. An aspiring pupil at a business college worships Lord Nuffield. A *New Statesman* reader worships Stalin. There is a difference in intellectual maturity, but none in moral outlook. Thirty years ago the heroes of popular fiction had nothing in common with Mr Chase's gangsters and detectives, and the idols of the English liberal intelligentsia were also comparatively sympathetic figures. Between Holmes and Fenner on the one hand, and between Abraham Lincoln and Stalin on the other, there is a similar gulf.

One ought not to infer too much from the success of Mr Chase's books. It is possible that it is an isolated phenomenon, brought about by the mingled boredom and brutality of war. But if such books should definitely acclimatise themselves in England, instead of being merely a half-understood import from America, there would be good grounds for dismay. In choosing *Raffles* as a background for *No Orchids* I deliberately chose a book which by the standards of its time was morally equivocal. Raffles, as I have pointed out, has no real moral code, no religion, certainly no social consciousness. All he has is a set of reflexes—the nervous system, as it were, of a gentleman. Give him a sharp tap on this reflex or that (they are called "sport", "pal", "woman", "king and country" and so forth), and you get a predictable reaction. In Mr Chase's books there are no gentlemen and no taboos. Emancipation is complete, Freud and Machiavelli have reached the outer suburbs. Comparing the schoolboy atmosphere of the one book with the cruelty and corruption of the other, one is driven to feel that snobbishness, like hypocrisy, is a check upon behaviour whose value from a social point of view has been underrated.

Horizon, October 1944; *Politics*, November 1944; CrE; DD; CE

65. As I Please

It is not my primary job to discuss the details of contemporary politics, but this week there is something that cries out to be said. Since, it seems, nobody else will do so, I want to protest against the

mean and cowardly attitude adopted by the British press towards
the recent rising in Warsaw.

As soon as the news of the rising broke, the *News Chronicle* and
kindred papers adopted a markedly disapproving attitude. One was
left with the general impression that the Poles deserved to have their
bottoms smacked for doing what all the Allied wirelesses had been
urging them to do for years past, and that they would not be given
and did not deserve to be given any help from outside. A few papers
tentatively suggested that arms and supplies might be dropped by the
Anglo-Americans, a thousand miles away: no one, so far as I know,
suggested that this might be done by the Russians, perhaps twenty
miles away. The *New Statesman*, in its issue of August 18, even went
so far as to doubt whether appreciable help could be given from the
air in such circumstances. All or nearly all the papers of the Left were
full of blame for the *émigré* London Government which had "prematurely" ordered its followers to rise when the Red army was at
the gates. This line of thought is adequately set forth in a letter to
last week's *Tribune* from Mr G. Barraclough. He makes the following
specific charges:

1. The Warsaw rising was "not a spontaneous popular rising", but
was "begun on orders from the *soi-disant* Polish Government in
London".

2. The order to rise was given "without consultation with either
the British or Soviet Governments", and "no attempt was made to
co-ordinate the rising with Allied action".

3. The Polish resistance movement is no more united round the
London Government than the Greek resistance movement is united
round King George of the Hellenes. (This is further emphasised by
frequent use of the words *émigré*, *soi-disant*, etc applied to the
London Government.)

4. The London Government precipitated the rising in order to be
in possession of Warsaw when the Russians arrived, because in that
case "the bargaining position of the *émigré* Government would be
improved". The London Government, we are told, "is ready to
betray the Polish people's cause to bolster up its own tenure of
precarious office", with much more to the same effect.

No shadow of proof is offered for any of these charges, though 1
and 2 are of a kind that could be verified and may well be true. My
own guess is that 2 is true and 1 partly true. The third charge makes
nonsense of the first two. If the London Government is not accepted

by the mass of the people in Warsaw, why should they raise a desperate insurrection on its orders? By blaming Sosnkowski and the rest for the rising, you are automatically assuming that it is to them that the Polish people looks for guidance. This obvious contradiction has been repeated in paper after paper, without, so far as I know, a single person having the honesty to point it out. As for the use of such expressions as *émigré*, it is simply a rhetorical trick. If the London Poles are *émigrés*, so are the Polish National Committee of Liberation, besides the "free" Governments of all the occupied countries. Why does one become an *émigré* by emigrating to London and not by emigrating to Moscow?

Charge No. 4 is morally on a par with the *Osservatore Romano's* suggestion that the Russians held up their attack on Warsaw in order to get as many Polish resisters as possible killed off. It is the unproved and unprovable assertion of a mere propagandist who has no wish to establish the truth, but is simply out to do as much dirt on his opponent as possible. And all that I have read about this matter in the press—except for some very obscure papers and some remarks in *Tribune*, the *Economist* and the *Evening Standard*—is on the same level as Mr Barraclough's letter.

Now, I know nothing of Polish affairs, and even if I had the power to do so I would not intervene in the struggle between the London Polish Government and the Moscow National Committee of Liberation. What I am concerned with is the attitude of the British intelligentsia, who cannot raise between them one single voice to question what they believe to be Russian policy, no matter what turn it takes, and in this case have had the unheard-of meanness to hint that our bombers ought not to be sent to the aid of our comrades fighting in Warsaw. The enormous majority of left-wingers who swallow the policy put out by the *News Chronicle* etc know no more about Poland than I do. All they know is that the Russians object to the London Government and have set up a rival organisation, and so far as they are concerned that settles the matter. If tomorrow Stalin were to drop the Committee of Liberation and recognise the London Government, the whole British intelligentsia would flock after him like a troop of parrots. Their attitude towards Russian foreign policy is not "Is this policy right or wrong?" but "This is Russian policy: how can we make it appear right?" And this attitude is defended, if at all, solely on grounds of power. The Russians are powerful in eastern Europe, we are not: therefore we must not oppose them. This involves the principle, of its nature alien to Socialism, that you must not protest against an evil which you cannot prevent.

I cannot discuss here why it is that the British intelligentsia, with few exceptions, have developed a nationalistic loyalty towards the USSR and are dishonestly uncritical of its policies. In any case, I have discussed it elsewhere. But I would like to close with two considerations which are worth thinking over.

First of all, a message to English left-wing journalists and intellectuals generally: "Do remember that dishonesty and cowardice always have to be paid for. Don't imagine that for years on end you can make yourself the boot-licking propagandist of the Soviet régime, or any other régime, and then suddenly return to mental decency. Once a whore, always a whore."

Secondly, a wider consideration. Nothing is more important in the world today than Anglo-Russian friendship and co-operation, and that will not be attained without plain speaking. The best way to come to an agreement with a foreign nation is *not* to refrain from criticising its policies, even to the extent of leaving your own people in the dark about them. At present, so slavish is the attitude of nearly the whole British press that ordinary people have very little idea of what is happening, and may well be committed to policies which they will repudiate in five years' time. In a shadowy sort of way we have been told that the Russian peace terms are a super-Versailles, with partition of Germany, astronomical reparations, and forced labour on a huge scale. These proposals go practically uncriticised, while in much of the left-wing press hack writers are even hired to extol them. The result is that the average man has no notion of the enormity of what is proposed. I don't know whether, when the time comes, the Russians will really want to put such terms into operation. My guess is that they won't. But what I do know is that if any such thing were done, the British and probably the American public would never support it when the passion of war had died down. Any flagrantly unjust peace settlement will simply have the result, as it did last time, of making the British people unreasonably sympathetic with the victims. Anglo-Russian friendship depends upon there being a policy which both countries can agree upon, and this is impossible without free discussion and genuine criticism *now*. There can be no real alliance on the basis of "Stalin is always right". The first step towards a real alliance is the dropping of illusions.

Finally, a word to the people who will write me letters about this. May I once again draw attention to the title of this column and remind everyone that the Editors of *Tribune* are not necessarily in agreement with all that I say, but are putting into practice their belief in freedom of speech?

(This column was written some days before the appearance of Vernon Bartlett's article in the *News Chronicle* of August 29, which gives at any rate a hint of disagreement with the policy prevailing throughout the press.) [Author's note.]

Tribune, 1 September 1944

66. As I Please

For a book of 32 pages, Sir Osbert Sitwell's *A Letter to My Son* contains a quite astonishing quantity of invective. I imagine that it is the invective, or rather the eminence of the people it is directed against, that has led Sir Osbert to change his publisher. But in among passages that are sometimes unfair and occasionally frivolous, he manages to say some penetrating things about the position of the artist in a modern centralised society. Here, for instance, are some excerpts:

> The true artist has always had to fight, but it is, and will be, a more ferocious struggle for you, and the artists of your generation, than ever before. The working man, this time, will be better looked after, he will be flattered by the press and bribed with Beveridge schemes, because he possesses a plurality of votes. But who will care for you or your fate, who will trouble to defend the cause of the young writer, painter, sculptor, musician? And what inspiration will you be offered when theatre, ballet, concert-hall lie in ruins, and, owing to the break in training, there are no great executant artists for several decades? Above all, do not underestimate the amount and intensity of genuine ill-will that people will feel for you; not the working man, for though not highly educated he has a mild respect for the arts and no preconceived notions, not the few remaining patricians, but the vast army between, the fat middle classes and the little men. And here I must make special mention of the

civil servant as enemy. . . . At the best, you will be ground down between the small but powerful authoritarian minority of art directors, museum racketeers, the chic, giggling modistes who write on art and literature, publishers, journalists and dons (who will, to do them justice, try to help you, if you will write as they tell you)—and the enormous remainder who would not mind, who would indeed be pleased, if they saw you starve. For we English are unique in that, albeit an art-producing nation, we are not an art-loving one. In the past the arts depended on a small number of very rich patrons. The enclave they formed has never been re-established. The very name "art-lover" stinks. . . . The privileges you hold today, then, as an artist, are those of Ishmael, the hand of every man is against you. Remember, therefore, that outcasts must never be afraid.

These are not my views. They are the views of an intelligent Conservative who underrates the virtues of democracy and attributes to feudalism certain advantages which really belong to capitalism. It is a mistake, for instance, to yearn after an aristocratic patron. The patron could be just as hard a master as the BBC, and he did not pay your salary so regularly. François Villon had, I suppose, as rough a time as any poet in our own day, and the literary man starving in a garret was one of the characteristic figures of the eighteenth century. At best, in an age of patronage you had to waste time and talent on revolting flatteries, as Shakespeare did. Indeed, if one thinks of the artist as an Ishmael, an autonomous individual who owes nothing to society, then the golden age of the artist was the age of capitalism. He had then escaped from the patron and not yet been captured by the bureaucrat. He could—at any rate a writer, a musician, an actor and perhaps even a painter could—make his living off the big public, who were uncertain of what they wanted and would to a great extent take what they were given. Indeed, for about a hundred years it was possible to make your livelihood by openly insulting the public, as the careers of, say, Flaubert, Tolstoy, D. H. Lawrence, and even Dickens, show.

But all the same there is much in what Sir Osbert Sitwell says. *Laissez-faire* capitalism is passing away, and the independent status of the artist must necessarily disappear with it. He must become either a spare-time amateur or an official. When you see what has happened to the arts in the totalitarian countries, and when you see the same thing happening here in a more veiled way through the MOI, the BBC and the film companies—organisations which not only buy up promising young writers and geld them and set them to work like cab-horses, but manage to rob literary creation of its individual character and turn it into a sort of conveyor-belt process—the prospects are not encouraging. Yet it remains true that capitalism, which in many ways was kind to the artist and the intellectual generally, is doomed and is not worth saving anyway. So you arrive at these two antithetical facts: (1) Society cannot be arranged for the benefit of artists; (2) without artists civilisation perishes. I have never yet seen this dilemma solved (there must be a solution), and it is not often that it is honestly discussed.

I have before me an exceptionally disgusting photograph, from the *Star* of August 29, of two partially undressed women, with shaven heads and with swastikas painted on their faces, being led through the streets of Paris amid grinning onlookers. The *Star*—not that I am picking on the *Star*, for most of the press has behaved likewise—reproduces this photograph with seeming approval.

I don't blame the French for doing this kind of thing. They have had four years of suffering, and I can partially imagine how they feel towards the collaborators. But it is a different matter when newspapers in this country try to persuade their readers that shaving women's heads is a nice thing to do. As soon as I saw this *Star* photograph, I thought, "Where have I seen something like this before?" Then I remembered. Just about ten years ago, when the Nazi régime was beginning to get into its stride, very similar pictures of humiliated Jews being led through the streets of German cities were exhibited in the British press—but with this difference, that on that occasion we were not expected to approve.

Recently another newspaper published photographs of the dangling corpses of Germans hanged by the Russians in Kharkov, and carefully informed its readers that these executions had been filmed and that the public would shortly be able to witness them at the news theatres. (Were children admitted, I wonder?)

There is a saying of Nietzsche which I have quoted before (not in this column, I think), but which is worth quoting again:

> He who fights too long against dragons becomes a dragon himself: and if thou gaze too long into the abyss, the abyss will gaze into thee.

"Too long", in this context, should perhaps be taken as meaning "after the dragon is beaten".

Tribune, 8 September 1944

67. As I Please

About the end of 1936, as I was passing through Paris on the way to Spain, I had to visit somebody at an address I did not know, and I thought that the quickest way of getting there would probably be to take a taxi. The taxi-driver did not know the address either. However, we drove up the street and asked the nearest policeman, whereupon it turned out that the address I was looking for was only about a hundred yards away. So I had taken the taxi-driver off the rank for a fare which in English money was about threepence.

The taxi-driver was furiously angry. He began accusing me, in a roaring voice and with the maximum of offensiveness, of having "done it on purpose". I protested that I had not known where the place was, and that I obviously would not have taken a taxi if I had known. "You knew very well!" he yelled back at me. He was an old, grey, thick-set man, with ragged grey moustaches and a face of quite unusual malignity. In the end I lost my temper, and, my command of French coming back to me in my rage, I shouted at him, "You think you're too old for me to smash your face in. Don't be too sure!" He backed up against the taxi, snarling and full of fight, in spite of his sixty years.

Then the moment came to pay. I had taken out a ten-franc note. "I've no change!" he yelled as soon as he saw the money. "Go and change it for yourself!"

"Where can I get change?"

"How should I know? That's your business."

So I had to cross the street, find a tobacconist's shop and get change. When I came back I gave the taxi-driver the exact fare, telling him that after his behaviour I saw no reason for giving him anything extra; and after exchanging a few more insults we parted.

This sordid squabble left me at the moment violently angry, and a little later saddened and disgusted. "Why do people have to behave like that?" I thought.

But that night I left for Spain. The train, a slow one, was packed with Czechs, Germans, Frenchmen, all bound on the same mission. Up and down the train you could hear one phrase repeated over and over again, in the accents of all the languages of Europe—*là-bas* (down there). My third-class carriage was full of very young, fair-haired, underfed Germans in suits of incredible shoddiness—the first *ersatz* cloth I had seen—who rushed out at every stopping-place to buy bottles of cheap wine and later fell asleep in a sort of pyramid on the floor of the carriage. About halfway down France the ordinary passengers dropped off. There might still be a few nondescript journalists like myself, but the train was practically a troop train, and the countryside knew it. In the morning, as we crawled across southern France, every peasant working in the fields turned round, stood solemnly upright and gave the anti-Fascist salute. They were like a guard of honour, greeting the train mile after mile.

As I watched this, the behaviour of the old taxi-driver gradually fell into perspective. I saw now what had made him so unnecessarily offensive. This was 1936, the year of the great strikes, and the Blum Government was still in office. The wave of revolutionary feeling which had swept across France had affected people like taxi-drivers as well as factory workers. With my English accent I had appeared to him as a symbol of the idle, patronising foreign tourists who had done their best to turn France into something midway between a museum and a brothel. In his eyes an English tourist meant a bourgeois. He was getting a bit of his own back on the parasites who were normally his employers. And it struck me that the motives of the polyglot army that filled the train, and of the peasants with raised fists out there in the fields, and my own motive in going to Spain, and the motive of the old taxi-driver in insulting me, were at bottom all the same.

The official statement on the doodlebug,[1] even taken together with Churchill's earlier statement, is not very revealing, because no clear figures have been given of the number of people affected. All we are told is that on average something under thirty bombs have hit London daily. My own estimate, based simply on such "incidents"

---

[1] Doodlebug was the name given by Londoners to the V1, an unmanned aircraft developed by the Germans. It made an irregular chugging noise as it approached, but the motor cut out and it was completely silent for the few seconds before its bomb fell and exploded.

as I have witnessed, is that on average every doodlebug hitting London makes thirty houses uninhabitable, and that anything up to five thousand people have been rendered homeless daily. At that rate between a quarter and half a million people will have been blitzed out of their homes in the last three months.

It is said that good billiard-players chalk their cues before making a stroke, and bad players afterwards. In the same way, we should have got on splendidly in this war if we had prepared for each type of blitz before and not after it happened. Shortly before the outbreak of war an official, returning from some conference with other officials in London, told me that the authorities were prepared for air-raid casualties of the order of 200,000 in the first week. Enormous supplies of collapsible cardboard coffins had been laid in, and mass graves were being dug. There were also special preparations for a great increase in mental disorders. As it turned out the casualties were comparatively few, while mental disorders, I believe, actually declined. On the other hand, the authorities had failed to foresee that blitzed people would be homeless and would need food, clothes, shelter and money. They had also, while foreseeing the incendiary bomb, failed to realise that you would need an alternative water supply if the mains were burst by bombs.

By 1942 we were all set for the blitz of 1940. Shelter facilities had been increased, and London was dotted with water tanks which would have saved its historic buildings if only they had been in existence when the fires were happening. And then along came the doodlebug, which, instead of blowing three or four houses out of existence, makes a large number uninhabitable, while leaving their interiors more or less intact. Hence another unforeseen headache—storage of furniture. The furniture from a doodlebugged house is nearly always salvaged, but finding places to put it in, and labour to move it, has been almost too much for the local authorities. In general it has to be dumped in derelict and unguarded houses, where such of it as is not looted is ruined by damp.

The most significant figures in Duncan Sandys's speech were those dealing with the Allied counter-measures. He stated, for instance, that whereas the Germans shot off 8,000 doodlebugs, or something under 8,000 tons of high explosive, we dropped 100,000 tons of bombs on the bases, besides losing 450 aeroplanes and shooting off hundreds of thousands or millions of AA shells. One can only make rough calculations at this date, but it looks as though the doodle-

bug may have a big future before it in forthcoming wars. Before
writing it off as a flop, it is worth remembering that artillery scored
only a partial success at the battle of Crécy.

Tribune, 15 September 1944

68. Arthur Koestler

One striking fact about English literature during the present century
is the extent to which it has been dominated by foreigners—for
example, Conrad, Henry James, Shaw, Joyce, Yeats, Pound and
Eliot. Still, if you chose to make this a matter of national prestige
and examine our achievement in the various branches of literature,
you would find that England made a fairly good showing until you
came to what may be roughly described as political writing, or
pamphleteering. I mean by this the special class of literature that has
arisen out of the European political struggle since the rise of Fascism.
Under this heading novels, autobiographies, books of "reportage",
sociological treatises and plain pamphlets can all be lumped together,
all of them having a common origin and to a great extent the same
emotional atmosphere.

Some out of the outstanding figures in this school of writers are
Silone, Malraux, Salvemini, Borkenau, Victor Serge and Koestler
himself. Some of these are imaginative writers, some not, but they
are all alike in that they are trying to write contemporary history,
but *unofficial* history, the kind that is ignored in the text-books and
lied about in the newspapers. Also they are all alike in being continental Europeans. It may be an exaggeration, but it cannot be a
very great one, to say that whenever a book dealing with totalitarianism appears in this country, and still seems worth reading six months
after publication, it is a book translated from some foreign language.
English writers, over the past dozen years, have poured forth an
enormous spate of political literature, but they have produced almost
nothing of aesthetic value, and very little of historical value either.
The Left Book Club, for instance, has been running ever since 1936.
How many of its chosen volumes can you even remember the names
of? Nazi Germany, Soviet Russia, Spain, Abyssinia, Austria,
Czechoslovakia—all that these and kindred subjects have produced,
in England, are slick books of reportage, dishonest pamphlets in

which propaganda is swallowed whole and then spewed up again, half digested, and a very few reliable guide books and text-books. There has been nothing resembling, for instance, *Fontamara* or *Darkness at Noon*, because there is almost no English writer to whom it has happened to see totalitarianism from the inside. In Europe, during the past decade and more, things have been happening to middle-class people which in England do not even happen to the working class. Most of the European writers I mentioned above, and scores of others like them, have been obliged to break the law in order to engage in politics at all; some of them have thrown bombs and fought in street battles, many have been in prison or the concentration camp, or fled across frontiers with false names and forged passports. One cannot imagine, say, Professor Laski indulging in activities of that kind. England is lacking, therefore, in what one might call concentration-camp literature. The special world created by secret-police forces, censorship of opinion, torture and frame-up trials is, of course, known about and to some extent disapproved of, but it has made very little emotional impact. One result of this is that there exists in England almost no literature of disillusionment about the Soviet Union. There is the attitude of ignorant disapproval, and there is the attitude of uncritical admiration, but very little in between. Opinion on the Moscow sabotage trials, for instance, was divided, but divided chiefly on the question of whether the accused were guilty. Few people were able to see that, whether justified or not, the trials were an unspeakable horror. And English disapproval of the Nazi outrages has also been an unreal thing, turned on and off like a tap according to political expediency. To understand such things one has to be able to imagine oneself as the victim, and for an Englishman to write *Darkness at Noon* would be as unlikely an accident as for a slave-trader to write *Uncle Tom's Cabin*.

Koestler's published work really centres about the Moscow trials. His main theme is the decadence of revolutions owing to the corrupting effects of power, but the special nature of the Stalin dictatorship has driven him back into a position not far removed from pessimistic Conservatism. I do not know how many books he has written in all. He is a Hungarian whose earlier books were written in German, and five books have been published in England: *Spanish Testament*, *The Gladiators*, *Darkness at Noon*, *Scum of the Earth*, and *Arrival and Departure*. The subject-matter of all of them is similar, and none of them ever escapes for more than a few pages from the atmosphere of nightmare. Of the five books, the action of three takes place entirely or almost entirely in prison.

In the opening months of the Spanish civil war Koestler was the *News Chronicle's* correspondent in Spain, and early in 1937 he was taken prisoner when the Fascists captured Malaga. He was nearly shot out of hand, then spent some months imprisoned in a fortress, listening every night to the roar of rifle fire as batch after batch of Republicans was executed, and being most of the time in acute danger of execution himself. This was not a chance adventure which "might have happened to anybody", but was in accordance with Koestler's life-style. A politically indifferent person would not have been in Spain at that date, a more cautious observer would have got out of Malaga before the Fascists arrived, and a British or American newspaper man would have been treated with more consideration. The book that Koestler wrote about this, *Spanish Testament*, has remarkable passages, but apart from the scrappiness that is usual in a book of reportage, it is definitely false in places. In the prison scenes Koestler successfully establishes the nightmare atmosphere which is, so to speak, his patent, but the rest of the book is too much coloured by the Popular Front orthodoxy of the time. One or two passages even look as though they had been doctored for the purposes of the Left Book Club. At that time Koestler still was, or recently had been, a member of the Communist Party, and the complex politics of the civil war made it impossible for any Communist to write honestly about the internal struggle on the Government side. The sin of nearly all left-wingers from 1933 onwards is that they have wanted to be anti-Fascist without being anti-totalitarian. In 1937 Koestler already knew this, but did not feel free to say so. He came much nearer to saying it—indeed, he did say it, though he put on a mask to do so—in his next book, *The Gladiators*, which was published about a year before the war and for some reason attracted very little attention.

The Gladiators is in some ways an unsatisfactory book. It is about Spartacus, the Thracian gladiator who raised a slaves' rebellion in Italy round about 65 BC, and any book on such a subject is handicapped by challenging comparison with *Salammbô*. In our own age it would not be possible to write a book like *Salammbô* even if one had the talent. The great thing about *Salammbô*, even more important than its physical detail, is its utter mercilessness. Flaubert could think himself into the stony cruelty of antiquity, because in the mid-nineteenth century one still had peace of mind. One had time to travel in the past. Nowadays the present and the future are too terrifying to be escaped from, and if one bothers with history it is in order to find modern meanings there. Koestler makes Spartacus into an allegorical figure, a primitive version of the proletarian dictator. Whereas Flaubert has been able, by a prolonged effort of the imagination, to make his mercenaries truly pre-Christian, Spartacus is a modern man dressed up. But this might not matter if Koestler were fully aware of what his allegory means. Revolutions always go wrong —that is the main theme. It is on the question of *why* they go wrong that he falters, and his uncertainty enters into the story and makes the central figures enigmatic and unreal.

For several years the rebellious slaves are uniformly successful. Their numbers swell to a hundred thousand, they overrun great areas of Southern Italy, they defeat one punitive expedition after another, they ally themselves with the pirates who at that time were the masters of the Mediterranean, and finally they set to work to build a city of their own, to be named the City of the Sun. In this city human beings are to be free and equal, and above all, they are to be happy: no slavery, no hunger, no injustice, no floggings, no executions. It is the dream of a just society which seems to haunt the human imagination ineradicably and in all ages, whether it is called the Kingdom of Heaven or the classless society, or whether it is thought of as a Golden Age which once existed in the past and from which we have degenerated. Needless to say, the slaves fail to achieve it. No sooner have they formed themselves into a community than their way of life turns out to be as unjust, laborious and fear-ridden as any other. Even the cross, symbol of slavery, has to be revived for the punishment of malefactors. The turning-point comes when Spartacus finds himself obliged to crucify twenty of his oldest and most faithful followers. After that the City of the Sun is doomed, the slaves split up and are defeated in detail, the last fifteen thousand of them being captured and crucified in one batch.

The serious weakness of this story is that the motives of Spartacus himself are never made clear. The Roman lawyer Fulvius, who joins the rebellion and acts as its chronicler, sets forth the familiar dilemma of ends and means. You can achieve nothing unless you are willing to use force and cunning, but in using them you pervert your original aims. Spartacus, however, is not represented as power hungry, nor, on the other hand, as a visionary. He is driven onwards by some obscure force which he does not understand, and he is frequently in two minds as to whether it would not be better to throw up the whole adventure and flee to Alexandria while the going is good. The slaves' republic is in any case wrecked rather by hedonism than by the struggle for power. The slaves are discontented with their liberty because they still have to work, and the final break-up happens because the more turbulent and less civilised slaves, chiefly Gauls and Germans, continue to behave like bandits after the republic has been established. This may be a true account of events—naturally we know very little about the slave rebellions of antiquity—but by allowing the Sun City to be destroyed because Crixus the Gaul cannot be prevented from looting and raping, Koestler has faltered between allegory and history. If Spartacus is the prototype of the modern revolutionary—and obviously he is intended as that—he should have gone astray because of the impossibility of combining power with righteousness. As it is, he is an almost passive figure, acted upon rather than acting, and at times not convincing. The story partly fails because the central problem of revolution has been avoided or, at least, has not been solved.

It is again avoided in a subtler way in the next book, Koestler's masterpiece, *Darkness at Noon*. Here, however, the story is not spoiled, because it deals with individuals and its interest is psychological. It is an episode picked out from a background that does not have to be questioned. *Darkness at Noon* describes the imprisonment and death of an Old Bolshevik, Rubashov, who first denies and ultimately confesses to crimes which he is well aware he has not committed. The grown-upness, the lack of surprise or denunciation, the pity and irony with which the story is told, show the advantage, when one is handling a theme of this kind, of being a European. The book reaches the stature of tragedy, whereas an English or American writer could at most have made it into a polemical tract. Koestler has digested his material and can treat it on the aesthetic level. At the same time his handling of it has a political implication, not important in this case but likely to be damaging in later books.

Naturally the whole book centres round one question: Why did Rubashov confess? He is not guilty—that is, not guilty of anything except the essential crime of disliking the Stalin régime. The concrete acts of treason in which he is supposed to have engaged are all imaginary. He has not even been tortured, or not very severely.

He is worn down by solitude, toothache, lack of tobacco, bright lights glaring in his eyes, and continuous questioning, but these in themselves would not be enough to overcome a hardened revolutionary. The Nazis have previously done worse to him without breaking his spirit. The confessions obtained in the Russian state trials are capable of three explanations:

1. That the accused were guilty.

2. That they were tortured, and perhaps blackmailed by threats to relatives and friends.

3. That they were actuated by despair, mental bankruptcy and the habit of loyalty to the Party.

For Koestler's purpose in *Darkness at Noon* 1 is ruled out, and though this is not the place to discuss the Russian purges, I must add that what little verifiable evidence there is suggests that the trials of the Bolsheviks were frame-ups. If one assumes that the accused were not guilty—at any rate, not guilty of the particular things they confessed to—then 2 is the common-sense explanation. Koestler, however, plumps for 3, which is also accepted by the Trotskyist Boris Souvarine, in his pamphlet *Cauchemar en URSS*. Rubashov ultimately confesses because he cannot find in his own mind any reason for not doing so. Justice and objective truth have long ceased to have any meaning for him. For decades he has been simply the creature of the Party, and what the Party now demands is that he shall confess to non-existent crimes. In the end, though he had to be bullied and weakened first, he is somewhat proud of his decision to confess. He feels superior to the poor Czarist officer who inhabits the next cell and who talks to Rubashov by tapping on the wall. The Czarist officer is shocked when he learns that Rubashov intends to capitulate. As he sees it from his "bourgeois" angle, everyone ought to stick to his guns, even a Bolshevik. Honour, he says, consists in doing what you think right. "Honour is to be useful without fuss," Rubashov taps back; and he reflects with a certain satisfaction that he is tapping with his pince-nez while the other, the relic of the past, is tapping with a monocle. Like Bukharin, Rubashov is "looking out upon black darkness". What is there, what code, what loyalty, what notion of good and evil, for the sake of which he can defy the Party and endure further torment? He is not only alone, he is also hollow. He has himself committed worse crimes than the one that is now being perpetrated against him. For example, as a secret envoy of the Party in Nazi Germany, he has got rid of disobedient followers by betraying them to the Gestapo. Curiously enough, if he has any inner strength to draw upon, it is the memories of his boyhood when he was the son of a landowner. The last thing he remembers, when he is shot from behind, is the leaves of poplar trees on his father's estate. Rubashov belongs to the older generation of Bolsheviks that was largely wiped out in the purges. He is aware of art and literature, and of the world outside Russia. He contrasts sharply with Gletkin, the young GPU man who conducts his interrogation, and who is the typical "good party man", completely without scruples or curiosity, a thinking gramophone. Rubashov, unlike Gletkin, does not have the Revolution as his starting-point. His mind was not a blank sheet when the Party got hold of it. His superiority to the other is finally traceable to his bourgeois origin.

One cannot, I think, argue that *Darkness at Noon* is simply a story dealing with the adventures of an imaginary individual. Clearly it is a political book, founded on history and offering an interpretation of disputed events. Rubashov might be called Trotsky, Bukharin Rakovsky or some other relatively civilised figure among the Old Bolsheviks. If one writes about the Moscow trials one must answer the question, "Why did the accused confess?" and which answer one makes is a political decision. Koestler answers, in effect, "Because these people had been rotted by the Revolution which they served", and in doing so he comes near to claiming that revolutions are of their nature bad. If one assumes that the accused in the Moscow trials were made to confess by means of some kind of terrorism, one is only saying that one particular set of revolutionary leaders has gone astray. Individuals, and not the situation, are to blame. The implication of Koestler's book, however, is that Rubashov in power would be no better than Gletkin: or rather, only better in that his outlook is still partly pre-revolutionary. Revolution, Koestler seems to say, is a corrupting process. Really enter into the Revolution and you must end up as either Rubashov or Gletkin. It is not merely that "power corrupts": so also do the ways of attaining power. Therefore, all efforts to regenerate society *by violent means* lead to the cellars of the OGPU, Lenin leads to Stalin, and would have come to resemble Stalin if he had happened to survive.

Of course, Koestler does not say this quite explicitly, and perhaps is not altogether conscious of it. He is writing about darkness, but it is darkness at what ought to be noon. Part of the time he feels that things might have turned out differently. The notion that so-and-so has "betrayed", that things have only gone wrong because of individual wickedness, is ever present in left-wing thought. Later, in *Arrival and Departure*, Koestler swings over much further towards the anti-revolutionary position, but in between these two books there is another, *Scum of the Earth*, which is straight autobiography and has only an indirect bearing upon the problems raised by *Darkness at Noon*. True to his life-style, Koestler was caught in France by the outbreak of war and, as a foreigner and a known anti-Fascist, was promptly arrested and interned by the Daladier Government. He spent the first nine months of war mostly in a prison camp, then, during the collapse of France, escaped and travelled by devious routes to England, where he was once again thrown into prison as an enemy alien. This time he was soon released, however. The book is a valuable piece of reportage, and together with a few other scraps of honest writing that happened to be produced at the time of the débâcle, it is a reminder of the depths that bourgeois democracy can descend to. At this moment, with France newly liberated and the witch-hunt after collaborators in full swing, we are apt to forget that in 1940 various observers on the spot considered that about forty per cent of the French population was either actively pro-German or completely apathetic. Truthful war books are never acceptable to non-combatants, and Koestler's book did not have a very good reception. Nobody came well out of it—neither the bourgeois politicians, whose idea of conducting an anti-Fascist war was to jail every left-winger they could lay their hands on, nor the French Communists, who were effectively pro-Nazi and did their best to sabotage the French war effort, nor the common people, who were just as likely to follow mountebanks like Doriot as responsible leaders. Koestler records some fantastic conversations with fellow victims in the concentration camp, and adds that till then, like most middle-class Socialists and Communists, he had never made contact with real proletarians, only with the educated minority. He draws the pessimistic conclusion: "Without education of the masses, no social progress; without social progress, no education of the masses". In *Scum of the Earth* Koestler ceases to idealise the common people. He has abandoned Stalinism, but he is not a Trotskyist either. This is the book's real link with *Arrival and Departure*, in which what is normally called a revolutionary outlook is dropped, perhaps for good.

Arrival and Departure is not a satisfactory book. The pretence that it is a novel is very thin; in effect it is a tract purporting to show that revolutionary creeds are rationalisations of neurotic impulses. With all too neat a symmetry, the book begins and ends with the same action—a leap into a foreign country. A young ex-Communist who has made his escape from Hungary jumps ashore in Portugal, where he hopes to enter the service of Britain, at that time the only power fighting against Germany. His enthusiasm is somewhat cooled by the fact that the British Consulate is uninterested in him and almost ignores him for a period of several months, during which his money runs out and other astuter refugees escape to America. He is successively tempted by the World in the form of a Nazi propagandist, the Flesh in the form of a French girl, and—after a nervous breakdown—the Devil in the form of a psychoanàlyst. The psychoanalyst drags out of him the fact that his revolutionary enthusiasm is not founded on any real belief in historical necessity, but on a morbid guilt complex arising from an attempt in early childhood to blind his baby brother. By the time that he gets an opportunity of serving the Allies he has lost all reason for wanting to do so, and he is on the point of leaving for America when his irrational impulses seize hold of him again. In practice he cannot abandon the struggle. When the book ends, he is floating down in a parachute over the dark landscape of his native country, where he will be employed as a secret agent of Britain.

As a political statement (and the book is not much more), this is insufficient. Of course it is true in many cases, and it may be true in all cases, that revolutionary activity is the result of personal maladjustment. Those who struggle against society are, on the whole, those who have reason to dislike it, and normal healthy people are no more attracted by violence and illegality than they are by war. The young Nazi in *Arrival and Departure* makes the penetrating remark that one can see what is wrong with the left-wing movement by the ugliness of its women. But after all, this does not invalidate the Socialist case. Actions have results, irrespective of their motives. Marx's ultimate motives may well have been envy and spite, but this does not prove that his conclusions were false. In making the hero of *Arrival and Departure* take his final decision from a mere instinct not to shirk action and danger, Koestler is making him suffer a sudden loss of intelligence. With such a history as he has behind him, he would be able to see that certain things have to be done, whether our reasons for doing them are "good" or "bad". History has to move in a certain direction, even if it has to be pushed that

way by neurotics. In *Arrival and Departure* Peter's idols are overthrown one after the other. The Russian Revolution has degenerated,
Britain, symbolised by the aged consul with gouty fingers, is no
better, the international class-conscious proletariat is a myth. But
the conclusion (since, after all, Koestler and his hero "support" the
war) ought to be that getting rid of Hitler is still a worth-while objective, a necessary bit of scavenging in which motives are almost
irrelevant.

To take a rational political decision one must have a picture of
the future. At present Koestler seems to have none, or rather to have
two which cancel out. As an ultimate objective he believes in the
Earthly Paradise, the Sun State which the gladiators set out to
establish, and which has haunted the imagination of Socialists,
Anarchists and religious heretics for hundreds of years. But his
intelligence tells him that the Earthly Paradise is receding into the
far distance and that what is actually ahead of us is bloodshed,
tyranny and privation. Recently he described himself as a "short-
term pessimist". Every kind of horror is blowing up over the horizon,
but somehow it will all come right in the end. This outlook is probably gaining ground among thinking people: it results from the very
great difficulty, once one has abandoned orthodox religious belief,
of accepting life on earth as inherently miserable, and on the other
hand, from the realisation that to make life liveable is a much bigger
problem than it recently seemed. Since about 1930 the world has
given no reason for optimism whatever. Nothing is in sight except
a welter of lies, hatred, cruelty and ignorance, and beyond our present
troubles loom vaster ones which are only now entering into the
European consciousness. It is quite possible that man's major problems will *never* be solved. But it is also unthinkable! Who is there who
dares to look at the world of today and say to himself, "It will
always be like this: even in a million years it cannot get appreciably
better?" So you get the quasi-mystical belief that for the present there
is no remedy, all political action is useless, but that somewhere in
space and time human life will cease to be the miserable brutish
thing it now is.

The only easy way out is that of the religious believer, who regards
this life merely as a preparation for the next. But few thinking people
now believe in life after death, and the number of those who do is
probably diminishing. The Christian churches would probably not
survive on their own merits if their economic basis were destroyed.

The real problem is how to restore the religious attitude while accepting death as final. Men can only be happy when they do not assume that the object of life is happiness. It is most unlikely, however, that Koestler would accept this. There is a well-marked hedonistic strain in his writings, and his failure to find a political position after breaking with Stalinism is a result of this.

The Russian Revolution, the central event in Koestler's life, started out with high hopes. We forget these things now, but a quarter of a century ago it was confidently expected that the Russian Revolution would lead to Utopia. Obviously this has not happened. Koestler is too acute not to see this, and too sensitive not to remember the original objective. Moreover, from his European angle he can see such things as purges and mass deportations for what they are; he is not, like Shaw or Laski, looking at them through the wrong end of the telescope. Therefore he draws the conclusion: This is what revolutions lead to. There is nothing for it except to be a "short-term pessimist", i.e. to keep out of politics, make a sort of oasis within which you and your friends can remain sane, and hope that somehow things will be better in a hundred years. At the basis of this lies his hedonism, which leads him to think of the Earthly Paradise as desirable. Perhaps, however, whether desirable or not, it isn't possible. Perhaps some degree of suffering is ineradicable from human life, perhaps the choice before man is always a choice of evils, perhaps even the aim of Socialism is not to make the world perfect but to make it better. All revolutions are failures, but they are not all the same failure. It is his unwillingness to admit this that has led Koestler's mind temporarily into a blind alley and that makes *Arrival and Departure* seem shallow compared with the earlier books.

Written [September] 1944; CTE; DD; *Focus 2* 1946; CE

69. Tobias Smollett: Scotland's Best Novelist

"Realism", a much abused word, has at least four current meanings, but when applied to novels it normally means a photographic imitation of everyday life. A "realistic" novel is one in which the dialogue is colloquial and physical objects are described in such a way that you can visualise them. In this sense almost all modern novels are more "realistic" than those of the past, because the describing of everyday scenes and the construction of natural-sounding dialogue are largely a matter of technical tricks which are passed on from one generation to another, gradually improving in the process. But there is another sense in which the stilted, artificial novelists of the eighteenth century are more "realistic" than almost any of their successors, and that is in their attitude towards human motives. They may be weak at describing scenery, but they are extraordinarily good at describing scoundrelism. This is true even of Fielding, who in *Tom Jones* and *Amelia* already shows the moralising tendency which was to mark English novels for a hundred and fifty years. But it is much truer of Smollett, whose outstanding intellectual honesty may have been connected with the fact that he was not an Englishman.

Smollett is a picaresque novelist, a writer of long, formless tales full of farcical and improbable adventures. He derives to some extent from Cervantes whom he translated into English and whom he also plagiarised in *Sir Lancelot Greaves*. Inevitably a great deal that he wrote is no longer worth reading, even including, perhaps, his most-praised book, *Humphrey Clinker*, which is written in the form of letters and was considered comparatively respectable in the nineteenth century, because most of its obscenities are hidden under puns. But Smollett's real masterpieces are *Roderick Random* and *Peregrine Pickle*, which are frankly pornographic in a harmless way and which contain some of the best passages of sheer farce in the English language.

Dickens, in *David Copperfield*, names these two books among his childhood favourites, but the resemblance sometimes claimed as existing between Smollett and Dickens is very superficial. In *Pickwick Papers*, and in several others of Dickens's early books, you have the picaresque form, the endless travelling to and fro, the fantastic adventures, the willingness to sacrifice no matter what amount of probability for the sake of a joke; but the moral atmosphere has greatly altered. Between Smollett's day and Dickens's there had happened not only the French Revolution, but the rise of a new industrial middle class, Low Church in its theology and puritanical in its outlook. Smollett writes of the middle class, but the mercantile and professional middle class, the kind of people who are cousins to a landowner and take their manners from the aristocracy.

Duelling, gambling and fornication seem almost morally neutral to him. It so happens that in private life he was a better man than the majority of writers. He was a faithful husband who shortened his life by overworking for the sake of his family, a sturdy republican who hated France as the country of the Grand Monarchy, and a patriotic Scotsman at a time when—the 1745 rebellion being a fairly recent memory—it was far from fashionable to be a Scotsman. But he has very little sense of sin. His heroes do things, and do them on almost every page, which in any nineteenth-century English novel would instantly call forth vengeance from the skies. He accepts as a law of nature the viciousness, the nepotism and the disorder of eighteenth-century society, and therein lies his charm. Many of his best passages would be ruined by any intrusion of the moral sense.

Both *Peregrine Pickle* and *Roderick Random* follow roughly the same course. Both heroes go through great vicissitudes of fortune, travel widely, seduce numerous women, suffer imprisonment for debt, and end up prosperous and happily married. Of the two, Peregrine is somewhat the greater blackguard, because he has no profession—Roderick is a naval surgeon, as Smollett himself had been for a while—and can consequently devote more time to seductions and practical jokes. But neither is ever shown acting from an unselfish motive, nor is it admitted that such things as religious belief, political conviction or even ordinary honesty are serious factors in human affairs.

In the world of Smollett's novels there are only three virtues. One is feudal loyalty (Roderick and Peregrine each have a retainer who is faithful through thick and thin), another is masculine "honour", i.e. willingness to fight on any provocation, and another is female "chastity", which is inextricably mixed up with the idea of capturing a husband. Otherwise anything goes. It is nothing out of the way to cheat at cards, for instance. It seems quite natural to Roderick, when he has got hold of £1,000 from somewhere, to buy himself a smart outfit of clothes and go to Bath posing as a rich man, in hopes of entrapping an heiress. When he is in France and out of a job, he decides to join the army, and as the French army happens to be the nearest one, he joins that, and fights against the British at the battle of Dettingen: he is nevertheless ready soon afterwards to fight a duel with a Frenchman who has insulted Britain.

Peregrine devotes himself for months at a time to the elaborate and horribly cruel practical jokes in which the eighteenth century delighted. When, for instance, an unfortunate English painter is thrown into the Bastille for some trifling offence and is about to be released, Peregrine and his friends, playing on his ignorance of the language, let him think that he has been sentenced to be broken on a wheel. A little later they tell him that this punishment has been commuted to castration, and then extract a last bit of fun out of his terrors by letting him think that he is escaping in disguise when he is merely being released from the prison in the normal way.

Why are these petty rogueries worth reading about? In the first place because they are funny. In the continental writers from whom Smollett derived there may be better things than the description of Peregrine Pickle's adventures on the Grand Tour, but there is nothing better of that particular kind in English. Secondly, by simply ruling out "good" motives and showing no respect whatever for human dignity, Smollett often attains a truthfulness that more serious novelists have missed. He is willing to mention things which do happen in real life but are almost invariably kept out of fiction. Roderick Random, for instance, at one stage of his career, catches a venereal disease—the only English novel hero, I believe, to whom this has happened. And the fact that Smollett, in spite of his fairly enlightened views, takes patronage, official jobbery and general corruption for granted gives great historical interest to certain passages in his books.

Smollett had been for a while in the navy, and in *Roderick Random* we are given not only an unvarnished account of the Cartagena expedition, but an extraordinarily vivid and disgusting description of the inside of a warship, in those days a sort of floating compendium of disease, discomfort, tyranny and incompetence. The command of Roderick's ship is for a while given to a young man of family, a scented homosexual fop who has hardly seen a ship in his life, and who spends the whole voyage in his cabin to avoid contact with the vulgar sailormen, almost fainting when he smells tobacco. The scenes in the debtors' prison are even better. In the prisons of those days, a debtor who had no resources might actually starve to death unless he could keep alive by begging from more fortunate prisoners. One of Roderick's fellow prisoners is so reduced that he has no clothes at all and preserves decency as best he can by wearing a very long beard. Some of the prisoners, needless to say, are poets, and the book includes a self-contained story, "Mr Melopoyn's Tragedy", which should make anyone who thinks aristocratic patronage a good basis for literature think twice.

Smollett's influence on subsequent English writers has not been as great as that of his contemporary, Fielding. Fielding deals in the same kind of boisterous adventure, but his sense of sin never quite leaves him. It is interesting, in *Joseph Andrews*, to watch Fielding start out with the intention of writing a pure farce, and then, in spite of himself as it were, begin punishing vice and rewarding virtue in the way that was to be customary in English novels until almost yesterday. Tom Jones would fit into a novel by Meredith, or for that matter by Ian Hay, whereas Peregrine Pickle seems to belong to a more European background. The writers nearest to Smollett are perhaps Surtees and Marryat, but when sexual frankness ceased to be possible, picaresque literature was robbed of perhaps half of its subject-matter. The eighteenth-century inn where it was almost abnormal to go into the right bedroom was a lost dominion.

In our own day various English writers—Evelyn Waugh, for instance, and Aldous Huxley in his early novels—drawing on other sources, have tried to revive the picaresque tradition. One has only to watch their eager efforts to be shocking, and their readiness to be shocked themselves—whereas Smollett was merely trying to be funny in what seemed to him the natural way—to see what an accumulation of pity, decency and public spirit lies between that age and ours.

Tribune, 22 September 1944

70. As I Please

By permission of a correspondent, I quote passages from a letter of instruction which she recently received from a well-known school of journalism. I should explain that when she undertook her "course" the instructor asked her to supply the necessary minimum of information about her background and experience, and then told her to write a couple of specimen essays on some subject interesting to her. Being a miner's wife, she chose to write about coal-mining. Here is the reply she got from someone calling himself the "Assistant Director of Studies". I shall have to quote from it at some length:

> I have read your two exercises with care and interest. You should have a good deal to write about: but do be careful of getting a bee in your bonnet. Miners are not the only men who have a hard time. How about young naval officers, earning less

than a skilled miner—who must spend three or four years from home and family, in ice or the tropics? How about the many retired folks on a tiny pension or allowance, whose previous £2 or £3 have been reduced by *half* by the income tax? We all make sacrifices in this war—and the so-called upper classes are being hard hit indeed.

Instead of writing propaganda for Socialist newspapers you will do better to describe—for the housewives—what life is like in a mining village. Do not go out of your way to be hostile to owners and managers—who are ordinary fellow creatures—but, if you must air a grievance, do so tolerantly, and fit it in with your plot or theme.

Many of your readers will be people who are not in the least inclined to regard employers as slave drivers and capitalist villains of society. . . . Write simply and naturally, without any attempt at long words or sentences. Remember that your task is to *entertain*. No reader will bother after a hard day's work to read a list of somebody else's woes. Keep a strict eye on your inclination to write about the "wrongs" of mining. There are *millions* of people who will not forget that miners *did* strike while our sons and husbands were fighting the Germans. Where would the miners be if the troops had refused to fight? I mention this to help you keep a sense of perspective. I advise you against writing very controversial things. They are hard to sell. A plain account of mining life will stand a far better chance. . . . The average reader is willing to read facts about other ways of life—but unless he is a fool or knave, he will not listen to *one-sided* propaganda. So forget your grievances, and tell us something of how *you* manage in a typical mining village. One of the women's magazines will, I'm sure, consider a housewife's article on that subject.

My correspondent, who, it seems, had agreed in advance to pay £11 for this course, sent the letter on to me with the query: Did I think that her instructor was trying to influence her to give her writings an acceptable political slant? Was an attempt being made to talk her out of writing like a Socialist?

I do think so, of course, but the implications of this letter are worse than that. This is not a subtle capitalist plot to dope the workers. The writer of that slovenly letter is not a sinister plotter, but simply an ass (a female ass, I should say by the style) upon whom years of bombing and privation have made no impression. What it demonstrates is the unconquerable, weed-like vitality of pre-war habits of mind. The writer assumes, it will be seen, that the only purpose of journalism is to tickle money out of the pockets of tired businessmen, and that the best way of doing this is to avoid telling unpleasant truths about present-day society. The reading public, so he (or she) reasons, don't like being made to think: therefore don't make them think. You are after the big dough, and no other consideration enters.

Anyone who has had anything to do with "courses" in free-lance journalism, or has even come as near to them as studying the now-defunct *Writer* and the *Writer's and Artist's Yearbook*, will recognise the tone of that letter. "Remember that your task is to *entertain*," "No reader will bother after a hard day's work to read a list of somebody else's woes," and "I advise you against writing very controversial things. They are hard to sell." I pass over the fact that even from a commercial point of view such advice is misleading. What is significant is the assumption that nothing ever changes, that the public always will be and always must be the same mob of nit-wits wanting only to be doped, and that no sane person would sit down behind a typewriter with any other object than to produce saleable drivel.

When I started writing, about fifteen years ago, various people—who, however, didn't succeed in getting £11 out of me in return—gave me advice almost identical with what I have quoted above. Then too, it seemed, the public did not want to hear about "unpleasant" things like unemployment, and articles on "controversial" subjects were "hard to sell". The dreary sub-world of the free-lance journalist, the world of furnished bed-sitting rooms, hired typewriters and self-addressed envelopes, was entirely dominated by the theory that "your task is to entertain". But at that time there was some excuse. To begin with there was widespread unemployment, and every newspaper and magazine was besieged by hordes of amateurs struggling frantically to earn odd guineas; and in addition the press was incomparably sillier than it is now, and there was some truth in the claim that editors would not print "gloomy" contributions. If you looked on writing as simply and solely a way of making money, then cheer-up stuff was probably the best line. What is depressing is to see that for the —— school of journalism the world has stood still. The bombs have achieved nothing. And, indeed, when I read that letter I had the same feeling that the pre-war world is back upon us as I had a little while ago when, through the window of some chambers in the Temple, I watched somebody—with great care and evident pleasure in the process—polishing a top-hat.

It is superfluous to say that long railway journeys are not pleasant in these days, and for a good deal of the discomfort that people have to suffer, the railway companies are not to blame. It is not their fault that there is an enormous to-and-fro of civilian traffic at a time when the armed forces are monopolising most of the rolling stock, nor that an English railway carriage is built with the seeming object of wasting as much space as possible. But journeys which often entail standing for six or eight hours in a crowded corridor could be made less intolerable by a few reforms.

To begin with, the First Class nonsense should be scrapped once and for all. Secondly, any woman carrying a baby should have a priority right to a seat. Thirdly, waiting rooms should be left open at night. Fourthly, if time-tables cannot be adhered to, porters and other officials should be in possession of correct information, and not, as at present, tell you that you will have to change when you won't, and vice versa. Also—a thing that is bad enough in peace time but is even worse at this moment—why is it that there is no cheap way of moving luggage across a big town? What do you do if you have to move a heavy trunk from Paddington to Camden Town? You take a taxi. And suppose you can't afford a taxi, what do you do then? Presumably you borrow a hand-cart, or balance the trunk on a perambulator. Why are there not cheap luggage-vans, just as there are buses for human passengers? Or why not make it possible to carry luggage on the Underground?

This evening, as King's Cross discharged another horde of returned evacuees, I saw a man and woman, obviously worn out by a long journey, trying to board a bus. The woman carried a squalling baby and clutched a child of about six by the other hand; the man was carrying a broken suitcase tied with rope and the elder child's cot. They were refused by one bus after another. Of course, no bus could take a cot on board. How could it be expected to? But, on the other hand, how were those people to get home? It ended by the woman boarding a bus with the two children, while the man trailed off carrying the cot. For all I know he had a five-mile walk ahead of him.

In war-time one must expect this kind of thing. But the point is that if those people had made the same journey, similarly loaded, in peace time, their predicament would have been just the same. For:

> The rain it raineth every day
> Upon the just and unjust feller,
> But more upon the just because
> The unjust has the just's umbrella.

Our society is not only so arranged that if you have money you can buy luxuries with it. After all, that is what money is for. It is also so arranged that if you don't have money you pay for it at every hour of the day with petty humiliations and totally unnecessary discomforts—such as, for instance, walking home with a suitcase cutting your fingers off when a mere half-crown would get you there in five minutes.

Tribune, 6 October 1944

71. As I Please

Recently I was told the following story, and I have every reason to believe that it is true.

Among the German prisoners captured in France there are a certain number of Russians. Some time back two were captured who did not speak Russian or any other language that was known either to their captors or their fellow prisoners. They could, in fact, only converse with one another. A professor of Slavonic languages, brought down from Oxford, could make nothing of what they were saying. Then it happened that a sergeant who had served on the frontiers of India overheard them talking and recognised their language, which he was able to speak a little. It was Tibetan! After some questioning, he managed to get their story out of them.

Some years earlier they had strayed over the frontier into the Soviet Union and had been conscripted into a labour battalion, afterwards being sent to western Russia when the war with Germany broke out. They were taken prisoner by the Germans and sent to North Africa;

later they were sent to France, then exchanged into a fighting unit when the Second Front opened, and taken prisoner by the British. All this time they had been able to speak to nobody but one another, and had no notion of what was happening or who was fighting whom.

It would round the story off neatly if they were now conscripted into the British army and sent to fight the Japanese, ending up somewhere in Central Asia, quite close to their native village, but still very much puzzled as to what it is all about.

An Indian journalist sends me a cutting of an interview he had with Bernard Shaw. Shaw says one or two sensible things and does state that the Congress leaders ought not to have been arrested, but on the whole it is a disgusting exhibition. Here are some samples:

Q: Supposing you were a National Leader of India, how would you have dealt with the British? What would have been your methods to achieve Indian independence?

A: Please do not suppose a situation that can never happen. The achievement of Indian independence is not my business.

Q: What do you think is the most effective way of getting the British out of India? What should the Indian people do?

A: Make them superfluous by doing their work better. Or assimilate them by cross-fertilisation. British babies do not thrive in India.

What kind of answers are those to give to people who are labouring under a huge and justified grievance? Shaw also refuses to send birthday greetings to Gandhi, on the ground that this is a practice he never follows, and advises the Indian people not to bother if Britain repudiates the huge credit balance which India has piled up in this country during the war. I wonder what impression this interview would give to some young Indian student who has been a couple of years in jail and has dimly heard of Bernard Shaw as one of Britain's leading "progressive" thinkers? Is it surprising if even very level-headed Indians are liable to a recurrent suspicion that "all Englishmen are the same"?

Sir Osbert Sitwell's little book[1] and my remarks on it, brought in an unusually large amount of correspondence, and some of the points that were raised seem to need further comment.

One correspondent solved the whole problem by asserting that

[1] *A Letter to My Son.* See 66.

society can get along perfectly well without artists. It can also get along without scientists, engineers, doctors, bricklayers or road-menders—for the time being. It can even get along without sowing next year's harvest, provided it is understood that everyone is going to starve to death in about twelve months' time.

This notion, which is fairly widespread and has been encouraged by people who should know better, simply restates the problem in a new form. What the artist does is not immediately and obviously necessary in the same way as what the milkman or the coal miner does. Except in the ideal society which has not yet arrived, or in very chaotic and prosperous ages like the one that is just ending, this means in practice that the artist must have some kind of patron— a ruling class, the Church, the State, or a political party. And the question "Which is best?" normally means "Which interferes least?"

Several correspondents pointed out that one solution is for the artist to have an alternative means of livelihood. "It is quite feasible," says Mr P. Philips Price, "to write and devote oneself to Socialism whilst accepting the patronage of the BBC, MOI, Rank[1] or CEMA[2]. . . . the only way out is some minor form of prostitution, part time." The difficulty here is that the practice of writing or any other art takes up a lot of time and energy. Moreover, the kind of job that a writer gets in war-time, if he is not in the Forces (or even if he is—for there is always PR), usually has something to do with propaganda. But this is itself a kind of writing. To compose a propaganda pamphlet or a radio feature needs just as much work as to write something you believe in, with the difference that the finished product is worthless. I could give a whole list of writers of promise or performance who are now being squeezed dry like oranges in some official job or other. It is true that in most cases it is voluntary. They want the war to be won, and they know that everyone must sacrifice something. But still the result is the same. They will come out of the war with nothing to show for their labours and with not even the stored-up experience that the soldier gets in return for his physical suffering.

If a writer is to have an alternative profession, it is much better that it should have nothing to do with writing. A particularly success-ful holder of two jobs was Trollope, who produced two thousand words between seven and nine o'clock every morning before leaving

[1] J. Arthur Rank Film Productions.
[2] Council for the Encouragement of Music and the Arts.

for his work at the Post Office. But Trollope was an exceptional man, and as he also hunted three days a week and was usually playing whist till midnight, I suspect that he did not overwork himself in his official duties.

Other correspondents pointed out that in a genuinely Socialist society the distinction between the artist and the ordinary man would vanish. Very likely, but then no such society yet exists. Others rightly claimed that State patronage is a better guarantee against starvation than private patronage, but seemed to me too ready to disregard the censorship that this implies. The usual line was that it is better for the artist to be a responsible member of a community than an anarchic individualist. The issue, however, is not between irresponsible "self-expression" and discipline; it is between truth and lies.

Artists don't so much object to *aesthetic* discipline. Architects will design theatres or churches equally readily, writers will switch from the three-volume novel to the one-volume, or from the play to the film, according to the demand. But the point is that this is a political age. A writer inevitably writes—and less directly this applies to all the arts—about contemporary events, and his impulse is to tell what he believes to be the truth. But no government, no big organisation, will pay for the truth. To take a crude example: can you imagine the British Government commissioning E. M. Forster to write *A Passage to India*? He could only write it because he was *not* dependent on State aid. Multiply that instance by a million, and you see the danger that is involved—not, indeed, in a centralised economy as such, but in our going forward into a collectivist age without remembering that the price of liberty is eternal vigilance.

Tribune, 13 October 1944

72. A Controversy: Orwell: Agate

Some months ago Sir Osbert Sitwell wrote a little book entitled *A Letter to My Son*, which was in effect a plea for the independence, or even the irresponsibility, of the artist. The son (an imaginary son, thought of as an artist or writer) was counselled to regard himself as an Ishmael, and preserve his intellectual integrity at no matter what cost.

Now Mr James Agate has written a vigorous, not to say violent, reply,[1] in which he asserts that the artist is not to be treated as a special kind of being, but has the same obligations as any other citizen. Much of what Mr Agate says is justified. It is quite true that the artist cannot exist in a vacuum and that he has an interest in defending our own relatively free society against conquest from without. The plea that writers and artists ought to be exempted from military service has not much to recommend it.

All the same, Sir Osbert Sitwell's main point is only partly met, and the tone of Mr Agate's reply will antagonise many people who might be disposed to agree with him.

In a healthy society everyone would be an artist of sorts. In our own society the artist is an exceptional person, and he has to practise cunning—not, indeed, to keep alive, but to keep his soul his own. Instead of seeing this as a temporary and evil phenomenon Mr Agate chooses to regard it as a law of nature. The average person, he says, is totally unmoved by art or literature, and he implies that this will always be so. "Let me say," he says, "that I have little or no belief in the power of education. So far as I can see, it leads the child out of the darkness of healthy ignorance into the much denser night of soul-destroying commonness," and he implies all the way through that he sympathises, or partly sympathises, with the average man's contempt for the arts. There are the usual jeers against "highbrows", the people who compose "an unintelligible poem" or paint "a picture of three sardines swimming in a top-hat", while golf, cricket, and other pastimes are declared to have "moved the ordinary man more than all the poets put together."

What Mr Agate does not see is that it is exactly this attitude, common enough in the general public and encouraged by people like himself, that makes artists and intellectuals irresponsible. If you treat people as pariahs, they behave like pariahs.

Some of the younger English writers and artists have behaved in an unworthy way in the present war, and a species of individualism, usually calling itself Anarchism, is probably on the up-grade. But the solution is not to congratulate the ordinary man on his bad taste. The solution, ultimately, is through the education which Mr Agate disbelieves in. Sir Osbert Sitwell's pamphlet deserves a better answer.

Manchester Evening News, 30 November 1944

[1] *Noblesse Oblige—Another Letter to Another Son.*

[James Agate replied to George Orwell's review of his book in a later issue of the *Manchester Evening News*, and his reply is printed below.]

In his review of my book *Noblesse Oblige—Another Letter to Another Son*, Mr George Orwell provides yet one more example of the tangled web woven for themselves by those who mistake feeling for thinking. Here is Mr Orwell: "Mr Agate implies all the way through that he sympathises, or partly sympathises, with the average man's contempt for the arts . . . while golf, cricket, and other pastimes are declared to have moved the ordinary man more than all the poets put together."

Consider here this passage from my book: "To define the flame of ecstasy is to go back to the first principles of all art. Shortly, we may allege the passionate quest for beauty, the search for light that never was on sea or land, the expression of all that some mysterious madness has taught the artist to be supremely worth-while setting down in word or paint or sound, the effort to perpetrate beyond the grave and in terms of his art that consciousness of the world about him which has been said to be civilised man's 'Marvel and treasure'."

How can Mr Orwell think it possible that a man who has written this can sympathise or partly sympathise with contempt for the arts? And is it not a fact that our football stadiums, cricket grounds, boxing rings and race-courses draw more adherents than the Old Vic? Mr Orwell pretends that I congratulate the ordinary man on his bad taste. This shows how completely he has misread my book. Here in simple words is the argument of *Noblesse Oblige*, which is a reply to Sir Osbert Sitwell's *A Letter to My Son*. It would be easier perhaps if I tabulate it:

1. Sir Osbert says that a man should be prepared to fight and die for the flowers of his country's soil. I say that he should fight for his country's soil.

2. Sir Osbert would have all artists exempt from war service. I say that all artists should be conscripted, leaving it for other judgement to decide whether by continuing in their art they will serve their country better. Examples: William Walton, John Gielgud, Robert Helpmann, Tommy Trinder.

3. Sir Osbert maintains that art is more than life's most exquisite decoration, that it is life's "finest and most spiritual essence". I agree, but I also ask whom that finest essence affects and reaches? Obviously it is only those who are capable of appreciating art, say

ten per cent of the community. And I contend, just as Shakespeare imparts ecstasy to art-lovers, so Alec James imparted ecstasy to non-art-lovers. If actors are to be exempt, why not footballers?

4. War, says Sir Osbert, may kill a budding Shakespeare. Yes, but it may also kill a budding Churchill, Lutyens, Eddington, Horder, Augustus John. Wherefore, if artists are exempt, potentially great men of all kinds must be exempt. It is absurd to exempt a Malcolm Sargent and not a Malcolm Campbell.

5. Sir Osbert says that the best way of getting to understand another nation is to understand its works of art. To which I reply that Englishmen should not let their love of Goethe, Heine, Bach, Beethoven and Wagner blind them to the German mentality of war-making.

To conclude. I do not sympathise with the average man's contempt for the arts. I do not congratulate him on his lack of taste. The last page of my little book contains these words: "I realise that the taste of the Walworth Road is low, and I hold that ninety-five per cent of it cannot be improved. I may be wrong, but I am putting my case at its strongest. I maintain that it is the duty of the artist to fight for the Walworth Road, however low its taste, as manfully and resolutely as the Walworth Road fights for—heaven forgive me— its betters."

I cannot understand how a man of Mr Orwell's intelligence can take this for sympathy with low taste, or congratulation on its possession.

I deplore the standard of taste in this country. I say that it is the duty of those whose standard is higher to fight for those less happily endowed. If any reader of the above can find any words into which to put more plainly what I obviously mean, I promise to use them in my little book's next edition.

Manchester Evening News, 21 December 1944.

[To which George Orwell answered:]

It would take too long to answer Mr Agate's objections one by one, but there are two points that I would like to take up:

1. Contempt for the artist: Mr Agate's little book is sown all the way through with the usual contemptuous asides about "Blooms-bury", and remarks such as "even intellectuals are thinking beings", quite obviously with the purpose of enlisting the highbrow-baiting section of the public on his side. In addition he condones or even

approves the current lack of taste by stating that the pleasure that the spectators get out of cricket, horse-racing, etc is *of the same nature* as the pleasure that can be derived from poetry or music. "I say that cricket has moved the ordinary man to the top of his spiritual bent, and that all infinities are equal." This is repeated over and over again. It follows from this that a good cricketer is just as valuable a being as a good poet. The point Mr Agate doesn't meet, however, is that poets are a lot *rarer* than cricketers, and that what they do has a value, or can have a value, that is not purely ephemeral. Shakespeare has made life more worth living for ten generations of Englishmen, while W. G. Grace, even granting that his famous stroke which broke the clock in the Lord's pavilion was somehow the equivalent of *Macbeth* or *King Lear*, is already a fading memory.

In the decay of the Byzantine Empire, who can doubt that Mr Agate's then equivalent was pointing out that the mob got much more kick out of the chariot races than out of the verses of Homer? But Homer is still there while the chariot drivers are forgotten. And more than this, in looking back we can see the spectacles of the Roman arena for what they were—dope to keep the masses from thinking. Our own commercialised sport will have the same appearance when society regains its mental health.

Isn't there, therefore, some reason for thinking that poetry, music and painting, in spite of the hordes of charlatans they admittedly attract, are more important to the human race than cricket, golf or pugilism? I fully agree with Mr Agate—and I said so—that the artist as such has no right to claim exemption from National Service. But I notice that Mr Agate, while vociferously opposing exemption for poets, is in favour of exempting popular entertainers. "Obviously," he says, "a wise government will not put a bayonet into the hands of a William Walton, a Constant Lambert, a Clifford Curzon, a Noel Coward, a John Gielgud or a Tommy Trinder." In practice, of course, the Government does not put bayonets into the hands of people of that kind but does put them into the hands of writers, painters, etc if they are young enough. Several of our more promising younger writers have been killed already, and the war of 1914–18 caused a positive slaughter of poets. Looking back, I think it might have been better for the human race if the authorities had seen fit to exempt Wilfred Owen and conscript Horatio Bottomley.

2. Contempt for the common man: although calling the common man, or ordinary man, to his aid on almost every page, Mr Agate

shows his contempt for him by asserting that he not only has not but can never be expected to have any feelings for the arts. "I realise that the taste of the Walworth Road is low, and I hold that ninety-five per cent of it cannot be improved." And he firmly declares his disbelief in the power of education. It follows that the ugliness and vulgarity of modern machine civilisation are unalterable and that the artist, who caters for a tiny minority, is a mere excrescence on society, a producer of "pretty things".

Sir Osbert Sitwell, it is worth noticing, was less contemptuous of the ordinary man. The working classes, he said, are less actively hostile to the arts than the comfortable middle classes. But the point Mr Agate misses is that bad taste is *not* an ineradicable human characteristic. Shakespeare was a popular writer, the plays of Aristophanes were popular entertainments, and to this day there are primitive peoples among whom good taste is all but universal.

We in this country have bad taste, as we have bad teeth, because of complex but discoverable social causes. It is a thing to be fought against, and an important part of the fight devolves on the artist and the critic. The artist fights it by preserving his integrity: the critic fights against it by educating the public. And flattery is not a form of education. To assume that the big public is inevitably composed of fools, and then to imply that there is something lovable and even meritorious in being a fool, is less useful and less admirable than retreating to an ivory tower with all the windows barred.

Manchester Evening News, 21 December 1944.

73. As I Please

Reading recently a book on Brigadier-General Wingate, who was killed early this year in Burma, I was interested to note that Wingate's "Chindits", who marched across Upper Burma in 1943, were wearing not the usual clumsy and conspicuous pith helmets, but slouch hats like those worn in the Gurkha regiments. This sounds a very small point, but it is of considerable social significance, and twenty or even ten years ago it would have been impossible. Nearly everyone, including nearly any doctor, would have predicted that large numbers of these men would perish of sunstroke.

Till recently the Europeans in India had an essentially superstitious attitude towards heat apoplexy, or sunstroke as it is usually called. It was supposed to be something dangerous to Europeans but not to Asiatics. When I was in Burma I was assured that the Indian sun, even at its coolest, had a peculiar deadliness which could only be warded off by wearing a helmet of cork or pith. "Natives", their skulls being thicker, had no need of these helmets, but for a European even a double felt hat was not a reliable protection.

But why should the sun in Burma, even on a positively chilly day, be deadlier than in England? Because we were nearer to the equator and the rays of the sun were more perpendicular. This astonished me, for obviously the rays of the sun are only perpendicular round about noon. How about the early morning, when the sun is creeping over the horizon and the rays are parallel with the earth? It is exactly then, I was told, that they are at their most dangerous. But how about the rainy season, when one frequently does not see the sun for days at a time? Then of all times, the old-stagers told me, you should cling to your topi. (The pith helmet is called a "topi", which is Hindustani for "hat".) The deadly rays filter through the envelope of cloud just the same, and on a dull day you are in danger of forgetting it. Take your topi off in the open for one moment, even for one moment, and you may be a dead man. Some people, not content with cork and pith, believed in the mysterious virtues of red flannel and had little patches of it sewn into their shirts over the top vertebra. The Eurasian community, anxious to emphasise their white ancestry, used at that time to wear topis even larger and thicker than those of the British.

My own disbelief in all this dated from the day when my topi was blown off my head and carried away down a stream, leaving me to march bareheaded all day without ill effects. But I soon noticed other facts that conflicted with the prevailing belief. To begin with some Europeans (for instance sailors working in the rigging of ships) did habitually go bareheaded in the sun. Again, when cases of sunstroke occurred (for they do occur), they did not seem to be traceable to any occasion when the victim had taken his hat off. They happened to Asiatics as well as to Europeans, and were said to be commonest among stokers on coal-burning ships, who were subjected to fierce heat but not to sunshine. The final blow was the discovery that the topi, supposedly the only protection against the Indian sun, is quite a recent invention. The early Europeans in India knew nothing of it. In short, the whole thing was bunkum.

But why should the British in India have built up this superstition about sunstroke? Because an endless emphasis on the differences between the "natives" and yourself is one of the necessary props of imperialism. You can only rule over a subject race, especially when you are in a small minority, if you honestly believe yourself to be racially superior, and it helps towards this if you can believe that the subject race is *biologically* different. There were quite a number of ways in which Europeans in India used to believe, without any evidence, that Asiatic bodies differed from their own. Even quite considerable anatomical differences were supposed to exist. But this nonsense about Europeans being subject to sunstroke and Orientals not, was the most cherished superstition of all. The thin skull was the mark of racial superiority, and the pith topi was a sort of emblem of imperialism.

That is why it seems to me a sign of the changing times that Wingate's men, British, Indians and Burmese alike, set forth in ordinary felt hats. They suffered from dysentery, malaria, leeches, lice, snakes and Japanese, but I do not think any cases of sunstroke were recorded. And above all, there seems to have been no official protest and no feeling that the abandonment of the topi was a subtle blow at white prestige.

In Mr Stanley Unwin's recent pamphlet, *Publishing in Peace and War*, some interesting facts are given about the quantities of paper allotted by the Government for various purposes. Here are the present figures:

Newspapers	.	.	250,000 tons
HM Stationery Office	.	.	100,000 „
Periodicals	.	. (nearly)	50,000 „
Books	.	.	22,000 „

A particularly interesting detail is that out of the 100,000 tons allotted to the Stationery Office, the War Office gets no less than 25,000 tons, or more than the whole book trade put together.

I haven't personally witnessed, but I can imagine, the kind of wastage of paper that goes on in the War Office and the various ministries. I know what happens in the BBC. Would you credit, for instance, that of every radio programme that goes out on the air, even the inconceivable rubbish of cross-talk comedians, at least six copies are typed—sometimes as many as fifteen copies? For years past all this trash has been filed somewhere or other in enormous archives. At the same time paper for books is so short that even the most hackneyed "classic" is liable to be out of print, many schools are short of text-books, new writers get no chance to start and even established writers have to expect a gap of a year or two years between finishing a book and seeing it published. And incidentally the export trade in English books has been largely swallowed up by America.

This part of Mr Unwin's pamphlet is a depressing story. He writes with justified anger of the contemptuous attitude towards books shown by one government department after another. But in fact the English as a whole, though somewhat better in this respect than the Americans, have not much reverence for books. It is in the small countries, such as Finland and Holland, that the book consumption per head is largest. Is it not rather humiliating to be told that a few years before the war a remote town like Reykjavik had a better display of *British* books than any English town of comparable size?

Tribune, 20 October 1944

74. As I Please

Reading, a week or two ago, Mr C. S. Lewis's recently-published book, *Beyond Personality* (it is a series of reprinted broadcasts on theology), I learned from the blurb on the dust jacket that a critic who should, and indeed does, know better had likened an earlier book, *The Screwtape Letters*, to *The Pilgrim's Progress*. "I do not hesitate to compare Mr Lewis's achievement with *Pilgrim's Progress*" were his quoted words. Here is a sample, entirely representative, from the later book:

> Well, even on the human level, you know, there are two kinds of pretending. There's a bad kind, where the pretence is *instead of* the real thing, as when a man pretends he's going to help you instead of really helping you. But there's also a good kind, where the pretence *leads up to* the real thing. When you're not feeling particularly friendly but know you ought to be, the best thing you can do, very often, is to put on a friendly manner and behave as if you were a much nicer chap than you actually

are. And in a few minutes, as we've all noticed, you will be
really feeling friendlier than you were. Very often the only way
to get a quality is to start behaving as if you had it already. That's
why children's games are so important. They're always pretend-
ing to be grown-ups—playing soldiers, playing shop. But all the
time they are hardening their muscles and sharpening their
wits, so that the pretence of being grown-ups helps them in
earnest.

The book is like this all the way through, and I think most of us
would hesitate a long time before equating Mr Lewis with Bunyan.
One must make some allowance for the fact that these essays are
reprinted broadcasts, but even on the air it is not really necessary to
insult your hearers with homey little asides like "you know" and
"mind you", or Edwardian slang like "awfully", "jolly well",
"specially" for "especially", "awful cheek" and so forth. The idea, of
course, is to persuade the suspicious reader, or listener, that one can
be a Christian and a "jolly good chap" at the same time. I don't
imagine that the attempt would have much success, and in any case
the cotton wool with which the BBC stuffs its speakers' mouths
makes any real discussion of theological problems impossible, even
from an orthodox angle. But Mr Lewis's vogue at this moment, the
time allowed to him on the air and the exaggerated praise he has
received, are bad symptoms and worth noticing.

Students of popular religious apologetics will notice early in the
book a side-kick at "all these people who turn up every few years
with some patent simplified religion of their own", and various hints
that unbelief is "out of date", "old-fashioned" and so forth.
And they will remember Ronald Knox saying much the same thing
fifteen years ago, and R. H. Benson twenty or thirty years before
that, and they will know in which pigeon-hole Mr Lewis should be
placed.

A kind of book that has been endemic in England for quite sixty
years is the silly-clever religious book, which goes on the principle
not of threatening the unbeliever with Hell, but of showing him up as
an illogical ass, incapable of clear thought and unaware that everything he says has been said and refuted before. This school of literature started, I think, with W. H. Mallock's *New Republic*, which
must have been written about 1880, and it has had a long line of
practitioners—R. H. Benson, Chesterton, Father Knox, "Beach-

comber" and others, most of them Catholics, but some, like Dr Cyril
Alington and (I suspect) Mr Lewis himself, Anglicans. The line of
attack is always the same. Every heresy has been uttered before
(with the implication that it has also been refuted before); and theology is only understood by theologians (with the implication that
you should leave your thinking to the priests). Along these lines one
can, of course, have a lot of clean fun by "correcting loose thinking"
and pointing out that so-and-so is only saying what Pelagius said in
AD 400 (or whenever it was), and has in any case used the word
transubstantiation in the wrong sense. The special targets of these
people have been T. H. Huxley, H. G. Wells, Bertrand Russell,
Professor Joad, and others who are associated in the popular mind
with Science and Rationalism. They have never had much difficulty
in demolishing them—though I notice that most of the demolished
ones are still there, while some of the Christian apologists themselves
begin to look rather faded.

One reason for the extravagant boosting that these people always
get in the press is that their political affiliations are invariably reactionary. Some of them were frank admirers of Fascism as long as
it was safe to be so. That is why I draw attention to Mr C. S. Lewis
and his chummy little wireless talks, of which no doubt there will
be more. They are not really so unpolitical as they are meant to
look. Indeed they are an outflanking movement in the big counter-
attack against the Left which Lord Elton, A. P. Herbert, G. M.
Young, Alfred Noyes and various others have been conducting for
two years past.

I notice that in his new book, *Adam and Eve*, Mr Middleton Murry
instances the agitation against Mosley's release from internment as
a sign of the growth of totalitarianism, or the totalitarian habit of
mind, in this country. The common people, he says, still detest
totalitarianism: but he adds in a later footnote that the Mosley
business has shaken this opinion somewhat. I wonder whether he is
right.

On the face of it, the demonstrations against Mosley's release were
a very bad sign. In effect people were agitating against Habeas
Corpus. In 1940 it was a perfectly proper action to intern Mosley,
and in my opinion it would have been quite proper to shoot him if
the Germans had set foot in Britain. When it is a question of national
existence, no government can stand on the letter of the law: otherwise

a potential quisling has only to avoid committing any indictable offence, and he can remain at liberty, ready to go over to the enemy and act as their gauleiter as soon as they arrive. But by 1943 the situation was totally different. The chance of a serious German invasion had passed, and Mosley (though possibly he may make a come-back at some future date—I won't prophesy about that) was merely a ridiculous failed politician with varicose veins. To continue imprisoning him without trial was an infringement of every principle we are supposedly fighting for.

But there was also strong popular feeling against Mosley's release, and not, I think, for reasons so sinister as Mr Murry implies. The comment one most frequently heard was "They've only done it because he's a rich man", which was a simplified way of saying "Class privilege is on the up-grade again". It is a commonplace that the political advance we seemed to make in 1940 has been gradually filched away from us again. But though the ordinary man sees this happening, he is curiously unable to combat it: there seems to be nowhere to take hold. In a way, politics has stopped. There has been no General Election, the elector is conscious of being unable to influence his MP, Parliament has no control over the Government. You may not like the way things are going, but what exactly can you do about it? There is no concrete act against which you can plausibly protest.

But now and again something happens which is obviously symptomatic of the general trend—something round which existing discontents can crystallise. "Lock up Mosley" was a good rallying cry. Mosley, in fact, was a symbol, as Beveridge still is and as Cripps was in 1942. I don't believe Mr Murry need bother about the implications of this incident. In spite of all that has happened, the failure of any genuinely totalitarian outlook to gain ground among the ordinary people of this country is one of the most surprising and encouraging phenomena of the war.

Tribune, 27 October 1944

75. As I Please

Penguin Books have now started publishing books in French, very nicely got up, at half-a-crown each. Among those to appear shortly is the latest instalment of André Gide's *Journal,* which covers a year of the German occupation. As I glanced through an old favourite, Anatole France's *Les Dieux Ont Soif* (it is a novel about the Reign of Terror during the French Revolution), the thought occurred to me: what a remarkable anthology one could make of pieces of writing describing executions! There must be hundreds of them scattered through literature, and—for a reason I think I can guess—they must be far better written on average than battle pieces.

Among the examples I remember at the moment are Thackeray's description of the hanging of Courvoisier, the crucifixion of the gladiators in *Salammbô,* the final scene of *A Tale of Two Cities,* a piece from a letter or diary of Byron's, describing a guillotining, and the beheading of two Scottish noblemen after the 1745 rebellion, described by, I think, Horace Walpole. There is a very fine chapter describing a guillotining in Arnold Bennett's *Old Wives' Tale,* and a horrible one in one of Zola's novels (the one about the Sacré Coeur). Then there is Jack London's short story, "The Chinago", Plato's account of the death of Socrates—but one could extend the list indefinitely. There must also be a great number of specimens in verse, for instance the old hanging ballads, to which Kipling's "Danny Deever" probably owes something.

The thing that I think very striking is that no one, or no one I can remember, ever writes of an execution *with approval.* The dominant note is always horror. Society, apparently, cannot get along without capital punishment—for there are some people whom it is simply not safe to leave alive—and yet there is no one, when the pinch comes, who feels it right to kill another human being in cold blood. I watched a man hanged once. There was no question that everybody concerned knew this to be a dreadful, unnatural action. I believe it is always the same—the whole jail, warders and prisoners alike, is upset when there is an execution. It is probably the fact that capital punishment is accepted as necessary, and yet instinctively felt to be wrong, that gives so many descriptions of executions their tragic atmosphere. They are mostly written by people who have actually watched an execution and feel it to be a terrible and only partly comprehensible experience which they want to record; whereas battle literature is largely written by people who have never heard a gun go off and think of a battle as a sort of football match in which nobody gets hurt.

Perhaps it was a bit previous to say that no one writes of an execution with approval, when one thinks of the way our newspapers have been smacking their chops over the bumping-off of wretched quislings in France and elsewhere. I recall, in one paper, a whole series of photos showing the execution of Caruso, the ex-chief of the Rome police. You saw the huge, fat body being straddled across a chair with his back to the firing squad, then the cloud of smoke issuing from the rifle barrels and the body slumping sideways. The editor who saw fit to publish this thought it a pleasant titbit, I suppose, but then he had not had to watch the actual deed. I think I can imagine the feelings of the man who took the photographs, and of the firing squad.

To the lovers of useless knowledge (and I know there are a lot of them, from the number of letters I always get when I raise any question of this kind) I present a curious little problem arising out of the recent Pelican, *Shakespeare's England*. A writer named Fynes Morrison, touring England in 1607, describes melons as growing freely. Andrew Marvell, in a very well-known poem written about fifty years later, also refers to melons. Both references make it appear that the melons grew in the open, and indeed they must have done so if they grew at all. The hot-bed was a recent invention in 1600, and glass-houses, if they existed, must have been a very great rarity. I imagine it would be quite impossible to grow a melon in the open in England nowadays. They are hard enough to grow under glass, whence their price. Fynes Morrison also speaks of grapes growing in large enough quantities to make wine. Is it possible that our climate has changed radically in the last three hundred years? Or was the so-called melon actually a pumpkin?

Tribune, 3 November 1944

76. Review

The Vicar of Wakefield by Oliver Goldsmith

When Mark Twain said of *The Vicar of Wakefield*, "Nothing could be funnier than its pathos, and nothing could be sadder than its humour", he was probably not exaggerating his own feelings very greatly. To a man of Mark Twain's generation it was natural that the elegance of the eighteenth century should seem frigid and ridiculous, just as it was natural that Dr Johnson should see nothing to admire in the Robin Hood ballads. *The Vicar of Wakefield*, now reprinted by Penguin Books in the English Classics series, is essentially a period piece, and its charm is about equalled by its absurdity. It is impossible to be moved by its story, which has none of the psychological realism that can be found in some eighteenth-century novels—for instance, *Amelia*. Its characters are sticks and its plot is somewhat less probable than those of the serial stories in *Peg's Paper*. But it remains extremely readable, and it has never been quite out of print in the 177 years since its first appearance. Like a Japanese woodcut, it is something perfectly executed after its own fashion, and at this date there is an historical interest in the remoteness of the standards of conduct which it is trying to uphold.

The Vicar of Wakefield is intended as a "moral tale", a sermon in fiction form. Its theme is the familiar one, preached without much success by hundreds of writers from Horace to Thackeray, of the vanity of worldly ambitions and the pleasures of the simple life. Its hero, Dr Primrose (he tells his own story in the first person), is a clergyman in what used to be called "easy circumstances", who temporarily loses his fortune and has to remove to another parish, where he supports himself by farming his own land. Here a whole series of disasters fall upon the family, traceable in every case to their having ambitions "above their station" and trying to associate with the nobility instead of with the neighbouring farmers. The eldest daughter is seduced by a heartless rascal, the farm-house is burnt to the ground, the eldest son is arrested for manslaughter, Primrose himself is thrown into a debtors' prison, and various other calamities happen. In the end, of course, everything is put right in an outrageously improbable way, one detail after another clicking into place like the teeth of a zip-fastener. Primrose's fortune is restored, the seemingly seduced daughter turns out to be an "honest woman" after all, the suitor of the second daughter, who has been posing as a poor man in order to try her affections, is discovered to be a wealthy nobleman, and so on and so forth. Virtue is rewarded and vice punished with relentless thoroughness. But the confusion in Goldsmith's mind between simple goodness and financial prudence gives the book, at this date, a strange moral atmosphere.

The main incidents are the various marriages, and the cold-blooded eighteenth-century attitude towards marriage is indicated on the first page when Dr Primrose remarks (Goldsmith probably does not intend this ironically): "I had scarcely taken orders a year, before I began to think seriously of matrimony, and chose my wife, as she did her wedding gown, not for a fine glossy surface, but such qualities as would wear well." But quite apart from this notion of choosing a wife as one might choose a length of cloth, there is the fact that getting married is inextricably mixed up with the idea of making a good financial bargain. A thumping dowry or a secure settlement is the first consideration, and the most passionate love match is promptly called off if the expected cash is not forthcoming. But together with this mercenary outlook there goes a superstitious regard for the sanctity of marriage which makes the most dramatic episode in the book ridiculous and even slightly disgusting.

Olivia is seduced by a Mr Thornhill, a wealthy young squire who has dazzled the Primrose family with his fashionable clothes and London manners. He is represented as a complete scoundrel, the "betrayer", as it was called, of innumerable women, and with every possible vice, even including physical cowardice. To entrap Olivia he uses the favourite eighteenth-century device of a false marriage. A marriage licence is forged, somebody impersonates a priest, and the girl can then be "ruined" under the delusion that she is married. Today it seems almost incredible that anyone should go to such lengths, but stratagems like this are inevitable in a society where technical chastity is highly valued and a woman has in effect no profession except marriage. In such a society there is an endless struggle between the sexes—a struggle which from the woman's point of view resembles an egg-and-spoon race, and from the man's a game of ninepins. Having been deceived in this manner, Olivia is now finished for life. She herself is made to express the current outlook by singing the justly famous lyric which Goldsmith throws into the tale:

> When lovely woman stoops to folly,
> And finds too late that men betray,
> What charm can soothe her melancholy?
> What art can wash her guilt away?
>
> The only art her guilt to cover,
> To hide her shame from every eye,
> To give repentance to her lover,
> And wring his bosom, is—to die.

Olivia indeed ought to die, and does actually begin to die—of sheer grief, after the manner of novel heroines. But here comes the *dénouement*, the great stroke of fortune that puts everything right. It turns out that Olivia was *not* seduced; she was legally married! Mr Thornhill has been in the habit of "marrying" women with a false priest and a false licence, but on this occasion a confederate of his, for purposes of his own, has deceived him by bringing a genuine licence and a real priest in holy orders. So the marriage was valid after all! And at this glorious news "a burst of pleasure seemed to fill the whole apartment. . . . Happiness was expanded upon every face, and even Olivia's cheeks seemed flushed with pleasure. To be thus restored to reputation and fortune at once was a rapture sufficient to stop the progress of decay and restore former health and vivacity."

When Olivia was believed to have "lost her virtue" she had lost all reason for living, but when it is discovered that she is tied for life to a worthless scoundrel all is well. Goldsmith does not make the ending quite so ridiculous as he might, for it is explained that Olivia continues to live apart from her husband. But she has the all-important wedding-ring, and a comfortable settlement into the bargain. Thornhill's rich uncle punishes him by depriving him of his fortune and bestowing part of it on Olivia. We are never indeed allowed quite to forget the connection between cash and virtue. Olivia sees herself "restored to reputation *and fortune at once*", while Thornhill sees "a gulf of infamy *and want*" opening before him.

Except for a scene or two in the debtors' prison and a few minor adventures at horse fairs and on muddy country roads, there is no realistic detail in *The Vicar of Wakefield*. The dialogue is quite exceptionally improbable. But the main theme—the hollowness of fashionable life and the superiority of country pleasures and family affection—is not so false as the absurd incidents which are meant to illustrate it make it appear. In inveighing against social ambition, against absentee landlords, against fine clothes, gambling, duelling, cosmetics and urban raffishness generally, Goldsmith is attacking a real tendency of his time, which Swift and Fielding had also denounced after their own fashion.

A phenomenon he is very much aware of is the growth of a new moneyed class with no sense of responsibility. Thanks to the expansion of foreign trade and wealth accumulated in the capital, the aristocracy were ceasing to be rustics. England was becoming more and more of an oligarchy, and the life of the countryside was broken

up by the enclosure of the common lands and the magnetic pull of
London. The peasants were proletarianised, the petty gentry were
corrupted. Goldsmith himself described the process in the often-
quoted lines from "The Deserted Village":

> Ill fares the land, to hastening ills a prey,
> Where wealth accumulates and men decay;
> Princes and lords may flourish or may fade,
> A breath can make them, as a breath has made;
> But a bold peasantry, their country's pride,
> When once destroyed, can never be supplied.

Thornhill stands for the new kind of rich man, the Whig aristocrat;
the Primroses, who make their own gooseberry wine and even in the
days of their wealth have hardly been ten miles from home, stand
for the old type of yeoman farmer or small landlord.

In praising country life, Goldsmith was probably praising something that he did not know much about. His descriptions of country
scenes have an unreal, idyllic atmosphere, and the Primroses are
not shown as doing much work on their farm. More often they are
sitting under some shady tree, reciting ballads and listening to the
blackbirds—pastimes that a practical farmer would seldom have
time for. Nor do we hear much of Dr Primrose's ministrations as a
clergyman: indeed, he only seems to remember at intervals that he
is in orders. But the general moral of the book is clear enough, and
thrust rather irrelevantly into one chapter there is a long political
discourse against oligarchy and the accumulation of capital. Goldsmith's conclusion—no doubt it was a common Tory theory at the
time—is that the only defence against oligarchy is a strong monarchy. Dr Primrose's son George, returning from travels in Europe, is
made to come to the same conclusion: "I found that monarchy was
the best government for the poor to live in, and commonwealths for
the rich." Dictatorship is defended on the same grounds in our own
day, and it is an instance of the way in which the same political ideas
come up again and again in slightly different forms that George
continues: "I found that riches in general were in every country
another name for freedom; and that no man is so fond of liberty
himself as not to be desirous of subjecting the will of some individuals
in society to his own."

But though there is some serious social criticism buried under its
artificialities, it is not there that the enduring charm of *The Vicar*

of Wakefield lies. The charm is in its manner—in the story, which for all its absurdity is beautifully put together, in the simple and yet elegant language, in the poems that are thrown in here and there, and in certain minor incidents, such as the well-known story of Moses and the green spectacles. Most people who read at all have read this book once, and it repays a second reading. It is one of those books which you can enjoy in one way as a child and in another as an adult, and which do not seem any the worse because you are frequently inclined to laugh in the wrong places.

Tribune, 10 November 1944

77. As I Please

Some weeks ago, in the course of some remarks on schools of journalism, I carelessly described the magazine the *Writer* as being "defunct". As a result I have received a severe letter from its proprietors, who enclose a copy of the November issue of the *Writer* and call on me to withdraw my statement.

I withdraw it readily. The *Writer* is still alive and seems to be much the same as ever, though it has changed its format since I knew it. And I think this specimen copy is worth examining for the light it throws on schools of journalism and the whole business of extracting fees from struggling free-lance journalists.

The articles are of the usual type, "Plotting Technique" (fifteenth instalment) by William A. Bagley, etc, but I am more interested in the advertisements, which take up more than a quarter of the space. The majority of them are from people who profess to be able to teach you how to make money out of writing. A surprising number undertake to supply you with ready-made plots. Here are a few specimens:

Plotting without tears. Learn my way. The simplest method ever. Money returned if dissatisfied. 5/– post free.

Inexhaustible plotting method for women's press, 5/3d. Gives real mastery. Ten days' approval.

PLOTS. Our plots are set out in sequence all ready for write-up, with lengths for each sequence. No remoulding necessary—just the requisite clothing of words. All types supplied.

PLOTS: in vivid scenes. With striking opening lines for actual use in story. Specimen conversation, including authentic dialect. ... Short-short, 5/–. Short story, 6/6d. Long-complete (with tense, breathless "curtains") 8/6d: Radio plays, 10/6d. Serial, novel, novelette (chapter by chapter, appropriate prefix, prose or poetical quotations if desired) 15/6d—1 gn.

There are many others. Somebody called Mr Martin Walter claims to have reduced story-construction to an exact science and "eventually evolved the Plot Formula according to which his own stories and those of his students throughout the world are constructed. ... Whether you aspire to write the 'literary' story or the popular story, or to produce stories for any existing market, remember that Mr Walter's Formula *alone* tells you just what a 'plot' is and how to produce one." The Formula only costs you a guinea, it appears. Then there are the "Fleet Street journalists" who are prepared to revise your manuscripts for you at 2/6d per thousand words. Nor are the poets forgotten:

GREETINGS

Are you poets neglecting the great post-war demand for sentiments?

Do you specialise and do you know what is needed?

Aida Reuben's famous Greeting Card Course is available to approved students willing to work hard. Her book *Sentiment and Greeting Card Publishers*, published at 3/6d., may be obtained from, etc etc.

I do not wish to say anything offensive, but to anyone who is inclined to respond to the sort of advertisement quoted above, I offer this consideration. If these people really know how to make money out of writing, why aren't they just doing it instead of peddling their secret at 5/– a time? Apart from any other consideration, they would be raising up hordes of competitors for themselves. This number of the *Writer* contains about 30 advertisements of this stamp, and the *Writer* itself, besides giving advice in its articles, also runs its own Literary Bureau in which manuscripts are "criticised by acknowledged experts" at so much a thousand words. If each of these various teachers had even ten successful pupils a week, they would between them be letting loose on to the market some fifteen thousand successful writers per annum!

Also, isn't it rather curious that the "Fleet Street journalists", "established authors" and "well-known novelists" who either run these courses or write the testimonials for them are not named—or, when named, are seldom or never people whose published work you have seen anywhere. If Bernard Shaw or J. B. Priestley offered to teach you how to make money out of writing, you might feel that there was something in it. But who would buy a bottle of hair restorer from a bald man?

If the *Writer* wants some more free publicity it shall have it, but I dare say this will do to go on with.

One favourite way of falsifying history nowadays is to alter dates. Maurice Thorez, the French Communist, has just been amnestied by the French Government (he was under sentence for deserting from the army). Apropos of this, one London newspaper remarks that Thorez "will now be able to return from Moscow, where he has been living in exile for the last six years."

On the contrary, he has been in Moscow for at most five years, as the editor of this newspaper is well aware. Thorez, who for several years past has been proclaiming his anxiety to defend France against the Germans, was called up at the outbreak of war in 1939, and failed to make an appearance. Some time later he turned up in Moscow.

But why the alteration of date? In order to make it appear that Thorez deserted, if he did desert, a year *before* the war and not after the fighting had started. This is merely one act in the general effort to whitewash the behaviour of the French and other Communists during the period of the Russo-German Pact. I could name other similar falsifications in recent years. Sometimes you can give an event a quite different colour by switching its date only a few weeks. But it doesn't matter so long as we all keep our eyes open and see to it that the lies do not creep out of the newspapers and into the history books.

A correspondent who lacks the collecting instinct has sent a copy of *Principles or Prejudices*, a sixpenny pamphlet by Kenneth Pickthorn, the Conservative MP, with the advice (underlined in red ink): "Burn when read".

I wouldn't think of burning it. It has gone straight into my archives. But I agree that it is a disgusting piece of work, and that this whole series of pamphlets (the Signpost Booklets, by such authors

as G. M. Young, Douglas Woodruff and Captain L. D. Gammans)
is a bad symptom. Mr Pickthorn is one of the more intelligent of the
younger Tory MPs ("younger" in political circles means under
sixty), and in this pamphlet he is trying to present Toryism in a
homely and democratic light while casting misleading little smacks
at the Left. Look at this, for instance, for a misrepresentation of the
theory of Marxism:

> Not one of the persons who say that economic factors govern
> the world believes it about himself. If Karl Marx had been more
> economically than politically interested he could have done
> better for himself than by accepting the kindnesses of the capi-
> talist Engels and occasionally selling articles to American news-
> papers.

Aimed at ignorant people, this is meant to imply that Marxism
regards *individual* acquisitiveness as the motive force in history.
Marx not only did not say this, he said almost the opposite of it.
Much of the pamphlet is an attack on the notion of internationalism,
and is backed up by such remarks as: "No British statesman should
feel himself authorised to spend British blood for the promotion of
something superior to British interests." Fortunately, Mr Pickthorn
writes too badly to have a very wide appeal, but some of the other
pamphleteers in this series are cleverer. The Tory Party used always
to be known as "the stupid party". But the publicists of this group
have a fair selection of brains among them, and when Tories grow
intelligent it is time to feel for your watch and count your small
change.

Tribune, 17 November 1944

78. As I Please

There have been innumerable complaints lately about the rudeness
of shopkeepers. People say, I think with truth, that shopkeepers
appear to take a sadistic pleasure in telling you that they don't stock
the thing you ask for. To go in search of some really rare object,
such as a comb or a tin of boot polish, is a miserable experience. It
means trailing from shop to shop and getting a series of curt or
actually hostile negatives. But even the routine business of buying

the rations and the bread is made as difficult as possible for busy people. How is a woman to do her household shopping if she is working till six every day while most of the shops shut at five? She can only do it by fighting round crowded counters during her lunch hour. But it is the snubs that they get when they ask for some article which is in short supply that people dread most. Many shopkeepers seem to regard the customer as a kind of mendicant and to feel that they are conferring a favour on him by selling him anything. And there are other justified grievances—for instance, the shameless overcharging on uncontrolled goods such as second-hand furniture, and the irritating trick, now very common, of displaying in the window goods which are not on sale.

But before blaming the shopkeeper for all this, there are several things one ought to remember. To begin with, irritability and bad manners are on the increase everywhere. You have only to observe the behaviour of normally long-suffering people like bus conductors to realise this. It is a neurosis produced by the war. But, in addition, many small independent shopkeepers (in my experience you are treated far more politely in big shops) are people with a well-founded grievance against society. Some of them are in effect the ill-paid employees of wholesale firms, others are being slowly crushed by the competition of the chain stores, and they are often treated with the greatest inconsiderateness by the local authorities. Sometimes a rehousing scheme will rob a shopkeeper of half his customers at one swoop. In war-time this may happen even more drastically owing to bombing and the call-up. And war has other special irritations for the shopkeeper. Rationing puts a great deal of extra work on to grocers, butchers, etc and it is very exasperating to be be asked all day long for articles which you have not got.

But after all, the main fact is that at normal times both the shop assistant and the independent shopkeepers are downtrodden. They live to the tune of "the customer is always right". In peace time, in capitalist society, everyone is trying to sell goods which there is never enough money to buy, whereas in war-time money is plentiful and goods scarce. Matches, razor blades, torch batteries, alarm clocks and teats for babies' feeding bottles are precious rarities, and the man who possesses them is a powerful being, to be approached cap in hand. I don't think one can blame the shopkeeper for getting a bit of his own back, when the situation is temporarily reversed.

But I do agree that the behaviour of some of them is disgusting, and that when one is treated with more than normal haughtiness it is a duty to the rest of the public not to go to that shop again.

Examining recently a copy of *Old Moore's Almanac*, I was reminded of the fun I used to extract in my boyhood from answering advertisements. Increase your height, earn five pounds a week in your spare time, drink habit conquered in three days, electric belts, bust-developers and cures for obesity, insomnia, bunions, backache, red noses, stammering, blushing, piles, bad legs, flat feet and baldness—all the old favourites were there, or nearly all. Some of these advertisements have remained totally unchanged for at least thirty years.

You cannot, I imagine, get much benefit from any of these nostrums, but you can have a lot of fun by answering the advertisements and then, when you have drawn them out and made them waste a lot of stamps in sending successive wads of testimonials, suddenly leaving them cold. Many years ago I answered an advertisement from Winifred Grace Hartland (the advertisement used to carry a photograph of her—a radiant woman with a sylph-like figure), who undertook to cure obesity. In replying to my letter she assumed that I was a woman—this surprised me at the time, though I realise now that the dupes of these advertisements are almost all female. She urged me to come and see her at once. "Do come," she wrote, "before ordering your summer frocks, as after taking my course your figure will have altered out of recognition." She was particularly insistent that I should make a personal visit, and gave an address somewhere in the London Docks. This went on for a long time, during which the fee gradually sank from two guineas to half a crown, and then I brought the matter to an end by writing to say that I had been cured of my obesity by a rival agency.

Years later I came across a copy of the cautionary list which *Truth* used to issue from time to time in order to warn the public against swindlers. It revealed that there was no such person as Winifred Grace Hartland, this swindle being run by two American crooks named Harry Sweet and Dave Little. It is curious that they should have been so anxious for a personal visit, and indeed I have since wondered whether Harry Sweet and Dave Little were actually engaged in shipping consignments of fat women to the harems of Istanbul.

Everyone has a list of books which he is "always meaning to read", and now and again one gets round to reading one of them. One that I recently crossed off my list was George Bourne's *Memoirs of a Surrey Labourer*. I was slightly disappointed with it, because, though it is a true story, Bettesworth, the man it is about, was not quite an ordinary labourer. He had been a farm worker, but had become a jobbing gardener, and his relation with George Bourne was that of servant and master. Nevertheless there is some remarkable detail in it, and it gives a true picture of the cruel, sordid end with which a lifetime of heavy work on the land is often rewarded. The book was written more than thirty years ago, but things have not changed fundamentally. Immediately before the war, in my own village in Hertfordshire, two old men were ending their days in much the same bare misery as George Bourne describes.

Another book I recently read, or rather re-read, was *The Follies and Frauds of Spiritualism*, issued about twenty years ago by the Rationalist Press Association. This is probably not an easy book to get hold of, but I can equally recommend Mr Bechhofer-Roberts's book on the same subject. An interesting fact that these and similar books bring out is the number of scientists who have been taken in by spiritualism. The list includes Sir William Crookes, Wallace the biologist, Lombroso, Flammarion the astronomer (he afterwards changed his mind, however), Sir Oliver Lodge, and a whole string of German and Italian professors. These people are not, perhaps, the top-notchers of the scientific world, but you do not, find, for instance, poets in comparable numbers falling a prey to the mediums. Elizabeth Barrett Browning is supposed to have been taken in by the famous medium Home, but Browning himself saw through him at a glance and wrote a scarifying poem about him ("Sludge the Medium"). Significantly, the people who are *never* converted to spiritualism are conjurors.

Tribune, 24 November 1944

79. As I Please

V2[1] (I am told that you can now mention it in print so long as you just call it V2 and don't describe it too minutely) supplies another

[1] The V2 was the rocket bomb used by the Germans after the V1. The V2 was quite silent in its approach but made a tremendous noise on landing.

instance of the contrariness of human nature. People are complaining of the sudden unexpected wallop with which these things go off. "It wouldn't be so bad if you got a bit of warning" is the usual formula. There is even a tendency to talk nostalgically of the days of the V1. The good old doodlebug did at least give you time to get under the table, etc etc. Whereas, in fact, when the doodlebugs were actually dropping, the usual subject of complaint was the uncomfortable waiting period before they went off. Some people are never satisfied. Personally, I am no lover of the V2, especially at this moment when the house still seems to be rocking from a recent explosion, but what depresses me about these things is the way they set people talking about the next war. Every time one goes off I hear gloomy references to "next time", and the reflection: "I suppose they'll be able to shoot them across the Atlantic by that time". But if you ask who will be fighting whom when this universally expected war breaks out, you get no clear answer. It is just war in the abstract—the notion that human beings could ever behave sanely having apparently faded out of many people's memories.

Maurice Baring, in his book on Russian literature, which was published in 1907 and must have been the means of introducing many people in this country to the great Russian novelists, remarks that English books were always popular in Russia. Among other favourites he mentions *The Diary of a Nobody* (which, by the way, is reprinted by the Everyman Library, if you can run across a copy).

I have always wondered what on earth *The Diary of a Nobody* could be like in a Russian translation, and indeed I have faintly suspected that the Russians may have enjoyed it because when translated it was just like Chekhov. But in a way it would be a very good book to read if you wanted to get a picture of English life, even though it was written in the 'eighties and has an intensely strong smell of that period. Charles Pooter is a true Englishman both in native gentleness and his impenetrable stupidity. The interesting thing, however, is to follow this book up to its origins. What does it ultimately derive from? Almost certainly, I think, from *Don Quixote*, of which, indeed, it is a sort of modern anglicised version. Pooter is a high-minded, even adventurous man, constantly suffering disasters brought upon him by his own folly, and surrounded by a whole tribe of Sancho Panzas. But apart from the comparative mildness of the things that befall him, one can see in the endings of the two books the enormous difference between the age of Cervantes and our own.

In the end the Grossmiths have to take pity on poor Pooter. Everything, or nearly everything, comes right, and at the last there is a tinge of sentimentality which does not quite fit in with the rest of the book. The fact is that, in spite of way we actually behave, we cannot any longer feel that the infliction of pain is merely funny. Nietzsche remarks somewhere that the pathos of *Don Quixote* may well be a modern discovery. Quite likely Cervantes didn't mean Don Quixote to seem pathetic—perhaps he just meant him to be funny and intended it as a screaming joke when the poor old man has half his teeth knocked out by a sling-stone. However this may be with Don Quixote, I am fairly certain that it is true of Falstaff. Except possibly for the final scene in *Henry V*, there is nothing to show that Shakespeare sees Falstaff as a pathetic as well as a comic figure.[1] He is just a punching-bag for fortune, a sort of Billy Bunter with a gift for language. The thing that seems saddest to us is Falstaff's helpless dependence on his odious patron, Prince Harry, whom John Masefield aptly described as a "disgusting beefy brute". There is no sign, or, at any rate, no clear sign, that Shakespeare sees anything pathetic or degrading in such a relationship.

Say what you like, things *do* change. A few years ago I was walking

[1] In a theatre review in *Time and Tide*, 4 January 1941, Orwell wrote: ". . . *The Merry Wives* is traditionally supposed to have been written in a week at the command of Queen Elizabeth, and it is often objected against it that the Falstaff who appears in it is a different being from the Falstaff of *Henry IV*. It is true that the plot requires him to behave in an unbelievably stupid manner—in any case Falstaff is the kind of burlesque character who ought never to be involved in a "plot"—but in the opening scenes he is his old self and both he and Pistol have some of their best speeches. Mr Wolfit presents him in the usual slapstick manner, with a red nose as well as an unmanageable belly, which is a mistake. Falstaff is fat, and it is well known that fat people have no finer feelings; he is also dishonest and cowardly, and "the cause of wit in others". But he is nevertheless a highly intelligent man, one of the very few among Shakespeare's characters who can be described as "intellectuals". It would be a wonderful thing if some actor would some day recognise this and act Falstaff with as much care as is usually given to Hamlet. Falstaff always speaks in prose, but it is a highly poetical prose; Pistol speaks gibberish, but on purely musical grounds his lines are some of the best that Shakespeare ever wrote. Nevertheless the poetry of the Falstaff scenes never gets across, because it is the convention to treat them as very low farce, to be enlivened as much as possible by the throwing of bottles, attacks of hiccoughs, etc etc. . . ."

across Hungerford Bridge with a lady aged about sixty or perhaps less. The tide was out, and as we looked down at the beds of filthy, almost liquid mud, she remarked:

"When I was a little girl we used to throw pennies to the mudlarks down there."

I was intrigued and asked what mudlarks were. She explained that in those days professional beggars, known as mudlarks, used to sit under the bridge waiting for people to throw them pennies. The pennies would bury themselves deep in the mud, and the mudlarks would plunge in head first and recover them. This was considered a most amusing spectacle.

Is there anyone who would degrade himself in that way nowadays? And how many people are there who would get a kick out of watching it?

Shortly before his assassination, Trotsky had completed a *Life of Stalin*. One may assume that it was not an altogether unbiassed book, but obviously a biography of Stalin by Trotsky—or, for that matter, a biography of Trotsky by Stalin—would be a winner from a selling point of view. A very well-known American firm of publishers were to issue it. The book had been printed and—this is the point that I have been waiting to verify before mentioning this matter in my notes—the review copies had been sent out when the USA entered the war. The book was immediately withdrawn, and the reviewers were asked to co-operate in "avoiding any comment whatever regarding the biography and its postponement".

They have co-operated remarkably well. This affair has gone almost unmentioned in the American press and, as far as I know, entirely unmentioned in the British press, although the facts were well known and obviously worth a paragraph or two.

Since the American entry into the war made the USA and the USSR allies, I think that to withdraw the book was an understandable if not particularly admirable deed. What is disgusting is the general willingness to suppress all mention of it. A little while back I attended a meeting of the PEN Club, which was held to celebrate the tercentenary of *Areopagitica*, Milton's famous tract on the freedom of the press. There were countless speeches emphasising the importance of preserving intellectual liberty, even in war-time. If I remember rightly, Milton's phrase about the special sin of "murdering" a book was printed on the PEN leaflet for the occasion.

But I heard no reference to this particular murder, the facts of which were no doubt known to plenty of people there.

Here is another little brain-tickler. The following often-quoted passage comes from Act V of Shakespeare's tragedy, *Timon of Athens*:

> Come not to me again, but say to Athens,
> Timon hath made his everlasting mansion
> Upon the beachèd verge of the salt flood
> Who once a day with his embossed froth
> The turbulent surge shall cover.

This passage contains three errors. What are they?

Tribune, 1 December 1944

80. Funny, But Not Vulgar

The great age of English humorous writing—not witty and not satirical, but simply humorous—was the first three-quarters of the nineteenth century.

Within that period lie Dickens's enormous output of comic writings, Thackeray's brilliant burlesques and short stories, such as "The Fatal Boots" and "A Little Dinner at Timmins's", Surtees's *Handley Cross*, Lewis Carroll's *Alice in Wonderland*, Douglas Jerrold's *Mrs Caudle's Curtain Lectures*, and a considerable body of humorous verse by R. H. Barham, Thomas Hood, Edward Lear, Arthur Hugh Clough, Charles Stuart Calverley and others. Two other comic masterpieces, F. Anstey's *Vice Versa* and the two Grossmiths' *Diary of a Nobody*, lie only just outside the period I have named. And, at any rate until 1860 or thereabouts, there was still such a thing as comic draughtsmanship, witness Cruikshank's illustrations to Dickens, Leech's illustrations to Surtees, and even Thackeray's illustrations of his own work.

I do not want to exaggerate by suggesting that, within our own century, England has produced no humorous writing of any value. There have been, for instance, Barry Pain, W. W. Jacobs, Stephen Leacock, P. G. Wodehouse, H. G. Wells in his lighter moments, Evelyn Waugh, and—a satirist rather than a humorist—Hilaire

Belloc. Still, we have not only produced no laugh-getter of anything like the stature of *Pickwick Papers*, but, what is probably more significant, there is not and has not been for decades past, any such thing as a first-rate humorous periodical. The usual charge against *Punch*, that it "isn't what it was", is perhaps unjustified at this moment, since *Punch* is somewhat funnier than it was ten years ago: but it is also very much *less* funny than it was ninety years ago.

And comic verse has lost all its vitality—there has been no English light verse of any value within this century, except Mr Belloc's, and a poem or two by Chesterton—while a drawing that is funny in its own right, and not merely because of the joke it illustrates, is a great rarity.

All this is generally admitted. If you want a laugh you are likelier to go to a music hall or a Disney film, or switch on Tommy Handley, or buy a few of Donald McGill's postcards, than to resort to a book or a periodical. It is generally recognised, too, that American comic writers and illustrators are superior to our own. At present we have nobody to set against either James Thurber or Damon Runyon.

We do not know with certainty how laughter originated or what biological purpose it serves, but we do know, in broad terms, what causes laughter.

A thing is funny when—in some way that is not actually offensive or frightening—it upsets the established order. Every joke is a tiny revolution. If you had to define humour in a single phrase, you might define it as dignity sitting on a tin-tack. Whatever destroys dignity, and brings down the mighty from their seats, preferably with a bump, is funny. And the bigger the fall, the bigger the joke. It would be better fun to throw a custard pie at a bishop than at a curate. With this general principle in mind, one can, I think, begin to see what has been wrong with English comic writing during the present century.

Nearly all English humorists today are too genteel, too kind-hearted and too consciously lowbrow. P. G. Wodehouse's novels, or A. P. Herbert's verses, seem always to be aimed at prosperous stockbrokers whiling away an odd half hour in the lounge of some suburban golf course. They and all their kind are dominated by an anxiety not to stir up mud, either moral, religious, political or intellectual. It is no accident that most of the best comic writers of our time—Belloc, Chesterton, "Timothy Shy" and the recent "Beachcomber"—have been Catholic apologists; that is, people with a serious purpose and a noticeable willingness to hit below the belt. The silly-ass tradition in modern English humour, the avoidance of brutality and horror of intelligence, is summed up in the phrase *funny without being vulgar*. "Vulgar" in this context usually means "obscene", and it can be admitted at once that the best jokes are not necessarily dirty ones. Edward Lear and Lewis Carroll, for instance, never made jokes of that description, and Dickens and Thackeray very rarely.

On the whole, the early Victorian writers avoided sex jokes, though a few, for instance Surtees, Marryat and Barham, retained traces of eighteenth-century coarseness. But the point is that the modern emphasis on what is called "clean fun" is really the symptom of a general unwillingness to touch upon any serious or controversial subject. Obscenity is, after all, a kind of subversiveness. Chaucer's "Miller's Tale" is a rebellion in the moral sphere, as *Gulliver's Travels* is a rebellion in the political sphere. The truth is that you cannot be memorably funny without *at some point* raising topics which the rich, the powerful and the complacent would prefer to see left alone.

I named above some of the best comic writers of the nineteenth century, but the case becomes much stronger if one draws in the English humorists of earlier ages—for instance, Chaucer, Shakespeare, Swift and the picaresque novelists, Smollett, Fielding and Sterne. It becomes stronger again if one considers foreign writers, both ancient and modern—for example, Aristophanes, Voltaire, Rabelais, Boccaccio and Cervantes. All of these writers are remarkable for their brutality and coarseness. People are tossed in blankets, they fall through cucumber frames, they are hidden in washing baskets, they rob, lie, swindle, and are caught out in every conceivable humiliating situation. And all great humorous writers show a willingness to attack the beliefs and the virtues on which society necessarily rests. Boccaccio treats Hell and Purgatory as a ridiculous fable, Swift jeers at the very conception of human dignity, Shakespeare makes Falstaff deliver a speech in favour of cowardice in the middle of a battle. As for the sanctity of marriage, it was the principal subject of humour in Christian society for the better part of a thousand years.

All this is not to say that humour is, of its nature, immoral or antisocial. A joke is at most a temporary rebellion against virtue, and its aim is not to degrade the human being but to remind him that he is already degraded. A willingness to make extremely obscene jokes can co-exist with very strict moral standards, as in Shakespeare. Some comic writers, like Dickens, have a direct political purpose, others, like Chaucer or Rabelais, accept the corruption of society as something inevitable; but no comic writer of any stature has ever suggested that society is *good*.

Humour is the debunking of humanity, and nothing is funny except in relation to human beings. Animals, for instance, are only funny because they are caricatures of ourselves. A lump of stone could not of itself be funny; but it can become funny if it hits a human being in the eye, or if it is carved into human likeness.

However, there are subtler methods of debunking than throwing custard pies. There is also the humour of pure fantasy, which assaults man's notion of himself as not only a dignified but a rational being. Lewis Carroll's humour consists essentially in making fun of logic, and Edward Lear's in a sort of poltergeist interference with common sense. When the Red Queen remarks, "*I've* seen hills compared with which you'd call that one a valley", she is in her way attacking the bases of society as violently as Swift or Voltaire. Comic verse, as in Lear's poem "The Courtship of the Yonghy-Bonghy-Bò", often depends on building up a fantastic universe which is just similar enough to the real universe to rob it of its dignity. But more often it depends on anticlimax—that is, on starting out with a high-flown language and then suddenly coming down with a bump. For instance, Calverley's lines:

> Once, a happy child, I carolled
> On green lawns the whole day through,
> Not unpleasingly apparelled
> In a tightish suit of blue,

in which the first two lines would give the impression that this is going to be a sentimental poem about the beauties of childhood. Or Mr Belloc's various invocations to Africa in *The Modern Traveller*:

> O Africa, mysterious land,
> Surrounded by a lot of sand,
> And full of grass and trees . . .
> Far land of Ophir, mined for gold
> By lordly Solomon of old,

> Who, sailing northward to Perim,
> Took all the gold away with him
> And left a lot of holes, etc.

Bret Harte's sequel to "Maud Muller", with such couplets as:

> But the very day that they were mated
> Maud's brother Bob was intoxicated

plays essentially the same trick, and so in a different way do Voltaire's mock epic, *La Pucelle*, and many passages in Byron.

English light verse in the present century—witness the work of Owen Seaman, Harry Graham, A. P. Herbert, A. A. Milne and others —has mostly been poor stuff, lacking not only in fancifulness but in intellectuality. Its authors are too anxious not to be highbrows— even, though they are writing in verse, not to be poets. Early-Victorian light verse is generally haunted by the ghost of poetry; it is often extremely skilful as verse, and it is sometimes allusive and "difficult". When Barham wrote:

> The Callipyge's injured behind,
> Bloudie Jack !
> The de Medici's injured before;
> And the Anadyomene's injured in so many
> Places, I think there's a score,
> If not more,
> Of her fingers and toes on the floor.

he was performing a feat of sheer virtuosity which the most serious poet would respect. Or, to quote Calverley again, in his "Ode to Tobacco":

> Thou, who when fears attack,
> Bidst them avaunt, and Black
> Care, at the horseman's back
> Perching, unseatest;
> Sweet when the morn is grey,
> Sweet when they've cleared away
> Lunch, and at close of day
> Possibly sweetest!

Calverley is not afraid, it will be seen, to put a tax on his reader's attention and to drag in a recondite Latin allusion. He is not writing for lowbrows, and—particularly in his "Ode to Beer"—he can achieve magnificent anticlimaxes because he is willing to sail close to true poetry and to assume considerable knowledge in his readers.

It would seem that you *cannot* be funny without being vulgar— that is, vulgar by the standards of the people at whom English humorous writing in our own day seems mostly to be aimed. For it is not only sex that is "vulgar". So are death, childbirth and poverty, the other three subjects upon which the best music-hall humour turns. And respect for the intellect and strong political feeling, if not actually vulgar, are looked upon as being in doubtful taste. You cannot be really funny if your main aim is to flatter the comfortable classes: it means leaving out too much. To be funny, indeed, you have got to be serious. *Punch*, for at least forty years past, has given the impression of trying not so much to amuse as to reassure. Its implied message is that all is for the best and nothing will ever really change.

It was by no means with that creed that it started out.

Written [December 1944]; *Leader*, 28 July 1945

81. As I Please

For years past I have been an industrious collector of pamphlets, and a fairly steady reader of political literature of all kinds. The thing that strikes me more and more—and it strikes a lot of other people, too—is the extraordinary viciousness and dishonesty of political controversy in our time. I don't mean merely that controversies are acrimonious. They ought to be that when they are on serious subjects. I mean that almost nobody seems to feel that an opponent deserves a fair hearing or that the objective truth matters so long as you can score a neat debating point. When I look through my collection of pamphlets—Conservative, Communist, Catholic, Trotskyist, Pacifist, Anarchist or what-have-you—it seems to me that almost all of them have the same mental atmosphere, though the points of emphasis vary. Nobody is searching for the truth, everybody is putting forward a "case" with complete disregard for fairness or accuracy, and the most plainly obvious facts can be ignored by those who don't want to see them. The same propaganda tricks are to be found almost everywhere. It would take many pages of this paper merely to classify them, but here I draw attention to one very widespread controversial habit—disregard of an opponent's motives. The key-word here is "objectively".

We are told that it is only people's objective actions that matter, and their subjective feelings are of no importance. Thus pacifists, by obstructing the war effort, are "objectively" aiding the Nazis: and therefore the fact that they may be personally hostile to Fascism is irrelevant. I have been guilty of saying this myself more than once. The same argument is applied to Trotskyists. Trotskyists are often credited, at any rate by Communists, with being active and conscious agents of Hitler; but when you point out the many and obvious reasons why this is unlikely to be true, the "objectively" line of talk is brought forward again. To criticise the Soviet Union helps Hitler: therefore "Trotskyism is Fascism". And when this has been established, the accusation of conscious treachery is usually repeated.

This is not only dishonest; it also carries a severe penalty with it. If you disregard people's motives, it becomes much harder to foresee their actions. For there are occasions when even the most misguided person can see the results of what he is doing. Here is a crude but quite possible illustration. A pacifist is working in some job which gives him access to important military information, and is approached by a German secret agent. In those circumstances his subjective feelings *do* make a difference. If he is subjectively pro-Nazi he will sell his country, and if he isn't, he won't. And situations essentially similar though less dramatic are constantly arising.

In my opinion a few pacifists are inwardly pro-Nazi, and extremist left-wing parties will inevitably contain Fascist spies. The important thing is to discover *which* individuals are honest and which are not, and the usual blanket accusation merely makes this more difficult. The atmosphere of hatred in which controversy is conducted blinds people to considerations of this kind. To admit that an opponent might be both honest and intelligent is felt to be intolerable. It is more immediately satisfying to shout that he is a fool or a scoundrel, or both, than to find out what he is really like. It is this habit of mind, among other things, that has made political prediction in our time so remarkably unsuccessful.

The following leaflet (printed) was passed to an acquaintance of mine in a pub:

LONG LIVE THE IRISH!

The first American soldier to kill a Jap was Mike Murphy.

The first American pilot to sink a Jap battleship was Colin Kelly.

The first American family to lose five sons in one action and have a naval vessel named after them were the Sullivans.

The first American to shoot a Jap plane was Dutch O'Hara.

The first coastguardsman to spot a German spy was John Conlan.

The first American soldier to be decorated by the President was Pat Powers.

The first American admiral to be killed leading his ship into battle was Dan Callahan.

The first American son-of-a-bitch to get four new tyres from the Ration Board was Abie Goldstein.

The origin of this thing might just possibly be Irish, but it is much likelier to be American. There is nothing to indicate where it was printed, but it probably comes from the printing-shop of some American organisation in this country. If any further manifestos of the same kind turn up, I shall be interested to hear of them.

This number of *Tribune* includes a long letter from Mr Martin Walter, Controller of the British Institute of Fiction-Writing Science Ltd, in which he complains that I have traduced him. He says (a) that he did not claim to have reduced fiction-writing to an exact science, (b) that numbers of successful writers *have* been produced by his teaching methods, and (c) he asks whether *Tribune* accepts advertisements that it believes to be fraudulent.

With regard to (a) "It is claimed by this Institute that these problems (of fiction-writing) have been solved by Martin Walter, who, convinced of the truth of the hypothesis that *every art is a science at heart*, analysed over 5,000 stories and eventually evolved the Plot Formula according to which all his own stories and those of his students throughout the world are constructed." "I had established that the nature of the 'plot' is strictly scientific." Statements of this type are scattered throughout Mr Walter's booklets and advertisements. If this is not a claim to have reduced fiction-writing to an exact science, what the devil is it?

With regard to (b) Who are these successful writers whom Mr

Walter has launched upon the world? Let us hear their names, and the names of their published works, and then we shall know where we are.

With regard to (c) A periodical ought not to accept advertisements which have the appearance of being fraudulent, but it cannot sift everything beforehand. What is to be done, for instance, about publishers' advertisements, in which it is invariably claimed that every single book named is of the highest possible value? What is most important in this connection is that a periodical should not let its editorial columns be influenced by its advertisements. *Tribune* has been very careful not to do that—it has not done it in the case of Mr Walter himself, for instance.

It may interest Mr Walter to know that I should never have referred to him if he had not accompanied the advertisement he inserted some time ago with some free copies of his booklets (including the Plot Formula), and the suggestion that I might like to mention them in my column. It was this that drew my attention to him. Now I have given him his mention, and he does not seem to like it.

Answer to last week's problem. The three errors are:

(a) The "who" should be "whom".

(b) Timon was buried below the high-tide mark. The sea would cover him twice a day, not once, as there are always two high tides within the twenty-four hours.

(c) It wouldn't cover him at all, as there is no perceptible tide in the Mediterranean.

Tribune, 8 December 1944

82. Letter to Frank Barber

> 27B Canonbury Square
> Islington
> London N1
> 15 December 1944

Dear Mr Barber,[1]

Many thanks for your letter of 8th December. I am pretty sure it *was* a life of Stalin, not Lenin. I had heard of this from other sources, but

---

[1] Frank D. Barber (1917–), journalist, at this time assistant editor of the *Leeds Weekly Citizen*.

on looking up again the copy of the *Partisan Review* which is my authority for the recall of the review copies, I find it definitely referred to as a *Life of Stalin*. This number of *PR* mentions 3 books as having been withdrawn in this way, the Stalin book, Barmine's book, which was entitled *One Who Survived*, and *My Year in the USSR*, by G. E. R. Gedye, who used to be Moscow correspondent for the *New York Times*.[1] I suppose the British Trotskyists could give further confirmation, but I have no contacts with them.

I was very interested in your note about Barmine. In my small way I have been fighting for years against the systematic faking of history which now goes on. I think you will be interested in [an] article which a friend of mine will publish shortly in *World Review*,[2] dealing with some of the lies which have been used against Mihailovich.[3] A Russian acquaintance (I can't give his name) writes to give me some details of the official Soviet publication *Reference Calendar for 1944*. This consists of chronological tables of important events, and the Russo-German Pact of 1939 is not mentioned in it! My attention was first drawn to this deliberate falsification of history by my experiences in the Spanish civil war. One can't make too much noise about it while the man in the street identifies the cause of Socialism with the USSR, but I believe one can make a perceptible difference by seeing that the true facts get into print, even if it is only in some obscure place.

A person who could probably give you some interesting infor-

[1] "Three books, either critical or definitely hostile to the present régime in Russia, have been withdrawn from publication after having been publicly announced. Doubleday, Doran has cancelled the publication this spring of *One Who Survived*, the reminiscences of a former Soviet diplomat, Alexander Barmine. Harper has withdrawn *My Year in the USSR*, by the former *NY Times* Moscow correspondent, G. E. R. Gedye, and also Trotsky's *Life of Stalin*. The latter book was actually sent out for review, only to be recalled a few days later (on December 12) by a note signed by President Cass Canfield which concludes, 'We hope you will co-operate with us in the matter of avoiding any comment whatever regarding the biography and its postponement'." [Editorial note in *Partisan Review*, March–April, 1942.]

[2] "The Truth about Mihailovich" by R. V. Elson, *World Review*, January 1945.

[3] Draja Mihailovich (1893–1946), Jugoslav patriot and military leader of the nationalist guerilla (Chetnik) forces in Jugoslavia, formed in 1941 when the Germans had invaded the country. He later became involved in a struggle for the control of the guerilla movement with Tito, a Communist. In 1946 Mihailovich was captured and executed by the Tito Government.

mation along these lines is the veteran (ex) Communist Ruth
Fischer,[1] who is in America. She can be found care of *Politics*, 45
Astor Place, New York 3, NY, USA.

Yours sincerely
Geo. Orwell

83. London Letter to *Partisan Review*

[December 1944]

Dear Editors,

It is close on four years since I first wrote to you, and I have told you
several times that I would like to write one letter which should be a
sort of commentary on the previous ones. This seems to be a suitable
moment.

Now that we have seemingly won the war and lost the peace, it is
possible to see earlier events in a certain perspective, and the first
thing I have to admit is that up to at any rate the end of 1942 I was
grossly wrong in my analysis of the situation. It is because, so far as
I can see, everyone else was wrong too that my own mistakes are
worth commenting on.

I have tried to tell the truth in these letters, and I believe your
readers have got from them a not too distorted picture of what was
happening at any given moment. Of course there are many mistaken
predictions (e.g. in 1941 I prophesied that Russia and Germany
would go on collaborating and in 1942 that Churchill would fall
from power), many generalisations based on little or no evidence,
and also, from time to time, spiteful or misleading remarks about
individuals. For instance, I particularly regret having said in one
letter that Julian Symons "writes in a vaguely Fascist strain"—a
quite unjustified statement based on a single article which I probably
misunderstood. But this kind of thing results largely from the lunatic
atmosphere of war, the fog of lies and misinformation in which one
has to work and the endless sordid controversies in which a political
journalist is involved. By the low standards now prevailing I think I

---

[1] Ruth Fischer (1895–1961), former General Secretary of the German Communist Party 1923–6, when she was expelled as a Trotskyist. A refugee from Hitler
Germany, she lived in France and the United States and wrote on political
subjects. Her *Stalin and German Communism* was published in 1948.

have been fairly accurate about facts. Where I have gone wrong is in assessing the relative importance of different *trends*. And most of my mistakes spring from a political analysis which I had made in the desperate period of 1940 and continued to cling to long after it should have been clear that it was untenable.

The essential error is contained in my very first letter, written at the end of 1940, in which I stated that the political reaction which was already visibly under weigh "is not going to make very much ultimate difference". For about eighteen months I repeated this in various forms again and again. I not only assumed (what is probably true) that the drift of popular feeling was towards the Left, but that it would be quite impossible to win the war without democratising it. In 1940 I had written, "Either we turn this into a revolutionary war, or we lose it", and I find myself repeating this word for word as late as the middle of 1942. This probably coloured my judgement of actual events and made me exaggerate the depth of the political crisis in 1942, the possibilities of Cripps as a popular leader and of Common Wealth as a revolutionary party, and also the socially levelling process occurring in Britain as a result of the war. But what really matters is that I fell into the trap of assuming that "the war and the revolution are inseparable". There were excuses for this belief, but still it was a very great error. For after all we have not lost the war, unless appearances are very deceiving, and we have not introduced Socialism. Britain is moving towards a planned economy, and class distinctions tend to dwindle, but there has been no real shift of power and no increase in genuine democracy. The same people still own all the property and usurp all the best jobs. In the United States the development appears to be *away* from Socialism. The United States is indeed the most powerful country in the world, and the most capitalistic. When we look back at our judgements of a year or two ago, whether we "opposed" the war or whether we "supported" it, I think the first admission we ought to make is that *we were all wrong*.

Among the British and American intelligentsia, using the word in a wide sense, there were five attitudes towards the war:

1. The war is worth winning at any price, because nothing could be worse than a Fascist victory. We must support any régime which will oppose the Nazis.

2. The war is worth winning at any price, but in practice it cannot

be won while capitalism survives. We must support the war, and at the same time endeavour to turn it into a revolutionary war.

3. The war cannot be won while capitalism survives, but even if it could, such a victory would be worse than useless. It would merely lead to the establishment of Fascism in our own countries. We must overthrow our own government before lending our support to the war.

4. If we fight against Fascism, under no matter what government, we shall inevitably go Fascist ourselves.

5. It is no use fighting, because the Germans and the Japanese are bound to win anyway.

Position 1 was taken by radicals everywhere, and by Stalinists after the entry of the USSR. Trotskyists of various colours took either position 2 or position 4. Pacifists took position 4 and generally used 5 as an additional argument. 1 merely amounts to saying, "I don't like Fascism", and is hardly a guide to political action: it does not make any prediction about what will happen. But the other theories have all been completely falsified. The fact that we were fighting for our lives has not forced us to "go Socialist", as I foretold that it would, but neither has it driven us into Fascism. So far as I can judge, we are somewhat further from Fascism than we were at the beginning of the war. It seems to me very important to realise that we have been wrong, and say so. Most people nowadays, when their predictions are falsified, just impudently claim that they have been justified, and squeeze the facts accordingly. Thus many people who took the line that I did will in effect claim that the revolution has already happened, that class privilege and economic injustice can never return, etc etc. Pacifists claim with even greater confidence that Britain is already a Fascist country and indistinguishable from Nazi Germany, although the very fact they they are allowed to write and agitate contradicts them. From all sides there is a chorus of "I told you so", and complete shamelessness about past mistakes. Appeasers, Popular Fronters, Communists, Trotskyists, Anarchists, pacifists, all claim—and in almost exactly the same tone of voice— that *their* prophecies and no others have been borne out by events. Particularly on the Left, political thought is a sort of masturbation fantasy in which the world of facts hardly matters.

But to return to my own mistakes. I am not here concerned with correcting those mistakes, so much as with explaining why I made them. When I suggested to you that Britain was on the edge of drastic political changes, and had already made an advance from which there could be no drawing back, I was not trying to put a good face on things for the benefit of the American public. I expressed the same ideas, and much more violently, in books and articles only published at home. Here are a few samples:

"The choice is between Socialism and defeat. We must go forward, or perish". "*Laissez-faire* capitalism is dead". "The English revolution started several years ago, and it began to gather momentum when the troops came back from Dunkirk". "With its present social structure England cannot survive". "This war, unless we are defeated, will wipe out most of the existing class privileges". "Within a year, perhaps even within six months, if we are still unconquered, we shall see the rise of something that has never existed before, a specifically *English* Socialist movement". "The last thing the British ruling class wants is to acquire fresh territory". "The real quarrel of the Fascist powers with British imperialism is that they know that it is disintegrating". "The war will bankrupt the majority of the public schools if it continues for another year or two". "This war is a race between the consolidation of Hitler's empire and the growth of democratic consciousness".

And so on and so on. How could I write such things? Well, there is a clue in the fact that my predictions, especially about military events, were by no means always wrong. Looking back through my diaries and the news commentaries which I wrote for the BBC over a period of two years, I see that I was often right as against the bulk of the left-wing intelligentsia. I was right to the extent that I was not defeatist, and after all the war has not been lost. The majority of left-wing intellectuals, whatever they might say in print, were blackly defeatist in 1940 and again in 1942. In the summer of 1942, the turning-point of the war, most of them held it as an article of faith that Alexandria would fall and Stalingrad would not. I remember a fellow broadcaster, a Communist, saying to me with a kind of passion, "I would bet you anything, *anything*, that Rommel will be in Cairo in a month." What this person really meant, as I could see at a glance, was, "I *hope* Rommel will be in Cairo in a month." I myself didn't hope anything of the kind, and therefore I was able to see that the chances of holding on to Egypt were fairly good. You have here an example of the wish-thinking that underlies almost all political prediction at present.

I could be right on a point of this kind, because I don't share the average English intellectual's hatred of his own country and am not dismayed by a British victory. But just for the same reason I failed to form a true picture of political developments. I hate to see England either humiliated or humiliating anybody else. I wanted to think that we would not be defeated, and I wanted to think that the class distinctions and imperialist exploitation of which I am ashamed would not return. I over-emphasised the anti-Fascist character of the war, exaggerated the social changes that were actually occurring, and underrated the enormous strength of the forces of reaction. This unconscious falsification coloured all my earlier letters to you, though perhaps not the more recent ones.

So far as I can see, all political thinking for years past has been vitiated in the same way. People can foresee the future only when it coincides with their own wishes, and the most grossly obvious facts can be ignored when they are unwelcome. For example, right up to May of this year the more disaffected English intellectuals refused to believe that a Second Front would be opened. They went on refusing while, bang in front of their faces, the endless convoys of guns and landing-craft rumbled through London on their way to the coast. One could point to countless other instances of people hugging quite manifest delusions because the truth would be wounding to their pride. Hence the absence of reliable political prediction. To name just one easily isolated example: who foresaw the Russo-German Pact of 1939? A few pessimistic Conservatives foretold an agreement between Germany and Russia, but the wrong kind of agreement, and for the wrong reasons. So far as I am aware, no intellectual of the Left, whether russophile or russophobe, foresaw anything of the kind. For that matter, the Left as a whole failed to foresee the rise of Fascism and failed to grasp that the Nazis were dangerous even when they were on the verge of seizing power. To appreciate the danger of Fascism the Left would have had to admit its own shortcomings, which was too painful: so the whole phenomenon was ignored or misinterpreted, with disastrous results.

The most one can say is that people can be fairly good prophets when their wishes are realisable. But a truly objective approach is almost impossible, because in one form or another almost everyone is a nationalist. Left-wing intellectuals do not think of themselves as nationalist, because as a rule they transfer their loyalty to some foreign country, such as the USSR, or indulge it in a merely negative form, in hatred of their own country and its rulers. But their outlook is essentially nationalist, in that they think entirely in terms of power politics and competitive prestige. In looking at any situation they do not say, "What are the facts? What are the probabilities?" but, "How can I make it appear to myself and others that my faction is getting the better of some rival faction?" To a Stalinist it is *impossible* that Stalin could ever be wrong, and to a Trotskyist it is equally impossible that Stalin could ever be right. So also with Anarchists, pacifists, Tories or what-have-you. And the atomisation of the world, the lack of any real contact between one country and another, makes delusions easier to preserve. To an astonishing extent it is impossible to discover what is happening outside one's own immediate circle. An illustration of this is that no one, so far as I know, can calculate the casualties in the present war within ten millions. But one expects governments and newspapers to tell lies. What is worse, to me, is the contempt even of intellectuals for objective truth so long as their own brand of nationalism is being boosted. The most intelligent people seem capable of holding schizophrenic beliefs, or disregarding plain facts, of evading serious questions with debating-society repartees, or swallowing baseless rumours and of looking on indifferently while history is falsified. All these mental vices spring ultimately from the nationalistic habit of mind, which is itself, I suppose, the product of fear and of the ghastly emptiness of machine civilisation. But at any rate it is not surprising that in our age the followers of Marx have not been much more successful as prophets than the followers of Nostradamus.

I believe that it is possible to be more objective than most of us are, but that it involves a *moral* effort. One cannot get away from one's own subjective feelings, but at least one can know what they are and make allowance for them. I have made attempts to do this, especially latterly, and for that reason I think the later ones among my letters to you, roughly speaking from the middle of 1942 onwards, give a more truthful picture of developments in Britain than the earlier ones. As this letter has been largely a tirade against the left-wing intelligentsia, I would like to add, without flattery, that judging from such American periodicals as I see, the mental atmosphere in the USA is still a good deal more breathable than it is in England.

I began this letter three days ago. World-shaking events are happening all over the place, but in London nothing new. The change-over from the black-out to the so-called dim-out has made no difference as yet. The streets are still inky dark. On and off it is beastly cold and it looks as though fuel will be very short this winter. People's tempers get more and more ragged, and shopping is a misery. The shopkeepers treat you like dirt, especially if you want something that happens to be in short supply at the moment. The latest shortages are combs and teats for babies' feeding bottles. Teats have been actually unprocurable in some areas, and what do exist are made of reconditioned rubber. At the same time contraceptives are plentiful and made of good rubber. Whisky is rarer than ever, but there are more cars on the roads, so the petrol situation must have let up a little. The Home Guard has been stood down and firewatching greatly reduced. More US soldiers have looked me up, using *PR* as an introduction. I am always most happy to meet any reader of *PR*. I can generally be got at the *Tribune,* but failing that my home number is CAN 3751.

George Orwell

Partisan Review, Winter 1944

84. Oysters and Brown Stout

G. K. Chesterton said once that every novelist writes one book whose title seems to be a summing-up of his attitude to life. He instanced, for Dickens, *Great Expectations,* and for Scott, *Tales of a Grandfather.*

What title would one choose as especially representative of Thackeray? The obvious one is *Vanity Fair,* but I believe that if one looked more closely one would choose either *Christmas Books, Burlesques,* or *A Book of Snobs*—at any rate, one would choose the title of one of the collections of scraps which Thackeray had previously contributed to *Punch* and other magazines. Not only was he by nature a burlesque writer, but he was primarily a journalist, a writer of fragments, and his most characteristic work is not fully separable from the illustrations. Some of the best of these are by Cruikshank, but Thackeray was also a brilliant comic draughtsman himself, and in some of his very short sketches the picture and the letter-press belong organically together. All that is best in his full-length novels seems to have grown out of his contributions to *Punch*, and even *Vanity Fair* has a fragmentary quality that makes it possible to begin reading in it at almost any place, without looking back to see what has happened earlier.

At this date some of his major works—for instance, *Esmond* or *The Virginians*—are barely readable, and only once, in a rather short book, *A Shabby Genteel Story*, did he write what we should now regard as a serious novel. Thackeray's two main themes are snobbishness and extravagance, but he is at his best when he handles them in the comic vein, because—unlike Dickens, for instance—he has very little social insight and not even a very clear moral code. *Vanity Fair*, it is true, is a valuable social document as well as being an extremely readable and amusing book. It records, with remarkable fidelity so far as physical detail goes, the ghastly social competition of the early nineteenth century, when an aristocracy which could no longer pay its way was still the arbiter of fashion and of behaviour. In *Vanity Fair*, and indeed throughout Thackeray's writings, it is almost exceptional to find anyone living inside his income.

To live in a house which is too big for you, to engage servants whom you cannot pay, to ruin yourself by giving pretentious dinner parties with hired footmen, to bilk your tradesmen, to overdraw your banking account, to live permanently in the clutches of money-lenders—this is almost the norm of human behaviour. It is taken for granted that anyone who is not halfway to being a saint will ape the aristocracy if possible. The desire for expensive clothes, gilded carriages and hordes of liveried servants is assumed to be a natural instinct, like the desire for food and drink. And the people Thackeray is best able to describe are those who are living the fashionable life upon no income whatever—people like Becky Sharp and Rawdon Crawley in *Vanity Fair*, or the innumerable seedy adventurers, Major Loder, Captain Rook, Captain Costigan, Mr Deuceace, whose life is an endless to-and-fro between the card-table and the sponging-house.

So far as it goes, Thackeray's picture of society is probably true. The types he depicts, the mortgage-ridden aristocrats, the brandy-drinking army officers, the elderly bucks with their stays and their dyed whiskers, the match-making mothers, the vulgar City magnates, did exist. But he is observing chiefly externals. In spite of endless musings on the French Revolution, a subject that fascinated him, he does not see that the structure of society is altering: he sees the nation-wide phenomenon of snobbery and extravagance, without seeing its deeper causes. Moreover, unlike Dickens, he does not see that the social struggle is three-sided: his sympathies hardly extend to the working class, whom he is conscious of chiefly as servants. Nor is he ever certain where he himself stands. He cannot make up his mind whether the raffish upper class or the money-grubbing middle class is more objectionable. Not having any definite social, political or, probably, religious convictions, he can hardly imagine any virtues except simplicity, courage and, in the case of women, "purity". (Thackeray's "good" women, incidentally, are completely intolerable.) The implied moral of both *Vanity Fair* and *Pendennis* is the rather empty one: "Don't be selfish, don't be worldly, don't live outside your income". And *A Shabby Genteel Story* says the same thing in a more delicate way.

But Thackeray's narrow intellectual range is actually an advantage to him when he abandons the attempt to portray real human beings. A thing that is very striking is the vitality of his *minor* writings, even of things that he himself must have thought of as purely ephemeral. If you dip almost anywhere in his collected works—even in his book reviews, for instance—you come upon the characteristic flavour. Partly it is the atmosphere of surfeit which belongs to the early nineteenth century, an atmosphere compounded of oysters, brown stout, brandy and water, turtle soup, roast sirloin, haunch of venison, Madeira and cigar smoke, which Thackeray is well able to convey because he has a good grip on physical detail and is extremely interested in food.

He writes about food perhaps more often even than Dickens, and more accurately. His account of his dinners in Paris—not expensive dinners, either—in "Memorials of Gormandising" is fascinating reading. "The Ballad of the Bouillabaisse" is one of the best poems of that kind in English. But the characteristic flavour of Thackeray is the flavour of burlesque, of a world where no one is good and nothing is serious. It pervades all the best passages in his novels, and it reaches its perfection in short sketches and stories like "Dr Birch and his Young Friends", *The Rose and the Ring*, "The Fatal Boots" and "A Little Dinner at Timmins's".

The Rose and the Ring is a sort of charade, similar in spirit to *The Ingoldsby Legends*, "A Little Dinner at Timmins's" is a relatively naturalistic story, and "The Fatal Boots" is about midway between the two. But in all these and similar pieces Thackeray has got away from the difficulty that besets most novelists and has never been solved by any characteristically English novelist—the difficulty of combining characters who are meant to be real and exist "in the round" with mere figures of fun.

English writers from Chaucer onwards have found it very difficult to resist burlesque, but as soon as burlesque enters the reality of the story suffers. Fielding, Dickens, Trollope, Wells, even Joyce, have all stumbled over this problem. Thackeray, in the best of his short pieces, solves it by making *all* his characters into caricatures. There is no question of the hero of "The Fatal Boots" existing "in the round". He is as flat as an ikon. In "A Little Dinner at Timmins's"— one of the best comic short stories ever written, though it is seldom reprinted—Thackeray is really doing the same thing as he did in *Vanity Fair*, but without the complicating factor of having to simulate real life and introduce disinterested motives. It is a simple little story, exquisitely told and rising gradually to a sort of crescendo which stops at exactly the right moment. A lawyer who has received an unusually large fee decides to celebrate it by giving a dinner party. He is at once led into much greater expense than he can afford, and there follows a series of disasters which leave him heavily in debt, with his friends alienated and his mother-in-law permanently installed in his home. From start to finish no one has had anything from the dinner party except misery. And when, at the end, Thackeray remarks, "Why, in fact, did the Timminses give that party at all?" one feels the folly of social ambition has been more conclusively demonstrated than it is by *Vanity Fair*. This is the kind of thing that Thackeray could do perfectly, and it is the recurrence of farcical incidents like this, rather than their central story, that makes the longer novels worth reading.

Tribune, 22 December 1944

85. As I Please

I am indebted to an article by Mr Dwight Macdonald in the September number of *Politics*, the New York monthly, for some extracts from a book entitled *Kill—or Get Killed; a Manual of Hand-to-Hand Fighting* by Major Rex Applegate.

This book, a semi-official American publication, not only gives extensive information about knifing, strangling, and the various horrors that come under the heading of "unarmed combat", but describes the battle-schools in which soldiers are trained for house-to-house fighting. Here are some sample directions:

... Before entering the tunnel, the coach exposes dummy A and the student uses the knife on it. While the student is proceeding from target No. 1 to target No. 4, the "Gestapo Torture Scene" or the "Italian Cursing" sequence is played over the loudspeaker. . . . Target No. 9 is in darkness, and as the student enters this compartment the "Jap Rape" sequence is used. . . . While the coach is reloading the student's pistol, the "Get that American son-of-a-bitch" sequence is used. As the coach and student pass through the curtain into the next compartment, they are confronted by a dummy which has a knife stuck in its back, and represents a dead body. This dummy is illuminated by a green light and is not to be fired at by the student, although practically all of them do.

Mr Macdonald comments: "There is one rather interesting problem in operating the course. Although the writer never states so directly, it would seem there is danger that the student's inhibitions will be broken down so thoroughly that he will shoot or stab the coach who accompanies him. . . . The coach is advised to keep himself in a position to grab the student's gun arm 'at any instant'; after the three dummies along the course have been stabbed, 'the knife is taken away from the student to prevent accidents'; and finally: 'There is no place on the course where total darkness prevails while the instructor is near student.' "

I believe the similar battle-courses in the British army have now been discontinued or toned down, but it is worth remembering that *something like* this is inevitable if one wants military efficiency. No ideology, no consciousness of having "something to fight for", is fully a substitute for it. This deliberate brutalising of millions of human beings is part of the price of society in its present form. The Japanese, incidentally, have been experts at this kind of thing for hundreds of years. In the old days the sons of aristocrats used to be taken at a very early age to witness executions, and if any boy showed the slightest sign of nausea he was promptly made to swallow large quantities of rice stained the colour of blood.

The English common people are not great lovers of military glory, and I have pointed out elsewhere that when a battle poem wins really wide popularity, it usually deals with a disaster and not a victory. But the other day, when I repeated this in some connection, there came into my head the once popular song—it might be popular again if one of the gramophone companies would bother to record it—"Admiral Benbow". This rather jingoistic ballad seems to contradict my theory, but I believe it may have owed some of its popularity to the fact that it had a class-war angle which was understood at the time.

Admiral Benbow, when going into action against the French, was suddenly deserted by his subordinate captains and left to fight against heavy odds. As the ballad puts it:

> Said Kirby unto Wade, "We will run, we will run,"
> Said Kirby unto Wade, "We will run;
> For I value no disgrace
> Nor the losing of my place,
> But the enemy I won't face,
> Nor his guns, nor his guns."

So Benbow was left to fight single-handed and, though victorious, he himself was killed. There is a gory but possibly authentic description of his death:

> Brave Benbow lost his legs, by chain shot, by chain shot,
> Brave Benbow lost his legs, by chain shot;
> Brave Benbow lost his legs
> And all on his stumps he begs,
> "Fight on, my English lads,
> 'Tis our lot, 'tis our lot."

> The surgeon dressed his wounds, Benbow cries, Benbow cries,
> The surgeon dressed his wounds, Benbow cries;
> "Let a cradle now in haste
> On the quarter-deck be placed,
> That the enemy I may face
> Till I die, till I die."

The point is that Benbow was an ordinary seaman who had risen from the ranks. He had started off as a cabin boy. And his captains are supposed to have fled from the action because they did not want to see so plebeian a commander win a victory. I wonder whether it was this tradition that made Benbow into a popular hero and caused his name to be commemorated not only in the ballad but on the signs of innumerable public houses?

I believe no recording of this song exists, but—as I discovered when I was broadcasting and wanted to use similar pieces as five-minute fill-ups—it is only one of a long list of old popular songs and folk songs which have not been recorded. Until recently, at any rate, I believe there was not even a record of "Tom Bowling" or of "Greensleeves", i.e. the words as well as the music. Others that I failed to get hold of were "A cottage well thatched with straw", "Green grow the rushes, O", "Blow away the morning dew", and "Come lasses and lads". Other well-known songs are recorded in mutilated versions, and usually sung by professional singers with such a stale perfunctoriness that you seem to smell the whisky and cigarette smoke coming off the record. The collection of recorded carols is also very poor. You can't, I believe, get hold of "Minstrels and maid", or "Like silver lamps in a distant shrine", or "Dives and Lazarus", or other old favourites. On the other hand, if you want a record of "Roll out the barrel", "Boomps-a-daisy", etc, you would find quite a number of different renderings to choose from.

A correspondent in *Tribune* of December 15 expressed his "horror and disgust" at hearing that Indian troops had been used against the Greeks, and compared this to the action of Franco in using Moorish troops against the Spanish Republic.

It seems to me important that this ancient red herring should not be dragged across the trail. To begin with, the Indian troops are not strictly comparable to Franco's Moors. The reactionary Moorish chieftains, bearing rather the same relationship to Franco as the Indian Princes do to the British Conservative Party, sent their men to Spain with the conscious aim of crushing democracy. The Indian troops are mercenaries, serving the British from family tradition or for the sake of a job, though latterly a proportion of them have probably begun to think of themselves as an *Indian* army, nucleus of the armed forces of a future independent India. It is not likely that their presence in Athens had any political significance. Probably it was merely that they happened to be the nearest troops available.

But in addition, it is of the highest importance that Socialists should have no truck with colour prejudice. On a number of occasions —the Ruhr occupation of 1923 and the Spanish civil war, for instance —the cry "using coloured troops" has been raised as though it were somehow worse to be shot up by Indians or Negroes than by Europeans. Our crime in Greece is to have interfered in Greek internal affairs at all: the colour of the troops who carry out the orders is irrelevant. In the case of the Ruhr occupation, it was perhaps justifiable to protest against the use of Senegalese troops, because the Germans probably felt this as an added humiliation, and the French may have used black troops for that very reason. But such feelings are not universal in Europe, and I doubt whether there is anywhere any prejudice against Indian troops, who are conspicuously well-behaved.

Our correspondent might have made the point that in an affair of this kind it is particularly mean to make use of politically ignorant colonial troops who don't understand in what a dirty job they are being mixed up. But at least don't let us insult the Indians by suggesting that their presence in Athens is somehow more offensive than that of the British.

Tribune, 29 December 1944

1945

86. A New Year Message

For some months past we have intended to make some kind of explanatory statement about *Tribune's* literary policy, present and future, and the first week of the new year seems a suitable time to do it.

Regular readers of *Tribune* will have noted that during recent months we have printed short stories only intermittently, we have printed less verse than we used to do, and we have altered our system of reviewing, giving a full-length review each week to only one book, and 200-word "shorts" to all the others. The new system of reviewing seems to be giving general satisfaction. By means of it we can cover—including the books in Daniel George's column—anything up to fifteen books a week, and thus can keep more or less abreast of the current output, which was quite impossible before. We can also in this way make some mention of cheap reprints and even a certain number of pamphlets and periodicals. From time to time we are charged by our readers with concentrating on books which the average person cannot afford to buy, but anyone who chooses to look back through our columns will see that Penguins and other very cheap publications have had their fair share of notice.

The gradual dropping of short stories is deliberate. In future we shall probably abandon short stories almost completely, though we shall not refuse a *good* short story when we happen to get one. We shall also from time to time, as we have done once or twice already, print detachable excerpts from old books. This seems to us a useful thing to do at a time like the present, when so many standard books are unobtainable.

It was only unwillingly that we decided on the dropping of short stories, but the quality of the stories sent in to me makes them, in much more than nine cases out of ten, simply not worth ink and paper. For long past there had been a volume of justified complaints from readers that *Tribune's* stories were "always so gloomy". The trouble, as anyone who had my job would quickly appreciate, is that one almost never nowadays sees a story with any serious literary pretensions that is *not* gloomy. The reasons for this are many and complex, but I think literary fashion is one of them. A "happy ending", or indeed any admission that anything is right with the world anywhere, seems to be as out of date as Dundreary whiskers, and it hardly seems worth diffusing gloom from the final pages of the paper unless exceptional literary distinction goes with it. Many readers have told me, in writing and by word of mouth, how tired they are of the kind of story that begins "Marjorie's husband was to be hanged on Tuesday, and the children were starving", or "For seven years no ray of sunlight had penetrated the dusty room where William Grocock, a retired insurance agent, lay dying of cancer"; but I don't fancy they are more tired of them than I am myself, who have to work my way through round about twenty such stories every week.

By printing less stories we shall have more room for essays and articles on literary or general (i.e. not directly political) subjects. But upon all those readers who complain that we do not have enough articles on music, or painting, or the drama, or radio, or modern educational methods, or psychoanalysis, or what not, I urge one important consideration: that we have very little space. In most weeks we have well under five pages at our disposal, and we have already been driven into smaller print for the short reviews. It is principally lack of space that has prevented us from undertaking any notes on radio, gramophone records and music generally. We could not do it regularly, and therefore should not be able to keep sufficiently up to date. Nor can we notice concerts, exhibitions, etc, because these occur only in one place, usually London, and *Tribune's* readers are spread all over the country.

So far I have been dealing with details. But a more general defence, or at least explanation, of our literary policy is needed, because there are certain criticisms of an adverse kind that come up in varying forms over and over again. Our critics are divisible into two main schools. It would be manifestly impossible to satisfy both, and in practice, I should say, impossible to satisfy either.

The first school accuses us of being lowbrow, vulgar, ignorant, obsessed with politics, hostile to the arts, dominated by back-scratching cliques and anxious to prevent talented young writers from getting a hearing. The other school accuses us of being high-brow, arty, bourgeois, indifferent to politics and constantly wasting space on material that can be of no interest to a working man and of no direct use to the Socialist movement. Both points need meeting, because between them they express a difficulty that is inherent in running any paper that is not a pure propaganda sheet.

Against the first school, we point out that *Tribune* reaches a large, heterogeneous left-wing audience and cannot be turned into a sort of trade paper for young poets, or a tilting-ground on which rival gangs of Surrealists, Apocalyptics and what not can fight out their battles. We can assume that our public is intelligent, but not that its primary interests are literary or artistic, and still less that all of our readers have been educated in the same way and will know the same jokes and recognise the same allusions. The smaller literary magazines tend to develop a sort of family atmosphere—almost, indeed, a private language unintelligible to outsiders—and, at the risk of offending a contributor now and then, we have made efforts to prevent that kind of thing from being imported into *Tribune*. We never, for instance, review books written in foreign languages, and we try to cut out avoidable foreign quotations and obscure literary allusions. Nor will we print anything that is verbally unintelligible. I have had several angry letters because of this, but I refuse to be responsible for printing anything that I do not understand. If I can't understand it, the chances are that many of our readers will not be able to either. As to the charge that we are dominated by cliques (contributions sometimes arrive with a sarcastic enquiry as to whether "someone outside the clique" may put a word in), a quick glance through our back numbers would easily disprove it. The number of our contributors is much larger than is usual in a paper of these dimensions, and many of them are people whose work has hardly appeared elsewhere.

The other school of critics presents a more serious difficulty. Any Socialist paper which has a literary section is attacked from time to time by the person who says: "What is the use of all this literary stuff? Does it bring Socialism any nearer? If not, drop it. Surely our task should be to work for Socialism and not waste our time on bourgeois literature?" There are various quick answers to this person (he is easily quelled, for instance, by pointing out that Marx wrote some excellent criticism of Shakespeare), but nevertheless he has a case. Here it is, put in an extreme form by a correspondent in last week's issue:

> May I ask if the book reviews in your paper contribute largely (if at all) to its upkeep? If not, why is so much precious space taken up each week with descriptions of books which (I guess) few of your readers buy?
>
> As a Socialist, my aim in life is to destroy Toryism.
>
> For this purpose I require all the ammunition I can get, and I look to *Tribune* as the main source of supply.

You may reply that some of the books would be useful for that purpose, but I think it would be a very small percentage, and in any case I have neither the money to buy nor the time to read them.

This correspondent, by the way, like many others who write in the same vein, is under the misconception that in order to read books you have to buy them. Actually you could read most of the books mentioned in *Tribune* without ever buying a book from one year's end to the other. What else are libraries for—not merely Boots, Smith's, etc, but the public libraries at which anyone who numbers a householder among his acquaintances can get three tickets without any charge whatever? But our correspondent also assumes (a) that a Socialist needs no recreations, and (b) that books are of no use to the Socialist movement unless they consist of direct propaganda. It is this viewpoint that we tacitly challenge when, for instance, we use up a whole column on a poem, or print a popularisation of some little-known dead writer, or give a good review to a book written by a Conservative.

Even the most unpolitical book, even an outright reactionary book, can be of use to the Socialist movement if it provides reliable information or forces people to think. But we also assume that books are not to be regarded simply as propaganda, that literature exists in its own right—as a form of recreation, to put it no higher—and that a large number of our readers are interested in it. This involves, unavoidably, a slight divergence between the political and the literary sections of the paper. Obviously we cannot print contributions that grossly violate *Tribune's* policy. Even in the name of free speech a Socialist paper cannot, for instance, throw open its columns to antisemitic propaganda. But it is only in this negative sense that any pressure is put upon contributors to the literary end of the paper. Looking through the list of our contributors, I find among them Catholics, Communists, Trotskyists, Anarchists, pacifists, left-wing Conservatives, and Labour Party supporters of all colours. All of them knew, of course, what kind of paper they were writing for and what topics were best left alone, but I think it is true to say that none of them has ever been asked to modify what he had written on the ground that it was "not policy".

This is particularly important in the case of book reviews, in which it is often difficult for the reviewer to avoid indicating his own opinions. To my knowledge, some periodicals coerce their reviewers into following the political line of the paper, even when they have to falsify their own opinions to do so. *Tribune* has never done this. We hold that the reviewer's job is to say what he thinks of the book he is dealing with, and not what we think our readers ought to think. And if, as a result, unorthodox opinions are expressed from time to time—even, on occasion, opinions that contradict some editorial statement at the other end of the paper—we believe that our readers are tough enough to stand a certain amount of diversity. We hold that the most perverse human being is more interesting than the most orthodox gramophone record. And though, in this section of the paper, our main aim is to talk about books as books, we believe that anyone who upholds the freedom of the intellect, in this age of lies and regimentation, is not serving the cause of Socialism so badly either.

Tribune, 5 January 1945

87. As I Please

I have just been looking through a bound volume of the *Quarterly Review* for the year 1810, which was, I think, the second year of the *Quarterly Review's* existence.

1810 was not quite the blackest period, from the British point of view, of the Napoleonic war, but it was nearly the blackest. It perhaps corresponded to 1941 in the present war. Britain was completely isolated, its commerce barred from every European port by the Berlin decrees. Italy, Spain, Prussia, Denmark, Switzerland and the Low Countries had all been subjugated. Austria was in alliance with France. Russia was also in an uneasy agreement with France, but it was known that Napoleon intended to invade Russia shortly. The United States, though not yet in the war, was openly hostile to Britain. There was no visible cause for hope, except the revolt in Spain, which had once again given Britain a foothold on the continent and opened the South American countries to British trade. It is therefore interesting to observe the tone of voice in which the *Quarterly Review*—a conservative paper which emphatically supported the war—speaks about France and about Napoleon at this desperate moment.

Here is the *Quarterly* on the alleged war-making propensities of the French people. It is reviewing a pamphlet by a Mr Walsh, an American who had just returned from France:

> We doubt the continued action of those military propensities which Mr Walsh ascribes to the French people. Without at all questioning the lively picture which he has drawn of the exultation excited amongst the squalid and famished inhabitants of Paris at the intelligence of every fresh triumph of their armies, we may venture to observe that such exultation is, everywhere, the usual concomitant of such events; that the gratification of national vanity is something, and that the festivities which victory brings with it may afford a pleasing dissipation to wretches who are perfectly free from any feelings of ambition. Our belief indeed is, that those feelings are, at present, nearly confined to the breast of the great conqueror; and that amongst his subjects, we may almost say among his officers and armies, the universal wish is for PEACE.

Compare this with the utterances of Lord Vansittart, or, indeed, of the great part of the press. The same article contains several tributes to the military genius of Napoleon. But the thing I find most impressive is that this year's issue of the *Quarterly* contains numerous reviews of recently published French books—and they are careful, serious reviews, not different in tone from the rest of its articles. There is, for instance, an article of about 9,000 words on the publication of the French scientific body known as the Société d'Arcueil. The French scientists, Gay-Lussac, Laplace and the rest of them, are treated with the utmost respect, and given their "Monsieur" every time. From reading this article it would be impossible to discover that there was a war on.

Can you imagine current German books being reviewed in the British press during the present war? No, I don't think you can. I do not, indeed, remember hearing the name of a single book published in Germany throughout the war. And if a contemporary German book did get mentioned in the press, it would almost certainly be misrepresented in some way. Looking through the reviews of French books in the *Quarterly*, I note that only when they are on directly political subjects does any propaganda creep in, and even then it is extremely mild by our standards. As for art, literature and science, their international character is taken for granted. And yet, I suppose,

Britain was fighting for existence in the Napoleonic war just as surely as in this one, and relative to the populations involved the war was not much less bloody or exhausting.

I have been rereading with some interest *The Fairchild Family*, which was written in 1813 and was for fifty years or more a standard book for children. Unfortunately I only possess the first volume, but even that, in its unexpurgated state—for various pretty-pretty versions, with all the real meat cut out, have been issued in recent years—is enough of a curiosity.

The tone of the book is sufficiently indicated by the sentence: "Papa," said Lucy (Lucy was aged nine, by the way), "may we say some verses about mankind having bad hearts?" And, of course, Papa is only too willing, and out come the verses, all correctly memorised. Or here is Mrs Fairchild, telling the children how when she herself was a child she disobeyed orders by picking cherries in company with the servant girl:

> Nanny was given up to her mother to be flogged; and I was shut up in the dark room, where I was to be kept several days upon bread and water. At the end of three days my aunts sent for me, and talked to me for a long time.
>
> "You broke the Fourth Commandment," said my Aunt Penelope, "which is, 'Remember the Sabbath day to keep it holy.': and you broke the Fifth, which is, 'Honour your parents'. . . . You broke the Eighth too, which is, 'Thou shalt not steal'."
> "Besides," said my Aunt Grace, "the shame and disgrace of climbing trees in such low company, after all the care and pains we have taken with you, and the delicate manner in which we have reared you."

The whole book is in this vein, with a long prayer at the end of every chapter, and innumerable hymns and verses from the Bible interspersed through the text. But its chief feature is the fearful visitations from Heaven which fall upon the children whenever they misbehave themselves. If they swing in the swing without leave they fall out and break several teeth: if they forget to say their prayers they fall into the trough of pig-swill; the theft of a few damsons is punished by an attack of pneumonia and narrow escape from death. On one occasion Mr Fairchild catches his children quarrelling. After the usual flogging, he takes them for a long walk to see the rotting body of a murderer hanging on a gibbet—the result, as he points out, of a quarrel between two brothers.

A curious and interesting feature of the book is that the Fairchild children, reared upon these stern principles, seem to be rather exceptionally untrustworthy. As soon as their parents' backs are turned they invariably misbehave themselves, which suggests that flogging and bread and water are not a very satisfactory treatment after all. It is worth recording, by the way, that the author, Mrs Sherwood, brought up several children, and at any rate they did not actually die under her ministrations.

Tribune, 5 January 1945

88. As I Please

Some time back a correspondent wrote to ask whether I had seen the exhibition of waxworks, showing German atrocities, which has been on show in London for a year or more. It is advertised outside with such captions as: HORRORS OF THE CONCENTRATION CAMP. COME INSIDE AND SEE REAL NAZI TORTURES. FLOGGING, CRUCIFIXION, GAS CHAMBERS, ETC. CHILDREN'S AMUSEMENT SECTION NO EXTRA CHARGE.

I did go and see this exhibition a long time ago, and I would like to warn prospective visitors that it is most disappointing. To begin with many of the figures are not life-size, and I suspect that some of them are not even real waxworks, but merely dressmakers' dummies with new heads attached. And secondly, the tortures are not nearly so fearful as you are led to expect by the posters outside. The whole exhibition is grubby, unlifelike and depressing. But the exhibitors are, I suppose, doing their best, and the captions are interesting in the complete frankness of their appeal to sadism and masochism. Before the war, if you were a devotee of all-in wrestling, or wrote letters to your MP to protest against the abolition of flogging, or haunted second-hand bookshops in search of such books as *The Pleasures of the Torture Chamber*, you laid yourself open to very unpleasant suspicions. Moreover, you were probably aware of your own motives and somewhat ashamed of them. Now, however, you can wallow in the most disgusting descriptions of torture and massacre, not only without any sensation of guilt, but with the feeling that you are performing a praiseworthy political action.

I am not suggesting that the stories about Nazi atrocities are untrue. To a great extent I think they are true. These horrors certainly happened in German concentration camps before the war, and there is no reason why they should have stopped since. But they are played up largely because they give the newspapers a pretext for pornography. This morning's papers are splashing the official British Army Report on Nazi atrocities. They are careful to inform you that naked women were flogged, sometimes spotlighting this detail by means of a headline The journalists responsible know very well what they are doing. They know that innumerable people get a sadistic kick out of thinking about torture, especially the torture of women, and they are cashing in on this widespread neurosis. No qualms need be felt, because these deeds are committed by the enemy, and the enjoyment that one gets out of them can be disguised as disapproval. And one can get a very similar kick out of barbarous actions committed by one's own side so long as they are thought of as the just punishment of evildoers.

We have not actually got to the point of Roman gladiatorial shows yet, but we could do so if the necessary pretext were supplied. If, for instance, it were announced that the leading war criminals were to be eaten by lions or trampled to death by elephants in the Wembley Stadium, I fancy that the spectacle would be quite well attended.

I invite attention to an article entitled "The Truth about Mihailovich?" (the author of it also writes for *Tribune*, by the way) in the current *World Review*. It deals with the campaign in the British press and the BBC to brand Mihailovich as a German agent.

Jugoslav politics are very complicated and I make no pretence of being an expert on them. For all I know it was entirely right on the part of Britain as well as the USSR to drop Mihailovich and support Tito. But what interests me is the readiness, once this decision had been taken, of reputable British newspapers to connive at what amounted to forgery in order to discredit the man whom they had been backing a few months earlier. There is no doubt that this happened. The author of the article gives details of one out of a number of instances in which material facts were suppressed in the most impudent way. Presented with very strong evidence to show that Mihailovich was *not* a German agent, the majority of our newspapers simply refused to print it, while repeating the charges of treachery just as before. . . .

In the same number of *World Review* I note that Mr Edward Hulton remarks rather disapprovingly that "the small city of Athens possesses far more daily newspapers than London". All I can say is, good luck to Athens! It is only when there are large numbers of newspapers, expressing all tendencies, that there is some chance of getting at the truth. Counting evenings, London has only twelve daily papers, and they cover the whole of the south of England and penetrate as far north as Glasgow. When they all decide to tell the same lie, there is no minority press to act as a check. In pre-war France the press was largely venal and scurrilous, but you could dig more news out of it than out of the British press, because every political faction had its paper and every viewpoint got a hearing. I shall be surprised if Athens keeps its multiplicity of newspapers under the kind of government that we apparently intend to impose.

Tribune, 12 January 1945

89. Review
The Unquiet Grave: a Word Cycle by "Palinurus"

"Palinurus" is the easily penetrable pseudonym of a well-known literary critic, but even without knowing his identity one could infer that the writer of this book is about forty, is inclined to stoutness, has lived much in continental Europe, and has never done any real work. His book is a kind of diary, or rather journal, interspersed with quotations from Pascal, Lao-Tze, La Rochefoucauld, and others, and having as its dominant note a refined, rather pessimistic, hedonism. In his previous incarnations, the author says, he was "a melon, a lobster, a lemur, a bottle of wine, Aristippus", and the periods in which he lived were the Augustan age in Rome and "then in Paris and London from 1660 to 1740, and lastly from 1770 to 1850. . . . Afternoons at Holland House, dinners chez Magny".

With his background of classical culture, religious scepticism, travel, leisure, country houses, and civilised meals, "Palinurus" naturally contemplates the modern world without enthusiasm and even, at moments, with sheer aristocratic disdain: but also—and this is the peculiar mark of our age—with self-accusation and the consciousness of being an end-product, a mere ghost, like the cultivated pagans of AD 400. On almost every page this book exhibits that queer product of capitalist democracy, an inferiority complex resulting from a private income. The author wants his comforts and privileges, and is ashamed of wanting them: he feels that he has a right to them, and yet feels certain that they are doomed to disappear. Before very long the mob will rise and destroy its exploiters, but in doing so it will also destroy civilisation:

> The English masses are lovable: they are kind, decent, tolerant, practical, and not stupid. The tragedy is that there are too many of them, and that they are aimless, having outgrown the servile functions for which they were encouraged to multiply. One day these huge crowds will have to seize power because there will be nothing else for them to do, and yet they neither demand power nor are ready to make use of it: they will only learn to be bored in a new way. Sooner or later the population of England will turn Communist, and then it will take over. Some form of Communism is the only effective religion for the working class; its coming is therefore as inevitable as was that of Christianity. The Liberal Die-hard then comes to occupy historically the same position as the "good pagan": he is doomed to extinction.

Throughout the book this is repeated over and over again, in varying forms. The Beehive State is upon us, the individual will be stamped out of existence, the future is with the holiday camp, the doodlebug, and the secret police. "Palinurus", however, differs from most of his similarly placed contemporaries in not acquiescing in the process. He refuses to desert the sinking ship of individualism. To the statement that man "will find fulfilment only through participation in the communal life of an organised group" he answers "No" seven times over. Yet he sees no escape from the Beehive future. He sees, or thinks he sees, ways in which order and liberty, reason and myth, might be combined, but he does not believe that is the turn civilisation will take. Finally, he has no resource except a sort of lonely defiance, as of the last mammoth, or, like Faustus, trying to forget damnation in the embraces of Helen.

This outlook, product of totalitarianism and the perversion of science, is probably gaining ground, and if only for that reason this rather fragmentary book is a valuable document. It is a cry of despair from the *rentier* who feels that he has no right to exist, but also feels that he is a finer animal than the proletarian. Its error lies in assuming that a collectivist society would destroy human individuality. The ordinary English Communist or "fellow-traveller" makes the same assumption, and yields up his intellectual integrity in a frenzy of masochism. "Palinurus" refuses to yield, but just as blindly as the other he takes "Communism" at its own valuation.

The mechanism is the same in both cases. They are *told* that the aim of Socialism or Communism is to make men resemble insects they are conscious that they are privileged people, and that if they resist Socialism their motives must be doubtful: therefore, they look no deeper. It does not occur to them that the so-called collectivist systems now existing only try to wipe out the individual because they are *not* really collectivist and certainly not egalitarian—because, in fact, they are a sham covering a new form of class privilege. If one can see this, one can defy the insect-men with a good conscience. But certainly it is a lot harder to see it, or at any rate to say it aloud, if one is carrying the burden of an unearned income.

Observer, 14 January 1945

90. As I Please

Last week Henri Béraud, the French journalist, was sentenced to death—later commuted to life imprisonment—for collaboration with the Germans. Béraud used to contribute to the Fascist weekly paper *Gringoire*, which in its later years had become the most disgusting rag it is possible to imagine. I have seldom been so angered by anything in the press as by its cartoon when the wretched Spanish refugees streamed into France with Italian aeroplanes machine-gunning them all the way. The Spaniards were pictured as a procession of villainous-looking men, each pushing a hand-cart piled with jewellery and bags of gold. *Gringoire* kept up an almost continuous outcry for the suppression of the French Communist Party but it was equally fierce against even the mildest politicians of the Left. One can get an idea of the moral level at which it conducted political controversy from the fact that it once published a cartoon showing Léon Blum in bed with his own sister. Its advertisement columns were full of ads for clairvoyants and books of pornography. This piece of rubbish was said to have a circulation of 500,000.

At the time of the Abyssinian war Béraud wrote a violent pro-Italian article in which he proclaimed "I hate England", and gave his reasons for doing so. It is significant that it was mostly people of this type, who had made no secret of their Fascist sympathies for years beforehand, that the Germans had to make use of for press propaganda in France. A year or two ago Mr Raymond Mortimer published an article on the activity of French writers during the war, and there have been several similar articles in American magazines. When one pieces these together, it becomes clear that the French literary intelligentsia has behaved extremely well under the German occupation. I wish I could feel certain that the English literary intelligentsia as a whole would have behaved equally well if we had had the Nazis here. But it is true that if Britain had also been overrun, the situation would have been hopeless and the temptation to accept the New Order very much stronger.

I think I owe a small apology to the twentieth century. Apropos of my remarks about the *Quarterly Review* for 1810—in which I pointed out that French books could get favourable reviews in England at the height of the war with France—two correspondents have written to tell me that during the present war German scientific publications have had fair treatment in the scientific press in this country. So perhaps we aren't such barbarians after all.

But I still feel that our ancestors were better at remaining sane in war-time than we are. If you ever have to walk from Fleet Street to the Embankment, it is worth going into the office of the *Observer* and having a look at something that is preserved in the waiting-room. It is a framed page from the *Observer* (which is one of our oldest newspapers) for a certain day in June, 1815. In appearance it is very like a modern newspaper, though slightly worse printed, and with only five columns on the page. The largest letters used are not much more than a quarter of an inch high. The first column is given up to "Court and Society", then follow several columns of advertisements, mostly of rooms to let. Halfway down the last column is a headline SANGUINARY BATTLE IN FLANDERS. COMPLETE DEFEAT OF THE CORSICAN USURPER. This is the first news of Waterloo!

"Today there are only eighty people in the United Kingdom with net incomes of over six thousand pounds a year." (Mr Quintin Hogg, MP, in his pamphlet *The Times We Live In*.)

There are also about eighty ways in the English and American languages of expressing incredulity—for example, *garn, come off it, you bet, sez you, oh yeah, not half, I don't think, less of it* or *and the pudding!* But I think *and then you wake up* is the exactly suitable answer to a remark like the one quoted above.

Recently I read the biography of Edgar Wallace which was written by Margaret Lane some years ago. It is a real "log cabin to White House" story, and by implication a frightful commentary on our age. Starting off with every possible disadvantage—an illegitimate child, brought up by very poor foster-parents in a slum street—Wallace worked his way up by sheer ability, enterprise and hard work. His output was enormous. In his later years he was turning out eight books a year, besides plays, radio scripts and much journalism. He thought nothing of composing a full-length book in less than a week. He took no exercise, worked behind a glass screen in a super-heated room, smoked incessantly and drank vast quantities of sweetened tea. He died of diabetes at the age of 57.

It is clear from some of his more ambitious books that Wallace did in some sense take his work seriously, but his main aim was to make money, and he made it. Towards the end of his life he was earning round about £50,000 a year. But it was all fairy gold. Besides losing money by financing theatres and keeping strings of race-horses which seldom won, Wallace spent fantastic sums on his various houses, where he kept a staff of twenty servants. When he died very suddenly in Hollywood, it was found that his debts amounted to £140,000, while his liquid assets were practically nil. However, the sales of his books were so vast that his royalties amounted to £26,000 in the two years following his death.

The curious thing is that this utterly wasted life—a life of sitting almost continuously in a stuffy room and covering acres of paper with slightly pernicious nonsense—is what is called, or would have been called a few years ago, "an inspiring story". Wallace did what all the "get on or get out" books, from Smiles's *Self Help* onwards, have told you to do. And the world gave him the kind of rewards he would have asked for, after his death as well as in life. When his body was brought home:

He was carried on board the *Berengaria*. . . . They laid a Union Jack over him, and covered him with flowers. He lay alone in the empty saloon under his burden of wreaths, and no journey that he had ever taken had been made in such quiet dignity and state. When the ship crept into Southampton Water her flag was flying at half-mast, and the flags of Southampton slipped gently down to salute him. The bells of Fleet Street tolled, and Wyndham's was dark.

All that and £50,000 a year as well! They also gave Wallace a plaque on the wall at Ludgate Circus. It is queer to think that London could commemorate Wallace in Fleet Street and Barrie in Kensington Gardens, but has never yet got round to giving Blake a monument in Lambeth.

Tribune, 19 January 1945

91. As I Please

The other night I attended a mass meeting of an organisation called the League for European Freedom. Although offically an all-party organisation—there was one Labour MP on the platform—it is, I think it is safe to say, dominated by the anti-Russian wing of the Tory Party.

I am all in favour of European freedom, but I feel happier when it is coupled with freedom elsewhere—in India, for example. The people on the platform were concerned with the Russian actions in Poland, the Baltic countries, etc and the scrapping of the principles of the Atlantic Charter that those actions imply. More than half of what they said was justified, but curiously enough they were almost as anxious to defend our own coercion of Greece as to condemn the Russian coercion of Poland. Victor Raikes, the Tory MP, who is an able and outspoken reactionary, made a speech which I should have considered a good one if it had referred only to Poland and Jugoslavia. But after dealing with those two countries he went on to speak about Greece, and then suddenly black became white, and white black. There was no booing, no interjections from the quite large audience—no one there, apparently, who could see that the forcing of quisling governments upon unwilling peoples is equally undesirable whoever does it.

It is very hard to believe that people like this are really interested in political liberty as such. They are merely concerned because Britain did not get a big enough cut in the sordid bargain that appears to have been driven at Teheran. After the meeting I talked with a journalist whose contacts among influential people are much more extensive than mine. He said he thought it probable that British policy will shortly take a violent anti-Russian swing, and that it would be quite easy to manipulate public opinion in that direction if necessary. For a number of reasons I don't believe he was right, but if he does turn out to be right, then ultimately it is *our* fault and not that of our adversaries.

No one expects the Tory Party and its press to spread enlightenment. The trouble is that for years past it has been impossible to extract a grown-up picture of foreign politics from the left-wing press either. When it comes to such issues as Poland, the Baltic countries, Jugoslavia or Greece, what difference is there between the russophile press and the extreme Tory press? The one is simply the other standing on its head. The *News Chronicle* gives the big headlines to the fighting in Greece but tucks away the news that "force has had to be used" against the Polish Home Army in small print at the bottom of a column. The *Daily Worker* disapproves of dictatorship in Athens, the *Catholic Herald* disapproves of dictatorship in Belgrade. There is no one who is able to say—at least, no one who has the chance to say in a newspaper of big circulation—that this whole dirty game of spheres of influence, quislings, purges, deportations, one-party elections and hundred per cent plebiscites is morally the same whether it is done by ourselves, the Russians or the Nazis. Even in the case of such frank returns to barbarism as the use of hostages, disapproval is only felt when it happens to be the enemy and not ourselves who is doing it.

And with what result? Well, one result is that it becomes much easier to mislead public opinion. The Tories are able to precipitate scandals when they want to partly because on certain subjects the Left refuses to talk in a grown-up manner. An example was the Russo-Finnish war of 1940. I do not defend the Russian action in Finland, but it was not especially wicked. It was merely the same kind of thing as we ourselves did when we seized Madagascar. The public could be shocked by it, and indeed could be worked up into a dangerous fury about it, because for years they had been falsely taught that Russian foreign policy was morally different from that of other countries. And it struck me as I listened to Mr Raikes the other night that if the Tories do choose to start spilling the beans about the Lublin Committee, Marshal Tito and kindred subjects, there will be—thanks to prolonged self-censorship on the Left—plenty of beans for them to spill.

But political dishonesty has its comic side. Presiding over that meeting of the League for European Freedom was no less a person than the Duchess of Atholl. It is only about seven years since the Duchess—"the Red Duchess" as she was affectionately nicknamed— was the pet of the *Daily Worker* and lent the considerable weight of her authority to every lie that the Communists happened to be uttering at the moment. Now she is fighting against the monster that she helped to create. I am sure that neither she nor her Communist ex-friends see any moral in this.

I want to correct an error that I made in this column last week. It seems that there *is* a plaque to William Blake, and that it is some-where near St George's church in Lambeth. I had looked for one in that area and had failed to find it. My apologies to the LCC.

If one cares about the preservation of the English language, a point one often has to decide is whether it is worth putting up a struggle when a word changes its meaning.

Some words are beyond redemption. One could not, I imagine, restore "impertinent" to its original meaning, or "journal", or "decimate". But how about the use of "infer" for "imply" ("He didn't actually say I was a liar, but he inferred it"), which has been gaining ground for some years? Ought one to protest against it? And ought one to acquiesce when certain words have their meanings arbitrarily narrowed? Examples are "immoral" (nearly always taken as meaning sexually immoral), and "criticise" (always taken as meaning criticise unfavourably). It is astonishing what numbers of words have come to have a purely sexual significance, partly owing to the need of the newspapers for euphemisms. Constant use of such phrases as "intimacy took place twice" has practically killed the original meaning of "intimacy", and quite a dozen other words have been perverted in the same way.

Obviously this kind of thing ought to be prevented if possible, but it is uncertain whether one can achieve anything by struggling against the current usage. The coming and going of words is a mysterious process whose rules we do not understand. In 1940 the word "wallop", meaning mild beer, suddenly became current all over London. I had never heard it until that date, but it seems that it was not a new word, but had been peculiar to one quarter of London. Then it suddenly spread all over the place, and now it appears to have died out again. Words can also revive, for no very clear reason, after lying dormant for hundreds of years: for example the word "car", which had never had any currency in England except in high-flown classical poetry, but was resurrected about 1900 to describe the newly invented automobile.

Possibly, therefore, the degradation which is certainly happening to our language is a process which one cannot arrest by conscious action. But I would like to see the attempt made. And as a start I would like to see a few dozen journalists declare war on some obviously bad usage—for example, the disgusting verb "to contact", or the American habit of tying an unnecessary preposition on to every verb—and see whether they could kill it by their concerted efforts.

Tribune, 26 January 1945

92. As I Please

I have just been rereading, with great interest, an old favourite of my boyhood, *The Green Curve* by "Ole Luk-Oie". "Ole Luk-Oie" was the pseudonym of Major Swinton (afterwards General Swinton), who was, I believe, one of the rather numerous people credited with the invention of the tank. The stories in this book, written about 1908, are the forecasts of an intelligent professional soldier who had learned the lessons of the Boer war and the Russo-Japanese war, and it is interesting to compare them with what actually happened a few years later.

One story, written as early as 1907 (at which date no aeroplane had actually risen off the ground for more than a few seconds), describes an air raid. The aeroplanes carry eight-pounder bombs Another story, written in the same year, deals with a German invasion of England, and I was particularly interested to notice that in this story the Germans are already nicknamed "Huns". I had been inclined to attribute the use of the word "Hun", for German, to

Kipling, who certainly used it in the poem that he published during the first week of the last war.

In spite of the efforts of several newspapers, "Hun" has never caught on in this war, but we have plenty of other offensive nicknames. Someone could write a valuable monograph on the use of question-begging names and epithets, and their effect in obscuring political controversies. It would bring out the curious fact that if you simply accept and apply to yourself a name intended as an insult, it may end by losing its insulting character. This appears to be happening to "Trotskyist", which is already dangerously close to being a compliment. So also with "Conchy" during the last war. Another example is "Britisher". This word was used for years as a term of opprobrium in the anglophobe American press. Later on, Northcliffe and others, looking round for some substitute for "Englishman" which should have an imperialistic and jingoistic flavour, found "Britisher" ready to hand, and took it over. Since then the word has had an aura of gutter patriotism, and the kind of person who tells you that "what these natives need is a firm hand" also tells you that he is "proud to be a Britisher"—which is about equivalent to a Chinese Nationalist describing himself as a "Chink".

A leaflet recently received from the Friends' Peace Committee states that if the current scheme to remove all Poles from the areas to be taken over by the USSR, and, in compensation, all Germans from the portions of Germany to be taken over by Poland, is put into operation, "this will involve the transfer of not less than seven million people".

Some estimates, I believe, put it higher than this, but let us assume it to be seven millions. This is equivalent to uprooting and transplanting the entire population of Australia, or the combined populations of Scotland and Ireland. I am no expert on transport or housing, and I would like to hear from somebody better qualified a rough estimate (a) of how many wagons and locomotives, running for how long, would be involved in transporting those seven million people, plus their livestock, farm machinery and household goods; or, alternatively, (b) of how many of them are going to die of starvation and exposure if they are simply shipped off without their livestock, etc.

I fancy the answer to (a) would show that this enormous crime cannot actually be carried through, though it might be started, with confusion, suffering and the sowing of irreconcilable hatreds as the result. Meanwhile, the British people should be made to understand, with as much concrete detail as possible, what kind of policies their statesmen are committing them to.

A not-too-distant explosion shakes the house, the windows rattle in their sockets, and in the next room the 1964 class wakes up and lets out a yell or two. Each time this happens I find myself thinking, "Is it possible that human beings can continue with this lunacy very much longer?" You know the answer, of course. Indeed, the difficulty nowadays is to find anyone who thinks that there will *not* be another war in the fairly near future.

Germany, I suppose, will be defeated this year, and when Germany is out of the way Japan will not be able to stand up to the combined power of Britain and the USA. Then there will be a peace of exhaustion, with only minor and unofficial wars raging all over the place, and perhaps this so-called peace may last for decades. But after that, by the way the world is actually shaping, it may well be that war will *become permanent*. Already, quite visibly and more or less with the acquiescence of all of us, the world is splitting up into the two or three huge super-states forecast in James Burnham's *Managerial Revolution*. One cannot draw their exact boundaries as yet, but one can see more or less what areas they will comprise. And if the world does settle down into this pattern, it is likely that these vast states will be permanently at war with one another, though it will not necessarily be a very intensive or bloody kind of war. Their problems, both economic and psychological, will be a lot simpler if the doodlebugs are more or less constantly whizzing to and fro.

If these two or three super-states do establish themselves, not only will each of them be too big to be conquered, but they will be under no necessity to trade with one another, and in a position to prevent all contact between their nationals. Already, for a dozen years or so, large areas of the earth have been cut off from one another, although technically at peace.

Some months ago, in this column, I pointed out that modern scientific inventions have tended to prevent rather than increase international communication. This brought me several angry letters from readers, but none of them were able to show that what I had said was false. They merely retorted that if we had Socialism, the aeroplane, the radio, etc would not be perverted to wrong uses.

Very true, but then we haven't Socialism. As it is, the aeroplane is primarily a thing for dropping bombs and the radio primarily a thing for whipping up nationalism. Even before the war there was enormously less contact between the peoples of the earth than there had been thirty years earlier, and education was perverted, history rewritten and freedom of thought suppressed to an extent undreamed of in earlier ages. And there is no sign whatever of these tendencies being reversed.

Maybe I am pessimistic. But, at any rate those are the thoughts that cross my mind (and a lot of other people's too, I believe) every time the explosion of a V bomb booms through the mist.

A little story I came upon in a book.

Someone receives an invitation to go out lion-hunting. "But," he exclaims, "I haven't lost any lions!"

Tribune, 2 February 1945

93. As I Please

Every time I wash up a batch of crockery I marvel at the unimaginativeness of human beings who can travel under the sea and fly through the clouds, and yet have not known how to eliminate this sordid time-wasting drudgery from their daily lives. If you go into the Bronze Age room in the British Museum (when it is open again) you will notice that some of our domestic appliances have barely altered in three thousand years. A saucepan, say, or a comb, is very much the same thing as it was when the Greeks were besieging Troy. In the same period we have advanced from the leaky galley to the 50,000 ton liner, and from the ox-cart to the aeroplane.

It is true that in the modern labour-saving house in which a tiny percentage of human beings live, a job like washing-up takes rather less time than it used to. With soap flakes, abundant hot water, plate racks, a well-lighted kitchen, and—what very few houses in England have—an easy method of rubbish disposal, you can make it more tolerable than it used to be when copper dishes had to be scoured with sand in porous stone sinks by the light of a candle. But certain jobs (for instance, cleaning out a frying-pan which has had fish in it) are

inherently disgusting, and this whole business of messing about
with dish-mops and basins of hot water is incredibly primitive. At this
moment the block of flats I live in is partly uninhabitable: not because of enemy action, but because accumulations of snow have
caused water to pour through the roof and bring down the plaster
from the ceilings. It is taken for granted that this calamity will happen
every time there is an exceptionally heavy fall of snow. For three
days there was no water in the taps because the pipes were frozen:
that, too, is a normal, almost yearly experience. And the newspapers
have just announced that the number of burst pipes is so enormous
that the job of repairing them will not be completed till the end of
1945—when, I suppose, there will be another big frost and they will
all burst again. If our methods of making war had kept pace with
our methods of keeping house, we should be just about on the verge
of discovering gunpowder.

To come back to washing-up. Like sweeping, scrubbing and dust-
ing, it is of its nature an uncreative and life-wasting job. You cannot
make an art out of it as you can out of cooking or gardening. What,
then, is to be done about it? Well, this whole problem of housework
has three possible solutions. One is to simplify our way of living very
greatly; another is to assume, as our ancestors did, that life on earth
is inherently miserable, and that it is entirely natural for the average
woman to be a broken-down drudge at the age of thirty; and the
other is to devote as much intelligence to rationalising the interiors
of our houses as we have devoted to transport and communications.
I fancy we shall choose the third alternative. If one thinks simply
in terms of saving trouble and plans one's home as ruthlessly as
one would plan a machine, it is possible to imagine houses and flats
which would be comfortable and would entail very little work.
Central heating, rubbish chutes, proper consumption of smoke,
cornerless rooms, electrically warmed beds and elimination of carpets
would make a lot of difference. But as for washing-up, I see no
solution except to do it communally, like a laundry. Every morning
the municipal van will stop at your door and carry off a box of dirty
crocks, handing you a box of clean ones (marked with your initial,
of course) in return. This would be hardly more difficult to organise
than the daily diaper service which was operating before the war.
And though it would mean that some people would have to be full-
time washers-up, as some people are now full-time laundry-workers,

the all-over saving in labour and fuel would be enormous. The alternatives are to continue fumbling about with greasy dish-mops, or to eat out of paper containers.

A sidelight on the habits of book reviewers.

Some time ago I was commissioned to write an essay for an annual scrapbook which shall be nameless. At the very last minute (and when I had had the money, I am glad to say) the publishers decided that my essay must be suppressed.[1] By this time the book was actually in process of being bound. The essay was cut out of every copy, but for technical reasons it was impossible to remove my name from the list of contributors on the title page.

Since then I have received a number of press cuttings referring to this book. In each case I am mentioned as being "among the contributors", and not one reviewer has yet spotted that the contribution attributed to me is not actually there.

Now that "explore every avenue" and "leave no stone unturned" have been more or less laughed out of existence, I think it is time to start a campaign against some more of the worn-out and useless metaphors with which our language is littered.

Three that we could well do without are "cross swords with", "ring the changes on", and "take up the cudgels for". How lifeless these and similar expressions have become you can see from the fact that in many cases people do not even remember their original meaning. What is meant by "ringing the changes", for instance? Probably it once had something to do with church bells, but one could not be sure without consulting a dictionary. "Take up the cudgels for" possibly derives from the almost obsolete game of singlestick. When an expression has moved as far from its original meaning as this, its value as a metaphor—that is, its power of providing a concrete illustration—has vanished. There is no sense whatever in writing "X took up the cudgels for Y". One should either say "X defended Y" or think of a new metaphor which genuinely makes one's meaning more vivid.

In some cases these overworked expressions have actually been severed from their original meaning by means of a mis-spelling. An example is "plain sailing" (plane sailing). And the expression "toe the line" is now coming to be spelled quite frequently "tow the line".

[1] "Benefit of Clergy: Some Notes on Salvador Dali". See 42.

People who are capable of this kind of thing evidently don't attach any definite meaning to the words they use.

I wonder whether people read Bret Harte nowadays. I do not know why, but for an hour past some stanzas from "The Society upon the Stanislaus" have been running in my head. It describes a meeting of an archaeological society which ended in disorder:

> Then Abner Dean of Angel's raised a point of order, when
> A chunk of old red sandstone took him in the abdomen;
> And he smiled a kind of sickly smile, and curled upon the floor,
> And the subsequent proceedings interested him no more.

It has perhaps been unfortunate for Bret Harte's modern reputation that of his two funniest poems, one turns on colour prejudice and the other on class snobbery. But there are a number that are worth rereading, including one or two serious ones: especially "Dickens in Camp", the now almost forgotten poem which Bret Harte wrote after Dickens's death and which was about the finest tribute Dickens ever had.

Tribune, 9 February 1945

94. Antisemitism in Britain

There are about 400,000 known Jews in Britain, and in addition some thousands or, at most, scores of thousands of Jewish refugees who have entered the country from 1934 onwards. The Jewish population is almost entirely concentrated in half a dozen big towns and is mostly employed in the food, clothing and furniture trades. A few of the big monopolies, such as the ICI, one or two leading newspapers and at least one big chain of department stores are Jewish-owned or partly Jewish-owned, but it would be very far from the truth to say that British business life is dominated by Jews. The Jews seem, on the contrary, to have failed to keep up with the modern tendency towards big amalgamations and to have remained fixed in those trades which are necessarily carried out on a small scale and by old-fashioned methods.

I start off with these background facts, which are already known to any well-informed person, in order to emphasise that there is no real

Jewish "problem" in England. The Jews are not numerous or power-ful enough, and it is only in what are loosely called "intellectual circles" that they have any noticeable influence. Yet it is generally admitted that antisemitism is on the increase, that it has been greatly exacerbated by the war, and that humane and enlightened people are not immune to it. It does not take violent forms (English people are almost invariably gentle and law-abiding), but it is ill-natured enough, and in favourable circumstances it could have political results. Here are some samples of antisemitic remarks that have been made to me during the past year or two:

Middle-aged office employee: "I generally come to work by bus. It takes longer, but I don't care about using the Under-ground from Golders Green nowadays. There's too many of the Chosen Race travelling on that line."

Tobacconist (woman): "No, I've got no matches for you. I should try the lady down the street. *She's* always got matches. One of the Chosen Race, you see."

Young intellectual, Communist or near-Communist: "No, I do *not* like Jews. I've never made any secret of that. I can't stick them. Mind you, I'm not antisemitic, of course."

Middle-class woman: "Well, no one could call me antisemitic, but I do think the way these Jews behave is too absolutely stinking. The way they push their way to the head of queues, and so on. They're so abominably selfish. I think they're respon-sible for a lot of what happens to them."

Milk roundsman: "A Jew don't do no work, not the same as what an Englishman does. 'E's too clever. We work with this 'ere" (flexes his biceps). "They work with that there" (taps his forehead).

Chartered accountant, intelligent, left-wing in an undirected way: "These bloody Yids are all pro-German. They'd change sides tomorrow if the Nazis got here. I see a lot of them in my business. They admire Hitler at the bottom of their hearts. They'll always suck up to anyone who kicks them."

Intelligent woman, on being offered a book dealing with antisemitism and German atrocities: "Don't show it me, *please* don't show it to me. It'll only make me hate the Jews more than ever."

I could fill pages with similar remarks, but these will do to go on with. Two facts emerge from them. One—which is very important and which I must return to in a moment—is that above a certain intellectual level people are ashamed of being antisemitic and are careful to draw a distinction between "antisemitism" and "disliking Jews". The other is that antisemitism is an irrational thing. The Jews are accused of specific offences (for instance, bad behaviour in food queues) which the person speaking feels strongly about, but it is obvious that these accusations merely rationalise some deep-rooted prejudice. To attempt to counter them with facts and statistics is useless, and may sometimes be worse than useless. As the last of the above-quoted remarks shows, people can remain antisemitic, or at least anti-Jewish, while being fully aware that their outlook is indefensible. If you dislike somebody, you dislike him and there is an end of it: your feelings are not made any better by a recital of his virtues.

It so happens that the war has encouraged the growth of antisemitism and even, in the eyes of many ordinary people, given some justification for it. To begin with, the Jews are one people of whom it can be said with complete certainty that they will benefit by an Allied victory. Consequently the theory that "this is a Jewish war" has a certain plausibility, all the more so because the Jewish war effort seldom gets its fair share of recognition. The British Empire is a huge heterogeneous organisation held together largely by mutual consent, and it is often necessary to flatter the less reliable elements at the expense of the more loyal ones. To publicise the exploits of Jewish soldiers, or even to admit the existence of a considerable Jewish army in the Middle East, rouses hostility in South Africa, the Arab countries and elsewhere: it is easier to ignore the whole subject and allow the man in the street to go on thinking that Jews are exceptionally clever at dodging military service. Then again, Jews are to be found in exactly those trades which are bound to incur unpopularity with the civilian public in war-time. Jews are mostly concerned with selling food, clothes, furniture and tobacco—exactly the commodities of which there is a chronic shortage, with consequent overcharging, black-marketing and favouritism. And again, the common charge that Jews behave in an exceptionally cowardly way during air raids was given a certain amount of colour by the big raids of 1940. As it happened, the Jewish quarter of Whitechapel was one of the first areas to be heavily blitzed, with the natural result that swarms of

Jewish refugees distributed themselves all over London. If one judged merely from these war-time phenomena, it would be easy to imagine that antisemitism is a quasi-rational thing, founded on mistaken premises. And naturally the antisemite thinks of himself as a reasonable being. Whenever I have touched on this subject in a newspaper article, I have always had a considerable "come-back", and invariably some of the letters are from well-balanced, middling people—doctors, for example—with no apparent economic grievance. These people always say (as Hitler says in *Mein Kampf*) that they started out with no anti-Jewish prejudice but were driven into their present position by mere observation of the facts. Yet one of the marks of antisemitism is an ability to believe stories that could not possibly be true. One could see a good example of this in the strange accident that occurred in London in 1942, when a crowd, frightened by a bomb-burst nearby, fled into the mouth of an Underground station, with the result that something over a hundred people were crushed to death. The very same day it was repeated all over London that "the Jews were responsible". Clearly, if people will believe this kind of thing, one will not get much further by arguing with them. The only useful approach is to discover *why* they can swallow absurdities on one particular subject while remaining sane on others.

But now let me come back to that point I mentioned earlier—that there is widespread awareness of the prevalence of antisemitic feeling, and unwillingness to admit sharing it. Among educated people, antisemitism is held to be an unforgivable sin and in a quite different category from other kinds of racial prejudice. People will go to remarkable lengths to demonstrate that they are *not* antisemitic. Thus, in 1943 an intercession service on behalf of the Polish Jews was held in a synagogue in St John's Wood. The local authorities declared themselves anxious to participate in it, and the service was attended by the mayor of the borough in his robes and chain, by representatives of all the churches, and by detachments of RAF, Home Guards, nurses, Boy Scouts and what not. On the surface it was a touching demonstration of solidarity with the suffering Jews. But it was essentially a *conscious* effort to behave decently by people whose subjective feelings must in many cases have been very different. That quarter of London is partly Jewish, antisemitism is rife there, and, as I well knew, some of the men sitting round me in the synagogue were tinged by it. Indeed, the commander of my own platoon of Home Guards, who had been especially keen beforehand that we should "make a good show" at the intercession service, was an ex-member of Mosley's Blackshirts. While this division of feeling exists, tolerance of mass violence against Jews, or, what is more important, antisemitic legislation, are not possible in England. It is not at present possible, indeed, that antisemitism should *become respectable*. But this is less of an advantage than it might appear.

One effect of the persecutions in Germany has been to prevent antisemitism from being seriously studied. In England a brief inadequate survey was made by Mass Observation a year or two ago, but if there has been any other investigation of the subject, then its findings have been kept strictly secret. At the same time there has been conscious suppression, by all thoughtful people, of anything likely to wound Jewish susceptibilities. After 1934 the "Jew joke" disappeared as though by magic from postcards, periodicals and the music-hall stage, and to put an unsympathetic Jewish character into a novel or short story came to be regarded as antisemitism. On the Palestine issue, too, it was *de rigueur* among enlightened people to accept the Jewish case as proved and avoid examining the claims of the Arabs—a decision which might be correct on its own merits, but which was adopted primarily because the Jews were in trouble and it was felt that one must not criticise them. Thanks to Hitler, therefore, you had a situation in which the press was in effect censored in favour of the Jews while in private antisemitism was on the up-grade, even, to some extent, among sensitive and intelligent people. This was particularly noticeable in 1940 at the time of the internment of the refugees. Naturally, every thinking person felt that it was his duty to protest against the wholesale locking-up of unfortunate foreigners who for the most part were only in England because they were opponents of Hitler. Privately, however, one heard very different sentiments expressed. A minority of the refugees behaved in an exceedingly tactless way, and the feeling against them necessarily had an antisemitic undercurrent, since they were largely Jews. A very eminent figure in the Labour Party—I won't name him, but he is one of the most respected people in England—said to me quite violently: "We never asked these people to come to this country. If they choose to come here, let them take the consequences." Yet this man would as a matter of course have associated himself with any kind of petition or manifesto against the internment of aliens. This feeling that antisemitism is something sinful and disgraceful, something that a civilised person does not suffer from, is unfavourable to a scientific approach, and indeed many people will admit that they are frightened of probing too deeply into the subject. They are frightened, that is to say, of discovering not only that antisemitism is spreading, but that they themselves are infected by it.

To see this in perspective one must look back a few decades, to the days when Hitler was an out-of-work house-painter whom nobody had heard of. One would then find that though antisemitism is sufficiently in evidence now, it is probably *less* prevalent in England than it was thirty years ago. It is true that antisemitism as a fully thought-out racial or religious doctrine has never flourished in England. There has never been much feeling against intermarriage, or against Jews taking a prominent part in public life. Nevertheless, thirty years ago it was accepted more or less as a law of nature that a Jew was a figure of fun and—though superior in intelligence—slightly deficient in "character". In theory a Jew suffered from no legal disabilities, but in effect he was debarred from certain professions. He would probably not have been accepted as an officer in the navy, for instance, nor in what is called a "smart" regiment in the army. A Jewish boy at a public school almost invariably had a bad time. He could, of course, live down his Jewishness if he was exceptionally charming or athletic, but it was an initial disability comparable to a stammer or a birthmark. Wealthy Jews tended to disguise themselves under aristocratic English or Scottish names, and to the average person it seemed quite natural that they should do this, just as it seems natural for a criminal to change his identity if possible. About twenty years ago, in Rangoon, I was getting into a taxi with a friend when a small ragged boy of fair complexion rushed up to us and began a complicated story about having arrived from Colombo on a ship and wanting money to get back. His manner and appearance were difficult to "place", and I said to him:

"You speak very good English. What nationality are you?"

He answered eagerly in his chi-chi accent: "I am a *Joo*, sir!"

And I remember turning to my companion and saying, only partly in joke, "He admits it openly." All the Jews I had known till then were people who were ashamed of being Jews, or at any rate preferred not to talk about their ancestry, and if forced to do so tended to use the word "Hebrew".

The working-class attitude was no better. The Jew who grew up in Whitechapel took it for granted that he would be assaulted, or at least hooted at, if he ventured into one of the Christian slums nearby, and the "Jew joke" of the music halls and the comic papers was almost consistently ill-natured.[1] There was also literary Jew-baiting, which in the hands of Belloc, Chesterton and their followers reached an almost continental level of scurrility. Non-Catholic writers were sometimes guilty of the same thing in a milder form. There has been a perceptible antisemitic strain in English literature from Chaucer onwards, and without even getting up from this table to consult a book I can think of passages which *if written now* would be stigmatised as antisemitism, in the works of Shakespeare, Smollett, Thackeray, Bernard Shaw, H. G. Wells, T. S. Eliot, Aldous Huxley and various others. Offhand, the only English writers I can think of who, before the days of Hitler, made a definite effort to stick up for Jews are Dickens and Charles Reade. And however little the average intellectual may have agreed with the opinions of Belloc and Chesterton, he did not acutely disapprove of them. Chesterton's endless tirades against Jews, which he thrust into stories and essays upon the flimsiest pretexts, never got him into trouble—indeed Chesterton was one of the most generally respected figures in English literary life. Anyone who wrote in that strain *now* would bring down a storm of abuse upon himself, or more probably would find it impossible to get his writings published.

If, as I suggest, prejudice against Jews has always been pretty widespread in England, there is no reason to think that Hitler has genuinely diminished it. He has merely caused a sharp division between the politically conscious person who realises that this is not a time to throw stones at the Jews, and the unconscious person whose native antisemitism is increased by the nervous strain of the war. One can assume, therefore, that many people who would perish rather than admit to antisemitic feelings are secretly prone to them. I have

[1] It is interesting to compare the "Jew joke" with that other stand-by of the music halls, the "Scotch joke", which superficially it resembles. Occasionally a story is told (e.g. the Jew and the Scotsman who went into a pub together and both died of thirst) which puts both races on an equality, but in general the Jew is credited *merely* with cunning and avarice while the Scotsman is credited with physical hardihood as well. This is seen, for example, in the story of the Jew and the Scotsman who go together to a meeting which has been advertised as free. Unexpectedly there is a collection, and to avoid this the Jew faints and the Scotsman carries him out. Here the Scotsman performs the athletic feat of carrying the other. It would seem vaguely wrong if it were the other way about. [Author's footnote.]

already indicated that I believe antisemitism to be essentially a neurosis, but of course it has its rationalisations, which are sincerely believed in and are partly true. The rationalisation put forward by the common man is that the Jew is an exploiter. The partial justification for this is that the Jew, in England, is generally a small businessman—that is to say a person whose depredations are more obvious and intelligible than those of, say, a bank or an insurance company. Higher up the intellectual scale, antisemitism is rationalised by saying that the Jew is a person who spreads disaffection and weakens national morale. Again there is some superficial justification for this. During the past twenty-five years the activities of what are called "intellectuals" have been largely mischievous. I do not think it an exaggeration to say that if the "intellectuals" had done their work a little more thoroughly, Britain would have surrendered in 1940. But the disaffected intelligentsia inevitably included a large number of Jews. With some plausibility it can be said that the Jews are the enemies of our native culture and our national morale. Carefully examined, the claim is seen to be nonsense, but there are always a few prominent individuals who can be cited in support of it. During the past few years there has been what amounts to a counter-attack against the rather shallow Leftism which was fashionable in the previous decade and which was exemplified by such organisations as the Left Book Club. This counter-attack (see for instance such books as Arnold Lunn's *The Good Gorilla* or Evelyn Waugh's *Put Out More Flags*) has an antisemitic strain, and it would probably be more marked if the subject were not so obviously dangerous. It so happens that for some decades past Britain has had no nationalist intelligentsia worth bothering about. But British nationalism, i.e. nationalism of an intellectual kind, may revive, and probably will revive if Britain comes out of the present war greatly weakened. The young intellectuals of 1950 may be as naively patriotic as those of 1914. In that case the kind of antisemitism which flourished among the anti-Dreyfusards in France, and which Chesterton and Belloc tried to import into this country, might get a foothold.

I have no hard-and-fast theory about the origins of antisemitism. The two current explanations, that it is due to economic causes, or on the other hand, that it is a legacy from the Middle Ages, seem to me unsatisfactory, though I admit that if one combines them they can be made to cover the facts. All I would say with confidence is that antisemitism is part of the larger problem of nationalism, which has not yet been seriously examined, and that the Jew is evidently a scapegoat, though *for what* he is a scapegoat we do not yet know. In this essay I have relied almost entirely on my own limited experience, and perhaps every one of my conclusions would be negatived by other observers. The fact is that there are almost no data on this subject. But for what they are worth I will summarise my opinions. Boiled down, they amount to this:

There is more antisemitism in England than we care to admit, and the war has accentuated it, but it is not certain that it is on the increase if one thinks in terms of decades rather than years.

It does not at present lead to open persecution, but it has the effect of making people callous to the sufferings of Jews in other countries.

It is at bottom quite irrational and will not yield to argument.

The persecutions in Germany have caused much concealment of antisemitic feeling and thus obscured the whole picture.

The subject needs serious investigation.

Only the last point is worth expanding. To study any subject scientifically one needs a detached attitude, which is obviously harder when one's own interests or emotions are involved. Plenty of people who are quite capable of being objective about sea urchins, say, or the square root of 2, become schizophrenic if they have to think about the sources of their own income. What vitiates nearly all that is written about antisemitism is the assumption in the writer's mind that *he himself* is immune to it. "Since I know that antisemitism is irrational," he argues, "it follows that I do not share it." He thus fails to start his investigation in the one place where he could get hold of some reliable evidence—that is, in his own mind.

It seems to me a safe assumption that the disease loosely called nationalism is now almost universal. Antisemitism is only one manifestation of nationalism, and not everyone will have the disease in that particular form. A Jew, for example, would not be antisemitic: but then many Zionist Jews seem to me to be merely antisemites turned upside-down, just as many Indians and Negroes display the normal colour prejudices in an inverted form. The point is that something, some psychological vitamin, is lacking in modern civilisation, and as a result we are all more or less subject to this lunacy of believing that whole races or nations are mysteriously good or mysteriously evil. I defy any modern intellectual to look closely and honestly into his own mind without coming upon nationalistic loyalties and hatreds of one kind or another. It is the fact that he can feel the emotional tug of such things, and yet see them dispassionately for what they are, that gives him his status as an intellectual. It will be seen, therefore, that the starting point for any investigation of antisemitism should not be "Why does this obviously irrational belief appeal to other people?" but "Why does antisemitism appeal to *me*? What is there about it that I feel to be true?" If one asks this question one at least discovers one's own rationalisations, and it may be possible to find out what lies beneath them. Antisemitism should be investigated—and I will not say by antisemites, but at any rate by people who know that they are not immune to that kind of emotion. When Hitler has disappeared a real enquiry into this subject will be possible, and it would probably be best to start not by debunking antisemitism, but by marshalling all the justifications for it that can be found, in one's own mind or anybody else's. In that way one might get some clues that would lead to its psychological roots. But that antisemitism will be definitively *cured*, without curing the larger disease of nationalism, I do not believe.

Written [early February 1945]; *Contemporary Jewish Record*, April 1945; SJ; EYE; CE

95. In Defence of P. G. Wodehouse

When the Germans made their rapid advance through Belgium in the early summer of 1940, they captured, among other things, Mr P. G. Wodehouse, who had been living throughout the early part of the war in his villa at Le Touquet, and seems not to have realised until the last moment that he was in any danger. As he was led away into captivity, he is said to have remarked, "Perhaps after this I shall write a serious book." He was placed for the time being under house arrest, and from his subsequent statements it appears that he was treated in a fairly friendly way, German officers in the neighbourhood frequently "dropping in for a bath or a party".

Over a year later, on 25th June 1941, the news came that Wodehouse had been released from internment and was living at the Adlon Hotel in Berlin. On the following day the public was astonished to learn that he had agreed to do some broadcasts of a "non-political" nature over the German radio. The full texts of these broadcasts are not easy to obtain at this date, but Wodehouse seems to have done five of them between 26th June and 2nd July, when the Germans took him off the air again. The first broadcast, on 26th June, was not made on the Nazi radio but took the form of an interview with Harry Flannery, the representative of the Columbia Broadcasting System, which still had its correspondents in Berlin. Wodehouse also published in the *Saturday Evening Post* an article which he had written while still in the internment camp.

The article and the broadcasts dealt mainly with Wodehouse's experiences in internment, but they did include a very few comments on the war. The following are fair samples:

> I never was interested in politics. I'm quite unable to work up any kind of belligerent feeling. Just as I'm about to feel belligerent about some country I meet a decent sort of chap. We go out together and lose any fighting thoughts or feelings.

> A short time ago they had a look at us on parade and got the right idea; at least they sent us to the local lunatic asylum. And I have been there forty-two weeks. There is a good deal to be said for internment. It keeps you out of the saloon and helps you to keep up with your reading. The chief trouble is that it means you are away from home for a long time. When I join my wife I had better take along a letter of introduction to be on the safe side.

> In the days before the war I had always been modestly proud of being an Englishman, but now that I have been some months resident in this bin or repository of Englishmen I am not so sure. . . . The only concession I want from Germany is that she gives me a loaf of bread, tells the gentlemen with muskets at the main gate to look the other way, and leaves the rest to me. In return I am prepared to hand over India, an autographed set of my books, and to reveal the secret process of cooking sliced potatoes on a radiator. This offer holds good till Wednesday week.

The first extract quoted above caused great offence. Wodehouse was also censured for using (in the interview with Flannery) the phrase "whether Britain wins the war or not", and he did not make things better by describing in another broadcast the filthy habits of some Belgian prisoners among whom he was interned. The Germans recorded this broadcast and repeated it a number of times. They seem to have supervised his talks very lightly, and they allowed him not only to be funny about the discomforts of internment but to remark that "the internees at Trost camp all fervently believe that Britain will eventually win." The general upshot of the talks, however, was that he had not been ill treated and bore no malice.

These broadcasts caused an immediate uproar in England. There were questions in Parliament, angry editorial comments in the press, and a stream of letters from fellow authors, nearly all of them disapproving, though one or two suggested that it would be better to suspend judgement, and several pleaded that Wodehouse probably did not realise what he was doing. On 15th July, the Home Service of the BBC carried an extremely violent Postscript by "Cassandra" of the *Daily Mirror*, accusing Wodehouse of "selling his country". This postscript made free use of such expressions as "quisling" and "worshipping the Fuehrer". The main charge was that Wodehouse had agreed to do German propaganda as a way of buying himself out of the internment camp.

"Cassandra's" Postscript caused a certain amount of protest, but on the whole it seems to have intensified popular feeling against Wodehouse. One result of it was that numerous lending libraries withdrew Wodehouse's books from circulation. Here is a typical news item:

> Within twenty-four hours of listening to the broadcast of Cassandra, the *Daily Mirror* columnist, Portadown (North Ireland) Urban District Council banned P. G. Wodehouse's books from their public library. Mr Edward McCann said that Cassandra's broadcast had clinched the matter. Wodehouse was funny no longer. (*Daily Mirror.*)

In addition the BBC banned Wodehouse's lyrics from the air and was still doing so a couple of years later. As late as December 1944 there were demands in Parliament that Wodehouse should be put on trial as a traitor.

There is an old saying that if you throw enough mud some of it will stick, and the mud has stuck to Wodehouse in a rather peculiar way. An impression has been left behind that Wodehouse's talks (not that anyone remembers what he said in them) showed him up not merely as a traitor but as an ideological sympathiser with Fascism. Even at the time several letters to the press claimed that "Fascist tendencies" could be detected in his books, and the charge has been repeated since. I shall try to analyse the mental atmosphere of those books in a moment, but it is important to realise that the events of 1941 do not convict Wodehouse of anything worse than stupidity. The really interesting question is how and why he could be so stupid. When Flannery met Wodehouse (released, but still under guard) at the Adlon Hotel in June 1941, he saw at once that he was dealing with a political innocent, and when preparing him for their broadcast interview he had to warn him against making some exceedingly unfortunate remarks, one of which was by implication slightly anti-Russian. As it was, the phrase "whether England wins or not" did get through. Soon after the interview Wodehouse told him that he was also going to broadcast on the Nazi radio, apparently not realising that this action had any special significance. Flannery comments:[1]

> By this time the Wodehouse plot was evident. It was one of the best Nazi publicity stunts of the war, the first with a human angle. . . . Plack (Goebbels's assistant) had gone to the camp near Gleiwitz to see Wodehouse, found that the author was completely without political sense, and had an idea. He suggested to Wodehouse that in return for being released from the prison camp he write a series of broadcasts about his experiences; there would be no censorship and he would put them on the air himself. In making that proposal Plack showed that he knew his man. He knew that Wodehouse made fun of the English in all his stories and that he seldom wrote in any other way, that he was still living in the period about which he wrote and had no conception of Nazism and all it meant. Wodehouse was his own Bertie Wooster.

The striking of an actual bargain between Wodehouse and Plack seems to be merely Flannery's own interpretation. The arrangement may have been of a much less definite kind, and to judge from the broadcasts themselves, Wodehouse's main idea in making them was to keep in touch with his public and—the comedian's ruling passion —to get a laugh. Obviously they are not the utterances of a quisling of the type of Ezra Pound or John Amery,[2] nor, probably, of a

---

[1] *Assignment to Berlin* by Harry W. Flannery. [Author's footnote.]

[2] John Amery (1912–1945), right-wing politician and son of Leo Amery, who was a Conservative and patriotic MP and Secretary of State for India 1940–5. John Amery was an ardent admirer of Hitler, and had broadcast from Germany

person capable of understanding the nature of quislingism. Flannery
seems to have warned Wodehouse that it would be unwise to broadcast, but not very forcibly. He adds that Wodehouse (though in one
broadcast he refers to himself as an Englishman) seemed to regard
himself as an American citizen. He had contemplated naturalisation,
but had never filled in the necessary papers. He even used, to
Flannery, the phrase, "We're not at war with Germany."

I have before me a bibliography of P. G. Wodehouse's works.
It names round about fifty books, but is certainly incomplete. It is
as well to be honest, and I ought to start by admitting that there are
many books by Wodehouse—perhaps a quarter or a third of the
total—which I have not read. It is not, indeed, easy to read the
whole output of a popular writer who is normally published in
cheap editions. But I have followed his work fairly closely since 1911,
when I was eight years old, and am well acquainted with its peculiar
mental atmosphere—an atmosphere which has not, of course,
remained completely unchanged, but shows little alteration since
about 1925. In the passage from Flannery's book which I quoted
above there are two remarks which would immediately strike any
attentive reader of Wodehouse. One is to the effect that Wodehouse
"was still living in the period about which he wrote", and the other
that the Nazi Propaganda Ministry made use of him because he
"made fun of the English". The second statement is based on a
misconception to which I will return presently. But Flannery's
other comment is quite true and contains in it part of the clue to
Wodehouse's behaviour.

A thing that people often forget about P. G. Wodehouse's novels
is how long ago the better-known of them were written. We think of
him as in some sense typifying the silliness of the nineteen-twenties
and nineteen-thirties, but in fact the scenes and characters by which
he is best remembered had all made their appearance before 1925.
Psmith first appeared in 1909, having been foreshadowed by other
characters in early school stories. Blandings Castle, with Baxter and
the Earl of Emsworth both in residence, was introduced in 1915.
The Jeeves-Wooster cycle began in 1919, both Jeeves and Wooster
having made brief appearances earlier. Ukridge appeared in 1924.

---

during the war urging British subjects in captivity to fight for Germany against
England and Russia, and also made public speeches throughout occupied Europe
on behalf of the German régime. He was executed for treason by the British in
December 1945.

When one looks through the list of Wodehouse's books from 1902 onwards, one can observe three fairly well-marked periods. The first is the school-story period. It includes such books as *The Gold Bat*, *The Pothunters*, etc and has its high-spot in *Mike* (1909). *Psmith in the City*, published in the following year, belongs in this category, though it is not directly concerned with school life. The next is the American period. Wodehouse seems to have lived in the United States from about 1913 to 1920, and for a while showed signs of becoming americanised in idiom and outlook. Some of the stories in *The Man with Two Left Feet* (1917) appear to have been influenced by O. Henry, and other books written about this time contain Americanisms (e.g. "highball" for "whisky and soda") which an Englishman would not normally use *in propria persona*. Nevertheless, almost all the books of this period—*Psmith, Journalist; The Little Nugget; The Indiscretions of Archie; Piccadilly Jim* and various others—depend for their effect on the *contrast* between English and American manners. English characters appear in an American setting, or vice versa: there is a certain number of purely English stories, but hardly any purely American ones. The third period might fitly be called the country-house period. By the early nineteen-twenties Wodehouse must have been making a very large income, and the social status of his characters moved upwards accordingly, though the Ukridge stories form a partial exception. The typical setting is now a country mansion, a luxurious bachelor flat or an expensive golf club. The schoolboy athleticism of the earlier books fades out, cricket and football giving way to golf, and the element of farce and burlesque becomes more marked. No doubt many of the later books, such as *Summer Lightning*, are light comedy rather than pure farce, but the occasional attempts at moral earnestness which can be found in *Psmith, Journalist; The Little Nugget; The Coming of Bill; The Man with Two Left Feet* and some of the school stories, no longer appear. Mike Jackson has turned into Bertie Wooster. That, however, is not a very startling metamorphosis, and one of the most noticeable things about Wodehouse is his *lack* of development. Books like *The Gold Bat* and *Tales of St Austin's*, written in the opening years of this century, already have the familiar atmosphere. How much of a formula the writing of his later books had become one can see from the fact that he continued to write stories of English life although throughout the sixteen years before his internment he was living at Hollywood and Le Touquet.

Mike, which is now a difficult book to obtain in an unabridged form, must be one of the best "light" school stories in English. But though its incidents are largely farcical, it is by no means a satire on the public-school system, and *The Gold Bat*, *The Pothunters*, etc are even less so. Wodehouse was educated at Dulwich, and then worked in a bank and graduated into novel writing by way of very cheap journalism. It is clear that for many years he remained "fix-ated" on his old school and loathed the unromantic job and the lower-middle-class surroundings in which he found himself. In the early stories the "glamour" of public-school life (house matches, fagging, teas round the study fire, etc) is laid on fairly thick, and the "play the game" code of morals is accepted with not many reservations. Wrykyn, Wodehouse's imaginary public school, is a school of a more fashionable type than Dulwich, and one gets the impression that between *The Gold Bat* (1904) and *Mike* (1908) Wrykyn itself has become more expensive and moved farther from London. Psychologically the most revealing book of Wodehouse's early period is *Psmith in the City*. Mike Jackson's father has suddenly lost his money, and Mike, like Wodehouse himself, is thrust at the age of about eighteen into an ill-paid subordinate job in a bank. Psmith is similarly employed, though not from financial necessity. Both this book and *Psmith, Journalist* (1915) are unusual in that they display a certain amount of political consciousness. Psmith at this stage chooses to call himself a Socialist—in his mind, and no doubt in Wodehouse's, this means no more than ignoring class distinctions—and on one occasion the two boys attend an open-air meeting on Clapham Common and go home to tea with an elderly Socialist orator, whose shabby-genteel home is described with some accuracy. But the most striking feature of the book is Mike's inability to wean himself from the atmosphere of school. He enters upon his job without any pretence of enthusiasm, and his main desire is not, as one might expect, to find a more interesting and useful job, but simply to be playing cricket. When he has to find himself lodgings he chooses to settle at Dulwich, because there he will be near a school and will be able to hear the agreeable sound of the ball striking against the bat. The climax of the book comes when Mike gets the chance to play in a county match and simply walks out of his job in order to do so. The point is that Wodehouse here sympa-thises with Mike: indeed he identified himself with him, for it is clear enough that Mike bears the same relation to Wodehouse as

Julien Sorel to Stendhal. But he created many other heroes essentially similar. Through the books of this and the next period there passes a whole series of young men to whom playing games and "keeping fit" are a sufficient life-work. Wodehouse is almost incapable of imagining a desirable job. The great thing is to have money of your own, or, failing that, to find a sinecure. The hero of *Something Fresh* (1915) escapes from low-class journalism by becoming physical-training instructor to a dyspeptic millionaire: this is regarded as a step up, morally as well as financially.

In the books of the third period there is no narcissism and no serious interludes, but the implied moral and social background has changed much less than might appear at first sight. If one compares Bertie Wooster with Mike, or even with the rugger-playing prefects of the earliest school stories, one sees that the only real difference between them is that Bertie is richer and lazier. His ideals would be almost the same as theirs, but he fails to live up to them. Archie Moffam, in *The Indiscretions of Archie* (1921), is a type intermediate between Bertie and the earlier heroes: he is an ass, but he is also honest, kind-hearted, athletic and courageous. From first to last Wodehouse takes the public-school code of behaviour for granted, with the difference that in his later, more sophisticated period he prefers to show his characters violating it or living up to it against their will:

> "Bertie! You wouldn't let down a pal?"
> "Yes, I would."
> "But we were at school together, Bertie."
> "I don't care."
> "The old school, Bertie, the old school!"
> "Oh, well—dash it!"

Bertie, a sluggish Don Quixote, has no wish to tilt at windmills, but he would hardly think of refusing to do so when honour calls. Most of the people whom Wodehouse intends as sympathetic characters are parasites, and some of them are plain imbeciles, but very few of them could be described as immoral. Even Ukridge is a visionary rather than a plain crook. The most immoral, or rather un-moral, of Wodehouse's characters is Jeeves, who acts as a foil to Bertie Wooster's comparative high-mindedness and perhaps symbolises the widespread English belief that intelligence and unscrupulousness are much the same thing. How closely Wodehouse sticks to conventional morality can be seen from the fact that nowhere in his books is there anything in the nature of a sex joke. This is an enormous sacrifice for a farcical writer to make. Not only are there no dirty jokes, but there are hardly any compromising situations: the horns-on-the-forehead motif is almost completely avoided. Most of the full-length books, of course, contain a "love interest", but it is always at the light-comedy level: the love affair, with its complications and its idyllic scenes, goes on and on, but, as the saying goes "nothing happens". It is significant that Wodehouse, by nature a writer of farces, was able to collaborate more than once with Ian Hay, a serio-comic writer and an exponent (*vide Pip*, etc) of the "clean-living Englishman" tradition at its silliest.

In *Something Fresh* Wodehouse had discovered the comic possibilities of the English aristocracy, and a succession of ridiculous but, save in a very few instances, not actually contemptible barons, earls and what not followed accordingly. This had the rather curious effect of causing Wodehouse to be regarded, outside England, as a penetrating satirist of English society. Hence Flannery's statement that Wodehouse "made fun of the English", which is the impression he would probably make on a German or even an American reader. Some time after the broadcasts from Berlin I was discussing them with a young Indian Nationalist who defended Wodehouse warmly. He took it for granted that Wodehouse *had* gone over to the enemy, which from his own point of view was the right thing to do. But what interested me was to find that he regarded Wodehouse as an anti-British writer who had done useful work by showing up the British aristocracy in their true colours. This is a mistake that it would be very difficult for an English person to make, and is a good instance of the way in which books, especially humorous books, lose their finer nuances when they reach a foreign audience. For it is clear enough that Wodehouse is not anti-British, and not anti-upper-class either. On the contrary, a harmless old-fashioned snobbishness is perceptible all through his work. Just as an intelligent Catholic is able to see that the blasphemies of Baudelaire or James Joyce are not seriously damaging to the Catholic faith, so an English reader can see that in creating such characters as Hildebrand Spencer Poyns de Burgh John Hanneyside Coombe-Crombie, 12th Earl of Dreever, Wodehouse is not really attacking the social hierarchy. Indeed, no one who genuinely despised titles would write of them so much. Wodehouse's attitude towards the English social system is the same as his attitude towards the public-school moral code—a mild facetiousness covering an unthinking acceptance. The Earl of Emsworth is funny because an earl ought to have more dignity, and Bertie Wooster's helpless dependence on Jeeves is funny partly because the servant ought not to be superior to the master. An American reader can mistake these two, and others like them, for hostile caricatures because he is inclined to be anglophobe already and they correspond to his preconceived ideas about a decadent aristocracy. Bertie Wooster, with his spats and his cane, is the traditional stage Englishman. But, as any English reader would see, Wodehouse intends him as a sympathetic figure, and Wodehouse's real sin has been to present the English upper classes as much nicer people than they are. All through his books certain problems are consistently avoided. Almost without exception his moneyed young men are unassuming, good mixers, not avaricious: their tone is set for them by Psmith, who retains his own upper-class exterior but bridges the social gap by addressing everyone as "Comrade".

But there is another important point about Bertie Wooster: his out-of-dateness. Conceived in 1917 or thereabouts, Bertie really belongs to an epoch earlier than that. He is the "knut" of the pre-1914 period, celebrated in such songs as "Gilbert the Filbert" or "Reckless Reggie of the Regent's Palace". The kind of life that Wodehouse writes about by preference, the life of the "clubman" or "man about town", the elegant young man who lounges all the morning in Piccadilly with a cane under his arm and a carnation in his buttonhole, barely survived into the nineteen-twenties. It is significant that Wodehouse could publish in 1936 a book entitled *Young Men in Spats*. For who was wearing spats at that date? They had gone out of fashion quite ten years earlier. But the traditional "knut", the "Piccadilly Johnny", *ought* to wear spats, just as the pantomime Chinese ought to wear a pigtail. A humorous writer is not obliged to keep up to date, and having struck one or two good veins, Wodehouse continued to exploit them with a regularity that was no doubt all the easier because he did not set foot in England during the sixteen years that preceded his internment. His picture of English society had been formed before 1914, and it was a naive, traditional and, at bottom, admiring picture.Nor did he ever become genuinely americanised. As I have pointed out, spontaneous Americanisms do occur in the books of the middle period, but Wodehouse remained English enough to find American slang an amusing and slightly

shocking novelty. He loves to thrust a slang phrase or a crude fact
in among Wardour Street English ("With a hollow groan Ukridge
borrowed five shillings from me and went out into the night"), and
expressions like "a piece of cheese" or "bust him on the noggin"
lend themselves to this purpose. But the trick had been developed
before he made any American contacts, and his use of garbled
quotations is a common device of English writers running back to
Fielding. As Mr John Hayward has pointed out,[1] Wodehouse owes
a good deal to his knowledge of English literature and especially of
Shakespeare. His books are aimed, not, obviously, at a highbrow
audience, but at an audience educated along traditional lines. When,
for instance, he describes somebody as heaving "the kind of sigh
that Prometheus might have heaved when the vulture dropped in for
its lunch", he is assuming that his readers will know something of
Greek mythology. In his early days the writers he admired were
probably Barry Pain, Jerome K. Jerome, W. W. Jacobs, Kipling and
F. Anstey, and he has remained closer to them than to the quick-
moving American comic writers such as Ring Lardner or Damon
Runyon. In his radio interview with Flannery, Wodehouse wondered
whether "the kind of people and the kind of England I write about
will live after the war", not realising that they were ghosts already.
"He was still living in the period about which he wrote," says Flannery, meaning, probably, the nineteen-twenties. But the period was
really the Edwardian age, and Bertie Wooster, if he ever existed, was
killed round about 1915.

If my analysis of Wodehouse's mentality is accepted, the idea that
in 1941 he consciously aided the Nazi propaganda machine becomes
untenable and even ridiculous. He *may* have been induced to broadcast by the promise of an earlier release (he was due for release a
few months later, on reaching his sixtieth birthday), but he cannot
have realised that what he did would be damaging to British interests.
As I have tried to show, his moral outlook has remained that of a
public-school boy, and according to the public-school code, treachery
in time of war is the most unforgivable of all the sins. But how could
he fail to grasp that what he did would be a big propaganda score for
the Germans and would bring down a torrent of disapproval on his
own head? To answer this one must take two things into consideration. First, Wodehouse's complete lack—so far as one can judge from

[1] "P. G. Wodehouse" by John Hayward. (*The Saturday Book*, 1942.) I believe
this is the only full-length critical essay on Wodehouse. [Author's footnote.]

his printed works—of political awareness. It is nonsense to talk of "Fascist tendencies" in his books. There are no post-1918 tendencies at all. Throughout his work there is a certain uneasy awareness of the problem of class distinctions, and scattered through it at various dates there are ignorant though not unfriendly references to Socialism. In *The Heart of a Goof* (1926) there is a rather silly story about a Russian novelist, which seems to have been inspired by the factional struggle then raging in the USSR. But the references in it to the Soviet system are entirely frivolous and, considering the date, not markedly hostile. That is about the extent of Wodehouse's political consciousness, so far as it is discoverable from his writings. Nowhere, so far as I know, does he so much as use the word "Fascism" or "Nazism". In left-wing circles, indeed in "enlightened" circles of any kind, to broadcast on the Nazi radio, to have any truck with Nazis whatever, would have seemed just as shocking an action before the war as during it. But that is a habit of mind that had been developed during nearly a decade of ideological struggle against Fascism. The bulk of the British people, one ought to remember, remained anaesthetic to that struggle until late into 1940. Abyssinia, Spain, China, Austria, Czechoslovakia—the long series of crimes and aggressions had simply slid past their consciousness or were dimly noted as quarrels occurring among foreigners and "not our business". One can gauge the general ignorance from the fact that the ordinary Englishman thought of "Fascism" as an exclusively Italian thing and was bewildered when the same word was applied to Germany. And there is nothing in Wodehouse's writings to suggest that he was better informed, or more interested in politics, than the general run of his readers.

The other thing one must remember is that Wodehouse happened to be taken prisoner at just the moment when the war reached its desperate phase. We forget these things now, but until that time feelings about the war had been noticeably tepid. There was hardly any fighting, the Chamberlain Government was unpopular, eminent publicists were hinting that we should make a compromise peace as quickly as possible, trade union and Labour Party branches all over the country were passing anti-war resolutions. Afterwards, of course, things changed. The army was with difficulty extricated from Dunkirk, France collapsed, Britain was alone, the bombs rained on London, Goebbels announced that Britain was to be "reduced to degradation and poverty". By the middle of 1941 the British people knew what they were up against and feelings against the enemy were far fiercer than before. But Wodehouse had spent the intervening year in internment, and his captors seem to have treated him reasonably well. He had missed the turning-point of the war, and in 1941 he was still reacting in terms of 1939. He was not alone in this. On several occasions about this time the Germans brought captured British soldiers to the microphone, and some of them made remarks at least as tactless as Wodehouse's. They attracted no attention, however. And even an outright quisling like John Amery was afterwards to arouse much less indignation than Wodehouse had done.

But why? Why should a few rather silly but harmless remarks by an elderly novelist have provoked such an outcry? One has to look for the probable answer amid the dirty requirements of propaganda warfare.

There is one point about the Wodehouse broadcasts that is almost certainly significant—the date. Wodehouse was released two or three days before the invasion of the USSR, and at a time when the higher ranks of the Nazi party must have known that the invasion was imminent. It was vitally necessary to keep America out of the war as long as possible, and in fact, about this time, the German attitude towards the USA did become more conciliatory than it had been before. The Germans could hardly hope to defeat Russia, Britain and the USA in combination, but if they could polish off Russia quickly—and presumably they expected to do so—the Americans might never intervene. The release of Wodehouse was only a minor move, but it was not a bad sop to throw to the American isolationists. He was well known in the United States, and he was—or so the Germans calculated—popular with the anglophobe public as a caricaturist who made fun of the silly-ass Englishman with his spats and his monocle. At the microphone he could be trusted to damage British prestige in one way or another, while his release would demonstrate that the Germans were good fellows and knew how to treat their enemies chivalrously. That presumably was the calculation, though the fact that Wodehouse was only broadcasting for about a week suggests that he did not come up to expectations.

But on the British side similar though opposite calculations were at work. For the two years following Dunkirk, British morale depended largely upon the feeling that this was not only a war for democracy but a war which the common people had to win by their own efforts. The upper classes were discredited by their appeasement policy and by the disasters of 1940, and a social-levelling process appeared to be taking place. Patriotism and left-wing sentiments were associated in the popular mind, and numerous able journalists were at work to tie the association tighter. Priestley's 1940 broadcasts and "Cassandra's" articles in the *Daily Mirror* were good examples of the demagogic propaganda flourishing at that time. In this atmosphere, Wodehouse made an ideal whipping-boy. For it was generally felt that the rich were treacherous, and Wodehouse—as "Cassandra" vigorously pointed out in his broadcast—was a rich man. But he was the kind of rich man who could be attacked with impunity and without risking any damage to the structure of society. To denounce Wodehouse was not like denouncing, say, Beaverbrook. A mere novelist, however large his earnings may happen to be, is not *of* the possessing class. Even if his income touches £50,000 a year he has only the outward semblance of a millionaire. He is a lucky outsider who has fluked into a fortune—usually a very temporary fortune—like the winner of the Calcutta Derby Sweep. Consequently, Wodehouse's indiscretion gave a good propaganda opening. It was a chance to "expose" a wealthy parasite without drawing attention to any of the parasites who really mattered.

In the desperate circumstances of the time, it was excusable to be angry at what Wodehouse did, but to go on denouncing him three or four years later—and more, to let an impression remain that he acted with conscious treachery—is not excusable. Few things in this war have been more morally disgusting than the present hunt after traitors and quislings. At best it is largely the punishment of the guilty by the guilty. In France, all kinds of petty rats—police officials, penny-a-lining journalists, women who have slept with German soldiers—are hunted down while almost without exception the big rats escape. In England the fiercest tirades against quislings are uttered by Conservatives who were practising appeasement in 1938 and Communists who were advocating it in 1940. I have striven to show how the wretched Wodehouse—just because success and expatriation had allowed him to remain mentally in the Edwardian age—became the *corpus vile* in a propaganda experiment, and I suggest that it is now time to regard the incident as closed. If Ezra Pound is caught and shot by the American authorities, it will have the effect of establishing his reputation as a poet for hundreds of years; and even in the case of Wodehouse, if we drive him to retire to the

United States and renounce his British citizenship, we shall end by being horribly ashamed of ourselves. Meanwhile, if we really want to punish the people who weakened national morale at critical moments, there are other culprits who are nearer home and better worth chasing.

Written [February] 1945; *Windmill*, No. 2 [July] 1945; CTE; DD; OR;CE

96. As I Please

Last week I received a copy of a statement on the future of Burma, issued by the Burma Association, an organisation which includes most of the Burmese resident in this country. How representative this organisation is I am not certain, but probably it voices the wishes of a majority of politically-conscious Burmese. For reasons I shall try to make clear presently, the statement just issued is an important document. Summarised as shortly as possible, it makes the following demands:

(a) An amnesty for Burmese who have collaborated with the Japs during the occupation. (b) A statement by the British Government of a definite date at which Burma shall attain Dominion status. The period, if possible, to be less than six years. The Burmese people to summon a Constituent Assembly in the meantime. (c) No interim of "direct rule". (d) The Burmese people to have a greater share in the economic development of their own country. (e) The British Government to make an immediate unequivocal statement of its intentions towards Burma.

The striking thing about these demands is how moderate they are. No political party with any tinge of nationalism, or any hope of getting a mass following, could possibly ask for less. But why do these people pitch their claims so low? Well, I think one can guess at two reasons. To begin with, the experience of Japanese occupation has probably made Dominion status seem a more tempting goal than it seemed three years ago. But—much more important—if they demand so little it is probably because they expect to be offered even less. And I should guess that they expect right. Indeed, of the very modest suggestions listed above, only the first is likely to be carried out.

The Government has never made any clear statement about the future of Burma, but there have been persistent rumours that when the Japs are driven out there is to be a return to "direct rule", which is a polite name for military dictatorship. And what is happening, politically, in Burma at this moment? We simply don't know: nowhere have I seen in any newspaper one word about the way in which the reconquered territories are being administered. To grasp the significance of this one has to look at the map of Burma. A year ago Burma proper was in Japanese hands and the Allies were fighting in wild territories thinly populated by rather primitive tribes who have never been much interfered with and are traditionally pro-British. Now they are penetrating into the heart of Burma, and some fairly important towns, centres of administration, have fallen into their hands. Several million Burmese must be once again under the British flag. Yet we are told nothing whatever about the form of administration that is being set up. Is it surprising if every thinking Burmese fears the worst?

It is vitally important to interest the British public in this matter, if possible. Our eyes fixed on Europe, we forget that at the other end of the world there is a whole string of countries awaiting liberation and in nearly every case hoping for something better than a mere change of conquerors. Burma will probably be the first British territory to be reconquered, and it will be a test case: a more important test than Greece or Belgium, not only because more people are involved, but because it will be almost wholly a British responsibility. It will be a fearful disaster if through apathy and ignorance we let Churchill, Amery and Co put across some reactionary settlement which will lose us the friendship of the Burmese people for good.

For a year or two after the Japanese have gone, Burma will be in a receptive mood and more pro-British than it has been for a dozen years past. Then is the moment to make a generous gesture. I don't know whether Dominion status is the best possible solution. But if the politically conscious section of the Burmese ask for Dominion status, it would be monstrous to let the Tories refuse it in a hopeless effort to bring back the past. And there must be a date attached to it, a not too distant date. Whether these people remain inside the British Commonwealth or outside it, what matters in the long run is that we should have their friendship—and we *can* have it if we do not play them false at the moment of crisis. When the moment comes for Burma's future to be settled, thinking Burmese will not turn their eyes towards Churchill. They will be looking at *us*, the Labour movement, to see whether our talk about democracy, self-determination, racial equality and what not has any truth in it. I do not know whether it will be in our power to force a decent settlement upon the Government; but I do know that we shall harm ourselves irreparably if we do not make at least as much row about it as we did in the case of Greece.

When asked, "Which is the wisest of the animals?" a Japanese sage replied, "The one that man has not yet discovered."

I have just seen in a book the statement that the grey seals, the kind that are found round the coasts of Britain, number only ten thousand. Presumably there are so few of them because they have been killed off, like many another over-trustful animal. Seals are quite tame, and appear to be very inquisitive. They will follow a boat for miles, and sometimes they will even follow you when you are walking round the shore. There is no good reason for killing them. Their coats are no use for fur, and except for eating a certain amount of fish they do no harm.

They breed mostly on uninhabited islands. Let us hope that some of the islands remain uninhabited, so that these unfortunate brutes may escape being exterminated entirely. However, we are not quite such persistent slaughterers of rare animals as we used to be. Two species of birds, the bittern and the spoonbill, extinct for many years, have recently succeeded in re-establishing themselves in Britain. They have even been encouraged to breed in some places. Thirty years ago, any bittern that dared to show its beak in this country would have been shot and stuffed immediately.

The Gestapo is said to have teams of literary critics whose job is to determine, by means of stylistic comparison, the authorship of anonymous pamphlets. I have always thought that, if only it were in a better cause, this is exactly the job I would like to have. . . .

Tribune, 16 February 1945

97. Letter to Leonard Moore

27B Canonbury Square
Islington N1
15 February 1945

Dear Mr Moore,

I am sending back these contracts after some delay as I have been very busy. . . .

I am just going to France for two months or more,[1] so I suppose I shall be away when *Animal Farm* comes out. I am sending Warburg a list of the people to send complimentary copies and special review copies to. I wonder if you could be kind enough to send my press cuttings and any other communications direct to my wife

Mrs Eric Blair
Greystone
Carlton
Stockton-on-Tees, Co. Durham

She has full powers to make decisions for me on any question that may come up. . . .

Yours sincerely
Eric Blair

98. Letter to Roger Senhouse

Room 329
Hotel Scribe
Rue Scribe
Paris 9e
17 March 1945

Dear Roger,[2]

Thanks so much for your letter, and for sending the copy of *Homage to Catalonia*. I didn't after all give it to André Malraux, who is not in Paris, but to, of all people, Jose Rovira, who was the commander of my division in Spain and whom I met at a friend's house here.

[1] As a war correspondent for the *Observer*.
[2] A director of Secker & Warburg, who had published *Homage to Catalonia* and *The Lion and the Unicorn*.

I don't know whether *Animal Farm* has definitively gone to press. If it has not actually been printed yet, there is one further alteration of one word that I would like to make. In Chapter VIII (I think it is VIII), when the windmill is blown up, I wrote "all the animals including Napoleon flung themselves on their faces." I would like to alter it to "all the animals except Napoleon." If the book has been printed it's not worth bothering about, but I just thought the alteration would be fair to J[oseph] S[talin], as he did stay in Moscow during the German advance.

I hope Fred[1] will have a good long rest. I know how long it takes to get one's strength back. I am trying to arrange to go to Cologne for a few days, but there keep being delays. I shall be back in England at the end of April.

Yours
George

99. Letter to Anthony Powell

Hotel Scribe
Rue Scribe
Paris 9e
13 April 1945

Dear Tony,[2]
I tried to get in touch with you when I was in London last week, but failed. I don't know whether you will have heard from some other source about what has happened. Eileen[3] is dead. She died very suddenly and unexpectedly on March 29th during an operation which was not supposed to be very serious. I was over here and had no expectation of anything going wrong, which indeed nobody seems to have had. I didn't see the final findings of the inquest and indeed don't want to, because it doesn't bring her back, but I think the anaesthetic was responsible. It was a most horrible thing to happen because she had had five really miserable years of bad health and overwork, and things were just beginning to get better. The only good thing is that I don't think she can have suffered or had any

---

[1] F. J. Warburg of Secker & Warburg.

[2] Anthony Powell (1905–), the novelist, who had begun corresponding with Orwell in 1936. They had met in 1941 and remained friends until Orwell's death.

[3] Eileen Blair, Orwell's wife.

apprehensions. She was actually looking forward to the operation to cure her trouble, and I found among her papers a letter she must have written only about an hour before she died and which she expected to finish when she came round. But it was terribly sad that she should die when she had become so devoted to Richard and was making such a good job of his upbringing. Richard I am glad to say is very well and for the moment is provided for. He is staying with his sort of aunt[1] who lives in the same square as me and has a young baby of her own, and I hope within a fairly short time to find a good nurse whom I can take on as a permanency. As soon as I can get a nurse and a house I shall remove him to the country, as I don't want him to learn to walk in London. I just got him settled in and then came straight back here, as I felt so upset at home I thought I would rather be on the move for a bit. I was in Germany for a few days recently and am now going back there for a week or two.

What I partly wrote for was to ask if you know Malcolm Muggeridge's address. He has left Paris and I have no idea how to get in touch with him. I vaguely heard there had been some kind of row in which l'affaire Wodehouse was mixed up, but have no idea what it is. Letters generally take about a fortnight, but the above address will find me. Please remember me to Violet.[2]

Yours
George

100. Letter to Lydia Jackson

Hotel Scribe
Rue Scribe
Paris 9e
11 May 1945

Dear Lydia,[3]
I just had letters from you and Pat about simultaneously. I don't want to re-let the cottage, because for the time being I want to keep

---

[1] Doreen Kopp, sister of Dr Gwen O'Shaughnessy, the widow of Eileen Blair's brother.

[2] The Lady Violet Powell, wife of Anthony Powell.

[3] Lydia Jackson, who writes under the pen name of "Elisaveta Fen", was born in 1899 in Russia and came to England in 1925. She met Eileen Blair in 1934 at University College London and they remained friends. Pat was a friend of Lydia Jackson's who shared Orwell's cottage at Wallington with her.

it on as a place to go down to for an occasional week-end. I can however make either of the following arrangements with you. Either I will lend you the cottage for a month in the summer at any time you choose to name, or else you can continue to use the cottage at all times, but on the understanding that I can come and have it for a week or so any time I want to. In either case I don't want you to pay me anything. I should be back in London about May 25th and we can make any final arrangements then. You could have it for June or July or really whenever you like provided I know beforehand. At present it seems impossible to get a house in the country and for that reason I want to keep on the cottage so that Richard can get a few days of country air now and then. Eileen and I had hoped that it would not be necessary for him to learn to walk in London, but it seems unavoidable, so I am going to keep on the flat.

Gwen[1] says you borrowed a refrigerator of hers. Do you think we could have it back, because it is so hard to keep milk from going sour in the summer months and that makes it so difficult with the children.

I came straight back here after Eileen's death and have felt somewhat better for being at work most of the time. The destruction in Germany is terrifying, far worse than people in England grasp, but my trips there have been quite interesting. I am making one more trip, to Austria I hope, and then coming back about the end of next week. I get bulletins about Richard from Doreen and it seems he is doing very well and has tripled his birth weight at 11 months. The next thing is to find a nurse for him which is next door to impossible at present. I don't know how long this letter will take getting to you— sometimes they take only 4 days, sometimes about 3 weeks—but if it gets to you before I get back, and you want to go down to the cottage, you can do so. Looking forward to seeing you both.

Yours
George

101. Notes on Nationalism

Somewhere or other Byron makes use of the French word *longueur*, and remarks in passing that though in England we happen not to

---

[1] Orwell's sister-in-law, Dr Gwen O'Shaughnessy.

have the *word*, we have the *thing* in considerable profusion. In the same way, there is a habit of mind which is now so widespread that it affects our thinking on nearly every subject, but which has not yet been given a name. As the nearest existing equivalent I have chosen the word "nationalism", but it will be seen in a moment that I am not using it in quite the ordinary sense, if only because the emotion I am speaking about does not always attach itself to what is called a nation—that is, a single race or a geographical area. It can attach itself to a church or a class, or it may work in a merely negative sense, *against* something or other and without the need for any positive object of loyalty.

By "nationalism" I mean first of all the habit of assuming that human beings can be classified like insects and that whole blocks of millions or tens of millions of people can be confidently labelled "good" or "bad".[1] But secondly—and this is much more important —I mean the habit of identifying oneself with a single nation or other unit, placing it beyond good and evil and recognising no other duty than that of advancing its interests. Nationalism is not to be confused with patriotism. Both words are normally used in so vague a way that any definition is liable to be challenged, but one must draw a distinction between them, since two different and even opposing ideas are involved. By "patriotism" I mean devotion to a particular place and a particular way of life, which one believes to be the best in the world but has no wish to force upon other people. Patriotism is of its nature defensive, both militarily and culturally. Nationalism, on the other hand, is inseparable from the desire for power. The abiding purpose of every nationalist is to secure more power and more prestige, *not* for himself but for the nation or other unit in which he has chosen to sink his own individuality.

So long as it is applied merely to the more notorious and identifiable nationalist movements in Germany, Japan and other countries, all this is obvious enough. Confronted with a phenomenon like

[1] Nations, and even vaguer entities such as the Catholic Church or the proletariat, are commonly thought of as individuals and often referred to as "she". Patently absurd remarks such as "Germany is naturally treacherous" are to be found in any newspaper one opens, and reckless generalisations about national character ("The Spaniard is a natural aristocrat" or "Every Englishman is a hypocrite") are uttered by almost everyone. Intermittently these generalisations are seen to be unfounded, but the habit of making them persists, and people of professedly international outlook, e.g. Tolstoy or Bernard Shaw, are often guilty of them. [Author's footnote.]

Nazism, which we can observe from the outside, nearly all of us would say much the same things about it. But here I must repeat what I said above, that I am only using the word "nationalism" for lack of a better. Nationalism, in the extended sense in which I am using the word, includes such movements and tendencies as Communism, political Catholicism, Zionism, Antisemitism, Trotskyism and Pacifism. It does not necessarily mean loyalty to a government or a country, still less to *one's own* country, and it is not even strictly necessary that the units in which it deals should actually exist. To name a few obvious examples, Jewry, Islam, Christendom, the Proletariat and the White Race are all of them the objects of passionate nationalistic feeling: but their existence can be seriously questioned, and there is no definition of any one of them that would be universally accepted.

It is also worth emphasising once again that nationalist feeling can be purely negative. There are, for example, Trotskyists who have become simply the enemies of the USSR without developing a corresponding loyalty to any other unit. When one grasps the implications of this, the nature of what I mean by nationalism becomes a good deal clearer. A nationalist is one who thinks solely, or mainly, in terms of competitive prestige. He may be a positive or a negative nationalist—that is, he may use his mental energy either in boosting or in denigrating—but at any rate his thoughts always turn on victories, defeats, triumphs and humiliations. He sees history, especially contemporary history, as the endless rise and decline of great power units, and every event that happens seems to him a demonstration that his own side is on the up-grade and some hated rival on the downgrade. But finally, it is important not to confuse nationalism with mere worship of success. The nationalist does not go on the principle of simply ganging up with the strongest side. On the contrary, having picked his side, he persuades himself that it *is* the strongest, and is able to stick to his belief even when the facts are overwhelmingly against him. Nationalism is power hunger tempered by self-deception. Every nationalist is capable of the most flagrant dishonesty, but he is also—since he is conscious of serving something bigger than himself—unshakeably certain of being in the right.

Now that I have given this lengthy definition, I think it will be admitted that the habit of mind I am talking about is widespread among the English intelligentsia, and more widespread there than among the mass of the people. For those who feel deeply about contemporary politics, certain topics have become so infected by considerations of prestige that a genuinely rational approach to them is almost impossible. Out of the hundreds of examples that one might choose, take this question: Which of the three great allies, the USSR, Britain and the USA, has contributed most to the defeat of Germany? In theory it should be possible to give a reasoned and perhaps even a conclusive answer to this question. In practice, however, the necessary calculations cannot be made, because anyone likely to bother his head about such a question would inevitably see it in terms of competitive prestige. He would therefore *start* by deciding in favour of Russia, Britain or America as the case might be, and only *after* this would begin searching for arguments that seemed to support his case. And there are whole strings of kindred questions to which you can only get an honest answer from someone who is indifferent to the whole subject involved, and whose opinion on it is probably worthless in any case. Hence, partly, the remarkable failure in our time of political and military prediction. It is curious to reflect that out of all the "experts" of all the schools, there was not a single one who was able to foresee so likely an event as the Russo-German Pact of 1939.[1] And when the news of the Pact broke, the most wildly divergent explanations of it were given, and predictions were made which were falsified almost immediately, being based in nearly every case not on a study of probabilities but on a desire to make the USSR seem good or bad, strong or weak. Political or military commentators, like astrologers, can survive almost any mistake, because their more devoted followers do not look to them for an appraisal of the facts but for the stimulation of nationalistic loyalties.[2] And

[1] A few writers of conservative tendency, such as Peter Drucker, foretold an agreement between Germany and Russia, but they expected an actual alliance or amalgamation which would be permanent. No Marxist or other left-wing writer, of whatever colour, came anywhere near foretelling the Pact. [Author's footnote.]

[2] The military commentators of the popular press can mostly be classified as pro-Russian or anti-Russian, pro-Blimp or anti-Blimp. Such errors as believing the Maginot Line impregnable, or predicting that Russia would conquer Germany in three months, have failed to shake their reputation, because they were always saying what their own particular audience wanted to hear. The two military critics most favoured by the intelligentsia are Captain Liddell Hart and Major-General Fuller, the first of whom teaches that the defence is stronger than the attack, and the second that the attack is stronger than the defence. This contradiction has not prevented both of them from being accepted as authorities by the same public. The secret reason for their vogue in left-wing circles is that both of them are at odds with the War Office. [Author's footnote.]

aesthetic judgements, especially literary judgements, are often corrupted in the same way as political ones. It would be difficult for an Indian Nationalist to enjoy reading Kipling or for a Conservative to see merit in Mayakovsky, and there is always a temptation to claim that any book whose tendency one disagrees with must be a bad book from a *literary* point of view. People of strongly nationalistic outlook often perform this sleight of hand without being conscious of dishonesty.

In England, if one simply considers the number of people involved, it is probable that the dominant form of nationalism is old-fashioned British jingoism. It is certain that this is still widespread, and much more so than most observers would have believed a dozen years ago. However, in this essay I am concerned chiefly with the reactions of the intelligentsia, among whom jingoism and even patriotism of the old kind are almost dead, though they now seem to be reviving among a minority. Among the intelligentsia, it hardly needs saying that the dominant form of nationalism is Communism—using this word in a very loose sense, to include not merely Communist Party members but "fellow-travellers" and russophiles generally. A Communist, for my purpose here, is one who looks upon the USSR as his Fatherland and feels it his duty to justify Russian policy and advance Russian interests at all costs. Obviously such people abound in England today, and their direct and indirect influence is very great. But many other forms of nationalism also flourish, and it is by noticing the points of resemblance between different and even seemingly opposed currents of thought that one can best get the matter into perspective.

Ten or twenty years ago, the form of nationalism most closely corresponding to Communism today was political Catholicism. Its most outstanding exponent—though he was perhaps an extreme case rather than a typical one—was G. K. Chesterton. Chesterton was a writer of considerable talent who chose to suppress both his sensibilities and his intellectual honesty in the cause of Roman Catholic propaganda. During the last twenty years or so of his life, his entire output was in reality an endless repetition of the same thing, under its laboured cleverness as simple and boring as "Great is Diana of the Ephesians". Every book that he wrote, every paragraph, every sentence, every incident in every story, every scrap of dialogue, had to demonstrate beyond possibility of mistake the superiority of the Catholic over the Protestant or the pagan. But

Chesterton was not content to think of this superiority as merely intellectual or spiritual: it had to be translated into terms of national prestige and military power, which entailed an ignorant idealisation of the Latin countries, especially France. Chesterton had not lived long in France, and his picture of it—as a land of Catholic peasants incessantly singing the *Marseillaise* over glasses of red wine—had about as much relation to reality as *Chu Chin Chow* has to everyday life in Baghdad. And with this went not only an enormous over-estimation of French military power (both before and after 1914–18 he maintained that France, by itself, was stronger than Germany), but a silly and vulgar glorification of the actual process of war. Chesterton's battle poems, such as "Lepanto" or "The Ballad of Saint Barbara", make "The Charge of the Light Brigade" read like a pacifist tract: they are perhaps the most tawdry bits of bombast to be found in our language. The interesting thing is that had the romantic rubbish which he habitually wrote about France and the French army been written by somebody else about Britain and the British army, he would have been the first to jeer. In home politics he was a Little Englander, a true hater of jingoism and imperialism, and according to his lights a true friend of democracy. Yet when he looked outwards into the international field, he could forsake his principles without even noticing that he was doing so. Thus, his almost mystical belief in the virtues of democracy did not prevent him from admiring Mussolini. Mussolini had destroyed the representative government and the freedom of the press for which Chesterton had struggled so hard at home, but Mussolini was an Italian and had made Italy strong, and that settled the matter. Nor did Chesterton ever find a word to say against imperialism and the conquest of coloured races when they were practised by Italians or Frenchmen. His hold on reality, his literary taste, and even to some extent his moral sense, were dislocated as soon as his nationalistic loyalties were involved.

Obviously there are considerable resemblances between political Catholicism, as exemplified by Chesterton, and Communism. So there are between either of these and, for instance, Scottish nationalism, Zionism, Antisemitism or Trotskyism. It would be an oversimplification to say that all forms of nationalism are the same, even in their mental atmosphere, but there are certain rules that hold good in all cases. The following are the principal characteristics of nationalist thought:

OBSESSION. As nearly as possible, no nationalist ever thinks, talks or writes about anything except the superiority of his own power unit. It is difficult if not impossible for any nationalist to conceal his allegiance. The smallest slur upon his own unit, or any implied praise of a rival organisation, fills him with uneasiness which he can only relieve by making some sharp retort. If the chosen unit is an actual country, such as Ireland or India, he will generally claim superiority for it not only in military power and political virtue, but in art, literature, sport, the structure of the language, the physical beauty of the inhabitants, and perhaps even in climate, scenery and cooking. He will show great sensitiveness about such things as the correct display of flags, relative size of headlines and the order in which different countries are named.[1] Nomenclature plays a very important part in nationalist thought. Countries which have won their independence or gone through a nationalist revolution usually change their names, and any country or other unit round which strong feelings revolve is likely to have several names, each of them carrying a different implication. The two sides in the Spanish civil war had between them nine or ten names expressing different degrees of love and hatred. Some of these names (e.g. "Patriots" for Franco-supporters, or "Loyalists" for Government-supporters) were frankly question-begging, and there was no single one of them which the two rival factions could have agreed to use. All nationalists consider it a duty to spread their own language to the detriment of rival languages, and among English-speakers this struggle reappears in subtler form as a struggle between dialects. Anglophobe Americans will refuse to use a slang phrase if they know it to be of British origin, and the conflict between Latinisers and Germanisers often has nationalist motives behind it. Scottish nationalists insist on the superiority of Lowland Scots, and Socialists whose nationalism takes the form of class hatred tirade against the BBC accent and even the broad A. One could multiply instances. Nationalist thought often gives the impression of being tinged by belief in sympathetic magic—a belief which probably comes out in the widespread custom of burning political enemies in effigy, or using pictures of them as targets in shooting galleries.

[1] Certain Americans have expressed dissatisfaction because "Anglo-American" is the normal form of combination of these two words. It has been proposed to substitute "America-British". [Author's footnote.]

INSTABILITY. The intensity with which they are held does not prevent nationalist loyalties from being transferable. To begin with, as I have pointed out already, they can be and often are fastened upon some foreign country. One quite commonly finds that great national leaders, or the founders of nationalist movements, do not even belong to the country they have glorified. Sometimes they are outright foreigners, or more often they come from peripheral areas where nationality is doubtful. Examples are Stalin, Hitler, Napoleon, de Valera, Disraeli, Poincaré, Beaverbrook. The Pan-German movement was in part the creation of an Englishman, Houston Chamberlain. For the past fifty or a hundred years, transferred nationalism has been a common phenomenon among literary intellectuals. With Lafcadio Hearne the transference was to Japan, with Carlyle and many others of his time to Germany, and in our own age it is usually to Russia. But the peculiarly interesting fact is that *re*-transference is also possible. A country or other unit which has been worshipped for years may suddenly become detestable, and some other object of affection may take its place with almost no interval. In the first version of H. G. Wells's *Outline of History*, and others of his writings about that time, one finds the United States praised almost as extravagantly as Russia is praised by Communists today: yet within a few years this uncritical admiration had turned into hostility. The bigoted Communist who changes in a space of weeks, or even of days, into an equally bigoted Trotskyist is a common spectacle. In continental Europe Fascist movements were largely recruited from among Communists, and the opposite process may well happen within the next few years. What remains constant in the nationalist is his own state of mind: the object of his feelings is changeable, and may be imaginary.

But for an intellectual, transference has an important function which I have already mentioned shortly in connection with Chesterton. It makes it possible for him to be much *more* nationalistic— more vulgar, more silly, more malignant, more dishonest—than he could ever be on behalf of his native country, or any unit of which he had real knowledge. When one sees the slavish or boastful rubbish that is written about Stalin, the Red army, etc by fairly intelligent and sensitive people, one realises that this is only possible because some kind of dislocation has taken place. In societies such as ours, it is unusual for anyone describable as an intellectual to feel a very deep attachment to his own country. Public opinion—that is, the section of public opinion of which he as an intellectual is aware—will not allow him to do so. Most of the people surrounding him are sceptical and disaffected, and he may adopt the same attitude from imitativeness or sheer cowardice: in that case he will have abandoned the form of nationalism that lies nearest to hand without getting any closer to a genuinely internationalist outlook. He still feels the need for a Fatherland, and it is natural to look for one somewhere abroad. Having found it, he can wallow unrestrainedly in exactly those emotions from which he believes that he has emancipated himself. God, the King, the Empire, the Union Jack—all the overthrown idols can reappear under different names, and because they are not recognised for what they are they can be worshipped with a good conscience. Transferred nationalism, like the use of scapegoats, is a way of attaining salvation without altering one's conduct.

INDIFFERENCE TO REALITY. All nationalists have the power of not seeing resemblances between similar sets of facts. A British Tory will defend self-determination in Europe and oppose it in India with no feeling of inconsistency. Actions are held to be good or bad, not on their own merits but according to who does them, and there is almost no kind of outrage—torture, the use of hostages, forced labour, mass deportations, imprisonment without trial, forgery, assassination, the bombing of civilians—which does not change its moral colour when it is committed by "our" side. The Liberal *News Chronicle* published, as an example of shocking barbarity, photographs of Russians hanged by the Germans, and then a year or two later published with warm approval almost exactly similar photographs of Germans hanged by the Russians.[1] It is the same with historical events. History is thought of largely in nationalist terms, and such things as the Inquisition, the tortures of the Star Chamber, the exploits of the English buccaneers (Sir Francis Drake, for instance, who was given to sinking Spanish prisoners alive), the Reign of Terror, the heroes of the Mutiny blowing hundreds of Indians from the guns, or Cromwell's soldiers slashing Irishwomen's faces with razors, become morally neutral or even meritorious when it is

[1] The *News Chronicle* advised its readers to visit the news film at which the entire execution could be witnessed, with close-ups. The *Star* published with seeming approval photographs of nearly naked female collaborationists being baited by the Paris mob. These photographs had a marked resemblance to the Nazi photographs of Jews being baited by the Berlin mob. [Author's footnote.]

felt that they were done in the "right" cause. If one looks back over the past quarter of a century, one finds that there was hardly a single year when atrocity stories were not being reported from some part of the world: and yet in not one single case were these atrocities—in Spain, Russia, China, Hungary, Mexico, Amritsar, Smyrna—believed in and disapproved of by the English intelligentsia as a whole. Whether such deeds were reprehensible, or even whether they happened, was always decided according to political predilection.

The nationalist not only does not disapprove of atrocities committed by his own side, but he has a remarkable capacity for not even hearing about them. For quite six years the English admirers of Hitler contrived not to learn of the existence of Dachau and Buchenwald. And those who are loudest in denouncing the German concentration camps are often quite unaware, or only very dimly aware, that there are also concentration camps in Russia. Huge events like the Ukraine famine of 1933, involving the deaths of millions of people, have actually escaped the attention of the majority of English russophiles. Many English people have heard almost nothing about the extermination of German and Polish Jews during the present war. Their own antisemitism has caused this vast crime to bounce off their consciousness. In nationalist thought there are facts which are both true and untrue, known and unknown. A known fact may be so unbearable that it is habitually pushed aside and not allowed to enter into logical processes, or on the other hand it may enter into every calculation and yet never be admitted as a fact, even in one's own mind.

Every nationalist is haunted by the belief that the past can be altered. He spends part of his time in a fantasy world in which things happen as they should—in which, for example, the Spanish Armada was a success or the Russian Revolution was crushed in 1918—and he will transfer fragments of this world to the history books whenever possible. Much of the propagandist writing of our time amounts to plain forgery. Material facts are suppressed, dates altered, quotations removed from their context and doctored so as to change their meaning. Events which, it is felt, ought not to have happened are left unmentioned and ultimately denied.[1] In 1927 Chiang Kai-

[1] An example is the Russo-German Pact, which is being effaced as quickly as possible from public memory. A Russian correspondent informs me that mention of the Pact is already being omitted from Russian year-books which table recent political events. [Author's footnote.]

Shek boiled hundreds of Communists alive, and yet within ten years he had become one of the heroes of the Left. The re-alignment of world politics had brought him into the anti-Fascist camp, and so it was felt that the boiling of the Communists "didn't count", or perhaps had not happened. The primary aim of propaganda is, of course, to influence contemporary opinion, but those who rewrite history do probably believe with part of their minds that they are actually thrusting facts into the past. When one considers the elaborate forgeries that have been committed in order to show that Trotsky did not play a valuable part in the Russian civil war, it is difficult to feel that the people responsible are merely lying. More probably they feel that their own version *was* what happened in the sight of God, and that one is justified in rearranging the records accordingly.

Indifference to objective truth is encouraged by the sealing-off of one part of the world from another, which makes it harder and harder to discover what is actually happening. There can often be a genuine doubt about the most enormous events. For example, it is impossible to calculate within millions, perhaps even tens of millions, the number of deaths caused by the present war. The calamities that are constantly being reported—battles, massacres, famines, revolutions—tend to inspire in the average person a feeling of unreality. One has no way of verifying the facts, one is not even fully certain that they have happened, and one is always presented with totally different interpretations from different sources. What were the rights and wrongs of the Warsaw rising of August 1944? Is it true about the German gas ovens in Poland? Who was really to blame for the Bengal famine? Probably the truth is discoverable, but the facts will be so dishonestly set forth in almost any newspaper that the ordinary reader can be forgiven either for swallowing lies or for failing to form an opinion. The general uncertainty as to what is really happening makes it easier to cling to lunatic beliefs. Since nothing is ever quite proved or disproved, the most unmistakable fact can be impudently denied. Moreover, although endlessly brooding on power, victory, defeat, revenge, the nationalist is often somewhat uninterested in what happens in the real world. What he wants is to *feel* that his own unit is getting the better of some other unit, and he can more easily do this by scoring off an adversary than by examining the facts to see whether they support him. All nationalist controversy is at the debating-society level. It is always entirely inconclusive, since each contestant invariably believes himself to have won the victory. Some nationalists are not far from schizophrenia, living quite happily amid dreams of power and conquest which have no connection with the physical world.

I have examined as best I can the mental habits which are common to all forms of nationalism. The next thing is to classify those forms, but obviously this cannot be done comprehensively. Nationalism is an enormous subject. The world is tormented by innumerable delusions and hatreds which cut across one another in an extremely complex way, and some of the most sinister of them have not yet even impinged on the European consciousness. In this essay I am concerned with nationalism as it occurs among the English intelligentsia. In them, much more often than in ordinary English people, it is unmixed with patriotism and can therefoie be studied pure. Below are listed the varieties of nationalism now flourishing among English intellectuals, with such comments as seem to be needed. It is convenient to use three headings, Positive, Transferred and Negative, though some varieties will fit into more than one category:

POSITIVE NATIONALISM

1. NEO-TORYISM. Exemplified by such people as Lord Elton, A. P. Herbert, G. M. Young, Professor Pickthorn, by the literature of the Tory Reform Committee, and by such magazines as the *New English Review* and the *Nineteenth Century and After*. The real motive force of neo-Toryism, giving it its nationalistic character and differentiating it from ordinary Conservatism, is the desire not to recognise that British power and influence have declined. Even those who are realistic enough to see that Britain's military position is not what it was, tend to claim that "English ideas" (usually left undefined) must dominate the world. All neo-Tories are anti-Russian, but sometimes the main emphasis is anti-American. The significant thing is that this school of thought seems to be gaining ground among youngish intellectuals, sometimes ex-Communists, who have passed through the usual process of disillusionment and become disillusioned with that. The anglophobe who suddenly becomes violently pro-British is a fairly common figure. Writers who illustrate this tendency are F. A. Voigt, Malcolm Muggeridge, Evelyn Waugh, Hugh Kingsmill, and a psychologically similar development can be observed in T. S. Eliot, Wyndham Lewis and various of their followers.

2. CELTIC NATIONALISM. Welsh, Irish and Scottish nationalism have points of difference but are alike in their anti-English orientation. Members of all three movements have opposed the war while continuing to describe themselves as pro-Russian, and the lunatic fringe has even contrived to be simultaneously pro-Russian and pro-Nazi. But Celtic nationalism is not the same thing as anglophobia. Its motive force is a belief in the past and future greatness of the Celtic peoples, and it has a strong tinge of racialism. The Celt is supposed to be spiritually superior to the Saxon—simpler, more creative, less vulgar, less snobbish, etc—but the usual power hunger is there under the surface. One symptom of it is the delusion that Eire, Scotland or even Wales could preserve its independence unaided and owes nothing to British protection. Among writers, good examples of this school of thought are Hugh MacDiarmid and Sean O'Casey. No modern Irish writer, even of the stature of Yeats or Joyce, is completely free from traces of nationalism.

3. ZIONISM. This has the usual characteristics of a nationalist movement, but the American variant of it seems to be more violent and malignant than the British. I classify it under Direct and not Transferred nationalism because it flourishes almost exclusively among the Jews themselves. In England, for several rather incongruous reasons, the intelligentsia are mostly pro-Jew on the Palestine issue, but they do not feel strongly about it. All English people of goodwill are also pro-Jew in the sense of disapproving of Nazi persecution. But any actual nationalistic loyalty, or belief in the innate superiority of Jews, is hardly to be found among Gentiles.

TRANSFERRED NATIONALISM

1. COMMUNISM.

2. POLITICAL CATHOLICISM.

3. COLOUR FEELING. The old-style contemptuous attitude towards "natives" has been much weakened in England, and various pseudo-scientific theories emphasising the superiority of the white race have been abandoned.[1] Among the intelligentsia, colour feeling only

[1] A good example is the sunstroke superstition. Until recently it was believed that the white races were much more liable to sunstroke than the coloured, and that a white man could not safely walk about in tropical sunshine without a

occurs in the transposed form, that is, as a belief in the innate superiority of the coloured races. This is now increasingly common among English intellectuals, probably resulting more often from masochism and sexual frustration than from contact with the Oriental and Negro nationalist movements. Even among those who do not feel strongly on the colour question, snobbery and imitation have a powerful influence. Almost any English intellectual would be scandalised by the claim that the white races are superior to the coloured, whereas the opposite claim would seem to him unexceptionable even if he disagreed with it. Nationalistic attachment to the coloured races is usually mixed up with the belief that their sex lives are superior, and there is a large underground mythology about the sexual prowess of Negroes.

4. CLASS FEELING. Among upper-class and middle-class intellectuals, only in the transposed form—i.e. as a belief in the superiority of the proletariat. Here again, inside the intelligentsia, the pressure of public opinion is overwhelming. Nationalistic loyalty towards the proletariat, and most vicious theoretical hatred of the bourgeoisie, can and often do co-exist with ordinary snobbishness in everyday life.

5. PACIFISM. The majority of pacifists either belong to obscure religious sects or are simply humanitarians who object to taking life and prefer not to follow their thoughts beyond that point. But there is a minority of intellectual pacifists whose real though unadmitted motive appears to be hatred of western democracy and admiration for totalitarianism. Pacifist propaganda usually boils down to saying that one side is as bad as the other, but if one looks closely at the writings of the younger intellectual pacifists, one finds that they do not by any means express impartial disapproval but are directed almost entirely against Britain and the United States. Moreover they do not as a rule condemn violence as such, but only violence used in defence of the western countries. The Russians, unlike the British, are not blamed for defending themselves by warlike means, and

---

pith helmet. There was no evidence whatever for this theory, but it served the purpose of accentuating the difference between "natives" and Europeans. During the present war the theory has been quietly dropped and whole armies manoeuvre in the tropics without pith helmets. So long as the sunstroke superstition survived, English doctors in India appear to have believed in it as firmly as laymen. [Author's footnote.]

indeed all pacifist propaganda of this type avoids mention of Russia or China. It is not claimed, again, that the Indians should abjure violence in their struggle against the British. Pacifist literature abounds with equivocal remarks which, if they mean anything, appear to mean that statesmen of the type of Hitler are preferable to those of the type of Churchill, and that violence is perhaps excusable if it is violent enough. After the fall of France, the French pacifists, faced by a real choice which their English colleagues have not had to make, mostly went over to the Nazis, and in England there appears to have been some small overlap of membership between the Peace Pledge Union and the Blackshirts. Pacifist writers have written in praise of Carlyle, one of the intellectual fathers of Fascism. All in all it is difficult not to feel that pacifism, as it appears among a section of the intelligentsia, is secretly inspired by an admiration for power and successful cruelty. The mistake was made of pinning this emotion to Hitler, but it could easily be retransferred.

NEGATIVE NATIONALISM

1. ANGLOPHOBIA. Within the intelligentsia, a derisive and mildly hostile attitude towards Britain is more or less compulsory, but it is an unfaked emotion in many cases. During the war it was manifested in the defeatism of the intelligentsia, which persisted long after it had become clear that the Axis powers could not win. Many people were undisguisedly pleased when Singapore fell or when the British were driven out of Greece, and there was a remarkable unwillingness to believe in good news, e.g. el Alamein, or the number of German planes shot down in the Battle of Britain. English left-wing intellectuals did not, of course, actually want the Germans or Japanese to win the war, but many of them could not help getting a certain kick out of seeing their own country humiliated, and wanted to feel that the final victory would be due to Russia, or perhaps America, and not to Britain. In foreign politics many intellectuals follow the principle that any faction backed by Britain must be in the wrong. As a result, "enlightened" opinion is quite largely a mirror-image of Conservative policy. Anglophobia is always liable to reversal, hence that fairly common spectacle, the pacifist of one war who is a bellicist in the next.

2. ANTISEMITISM. There is little evidence about this at present, because the Nazi persecutions have made it necessary for any thinking

person to side with the Jews against their oppressors. Anyone educated enough to have heard the word "antisemitism" claims as a matter of course to be free of it, and anti-Jewish remarks are carefully eliminated from all classes of literature. Actually antisemitism appears to be widespread, even among intellectuals, and the general conspiracy of silence probably helps to exacerbate it. People of Left opinions are not immune to it, and their attitude is sometimes affected by the fact that Trotskyists and Anarchists tend to be Jews. But antisemitism comes more naturally to people of Conservative tendency, who suspect the Jews of weakening national morale and diluting the national culture. Neo-Tories and political Catholics are always liable to succumb to antisemitism, at least intermittently.

3. TROTSKYISM. This word is used so loosely as to include Anarchists, democratic Socialists and even Liberals. I use it here to mean a doctrinaire Marxist whose main motive is hostility to the Stalin régime. Trotskyism can be better studied in obscure pamphlets or in papers like the *Socialist Appeal* than in the works of Trotsky himself, who was by no means a man of one idea. Although in some places, for instance in the United States, Trotskyism is able to attract a fairly large number of adherents and develop into an organised movement with a petty fuehrer of its own, its inspiration is essentially negative. The Trotskyist is *against* Stalin just as the Communist is *for* him, and, like the majority of Communists, he wants not so much to alter the external world as to feel that the battle for prestige is going in his own favour. In each case there is the same obsessive fixation on a single subject, the same inability to form a genuinely rational opinion based on probabilities. The fact that Trotskyists are everywhere a persecuted minority, and that the accusation usually made against them, i.e. of collaborating with the Fascists, is obviously false, creates an impression that Trotskyism is intellectually and morally superior to Communism; but it is doubtful whether there is much difference. The most typical Trotskyists, in any case, are ex-Communists, and no one arrives at Trotskyism except via one of the left-wing movements. No Communist, unless tethered to his party by years of habit, is secure against a sudden lapse into Trotskyism. The opposite process does not seem to happen equally often, though there is no clear reason why it should not.

In the classification I have attempted above, it will seem that I have often exaggerated, oversimplified, made unwarranted assumptions and have left out of account the existence of ordinarily decent motives. This was inevitable, because in this essay I am trying to isolate and identify tendencies which exist in all our minds and pervert our thinking, without necessarily occurring in a pure state or operating continuously. It is important at this point to correct the over-simplified picture which I have been obliged to make. To begin with, one has no right to assume that *everyone*, or even every intellectual, is infected by nationalism. Secondly, nationalism can be intermittent and limited. An intelligent man may half-succumb to a belief which attracts him but which he knows to be absurd, and he may keep it out of his mind for long periods, only reverting to it in moments of anger or sentimentality, or when he is certain that no important issue is involved. Thirdly, a nationalistic creed may be adopted in good faith from non-nationalist motives. Fourthly, several kinds of nationalism, even kinds that cancel out, can co-exist in the same person.

All the way through I have said "the nationalist does this" or "the nationalist does that", using for purposes of illustration the extreme, barely sane type of nationalist who has no neutral areas in his mind and no interest in anything except the struggle for power. Actually such people are fairly common, but they are not worth powder and shot. In real life Lord Elton, D. N. Pritt, Lady Houston, Ezra Pound, Lord Vansittart, Father Coughlin and all the rest of their dreary tribe have to be fought against, but their intellectual deficiencies hardly need pointing out. Monomania is not interesting, and the fact that no nationalist of the more bigoted kind can write a book which still seems worth reading after a lapse of years has a certain deodorising effect. But when one has admitted that nationalism has not triumphed everywhere, that there are still people whose judgements are not at the mercy of their desires, the fact does remain that the pressing problems—India, Poland, Palestine, the Spanish civil war, the Moscow trials, the American Negroes, the Russo-German Pact or what have you—cannot be, or at least never are, discussed upon a reasonable level. The Eltons and Pritts and Coughlins, each of them simply an enormous mouth bellowing the same lie over and over again, are obviously extreme cases, but we deceive ourselves if we do not realise that we can all resemble them in unguarded moments. Let a certain note be struck, let this or that corn be trodden on—and it may be a corn whose very existence has been unsuspected hitherto—and the most fair-minded and sweet-tempered person may suddenly be transformed into a vicious partisan, anxious only to "score" over his adversary and indifferent as to how many lies he tells or how many logical errors he commits in doing so. When Lloyd George, who was an opponent of the Boer war, announced in the House of Commons that the British communiqués, if one added them together, claimed the killing of more Boers than the whole Boer nation contained, it is recorded that Arthur Balfour rose to his feet and shouted "Cad!" Very few people are proof against lapses of this type. The Negro snubbed by a white woman, the Englishman who hears England ignorantly criticised by an American, the Catholic apologist reminded of the Spanish Armada, will all react in much the same way. One prod to the nerve of nationalism, and the intellectual decencies can vanish, the past can be altered, and the plainest facts can be denied.

If one harbours anywhere in one's mind a nationalistic loyalty or hatred, certain facts, although in a sense known to be true, are inadmissible. Here are just a few examples. I list below five types of nationalist, and against each I append a fact which it is impossible for that type of nationalist to accept, even in his secret thoughts:

BRITISH TORY. Britain will come out of this war with reduced power and prestige.

COMMUNIST. If she had not been aided by Britain and America, Russia would have been defeated by Germany.

IRISH NATIONALIST. Eire can only remain independent because of British protection.

TROTSKYIST. The Stalin régime is accepted by the Russian masses.

PACIFIST. Those who "abjure" violence can only do so because others are committing violence on their behalf.

All of these facts are grossly obvious if one's emotions do not happen to be involved: but to the kind of person named in each case they are also *intolerable*, and so they have to be denied, and false theories constructed upon their denial. I come back to the astonishing failure of military prediction in the present war. It is, I think, true to say that the intelligentsia have been more wrong about the progress of the war than the common people, and that they were more swayed by partisan feelings. The average intellectual of the Left believed, for instance, that the war was lost in 1940, that the Germans were bound to overrun Egypt in 1942, that the Japanese would never be driven out of the lands they had conquered, and that the Anglo-American bombing offensive was making no impression on Germany. He could believe these things because his hatred of the British ruling class forbade him to admit that British plans could succeed. There is no limit to the follies that can be swallowed if one is under the influence of feelings of this kind. I have heard it confidently stated, for instance, that the American troops had been brought to Europe not to fight the Germans but to crush an English revolution. One has to belong to the intelligentsia to believe things like that: no ordinary man could be such a fool. When Hitler invaded Russia, the officials of the MOI issued "as background" a warning that Russia might be expected to collapse in six weeks. On the other hand the Communists regarded every phase of the war as a Russian victory, even when the Russians were driven back almost to the Caspian Sea and had lost several million prisoners. There is no need to multiply instances. The point is that as soon as fear, hatred, jealousy and power worship are involved, the sense of reality becomes unhinged. And, as I have pointed out already, the sense of right and wrong becomes unhinged also. There is no crime, absolutely none, that cannot be condoned when "our" side commits it. Even if one does not deny that the crime has happened, even if one knows that it is exactly the same crime as one has condemned in some other case, even if one admits in an intellectual sense that it is unjustified—still one cannot *feel* that it is wrong. Loyalty is involved, and so pity ceases to function.

The reason for the rise and spread of nationalism is far too big a question to be raised here. It is enough to say that, in the forms in which it appears among English intellectuals, it is a distorted reflection of the frightful battles actually happening in the external world, and that its worst follies have been made possible by the break-down of patriotism and religious belief. If one follows up this train of thought, one is in danger of being led into a species of Conservatism, or into political quietism. It can be plausibly argued, for instance—it is even probably true—that patriotism is an inoculation against nationalism, that monarchy is a guard against dictatorship, and that organised religion is a guard against superstition. Or again it can be argued that *no* unbiassed outlook is possible, that *all* creeds and causes involve the same lies, follies and barbarities; and this is often advanced as a reason for keeping out of politics altogether. I do not accept this argument, if only because in the modern world no one describable as an intellectual *can* keep out of politics in the sense of not caring about them. I think one must engage in politics—using the word in a wide sense—and that one must have preferences: that is, one must recognise that some causes are objectively better than others, even if they are advanced by equally bad means. As for the nationalistic loves and hatreds that I have spoken of, they are part of the make-up of most of us, whether we like it or not. Whether it is possible to get rid of them I do not know, but I do believe that it is possible to struggle against them, and that this is essentially a *moral* effort. It is a question first of all of discovering what one really is, what one's own feelings really are, and then of making allowance for the inevitable bias. If you hate and fear Russia, if you are jealous of the wealth and power of America, if you despise Jews, if you have a sentiment of inferiority towards the British ruling class, you cannot get rid of those feelings simply by taking thought. But you can at least recognise that you have them, and prevent them from contaminating your mental processes. The emotional urges which are inescapable, and are perhaps even necessary to political action, should be able to exist side by side with an acceptance of reality. But this, I repeat, needs a *moral* effort, and contemporary English literature, so far as it is alive at all to the major issues of our time, shows how few of us are prepared to make it.

Written [May 1945]; *Polemic*, [No. 1, October 1945]; SJ; EYE; CE

102. London Letter to *Partisan Review*

[5 June 1945]

Dear Editors,

I have spent the last three months in France and Germany, but I must devote this letter to British affairs, because if I touch directly on anything I saw abroad I shall have to submit the letter to SHAEF censorship.

The forthcoming General Election is causing a fair amount of excitement, and many Labour Party supporters seem honestly confident that their party will win. Churchill is considered to have decided on an early election because this will probably mean a low

poll. Millions of soldiers and others will still be away from home
and, though not strictly speaking disenfranchised (the soldiers can
vote by proxy, for instance), out of touch with their local political
organisations. The votes lost in this way will be mostly potential
Labour votes. I have predicted all along that the Conservatives will
win by a small majority, and I still stick to this, though not quite so
confidently as before, because the tide is obviously running very
strongly in the other direction. It is even conceivable that Labour
may win the election against the will of its leaders. Any government
taking office now is in for an uncomfortable time, and a Left government especially so. War-time controls will have to be continued and
even tightened up, and demobilisation will inevitably be slower than
the general public expects. Then there is the coal problem, which is
simply not soluble until the mines have been nationalised and then
renovated by a process that will take several years. For the time being
any government, of whatever colour, will be obliged both to coerce
the miners and to let the public shiver through the winter. There is
also the impending show-down with Russia, which the people at the
top of the Labour Party no doubt realise to be unavoidable, but
which public opinion has not been prepared for. And above all there
is India. The Conservatives might be able to stave off an Indian
settlement for one more term of office, but a government calling
itself Socialist could hardly attempt to do so, while at the same time
it is very unlikely that Attlee, Morrison and the rest of them can make
any offer that the Indian Nationalists would accept. Some people
consider that a government taking office at this moment does not
risk unpopularity, because the security and semi-prosperity produced
by the war will still be operative, and that the really difficult time lies
about two years ahead, when there will be full demobilisation with
consequent unemployment and a calamitous housing shortage.
Nevertheless I believe that the fear of responsibility, which always
weighs heavily on the Labour Party, will be particularly strong when
the prospect ahead is of dragging an exhausted country through
another two years of war, and that there will be some pulling of
punches when the last-minute struggle begins. Of course one doesn't
know what piece of trickery the Conservatives have in store this time.
The election will be more or less a straight fight between Labour and
the Conservatives. Both Common Wealth and the Communists are
likely to increase their representation, but not to a significant extent,
and the come-back which the Liberal Party is attempting is not likely

to be much of a success. The Liberals have a big asset in Beveridge, but they no longer represent any definite bloc of interests or opinions, and they advocate several different policies which cancel out. It is thought that they may win another ten or twenty seats, but that their main achievement will be to split the Labour vote in town areas and the Conservative vote in rural ones.

I have only been home a week, and I cannot make up my mind whether the Russian *mythos* is as powerful as it was before. A good observer who has been in England throughout the past three months gives me his opinion that pro-Russian feeling is cooling off rapidly and that former sympathisers are much dismayed by Russian foreign policy and by such episodes as the arrest of the 16 Polish delegates. Certainly the press is less adulatory than it was before, but this does not necessarily indicate a change in popular feeling. I have always held that pro-Russian sentiment in England during the past ten years has been due much more to the need for an external paradise than to any real interest in the Soviet régime, and that it cannot be countered by an appeal to the facts, even when these are known. A thing that has much struck me in recent years is that the most enormous crimes and disasters—purges, deportations, massacres, famines, imprisonment without trial, aggressive wars, broken treaties—not only fail to excite the big public, but can actually escape notice altogether, so long as they do not happen to fit in with the political mood of the moment. Thus it is possible *now* to rouse a certain amount of indignation about Dachau, Buchenwald, etc and yet before the war it was impossible to get the average person to take the faintest interest in such things, although the most horrible facts had had abundant publicity. If you could have taken a Gallup poll in 1939 I imagine you would have found that a majority, or at least a very big minority, of adult English people had not even heard of the existence of the German concentration camps. The whole thing had slid off their consciousness, since it was not what they then wanted to hear. So also with the USSR. If it could be proven tomorrow that the Russian concentration camps in the Arctic actually exist, and that they contain eighteen million prisoners, as some observers claim, I doubt whether this would make much impression on the russophile section of the public. The Warsaw business last year went almost unnoticed, and I don't see why the Russian behaviour towards Poland should suddenly begin exciting indignation now.

It may be, however, that public opinion is beginning to alter for other reasons. One thing which, in a small way, probably affects working-class opinion is that latterly there has been more contact than before between British and Russians. From what I can hear, the British prisoners liberated by the Red army in eastern Germany often bring back anti-Russian reports, and there has been a trickle of similar reports from the crews of the ships which go to Archangel and the air crews which were for a while operating in the USSR. What is probably involved here is the question of relative cultural levels, to which working-class people are usually very sensitive. In Germany I was struck by the attitude of the American GIs towards the hordes of Russian forced labourers, and of the British and American prisoners in liberated camps towards their Russian fellow prisoners. It was not that there was a hostility, merely that the western industrial worker, confronted with a Slav peasant, immediately feels him to be less civilised—which he is, according to the western worker's standards. However, this kind of thing takes effect on the big public very slowly, if at all. Meanwhile, so far as I can judge, pro-Russian sentiment is still strong and will be an appreciable factor in the General Election. A lot of people remark that a real stand against Russian aggression in Europe can only be made by a government of the Left, just as, when Germany was to be opposed, it had to be under Conservative leadership.

I was not in England for V-Day, but I am told it was very decorous —huge crowds, but little enthusiasm and even less rowdiness—just as it was in France. No doubt in both cases this was partly due to the shortage of alcohol. The ending of the European part of the war has made extraordinarily little difference to anybody. Even the black-out is almost as black as ever, since few of the street lights have been restored and most people don't possess any curtains other than black-out curtains. The basic petrol ration has been restored and there is a scramble for cars which are being sold at fantastic prices, but as yet the streets are comparatively empty. Certain war-time amenities, such as British Restaurants and the excellent day nurseries at which working mothers can leave their children, are now to be scrapped, or at least there is talk of scrapping them, and already people are signing petitions against this. In general, people of left-wing views are in favour of continuing war-time controls (there were even some murmurs against the discontinuance of 18b), while the Right makes play with such slogans as "No more bureaucracy". The ordinary people in the street seem to me not only to have become entirely habituated to a planned, regimented sort of life, in which consumption goods of all kinds are scarce but are shared out with reasonable fairness, but actually to prefer it to what they had before. Clearly one can't verify such impressions, but I have believed all along that England has been *happier* during the war, in spite of the desperate tiredness of some periods. It is usual to say that war simply causes suffering, but I question whether this is so when the casualties are small, as they have been for this country on this occasion. What happens in total war is that the acute suffering—not merely danger and hardship but boredom and homesickness—is pushed on to the armed forces, who may number ten per cent of the population, while the rest enjoy a security and a social equality which they never know at other times. Of course there is also bombing, the break-up of families, anxiety over husbands and sons, overwork and lack of amusements, but these are probably much more tolerable than the haunting dread of unemployment against a background of social competitiveness.

Having come back from the Continent I can see England with fresh eyes, and I see that certain things—for instance, the pacifist habit of mind, respect for freedom of speech and belief in legality—have managed to survive here while seemingly disappearing on the other side of the Channel. But if I had to say what had most struck me about the behaviour of the British people during the war, I should point to the *lack* of reaction of any kind. In the face of terrifying dangers and golden political opportunities, people just keep on keeping on, in a sort of twilight sleep in which they are conscious of nothing except the daily round of work, family life, darts at the pub, exercising the dog, mowing the lawn, bringing home the supper beer, etc etc. I remember that during the worst moment of Dunkirk I was walking in a park with a friend, and I pointed out to him that in the behaviour of the crowds there was absolutely nothing to indicate that anything out of the ordinary was happening. Exactly as usual people were pushing their prams to and fro, young men were chasing girls, games of cricket were being played, etc. He said gloomily, "They'll behave like this until the bombs start dropping, and then they'll panic." Yet they didn't panic, and, as I noted at the time, they preserved the ordinary pattern of their lives to a surprising extent even amid the disorganisation caused by the bombing. As William Empson puts it, "Three fathoms down the sea is always calm." I think it is well established that this time there has been far less feeling either for or against the war than there was last time. It is true that this time the number of men registering as Conscientious Objectors has about doubled itself, but I don't think this is significant, because, unless one actually wanted to be a martyr, being a CO has not entailed either ill-treatment or social ostracism this time. It has been made easy for COs to choose non-military jobs, and the number refusing all kinds of national service has been tiny. One has to remember that last time the organised labour movement was more or less anti-war for the first two years, there was strong feeling against conscription, and by the end several parts of the country were not far from revolution. There were also military mutinies all over the place as soon as the fighting stopped. This time nothing of the kind has happened, but neither has there been anything like the insane enthusiasm of 1914, which I am old enough to remember, nor has hatred of the enemy gone to the same lengths. This time people haven't—except in the columns of the newspapers—referred to the Germans as Huns, they haven't looted German shops or lynched so-called spies in Hyde Park, and children's papers haven't been decorated with pictures of Germans wearing the faces of pigs: but on the other hand there has been less protest against the proposals to dismember Germany, make use of forced labour, etc than there was against the Versailles settlement. Considering what has happened in Europe, I think it is worth noticing that almost no English people have changed sides in this war. At most a few dozen individuals, mostly with a pre-war Fascist history, have quislingised. Towards the end of the war literally hundreds of thousands of Russians, Poles, Czechs and what not were fighting for the Germans or serving in the Todt organisation, but no British or Americans at all. It is the same with the development, or rather lack of development, on the home front. Never would I have prophesied that we could go through nearly six years of war without arriving at either Socialism or Fascism, and with our civil liberties almost intact. I don't know whether this semi-anaesthesia in which the British people contrive to live is a sign of decadence, as many observers believe, or whether on the other hand it is a kind of instinctive wisdom. It may well be that it is the best attitude when you live among endless horrors and calamities which you are powerless to prevent. Possibly we shall all have to develop it if war becomes continuous, which seems to me a likely development in the fairly near future.

I understand that with the ending of the war you are rearranging your foreign contributions, so this will be my last letter in this particular series, which started over four years ago. It doesn't seem worth making any winding-up remarks, since I did something of the kind in your last issue but one. I would merely like to finish up by telling you and your readers how much I have enjoyed writing these letters. In among the lunatic activities on which I have wasted the war years, they have given me a wonderful feeling of getting my nose above water. And finally, I think you all will agree that a word of praise is due to the censorship department, which has let these letters through with remarkably little interference. All the best.

George Orwell

Partisan Review, Summer 1945

103. Letter to F. J. Warburg

London N1
13 June 1945

Dear Fred,

Thanks for your letter of June 12th. I will send the blurb[1] as soon as possible.

As to the contract for a novel, I was in France when the two contracts reached me and I probably did not explain adequately why I did not sign the novel contract and struck out references to it in the other contract. To begin with, the novel referred to did not exist and does not exist yet. Secondly there was the question of my existing contract with Gollancz.[2] I still have a contract to give Gollancz the first refusal of my next two works of fiction, but I have no intention of keeping this as he has not kept his contract with me in spirit nor, I think, in the letter. However, I want to remain within my rights and this involves something which I had explained to Moore but which he had failed to understand. Gollancz was offered *Animal Farm*, which of course I knew in advance he would refuse, and he was only offered it on his own insistence. Having refused it he refused to regard it as one of the two contracted novels on the ground

---

[1] For *Animal Farm*.

[2] Victor Gollancz (1893–1967), Kt. 1965, who had published seven of Orwell's books, including his first, between 1933 and 1940, but rejected *Homage to Catalonia* and *Animal Farm* on political grounds.

that it was too short. It appeared that these two novels, of which he was to have first refusal, were to be of standard length. I then tried to get Moore to get from Gollancz a statement of what amounted to standard length. Moore failed to see what I was driving at and simply said that standard length is a trade expression meaning about 70,000 words and that 65,000 words could be regarded as a minimum. I then decided that I would make my next two novels, if any, less than 65,000 words, which would get me out of this contract. It was for that reason that I did not want to sign an ordinary novel contract with you, which might give Gollancz the chance to say I was defrauding him. If you like we can draw up another contract worded differently, but in any case you know I will bring you all my books except any which may be written for some special purpose.

I don't think the list of review copies needs adding to. I think it is best if you send them out, as your office will be able to do them more systematically than I can. Have you fixed a definite date for publication yet?

Victor Serge[1] now doesn't want to send his memoirs across the Atlantic because it seems he has only one copy and he is frightened of their getting lost or seized on the way. I have written suggesting that he should get another copy typed.

I could have lunch on June 19th as you suggest. I'll ring up about this between now and then.

Yours
George

104. Review

The Nigger of the Narcissus, Typhoon, The Shadow-Line, Within the Tides by Joseph Conrad

It has been said that a creative writer can only expect to remain at the top of his form for about fifteen years, and the bibliography which is included in the Everyman reprint of Conrad's short stories seems to bear this out. Conrad's great period was from 1902 to

[1] Victor Serge (1890–1947), Russian by parentage, French by adoption, one of the most literary of the early Communists and author of innumerable books; friendly with the POUM during the Spanish civil war. He became a Trotskyist and in 1941 he settled in Mexico.

1915. Within those years he produced not only *The Secret Agent,* *Chance* and *Victory,* but a whole string of brilliant short and long-short stories, such as "Youth", "The End of the Tether", "Falk", and "Heart of Darkness". Also, it is only in this period that stories *not* dealing with the sea predominate in his work.

Of the tales now reprinted (the Penguin book contains four), only one, *Typhoon,* shows Conrad at his best. His name is associated with the sea and with the "romance" of muddy islands in the eastern archipelagos, and in a time of paper shortage it was no doubt inevitable that the more obviously picturesque of his stories should be selected for reissue. But even if inevitable it was unfortunate. "The Planter of Malata", for instance, which occupies nearly half of *Within the Tides,* was not worth reprinting. It simply illustrates the vulgar theatricality which was the reverse side of Conrad's feeling for *noblesse oblige.*

"The Partner", on the other hand, which is included in the same volume, is in essence a very fine story, though it is marred by the queer shyness or clumsiness which made it difficult for Conrad to tell a story straightforwardly in the third person. *The Nigger of the Narcissus* contains magnificent descriptive passages, but curiously enough the most memorable things in it are certain irrelevant paragraphs in which Conrad goes out of his way to express his reactionary political and social opinions. In a penetrating essay published some years ago, the sailor writer, George Garrett, pointed out that the whole story can probably be traced back to some encounter which Conrad, as an officer, had had with a rebellious seaman. *The Shadow-Line* is a goodish story, not better or worse than about a dozen others that Conrad wrote. *Typhoon,* of course, was well worth reprinting, but one cannot help feeling sorry that it was not accompanied either by *Chance* or by *The Secret Agent* and some of the short stories on kindred subjects.

Nearly the whole of Conrad's charm springs from the fact that he was a European and not an Englishman. This is most obvious in his style of writing, which even at his best, and perhaps especially at his best, has the air of being a translation. It is said that for many years he was obliged to translate his thoughts from Polish into French and from French into English, and when he uses phrases like "his face of a sick goat", or puts the adjective after the noun ("it was a fate unique and their own"), it is possible to follow the process back at least as far as the French. But Conrad's romanticism, his love of the grand gesture and of the lonely Prometheus struggling against fate, is also somehow un-English. He had the outlook of a European aristocrat, and he believed in the existence of the "English gentleman" at a time when this type had been extinct for about two generations. As a result he was constantly creating characters in whom a capacity for having adventures, and a capacity for appreciating them, were combined in a way that is impossible in real life. *Lord Jim*, for instance, is an absurdity as a whole, in spite of the brilliant passages describing the scuttling of the ship. "The End of the Tether" is an example of a story in which Conrad's feeling for personal nobility produces a truly moving effect, but probably an Englishman could not have written it. To admire the English as much as Conrad did, one had to be a foreigner, seeing the English with fresh eyes and slightly misunderstanding them.

The other advantage Conrad derived from his European background was a considerable understanding of conspiratorial politics. He had an often-expressed horror of Anarchists and Nihilists, but he also had a species of sympathy with them, because he was a Pole—a reactionary in home politics, perhaps, but a rebel against Russia and Germany. His most colourful passages may have dealt with the sea, but he is at his most grown-up when he touches dry land.

Observer, 24 June 1945

105. Unpublished Letter to the Editor of *Tribune*[1]

I read with some disappointment your comment on the trial of the sixteen Poles in Moscow,[2] in which you seemed to imply that they had behaved in a discreditable manner and deserved punishment.

---

[1] An unpublished letter to *Tribune*, written [26? June 1945]. It was set up in type but on the printer's proof from which this text is taken a note in Orwell's hand says: "Withdrawn because *Tribune* altered attitude in following week".

[2] The British had called for a meeting of the leaders of the Polish underground to discuss the implementation of the Yalta decisions on the formation of a Polish Government of National Unity. The preliminary meeting was to be held in Moscow and a further meeting was planned for London. However when the Poles reached Moscow they were arrested by the Russians and put on trial.

Early in the proceedings I formed the opinion that the accused were technically guilty: only, just what were they guilty of? Apparently it was merely of doing what everyone thinks it right to do when his country is occupied by a foreign power—that is, of trying to keep a military force in being, of maintaining communication with the outside world, of committing acts of sabotage and occasionally killing people. In other words, they were accused of trying to preserve the independence of their country against an unelected puppet government, and of remaining obedient to a government which at that time was recognised by the whole world except the USSR. The Germans during their period of occupation could have brought exactly the same indictment against them, and they would have been equally guilty.

It will not do to say that the efforts of the Poles to remain independent "objectively" aided the Nazis, and leave it at that. Many actions which left-wingers do not disapprove of have "objectively" aided the Germans. How about EAM,[1] for instance. They also tried to keep their military force in being, and they, too, killed Allied soldiers—British in this case—and they were not even acting under the orders of a government which was recognised by anyone as legal. But what of it? We do not disapprove of their action, and if sixteen EAM leaders were now brought to London and sentenced to long terms of imprisonment we should rightly protest.

To be anti-Polish and pro-Greek is only possible if one sets up a double standard of political morality, one for the USSR and the other for the rest of the world. Before these sixteen Poles went to Moscow they were described in the press as political delegates, and it was stated that they had been summoned there to take part in discussions on the formation of a new government. After their arrest all mention of their status as political delegates was dropped from the British press—an example of the kind of censorship that is necessary if this double standard is to be made acceptable to the big public. Any well-informed person is aware of similar instances.

[1] Ethnikon Apeleutherotikon Metopon, the National Liberation Front formed in Greece in 1941 after the German invasion. It started as a truly national resistance movement with nearly the whole population as members. By early 1942 it was discovered that it was in fact Communist organised. A national guerilla army was then formed to fight the Germans but found itself also fighting the EAM. When the British returned to Greece in 1945 they also found themselves fighting the EAM.

To name just one: at this moment speakers up and down the country are justifying the Russian purges on the ground that Russia "had no quislings", at the same time as any mention of the considerable numbers of Russian troops, including several generals, who changed sides and fought for the Germans is being suppressed by cautious editors. This kind of whitewashing may be due to a number of different motives, some of them respectable ones, but its effect on the Socialist movement can be deadly if it is long continued.

When I wrote in your columns I repeatedly said that if one criticises this or that Russian action one is not obliged to put on airs of moral superiority. Their behaviour is not worse than that of capitalist governments, and its actual results may often be better. Nor is it likely that we shall alter the behaviour of the rulers of the USSR by telling them that we disapprove of them. The whole point is the effect of the Russian *mythos* on the Socialist movement *here*. At present we are all but openly applying the double standard of morality. With one side of our mouths we cry out that mass deportations, concentration camps, forced labour and suppression of freedom of speech are appalling crimes, while with the other we proclaim that these things are perfectly all right if done by the USSR or its satellite states: and where necessary we make this plausible by doctoring the news and cutting out unpalatable facts. One cannot possibly build up a healthy Socialist movement if one is obliged to condone no matter what crime when the USSR commits it. No one knows better than I do that it is unpopular to say anything anti-Russian *at this moment*. But what of it? I am only forty-two, and I can remember the time when it was as dangerous to say anything pro-Russian as it is to say anything anti-Russian now. Indeed, I am old enough to have seen working-class audiences booing and jeering at speakers who had used the word Socialism. These fashions pass away, but they can't be depended on to do so unless thinking people are willing to raise their voices against the fallacy of the moment. It is only because over the past hundred years small groups and lonely individuals have been willing to face unpopularity that the Socialist movement exists at all.

George Orwell

106. Letter to Leonard Moore

27B Canonbury Square
Islington, London N1
3 July 1945

Dear Mr Moore,

I had a talk with Warburg about the contract position. He is quite satisfied with my assurance that I will bring him all my future work, subject to books of a special nature (e.g. that "Britain in Pictures" book)[1] being allowed to go elsewhere. He is not pressing for a hard and fast contract, but he would no doubt prefer to have one when the other business is settled.

The real trouble is with Gollancz. The contract to bring him my next two novels is still extant, and as he refused to regard *Animal Farm* as working off one of these, it looks as if he wants to keep to it. At the same time I frankly would prefer not to give or offer him any more books if we can get out of it. I have no quarrel with him personally, he has treated me generously and published my work when no one else would, but it is obviously unsatisfactory to be tied to a publisher who accepts or refuses books partly on political grounds and whose own political views are constantly changing. When I wrote *Animal Farm*, for instance, I knew in advance that it would be a very difficult book to find a publisher for, and having to submit it to Gollancz simply meant that much time wasted. This might happen over and over again, and judging by some of the things he has published during the past year or two, I doubt whether I could now write anything that Gollancz would approve of. For instance, I recently started a novel.[2] Considering how much work I have to do elsewhere I don't expect to finish it till sometime in 1947, but I am pretty sure Gollancz would refuse it when the time comes, unless by that time his views have altered again. He might say that so far as novels go he does not mind what views they express, but it is a bad arrangement to take novels to one publisher and non-fiction to another. For example, that Spanish war book, which is about the best I have written, would probably have sold more if published by Gollancz, as by that time I was becoming known to the Gollancz public. With Warburg these difficulties don't arise. He is less interested in propaganda and in any case his views are near enough to mine to prevent serious disagreement. From Gollancz's

[1] Reprinted here as *The English People*. See 1.
[2] *Nineteen Eighty-Four*.

own point of view I do not imagine I am a good proposition either. Having me on his list simply means that from time to time he will publish a book which neither he nor his friends can disapprove of. It seems to me that if he will agree it would be better to scrap the contract. If he won't agree I will keep to the strict letter, i.e. as regards two more novels, and I have no doubt I can make this all right with Warburg. Perhaps you could approach Gollancz about this. You can quote this paragraph if you wish.

I saw W. J. Turner [1] the other day and asked him about the "Britain in Pictures" book. He said Edmund Blunden [2] is writing the companion volume and the two will be published simultaneously. I said that as they had had the MS a year I thought I ought to have some money. The agreed advance was £50 and I suggested they should give me £25 now. He said there would be no objection to this and I told him you would write to him, which you have perhaps done already.

Hamish Hamilton wrote to say Harper's would like to see something more of mine. I told him about the book of essays, [3] and perhaps if the Dial Press people turn it down it might be worth showing it to Harper's, though I shouldn't think it is much in their line.

Yours sincerely
Eric Blair

107. London Letter to *Partisan Review*

[15? August 1945]

Dear Editors,

I have put off starting this letter until today, hoping that some unmistakable symptom might indicate what the Labour Government intends doing. However, nothing very revealing has happened up to date, and I can discuss the situation only in general terms. In

[1] W. J. Turner (1889–1946), poet, novelist and music critic who did occasional publishing and journalistic work. When he asked Orwell to contribute to the series "Britain in Pictures" for Collins Ltd he was also literary editor of the *Spectator*.

[2] Edmund Blunden (1896–), CBE, MC, poet, man of letters and editor. Fellow and tutor in English literature, Merton College, Oxford, 1931–43. Professor of Poetry, Oxford University, 1966–68. His publications include *Poems 1914–30* and *Undertones of War*.

[3] *Critical Essays* (*Dickens, Dali and Others*).

order to see what the Labour Party is up against, one has to consider the background against which it won its victory.

It is fashionable to say that all the causes we fought for have been defeated, but this seems to me a gross exaggeration. The fact that after six years of war we can hold a General Election in a quite orderly way, and throw out a Prime Minister who has enjoyed almost dictatorial powers, shows that we *have* gained something by not losing the war. But still the general outlook is black enough. Western Europe is mostly on the verge of starvation. Throughout eastern Europe there is a "revolution from above", imposed by the Russians, which probably benefits the poorer peasants but kills in advance any possibility of democratic Socialism. Between the two zones there is an impenetrable barrier which runs slap across economic frontiers. Germany, already devastated to an extent that people in this country can't imagine, is to be plundered more effectively than after Versailles, and some twelve million of its population are to be evicted from their homes. Everywhere there is indescribable confusion, mix-up of populations, destruction of dwelling houses, bridges and railway tracks, flooding of coal mines, shortage of every kind of necessity, and lack of transport to distribute even such goods as exist. In the Far East hundreds of thousands of people, if the reports are truthful, have been blown to fragments by atomic bombs, and the Russians are getting ready to bite another chunk off the carcase of China. In India, Palestine, Persia, Egypt and other countries, troubles that the average person in England has not even heard of are just about ready to boil over.

And Britain's own situation is none too rosy. We have lost most of our markets and overseas investments, twelve million tons of our shipping have gone to the bottom, much of our industry is hopelessly antiquated, and our coal mines are in such a state that for years it will be impossible to get enough coal out of them. We have ahead of us the enormous job of reconstructing industry and recapturing markets in the teeth of overwhelming competition from the USA, and at the same time we have to build millions of houses and to keep up armed forces larger than we can afford in order to hold on to our precarious supplies of oil. No one, I think, expects the next few years to be easy ones, but on the whole people did vote Labour because of the belief that a Left government means family allowances, higher old-age pensions, houses with bathrooms, etc rather than from any internationalist consideration. They look to a Labour government to make them more secure and, after a few years, more comfortable, and the chief danger of the situation lies in the fact that English people have never been made to grasp that the sources of their prosperity lie outside England. The parochial outlook of the Labour Party itself is largely responsible for this.

I have already written on the election and I do not want to repeat what I said. But I must re-emphasise two points. One—not everyone agrees with me about this, but it is the impression I gathered in the London constituencies—is that the election was fought on domestic issues. Even russophile feeling was a secondary factor. The other is that the turn-over of votes was not enormous. Looking back at the last letter I sent you, I find that I was wrong on several points, and above all in predicting that the Conservatives would win. But everybody else, so far as I know, was also wrong, and even when the Gallup polls indicated that about 46 per cent would vote Labour, the newspapers of the Left would go only so far as predicting a stalemate. The anomalies of the English electoral system usually work in favour of the Conservatives, and everyone assumed that they would do so again. Actually they worked the other way, for once, and everyone was stunned with surprise when the results were announced. But I was also wrong in suggesting that the Labour leaders might flinch from power and hence fight the election half-heartedly. It was a genuine enough fight, and it turned on issues that were serious so far as they went. Everyone who took an interest saw that the only chance of getting the Tories out was to vote Labour, and the minor parties were ignored. The twenty candidates put up by the Communists only won about 100,000 votes between them, and Common Wealth did equally badly. I think that the democratic tradition came out of the election fairly well. Tory efforts to turn the whole thing into a sort of plebiscite only excited disgust, and though the big masses appeared uninterested, they did go into the polling booths and vote at the last minute—against Churchill, as it turned out. But one cannot take this slide to the Left as meaning that Britain is on the verge of revolution. In spite of the discontent smouldering in the armed forces, the mood of the country seems to me less revolutionary, less Utopian, even less hopeful, than it was in 1940 or 1942. Of the votes cast in the election, at most 50 per cent could be considered as outright votes for Socialism, and about another 10 per cent as votes for nationalisation of certain key industries.

A Labour government may be said to mean business if it (a) nationalises land, coal mines, railways, public utilities and banks, (b) offers India immediate Dominion Status (this is a minimum), and (c) purges the bureaucracy, the army, the diplomatic service, etc so thoroughly as to forestall sabotage from the Right. The symptoms to watch for are an all-round swapping of ambassadors, the abolition of the India Office and, after Parliament reassembles, a battle with the House of Lords. If these don't happen, it is a good bet that no really radical economic change is intended. But the success or failure of the Government does not depend solely on its willingness to fulfil its promises. It also has to re-educate public opinion at short notice, which to a large extent means fighting against its own past propaganda.

The weakness of all left-wing parties is their inability to tell the truth about the immediate future. When you are in opposition, and are trying to win support for a new economic and political programme, it is your job to make people discontented, and you almost inevitably do it by telling them that they will be better off in a material sense when the new programme is introduced. You probably don't tell them, what may very well be true, that they won't experience any benefit *immediately*, but only after, say, twenty years. The British people have never been warned, i.e. by the Left, that the introduction of Socialism may mean a serious drop in the standard of living. Nearly all left-wingers, from Labourites to Trotskyists, would regard it as political suicide to say any such thing. Yet in my opinion it is probably true, at least in the case of a country like Britain, which lives partly by exploiting the coloured peoples. To continue exploiting them is incompatible with the spirit of Socialism, while to stop doing so would entail a difficult reconstruction period during which our own standard of living might fall catastrophically. In one form and another this problem comes up again and again, and, except for the minority who have travelled outside Europe, I have never met an English Socialist who would face it. The stock answer is that we should lose nothing by liberating India and the colonies, since they would then develop more rapidly and their purchasing power would increase, which would be to our advantage—all true enough, but overlooking the interim period, which is the crux of the matter. The coloured peoples themselves are not to be fobbed off with such easy answers, and indeed they are inclined to think of British prosperity as more dependent on imperialist exploitation than it actually is. When the Beveridge Report was first published, it had to be somewhat soft-pedalled in the news bulletins to India. There was danger that it would cause serious resentment, the likeliest Indian reaction being: "They are making themselves comfortable at our expense."

Similarly, the calamity of the war, and the impoverishment of the world as a whole, have not been fully brought home to the British people. I think they grasp that the reconversion of industry will be a big job, involving rationing and "direction" of labour over a long period, but are less well aware that the devastation of Europe must react badly on our own economy. It is extraordinary how little protest there has been against the proposal to turn Germany into a sort of overcrowded rural slum. In looking to the future, people think in terms of redistributing the national income, and don't pause to reflect that that income is itself dependent on world conditions. They have had the Beveridge Scheme, raising of the school-leaving age, and so forth, whisked in front of their noses, and no one has told them that for a long time to come we may be unable to afford any improvement in our way of life. Sometimes at Labour meetings during the election I tried the experiment of asking at question time: "What is the Labour Party's policy towards India?" I always got some such perfunctory answer as "Of course the Labour Party is in the completest sympathy with the Indian people's aspiration towards independence", and there the subject dropped, neither speakers nor audiences having the faintest interest in it. I don't think throughout the election I heard a Labour speaker spontaneously mention India, and they rarely mentioned Europe except to make the demagogic and misleading claim that a government of the Left would be able to "come to an understanding with Soviet Russia". It is easy to see what dangers are contained in this optimism about home affairs and disregard of conditions abroad. The trouble could come to a head in dozens of ways—over India or the colonies, over the need to cut our rations further in order to prevent occupied Germany from starving, over mobility of labour, over the inevitable muddles and failures in rehousing, and so on and so forth. The great need of the moment is to make people aware of what is happening and why, and to persuade them that Socialism is a *better* way of life but not necessarily, in its first stages, a more comfortable one. I have no doubt they would accept this if it were put to them in the right way: but at present nothing of the kind is being attempted.

Up to date there has been no definite sign of a reorientation in foreign policy. A Labour government has fewer reasons than a Conservative one for propping up unpopular monarchs and dictators, but it cannot disregard British strategic interests. I think it is an error to suppose, as the public was allowed to suppose during the election, that the Labour leaders will be more subservient to the USSR than the Tories were. After the first few months it will probably be the other way about. Most of them—Laski, for instance, is an exception—have no illusions about the Soviet system. They are involved, as the Tories are not, in the ideological struggle between the eastern and western conceptions of Socialism, and if they choose to stand up to Russia public opinion will support them, whereas Tory motives for opposing Russia were always justly suspect. One probable source of trouble in the near future is Palestine. The Labour Party, and the Left generally, is very strongly committed to support the Jews against the Arabs, largely because it is only the Jewish case that ever gets a hearing in England. Few English people realise that the Palestine issue is partly a colour issue and that an Indian nationalist, for instance, would probably side with the Arabs. As to the long-term aspects of international policy, they are largely governed by geography. Britain, not strong enough to compete single-handed with Russia or America, has three alternatives. One is to carry on as at present, acquiescing in "spheres of interest" and holding the Empire together as well as possible; another is to move definitely into the orbit of the USA; and the other is to liberate India, cut the links with the Dominions, and form a solid bloc of the western European states and their African possessions. Various observers, including scientists, assure me that the third alternative is technically feasible and that such a bloc could be stronger than either the USA or the USSR. But it seems to me a pipe-dream. The centrifugal forces in both France and Britain, the two countries that would matter most, are far too strong.

In spite of the difficulties and dangers I have outlined above, the new Government starts off in a very strong position. Unless the Party suffers a major split, Labour is secure in office for at least five years, probably longer. Its one serious opponent, the Conservative Party, is discredited and bankrupt of ideas. Moreover the people who are in power this time are not a gang of easily-bribed weaklings like those of 1929. Like nearly everyone else in England, I know very little about Attlee. Someone who does know him tells me that he is in fact the colourless creature that he appears—one of those secondary figures who step into a leading position because of the death or resignation of somebody else, and hold on to it by being industrious and methodical. He certainly has not the magnetism that a statesman needs nowadays, and the cartoonists of the daily press are frankly puzzled to find some outstanding characteristic (cf Churchill's cigar, Chamberlain's umbrella, Lloyd George's hair) by which they can popularise him. But the other people in a commanding position in the Government, Bevin, Morrison, Greenwood, Cripps, Aneurin Bevan, are tougher and abler than their opposite numbers in the Conservative Party, Churchill's tendency having been to surround himself with yes-men. The composition of the House has altered greatly. For the first time the bulk of the Labour Party members are not trade union officials but come from the constituency parties. Of the 390 Labour members, about 90 are trade union officials and about another 40 are proletarians of one kind or another. The rest are mostly middle-class, and include large numbers of factory managers, doctors, lawyers and journalists. The salaried and professional middle class has now largely "gone left", and its votes were an important factor in swinging the election. It is difficult to believe that this Government will collapse in the same ignominious way as those of 1929 and 1923. Five years should be long enough to tide over the worst period. Heaven knows whether the Government has any serious intention of introducing Socialism, but if it has, I don't see what there is to stop it.

The news of the Japanese surrender came in yesterday about lunch-time, when I was in Fleet Street. There was quite a bit of jubilation in the streets, and people in upstairs offices instantly began tearing up old papers and throwing them out of the window. This idea occurred to everyone simultaneously, and for a couple of miles my bus travelled through a rain of paper fragments which glittered in the sunlight as they came down and littered the pavements ankle deep. It annoyed me rather. In England you can't get paper to print books on, but apparently there is always plenty of it for this kind of thing. Incidentally the British War Office alone uses more paper than the whole of the book trade.

The prompt surrender of Japan seems to have altered people's outlook on the atomic bomb. At the beginning everyone I spoke to about it, or overheard in the street, was simply horrified. Now they begin to feel that there's something to be said for a weapon that could end the war in two days. Much speculation as to "whether the Russians have got it too". Also, from some quarters, demands that Anglo-America should hand over the secret of the bomb to Russia, which does seem to be carrying trustfulness a bit far.

George Orwell

Partisan Review, Fall 1945

108. Letter to Herbert Read

27B Canonbury Square
Islington
London N1
18 August 1945

Dear Read,
Thanks for your letter. I'm glad you liked *Animal Farm*. If you're going to be back in London about the end of August we could perhaps meet shortly after that, as I would like to talk to you about this Freedom Defence Committee.[1] George Woodcock[2] asked me to be vice-chairman, which I agreed to, but I haven't been very active, because I am really not much good at that kind of thing, and it's all still a bit vague in my mind. I am going away for my holiday about September 10th, but shall be in London till then.

I lost my wife in March. I cannot remember whether you ever met her. It was a beastly, cruel business, however I don't think she expected to die (it happened during an operation), so perhaps it was not so bad as it might have been. I was in France at the time and only

[1] The Freedom Defence Committee was founded in 1945 to deal with cases of the infringement of the civil liberties of any citizens of the British Empire; it intervened in innumerable cases which were reported in its Bulletin. Herbert Read was its Chairman, with Orwell as Vice-Chairman and George Woodcock as Secretary.

[2] George Woodcock (1912–   ), author, Anarchist, editor of *Now* 1940–7, at present Professor of English at the University of British Columbia. After his controversy with Orwell (see II, 34) they corresponded and remained friends until Orwell's death.

got back after she was dead. My little son is now 15 months. Fortunately he has always had excellent health and I have got a very good nurse who looks after both him and me. I am trying to take a cottage on Jura and am going up to arrange about the rent and repairs in September. If I can fix it up and manage to transfer some furniture there, which is the most difficult thing, I can live there in the summers, and it would be a wonderful place for a child to learn to walk in.

Rayner Heppenstall is out of the army and is working at the BBC. *Tribune* is going through some changes now that Labour has won the election. Bevan [1] and Strauss [2] are severing their official connection with it and Michael Foot [3] is going on to the editorial board. It will thus be able to continue as a critical organ and not have to back up the Government all the time. I am probably going to continue my column, or something similar, after I come back from my holiday. I stopped it, of course, while I was in France, and didn't start again because Bevan was terrified there might be a row over *Animal Farm*, which might have been embarrassing if the book had come out before the election, as it was at first intended to.

Hoping to see you.

Yours
George

Animal Farm was published in London by Secker & Warburg on 17 August 1945 and in New York by Harcourt, Brace on 26 August 1946.

[1] Aneurin (Nye) Bevan (1897–1960), Socialist politician, Labour MP, and Minister of Health in the post-war Labour Government; one of England's greatest orators and the symbol of the Socialist aspirations of the Left. As director of *Tribune* he had given Orwell complete freedom to write as he pleased, however unpopular or inexpedient his anti-Soviet, etc line might be with the official Left.

[2] G. R. Strauss, a Labour MP and co-director with Bevan of *Tribune*.

[3] Michael Foot (1913–), politician, writer and journalist, on the extreme Left of the Labour Party. Labour MP for Devonport 1945–55. Since 1960 Labour MP for Ebbw Vale, the constituency formerly held by Bevan whose official biography he wrote and whose close friend he had been. He was assistant editor of *Tribune* 1937–8, editor 1948–52 and 1955–60, and is one of the ablest debaters in the post-war House of Commons.

109. Letter to Frank Barber

27B Canonbury Square
Islington
London N1
3 September 1945

Dear Mr Barber,

Many thanks for your letter, and thanks for the notice in the *Yorkshire Evening News*, which I had already seen. I am sorry you have left the *Leeds Weekly Citizen*, as it is so importantthatthere should be some Labour papers which are not taken in by Russian propaganda. However, I think the intellectual atmosphere is changing a bit. I have been surprised by the friendly reception *Animal Farm* has had, after lying in type for about a year because the publisher dared not bring it out till the war was over. I don't suppose there will be any more copies yet awhile, as the first edition sold out immediately. Warburg is printing a second edition of 6,000 copies, but I suppose there will be the usual delays before they appear.

No, I haven't severed connection with *Tribune*, though I have given up the literary editorship. I was, of course, obliged to stop the column while I went abroad, but I am going to start doing another weekly article for them in October.

Yours sincerely
Geo. Orwell

110. Author's Preface to the Ukrainian Edition of *Animal Farm*

[In March 1947 Orwell wrote a special preface for the Ukrainian edition of *Animal Farm*, distributed in November the same year by a Ukrainian Displaced Persons Organisation in Munich. Orwell's original text has not been traced and the version given here is a re-casting back into English from the Ukrainian translation.]

I have been asked to write a preface to the Ukrainian translation of *Animal Farm*. I am aware that I write for readers about whom I know nothing, but also that they too have probably never had the slightest opportunity to know anything about me.

In this preface they will most likely expect me to say something of how *Animal Farm* originated but first I would like to say something about myself and the experiences by which I arrived at my political position.

I was born in India in 1903. My father was an official in the English administration there, and my family was one of those ordinary middle-class families of soldiers, clergymen, government officials, teachers, lawyers, doctors, etc. I was educated at Eton, the most costly and snobbish of the English Public Schools. But I had only got in there by means of a scholarship; otherwise my father could not have afforded to send me to a school of this type.

Shortly after I left school (I wasn't quite twenty years old then) I went to Burma and joined the Indian Imperial Police. This was an armed police, a sort of *gendarmerie* very similar to the Spanish *Guardia Civil* or the *Garde Mobile* in France. I stayed five years in the service. It did not suit me and made me hate imperialism, although at that time nationalist feelings in Burma were not very marked, and relations between the English and the Burmese were not particularly bad. When on leave in England in 1927, I resigned from the service and decided to become a writer: at first without any especial success. In 1928–9 I lived in Paris and wrote short stories and novels that nobody would print (I have since destroyed them all). In the following years I lived mostly from hand to mouth, and went hungry on several occasions. It was only from 1934 onwards that I was able to live on what I earned from my writing. In the meantime I sometimes lived for months on end amongst the poor and half-criminal elements who inhabit the worst parts of the poorer quarters, or take to the streets, begging and stealing. At that time I associated with them through lack of money, but later their way of life interested me very much for its own sake. I spent many months (more systematically this time) studying the conditions of the miners in the north of England. Up to 1930 I did not on the whole look upon myself as a Socialist. In fact I had as yet no clearly defined political views. I became pro-Socialist more out of disgust with the way the poorer section of the industrial workers were oppressed and neglected than out of any theoretical admiration for a planned society.

In 1936 I got married. In almost the same week the civil war broke out in Spain. My wife and I both wanted go to to Spain and fight for the Spanish Government. We were ready in six months, as soon as I had finished the book I was writing. In Spain I spent almost six months on the Aragon front until, at Huesca, a Fascist sniper shot me through the throat.

In the early stages of the war foreigners were on the whole unaware of the inner struggles between the various political parties supporting the Government. Through a series of accidents I joined not the International Brigade like the majority of foreigners, but the POUM militia—i.e. the Spanish Trotskyists.

So in the middle of 1937, when the Communists gained control (or partial control) of the Spanish Government and began to hunt down the Trotskyists, we both found ourselves amongst the victims. We were very lucky to get out of Spain alive, and not even to have been arrested once. Many of our friends were shot, and others spent a long time in prison or simply disappeared.

These man-hunts in Spain went on at the same time as the great purges in the USSR and were a sort of supplement to them. In Spain as well as in Russia the nature of the accusations (namely, conspiracy with the Fascists) was the same and as far as Spain was concerned I had every reason to believe that the accusations were false. To experience all this was a valuable object lesson: it taught me how easily totalitarian propaganda can control the opinion of enlightened people in democratic countries.

My wife and I both saw innocent people being thrown into prison merely because they were suspected of unorthodoxy. Yet on our return to England we found numerous sensible and well-informed observers believing the most fantastic accounts of conspiracy, treachery and sabotage which the press reported from the Moscow trials.

And so I understood, more clearly than ever, the negative influence of the Soviet myth upon the western Socialist movement.

And here I must pause to describe my attitude to the Soviet régime.

I have never visited Russia and my knowledge of it consists only of what can be learned by reading books and newspapers. Even if I had the power, I would not wish to interfere in Soviet domestic affairs: I would not condemn Stalin and his associates merely for their barbaric and undemocratic methods. It is quite possible that, even with the best intentions, they could not have acted otherwise under the conditions prevailing there.

But on the other hand it was of the utmost importance to me that people in western Europe should see the Soviet régime for what it really was. Since 1930 I had seen little evidence that the USSR was progressing towards anything that one could truly call Socialism. On the contrary, I was struck by clear signs of its transformation into a hierarchical society, in which the rulers have no more reason to give up their power than any other ruling class. Moreover, the workers and intelligentsia in a country like England cannot understand that the USSR of today is altogether different from what it was in 1917. It is partly that they do not want to understand (i.e. they want to believe that, somewhere, a really Socialist country does actually exist), and partly that, being accustomed to comparative freedom and moderation in public life, totalitarianism is completely incomprehensible to them.

Yet one must remember that England is not completely democratic. It is also a capitalist country with great class privileges and (even now, after a war that has tended to equalise everybody) with great differences in wealth. But nevertheless it is a country in which people have lived together for several hundred years without knowing civil war, in which the laws are relatively just and official news and statistics can almost invariably be believed, and, last but not least, in which to hold and to voice minority views does not involve any mortal danger. In such an atmosphere the man in the street has no real understanding of things like concentration camps, mass deportations, arrests without trial, press censorship, etc. Everything he reads about a country like the USSR is automatically translated into English terms, and he quite innocently accepts the lies of totalitarian propaganda. Up to 1939, and even later, the majority of English people were incapable of assessing the true nature of the Nazi régime in Germany, and now, with the Soviet régime, they are still to a large extent under the same sort of illusion.

This has caused great harm to the Socialist movement in England, and had serious consequences for English foreign policy. Indeed, in my opinion, nothing has contributed so much to the corruption of the original idea of Socialism as the belief that Russia is a Socialist country and that every act of its rulers must be excused, if not imitated.

And so for the past ten years I have been convinced that the destruction of the Soviet myth was essential if we wanted a revival of the Socialist movement.

On my return from Spain I thought of exposing the Soviet myth in a story that could be easily understood by almost anyone and which could be easily translated into other languages. However the actual details of the story did not come to me for some time until one day (I was then living in a small village) I saw a little boy, perhaps ten years old, driving a huge cart-horse along a narrow path, whipping it whenever it tried to turn. It struck me that if only such animals became aware of their strength we should have no power over them, and that men exploit animals in much the same way as the rich exploit the proletariat.

I proceeded to analyse Marx's theory from the animals' point of view. To them it was clear that the concept of a class struggle between humans was pure illusion, since whenever it was necessary to exploit animals, all humans united against them: the true struggle is between animals and humans. From this point of departure, it was not difficult to elaborate the story. I did not write it out till 1943, for I was always engaged on other work which gave me no time; and in the end, I included some events, for example the Teheran Conference, which were taking place while I was writing. Thus the main outlines of the story were in my mind over a period of six years before it was actually written.

I do not wish to comment on the work; if it does not speak for itself, it is a failure. But I should like to emphasise two points: first, that although the various episodes are taken from the actual history of the Russian Revolution, they are dealt with schematically and their chronological order is changed; this was necessary for the symmetry of the story. The second point has been missed by most critics, possibly because I did not emphasise it sufficiently. A number of readers may finish the book with the impression that it ends in the complete reconciliation of the pigs and the humans. That was not my intention; on the contrary I meant it to end on a loud note of discord, for I wrote it immediately after the Teheran Conference which everybody thought had established the best possible relations between the USSR and the West. I personally did not believe that such good relations would last long; and, as events have shown, I wasn't far wrong. . . .

Appendix I

BOOKS BY OR CONTAINING CONTRIBUTIONS BY GEORGE ORWELL

Down and Out in Paris and London, London, 1933; New York, 1933.
Burmese Days, New York, 1934; London, 1935.
A Clergyman's Daughter, London, 1935; New York, 1936.
Keep the Aspidistra Flying, London, 1936; New York, 1956.
The Road to Wigan Pier, London, 1937; New York, 1958.
Homage to Catalonia, London, 1938; New York, 1952.
Coming Up for Air, London, 1939; New York, 1950.
Inside the Whale, London, 1940.
The Lion and the Unicorn, London, 1941.
The Betrayal of the Left, by Victor Gollancz, John Strachey, George Orwell and others, London, 1941.
Victory or Vested Interest? by G. D. H. Cole, George Orwell and others, London, 1942.
Talking to India, edited with an introduction by George Orwell, London, 1943.
Animal Farm, London, 1945; New York, 1946.
Critical Essays, London, 1946; (American title) *Dickens, Dali and Others*, New York, 1946.
James Burnham and the Managerial Revolution, London, 1946. (Pamphlet)
Love of Life and Other Stories, by Jack London. Introduction George Orwell, London, 1946.
The English People, London, 1947.
British Pamphleteers, Vol. I, edited by George Orwell and Reginal Reynolds. Introduction by George Orwell, London, 1948.
Nineteen-Eighty-Four, London, 1949; New York, 1949.

POSTHUMOUS COLLECTIONS

Shooting an Elephant, London, 1950; New York, 1950
Such, Such Were the Joys, New York, 1953.
England Your England, London, 1953.
The Orwell Reader, edited by Richard H. Rovere, New York, 1956.
Collected Essays, London, 1961.

Appendix II: Chronology

1943

On 24 November Orwell resigned from his post of Talks Producer in the Indian section of the BBC Eastern Service. Before the end of the month he had begun work as literary editor of *Tribune*, of which his friends, the Labour MPs Aneurin Bevan and G. R. Strauss, were co-directors and which had as its editor, Jon Kimche, whom Orwell had known since October 1934 when they had worked together at Booklovers' Corner in Hampstead. On 3 December Orwell's first "As I Please" appeared, the column he wrote in *Tribune* every week until 16 February 1945 and thereafter irregularly until April 1947. Aneurin Bevan allowed Orwell his head as literary editor, so that it was not uncommon for opinions, largely to do with Russia, then a war ally, or the nature of Socialism, in the literary section of the paper to controvert those in the front political section with the result, as Michael Foot has said, "How many readers [Orwell] offended no one can calculate (the circulation manager made her rough-and-ready weekly estimate)." Orwell wrote, "*Tribune* is not perfect, . . . but I do think it is the only existing weekly paper that makes a genuine effort to be both progressive and humane—that is, to combine a radical Socialist policy with a respect for freedom of speech and a civilised attitude towards literature and the arts."

On 9 December he began his series of book reviews in the *Manchester Evening News* which were normally to appear every other Thursday until 21 November 1946 under the heading "Life . . . People . . . and Books". Also in December Orwell's occasional book reviews for the *Observer* became a regular series, continuing fortnightly until 5 May 1946.

1944

In February Orwell finished *Animal Farm* which he had begun writing in November. During May he completed the manuscript of *The*

English People, a commissioned booklet, which did not appear in print until August 1947.

In early June Eileen Blair gave up her job organising the "Kitchen Front" broadcast talks for the Ministry of Food so that she and Orwell could adopt a baby who had been born on 14 May. They named him Richard Horatio Blair. On 28 June their flat, 10A Mortimer Crescent, Maida Vale was bombed and their friend, Inez Holden, the author and journalist, who was away ill in the country, lent Orwell and his wife her flat, 106 George Street, off Baker Street, until they were able to move into a flat, 27B Canonbury Square, Islington, at the beginning of October.

Orwell had a hard time finding a publisher for *Animal Farm* and by July Victor Gollancz, Jonathan Cape and Faber & Faber amongst others had turned it down on political grounds and it was only at the beginning of October that Fredric Warburg undertook to publish it. In the same month Orwell began planning the contents of *Critical Essays,* the manuscript of which he sent Leonard Moore on 22 January 1945, except for "In Defence of P. G. Wodehouse" which he completed by early February and included later.

1945

In February Orwell gave up the literary editorship of *Tribune* and on the fifteenth went to France as a war correspondent for the *Observer.* He used the Hotel Scribe in Paris as his base until the fourth week in March when he moved to Cologne, from which he hurriedly returned to England on learning of his wife's death.

Eileen Blair had been in poor health for some time and in early March she had gone to stay at Greystone, the house her sister-in-law, Gwen O'Shaughnessy, had at Carlton, Stockton-on-Tees, County Durham. Gwen O'Shaughnessy's children were evacuated to Greystone and had a nanny who had also been looking after young Richard Blair since the Blairs had been bombed out. Eileen Blair was to rest and build up her strength for an operation. On 29 March she died, aged 39, as the anaesthetic was being given.

Orwell returned to Paris about 8 April, then went to Nuremberg and Stuttgart. He was in Paris on VE Day, 8 May, and in Austria in the middle of the month, arriving back in London by 24 May. While on the continent he had sent despatches to the *Manchester Evening News* as well as to the *Observer.*

In late June and early July Orwell covered the General Election campaign in London for the *Observer*. On 3 July he signed a contract to write four long articles for *Polemic*, a new magazine of philosophy, psychology and aesthetics, edited by Humphrey Slater. On the same day he mentioned to Leonard Moore in a letter that he had "recently started a novel", his first attempt at *Nineteen Eighty-Four*.

In August Orwell accepted the vice-chairmanship of the Freedom Defence Committee, which had been formed in the spring of 1945 to deal with cases of the infringement of civil liberties. He gave it his support until it was dissolved early in 1949.

On 17 August, after eighteen months of set-backs, *Animal Farm* was published by Secker & Warburg.

Ian Angus

INDEX

Compiled by Oliver Stallybrass

All numbers refer to pages, not items. Footnotes are indicated by "n" or "(n)" after the page-number: "n" refers *only* to the footnote, "(n)" to text *and* footnote. The *first* footnote on any individual person usually includes a brief biographical outline.

Subheadings are arranged in order of first page reference, except where chronological order (e.g. Orwell: *chronology*) or alphabetical order (e.g. Orwell: *writings*: individual titles) is clearly more appropriate.

George Orwell is abbreviated to GO throughout.

AMG, *see* Allied Military Government

Abyssinia: Italian war, 8, 84, 152, 182, 234

Acland, Sir Richard, 76(n), 124

Action Stories, 218

Adelphi, The, 184(n), 202–3; GO's contribution, 191(n)

Advertising, 35, 89; in *Daily Worker*, 21; in relation to careers, 96–7; publishers', 168–9; and snobbery motif, 183–4, 194; of plots for stories, 273–4, 290–1; in *Old Moore's Almanac*, for curing obesity etc, 278

Aesop, 198

Africa, *see* Abyssinia; Egypt; North African campaign; South Africa

Agate, James: *Noblesse Oblige* reviewed by GO, 255–6; subsequent controversy, 257–60

"Age d'Or, L'", film, 160n

Agriculture: war-time revival, 2, 34

Air Raid Precautions, 4, 233–4; unsuitable language of posters, 135

Air raids: on Britain, 6, 67 ("Baedeker raids"), 201; on London, 3, 82, 88; (fictitious), 123, 131, 334–5; flying bombs, 179–80, 195–6, 232(n)–4; rocket bombs, 279–80, 328–9; shelters, 72–3; on Germany and Italy, 126; moral problem of, 150–2, 176–177, 181–3, 198–9, 204

Air Training Corps, 195

"Albion", 166

Alexandria, 296; destruction of libraries, 178

Alice's Adventures in Wonderland (Carroll), 283

Alington, Cyril, 265

Allied Military Government, 75(n)

Amelia (Fielding), 245, 269

America, *see* United States

American army: relations with the British, 54–5, 58–9, 76–7, 128, 153–4; left-wing view of, 379

American civil war, 8

American Notes (Dickens), 84

Americanisms, 27–9, 109, 326

Amery, John, 344(n), 353

Amery, Leo, 344n, 356

AMG, *see* Allied Military Government

Amiens, Peace of, 68

Amritsar, 370

Amusements, *see* Entertainments

Anarchism and Anarchists, 16, 112, 193, 256, 295, 376; and pessimism, 63

Anglophobia, 367, 375

Animal Farm, see Orwell, G.

Animals: English sentimentality about, 4, 175

Anstey, F.: *Vice Versa*, 283

Antisemitism, 153, 154, 199; Ezra Pound and, 85; in Britain, 89–91, 332–41; Roy Fuller and, 104–5; in Germany, 146, 230, 369n; in Russia, 146; antisemitic letter quoted, 152;

Mickaela Walsh
Rockefeller Bros. Foundation

Books by George Orwell

available in paperbound editions from
Harcourt Brace Jovanovich, Inc.

A CLERGYMAN'S DAUGHTER (HPL 37)

KEEP THE ASPIDISTRA FLYING (HPL 38)

HOMAGE TO CATALONIA (HB 162)

COMING UP FOR AIR (HPL 44)

DICKENS, DALI & OTHERS (HB 188)

A COLLECTION OF ESSAYS (HPL 48)

THE ORWELL READER: FICTION, ESSAYS AND REPORTAGE (HB 42)

THE COLLECTED ESSAYS, JOURNALISM AND LETTERS
OF GEORGE ORWELL:

I. An Age Like This, 1920–1940 (HB 209)
II. My Country Right or Left, 1940–1943 (HB 210)
III. As I Please, 1943–1945 (HB 211)
IV. In Front of Your Nose, 1945–1950 (HB 212)

Four volumes, boxed set (HB 218)